JOBS
WORLDWIDE

David Lay
Benedict A. Leerburger

IMPACT PUBLICATIONS
Manassas Park, VA

JOBS WORLDWIDE

Copyright © 1996 by David Lay and Benedict A. Leerburger

Distributed by:
Marvin Melnyk Assoc. Ltd.
Queenston, Ontario   L0S 1L0
905 262-4964 Fax 262-4974

CONTENTS

1

THE LURE OF FOREIGN EMPLOYMENT

*A*side from military personnel stationed outside the United States and some 50,000 students studying abroad, more than two million Americans live and work overseas. What's so appealing about leaving the comforts of one's home and experiencing a new and often totally different lifestyle? For many it is simply the thrill of adventure—something new and different. For others it is the experience of a different lifestyle: new foods, different customs, a foreign language. However, for many Americans who elect to spend several years away from home, one of the most important reasons is economic. More and more Americans have discovered that by combining the good salaries paid in many foreign countries with the tax advantages of living outside of the United States it is possible to save and return home with a substantial nest egg.

Perhaps the single most stated reason for leaving a good job in the States for a tour overseas is money. In our case, I was a typical young professional in the engineering/construction industry. I lived with my family in Southern California. I was in debt and had a problem saving a dime from the weekly paycheck. Sound familiar? Overseas employment

1

was a God-send. I not only found financial security but upward mobility, ending up as the corporate chief of a major Middle Eastern company. I never would have had comparable opportunities in the States.

By taking advantage of the tax laws and contractual bonuses offered abroad, an individual is hard pressed to find a better way to accumulate and save a significant amount of money—aside from winning a lottery. According to one management consultant, "The existing structure, devised specifically by hiring companies and participating governments to encourage Americans to work overseas, may be the last legal avenue, short of a large inheritance, for achieving financial security."

Not only are salaries up to 50 per cent higher abroad—depending on location—but **all** Americans who work abroad, except those with the federal government, and who are out of the United States for 330 days out of any 12 consecutive months, receive a tax exemption of $70,000. To encourage American know-how in the world's developing nations Congress passed the Economic Recovery Act of 1981. Any money earned above the $70,000 exemption is taxed at the current tax rate, for example, a worker earning $85,000 abroad is taxed only on $15,000—a very low tax bracket. All income below $70,000 is tax free. In addition to higher base salaries and significant tax breaks, many Americans working abroad also receive paid living expenses (food, housing and transportation), free travel, free medical benefits and a 5 to 30 percent bonus upon completing their contracted assignment. U.S. Government employees who live abroad are not able to take advantage of these tax advantages as their income is not treated as "foreign earned."

However, there is one big exception to this tax-free situation. Although Americans are exempt from U.S. taxes on a large portion of money earned abroad, they are not always tax exempt in the country in which they may be employed. Thus it is important to evaluate the entire tax picture. For example, an American earning $30,000 working at home may pay 25 per cent to the U.S. Government. Earn the same salary in Australia and the U.S. Government takes nothing—but the Australian government takes a third. Work in Saudi Arabia and all your income is yours. Saudi Arabia has no local taxes.

These figures must be evaluated as a total package. For example, many companies provide a complete subsidy to encourage skilled Americans to move abroad.

In addition to higher salaries most foreign companies provide living expenses as well as a contract completion bonus. Add such additional incentives as free vacation travel (ranging from two to six weeks a year) as well as free home leave travel and the total dollar package becomes far greater than the initial tax incentives.

As an example, let's evaluate three different country situations of single individuals doing a comparable job. (The data is taken from actual situations):

	UNITED STATES	AUSTRALIA	SAUDI ARABIA
Income	$30,000	$27,000	$45,000
Taxes	7,500	9,000	none
Housing	7,200	3,000	none
Utilities	1,000	1,000	none
Transportation	4,000	3,000	none
Food	4,800	4,000	none
Bankable	**$ 5,500**	**$ 7,000**	**$45,000**

To answer the obvious question, "How much money can I make?", one really must consider that "making" money and "banking" or saving money are two different questions. Working abroad is an excellent way to save money—to create a substantial nest egg. As for the amount of money you can put away, it really depends upon several basic factors: job location, bonuses and benefits, and tax liabilities.

Although the lure of generating a significant financial cache is a prime consideration, the opportunity to acquire invaluable job experience and add prestigious accomplishments to a resume is an appealing and valuable benefit. We can't overemphasize the added benefit of acquiring overseas work experience and adding attendant accomplishments to a resume. Two years as a Resident Manager on a large project, for example, put me in contention for Managing Director of the company. Fortunately, my foreign experience helped me land the job! This isn't to suggest that everyone will have the same luck; I was in the right place at the right time.

Yet a tour abroad may not be all wine and roses. In some developing nations you live in a compound miles from a major city. Working conditions are often more primitive than back home and cultural differences may require adjustments as well. For instance, living a single life in a Muslim country may severely restrict your social life. As a general rule, the higher the salaries and financial incentives, the greater the hardships whether physical or psychological.

Working overseas isn't for everyone. There is the old story of the man who left his native Poland for New York City at the turn of the century because he heard the streets were paved with gold. When his boat arrived in New York he discovered three things: the streets were not paved with gold; the streets weren't paved; his job was to pave them!

The individual who elects to leave his American job for a similar position abroad that pays significantly more may discover that the financial perks may not be worth the personal hardship of living in a developing nation. Balancing the many benefits with any negative factors is a most subjective analysis.

Each individual must consider all the factors. Are you an adventurer that thrives on the different and unusual? Would you enjoy being with people of a different culture? How about some of the more personal aspects of life outside the United States? For example: Would you mind living in a small town, village or isolated work site? How important is American TV or movies? Would there be a language problem? Is it important to be close to your house of worship? Would being apart from your American friends and relatives be a problem?

If you have a family that you plan to bring with you overseas, keep in mind that many foreign jobs are not available on a "family status" basis and those that are, usually are reserved for management or supervisory personnel. Let's look at some of the pros and cons of life abroad. Keep in mind that those who dream of a sweet, high-paying job on the French Riviera or a bachelor's pad in Paris or Rome will be in for a disappointment. Yes, there are plush jobs in romantic parts of the world, but for the most part these positions are in obvious demand and usually go to the first qualified national rather than to an unknown American. For an American to secure one of the more plush foreign assignments the best opportunities lie with a U.S. company doing business in the location of your choice. However, don't expect to have first crack at the best job with a U.S. company either—that goes to existing company employees.

Although the majority of employees that head for the high paying Middle East jobs or the adventuresome assignments in an underdeveloped country are single, there are many that seek the opportunity to experience life abroad with their families. Whereas the idea of family work and travel sounds good, be aware that it is far more difficult to get a foreign job as a family employee. From the employer's point of view the cost of bringing you, your spouse and possibly your children to a distant job site is considerable. To support a family overseas, the company has to provide larger living quarters, more food, schools, doctors, nurses, recreation and a large list of extras to keep you and your clan happy.

Even if all the facilities are already in place, the company must double or triple their up-front expenses to relocate you and your family before they know for sure what kind of a worker you are. The company has also learned from experience that if your spouse is not happy, the chances are extremely high that you won't be an employee long. Unless your skills are such that a company must hire you and your family as a package deal, you can be sure that they will opt for a single worker rather than put your resume on their short list.

Often times, a company will hire an employee on a single status and convert him to family status after he proves himself on the job. This may become a probationary period for several months or the status change may occur near the end of the contract period. It is important to know and understand these options before accepting the job if family status is your ultimate goal.

2

TEST YOUR OVERSEAS EMPLOYMENT APTITUDE

*H*ow successful will you be in obtaining an overseas job? The following test will give you some indication of your potential for success. It is a useful tool for determining how much of your time, effort, and money you should devote to your overseas job search.

Circle one answer for each question that best fits your situation:

1. **Why do you want to work overseas?**

   A. I've been unemployed for two (or more) months and I've got to do something.
   B. I've been unemployed for less than two months and I might as well do what I want to do.
   C. My current job is okay and I'm making ends meet, but I want to get ahead financially.
   D. I'm stalemated in my career currently and I want more opportunity for advancement and pay.

E. I enjoyed travel and excitement, not to mention the economic rewards when I worked overseas before.

2. **I understand that the search for an overseas job can be a time consuming task, but I am willing to devote:**

   A. 30 days or less.
   B. 60 to 90 days.
   C. 3 to 6 months.
   D. 6 to 12 months.
   E. Until I have exhausted all possibilities.

3. **Up to now, I have just:**

   A. Thought about looking for an overseas job.
   B. Made a few inquiries about overseas employment.
   C. Sent out a few resumes to overseas employers.
   D. Talked to employment agencies about it.
   E. Researched and contacted at least 10 leads a month.

4. **The work that I now do is considered;**

   A. Unskilled labor.
   B. Skilled craftsman.
   C. Supervisory/Technical
   D. Professional
   E. Management

5. **The industry in which I work is;**

   A. Manufacturing, sales, transportation, retail, trucking.
   B. Clerical, counseling, banking, residential construction.
   C. Commercial construction, data processing, electronics.
   D. Military, teaching, vocational training, agriculture.
   E. Engineering, heavy or industrial construction, medicine, defense.

6. **I have the following number of years experience working in my career field.**

   A. 0 to 2 years.

    B. 2 to 5 years.
    C. 5 to 10 years.
    D. 10 to 20 years
    E. 20 or more years.

7. My supervisory experience is as follows:

    A. I have never had a supervisory position.
    B. I have supervised 1 to 5 subordinates.
    C. I have supervised up to 10 subordinates.
    D. I have had other supervisors working for me.
    E. I have managed operations with more than two levels of supervision under me.

8. I have attained the following level of education:

    A. I never finished high school.
    B. High school or GED.
    C. Some college, technical training or apprenticeship.
    D. Bachelors degree.
    E. Advanced degree.

9. Licenses, registration, or certification I have held in the last five years.

    A. None.
    B. Course certificates, city licenses, etc.
    C. National professional organizations, craft union memberships.
    D. State board exam or registration, state license or certificate.
    E. National registration or certification.

10. Level of security clearance:

    A. Have been convicted of a crime.
    B. Never applied for a security clearance.
    C. Have had Secret clearance in the last five years.
    D. Currently have Secret clearance.
    E. Top Secret clearance in last five years.

11. Military history:

A. Dishonorable Discharge.
B. Never served or E-1 or E-2 only.
C. E-3 to E-5.
D. E-6 to E-8.
E. Officer.

12. Current or last earnings per annum:

A. Under $10,000 or over $150,000.
B. $10,000 to $20,000 or between $100,000 and $150,000.
C. $20,000 to $30,000 or between $80,000 and $100,000.
D. $30,000 to $40,000 or between $60,000 and $80,000.
E. $40,000 to $60,000.

13. I expect to earn the following working overseas.

A. Over $150,000 per annum.
B. $100,000 to $150,000 per annum.
C. $50,000 to $100,000 per annum.
D. 30-50% more than I earn in the U.S.
E. 10-30% more than I earn in the U.S.

14. My overseas experience is a s follows;

A. None.
B. I've traveled to Europe, Australia or the Far East.
C. I was stationed in Europe, the Far East, etc.
D. I grew up or went to school overseas.
E. I have completed at least one overseas contract.

15. My family status overseas would be:

A. Single parent.
B. Married with children.
C. Married with no children.
D. Negotiable, depending on location and contract package.
E. Single status.

16. I want to work in:

A. The Caribbean, Alaska, Hawaii.
B. Europe, Australia, or English speaking countries only.
C. A temperate climate with decent living conditions.
D. A developing country where pay equals the hardship.
E. Any country depending on safety, pay, and benefits.

17. My foreign language capability is:

A. None or high school French or Spanish.
B. Speak a foreign language.
C. Speak and write a foreign language.
D. Speak and write more than one foreign language.
E. Certified translator or teach English as a second language.

18. Citizenship/Immigration status:

A. Student/Visitor Visa to the U.S.
B. Permanent resident/Green card.
C. U.S. citizen
D. U.S. citizen with passport applied for.
E. U.S. citizen with active passport.

19. Current financial situation:

A. Eminent bankruptcy or foreclosure proceedings.
B. Working but getting deeper in debt.
C. Paying the bills but not saving much.
D. Currently saving 5% of income.
E. Saving 10% or more of income.

20. My technical or administrative job skills include:

A. None.
B. Operating trucks/backhoes, etc. or basic office machines.
C. Operating most heavy equipment or advanced office machines/computers.
D. Supervise heavy equipment operations or administrative office.
E. Manage technical operations or direct administrative officer.

ANSWER KEY

Count each of the capital letters you have circled, A through E, and multiply the number by the points for each letter shown below.

A = 0 points
B = 1 point
C = 3 points
D = 4 points
E = 5 points

SCORE:

0 to 20 points:	Poor chance of success; not really worth the time and effort required.
21 to 40 points:	Minimal chance; don't spend much time and money on the effort.
41 to 60 points:	Realistic opportunity but be objective; don't lose sight of domestic opportunities.
61 to 80 points:	Qualified for overseas work; will require diligent effort and commitment but may be worth the effort.
81 to 100 points:	Very qualified candidate; committed effort will result in success.

3

JOB OPPORTUNITIES

*J*ust as there are a host of employment opportunities in the United States—depending upon your particular field of expertise—so too are there a wide variety of job opportunities abroad. Basically, however, there are four broad delineations of overseas employment:

- Working for the government (either the U.S. government or the United Nations).

- Working for an American industrial concern or for a foreign company.

- Working for a non-profit organization.

- Working as an independent consultant.

As with all employers there are pros and cons for each of the above. A governmental organization, whether the U.N. or Uncle Sam, offers greater security, but the salaries are usually below that offered by industry. An American company often offers high salaries and benefits but may require you to work state-side for a period of time before being sent abroad. A foreign company may offer you a solid contract, but many of the familiar perks may not exist when compared with an American organization's employment contract.

As a free lance consultant, you face the risk of being left without work if your contract is canceled once you are overseas. Yet, being your own boss has many virtues. It so depends upon your needs and personality. Usually the greater the risk, the greater the gain. However, for a man or woman with a family, security and a guaranteed job complete with assured housing and that return ticket in your pocket may be worth a few dollars less in your monthly paycheck. The basic tax advantages remain the same regardless of who signs your check unless it is the U.S. government.

Let's look at a few of the many job opportunities afforded you:

FEDERAL JOBS

Without question, the largest employer of Americans abroad is the Federal government. Just leaving out the hundreds of thousands of American military personnel stationed outside the country, the numbers of Americans abroad working for Uncle Sam is staggering. An exact number is not possible because as so many are involved in operations that require secrecy. For example, the most secret of America's intelligence gathering organizations is the little known National Security Agency. It has been reported that more than 50,000 Americans are on the NSA payroll (receiving their pay check marked Department of Defense to assure their cover), but the actual number living outside the country is a top secret. (The same is true for the other major intelligence agencies with foreign employees: Central Intelligence Agency, Defense Intelligence Agency, Drug Enforcement Agency.) Of course there are a host of job opportunities in non-intelligence federal foreign operations as well. These foreign jobs are often in heavy demand, but considering the large numbers of Americans abroad on the federal payroll, it is well worth your while to consider the opportunities and benefits of a government job abroad. The needs are extremely diverse as so many agencies are involved in overseas operations. Keep in mind, however, if you choose to work for the federal government overseas, you will not qualify for the $70,000 tax exemption granted to employees of "foreign" companies abroad.

The best place to start your search for a U.S. government job overseas is to contact the Office of Personnel Management and request a copy of their highly informative booklet, *Federal Jobs Overseas*. (Forms and Publications, Office of Personnel Management, 1900 E Street NW, Washington DC 20415). Also request a copy of their current application forms (Standard Form 171, OF-612, OF-306) and information on the new application process.

The many agencies that employ Americans abroad include the following:

- **Department of State**—One of the largest employers of Americans abroad, the State Department is responsible for operating and maintaining the nearly 250 diplomatic and consular posts overseas. The work is extremely involved and job needs range from technical specialists in defense policy and diplomacy to secretarial and general office management. For example, many jobs are available for individuals who can operate data processing machines, communications equipment, or set up and maintain libraries.

   Requirements may vary depending upon the specific job you apply for, however, for all jobs you must be a 21 years or older, a U.S. citizen, a high school graduate, and be prepared for an extensive background check and thorough medical exam.

   The Foreign Service is what most people think of when considering a job with State. More than 3,700 Foreign Service Officers (FSO) are employed in consular posts in over 140 nations. Most work directly for the State Department but can either be hired or assigned to another federal agency involved in foreign operations. Most people choosing be become a FSO do so as a career move rather than as a temporary stint abroad. The median age of a beginning junior officer is about 31. Most have at least one advanced degree and many have had several years in the job market before deciding to switch to the foreign service. The professional backgrounds range from teaching, law, business, economics and business. At least half the FSO applicants are fluent in at least one foreign language but speaking a foreign language is not a requirement. Starting salaries can vary from $19,000 to $27,000 plus all benefits including full medical and a cost of living allowance which varies depending upon in which country you work. Once you complete the basic applications for a FSO assignment, plan to wait at least nine months before hearing whether you have a job. The background security checks, day-long personal assessment exam and general bureaucracy is very time consuming. All FSOs go through the process; there are no exceptions.

As a foreign service officer you probably would be initially involved in all of the following areas for a period of six months each: political, consular, economic, and administrative. After that two year broad indoctrination you could well be sent to a different foreign country or to a desk job in Washington. A foreign service officer can plan to spend at least half of his career abroad. In addition to working as a foreign service officer other jobs include:

Foreign service secretaries: As a secretary at a foreign embassy or consulate your routine usually would expand well beyond the clerical. Secretaries are often involved in coding and decoding the many messages received and transmitted, handling routine questions from both local nationals as well as visiting Americans, perhaps working with visiting Congressional representatives or other government officials. Often the perks include invitations to local national events and embassy parties.

General service officers: These are the individuals that are considered the nuts and bolts of running a foreign office. They are responsible for the widely dispersed physical resources and intricate logistical functions including procurement, supply, and building maintenance.

Foreign commercial service officers: A fairly new post in foreign embassies, the commercial officer works with both local and American business leaders in establishing closer business ties. Business experience and international trade is a most helpful prerequisite for the job.

Information on the range of foreign service jobs is contained in the 34 page brochure, Foreign Service Careers, (Department of State Publication 9202) available from The U.S. Department of State Publications, Rosslyn Station, Arlington, VA 22209. More specific job information as well as data on current needs and openings is available from the Foreign Service Officer Recruitment Branch, Department of State, Box # 9317, Rosslyn Station, Arlington, VA 22209.

- **US Information Agency (USIA)**—This independent agency under the executive branch employs more than 4,000 Americans as well as foreign nationals overseas. They seek specialists in public relations, broadcast journalism (to work for the Voice of America), management, finance, educational and cultural affairs, teachers, publishing, and library science. The US Information Service (USIS) as the USIA is known abroad operates libraries in most countries of the world, organizes cultural exchange programs, teaches English to foreign nationals, interfaces with the foreign media and in general, attempts to serve as America's best face abroad. The USIA also employees American guides who accompany U.S. exhibits as they travel to different parts of the world. This assignment is usually for no more than six months and requires a working knowledge of the language. Working for the USIA requires the same background and general employment procedures as the State Department. Jobs are highly competitive but the turnover necessitates new blood every year. More information is available from: Employment Branch, U.S. Information Agency, 301 Fourth Street NW, Washington, DC 20547 (202) 619-4700. If you want to pursue a career with the Voice of America, which also offers an internship program, they may be reached at 330 Independence Avenue SW, Washington, DC 20547.

- **Agency for International Development**—This independent agency administers the U.S. economic assistance programs in most Third World countries. Positions with AID are extremely varied and include program directors and managers; financial officers with a background in accounting and money management; economists (particularly with a background in political science or international relations); agronomists and those specializing in the production, distribution and consumption of food products; and family planning personnel with a knowledge of population and world health matters. An intern program usually selects about 50 applicants a year. Salaries vary from about $18,500 for a beginning level job or an intern to the upper levels of the civil service scale depending on experience. Contact: Office of Personnel and Management, Agency for International Development, 320 21st Street NW, Washington, DC 20523 (202) 647-1770.

- **International Development Cooperation Agency (IDCA)**— This small and little known agency is involved in policy planning and coordinating the various economic issues that impact on Third World nations. Those with a background in economics, international development, and trade should look into this group by writing to the Personnel Officer, International Development Cooperation Agency, 320 21st Street NW, Washington, DC 20523.

- **U.S. Trade Representative**—Most of the work in this office is handled in Washington, however, a growing staff in Geneva is always looking for experienced applicants with a knowledge of economics, trade negotiations, and international business. It is the U.S. Trade Representative's responsibility to formulate our international trade policies and establish the basic ground rules for all trade talks and negotiations. You may see a college professor taking a few years off to work in this office. Write: Office of the U.S. Trade Representative, 600 17th Street NW, Washington, DC 20506. This office works closely with the U.S. International Trade Commission, the group that is concerned with international trade and tariffs. A background in international economics, marketing, international law and economics is required for the few Civil Service jobs offered outside the U.S. More information is available from Office of Administration, U.S. International Trade Commission, 701 E Street NW, Washington, DC 20436. (202) 482-3301.

- **Department of Defense, Intelligence Operations**—Although there are many intelligence gathering agencies within the government, only a handful employ people specifically for work outside the country. The prime groups with a foreign flair all have interrelated objectives; they all keep contact with each other and funnel foreign intelligence information to the key decision and policy makers within the executive branch. Thus, the President's National Security Advisor requires input from various sources as does the chief decision makers within both the Departments of Defense and State. The interagency rivalry is keen and rarely does an operative in one agency speak kindly about the work of another. The Big Three consist of the Central Intelligence Agency (CIA), National Security Agency (NSA) and, the Defense Intelligence Agency (DIA). All are non-civil service agencies.

- **The Central Intelligence Agency** is almost exclusively involved outside the country. In fact, by Congressional mandate all domestic intelligence gathering is restricted to the Federal Bureau of Investigation while all foreign intelligence gathering is the bidding of the CIA. Of course not all agents in these esteemed departments are aware of the Congressional mandate, so it is not out of the question for the CIA to be involved with a local operation (Just don't expect them to be too quick to admit their "indiscretion"). The CIA is also directly involved in on-site investigations. They have agents (or operatives) stationed in every country in the world. For the most part agents are stationed at the embassy under the cover of Security Officer or Cultural Attaché. Those James Bond-type agents who work in secret under "deep cover" exist but little is published about their numbers or assignments. Although, the CIA employs about 24,000 individuals.

  An agent's job may be reading and clipping local newspapers and local government reports assembling data on economic production, military spending, business practices, or agricultural output and future planing. The job is rarely as romantic as many spy novels portray. It's long on leg work and research and short on back avenue bars and secret meetings with sexy counterspies. A background in one or more of the many world regions, i.e. Eastern Europe, Latin America, Middle East, Africa, or Asia is important as is an ability to read and translate a foreign language. The ability to research economic matters is a big plus as is a Ph.D. in international affairs.

  Like all secret federal agencies, there is an extensive background check, detailed psychological exams, and a polygraph test. After spending months either taking tests or waiting for word on your job status, it is often the case that applicants who appear to be a natural for the job receive a polite rejection letter. There is no appeal and the applicant never discovers why he or she didn't make the grade.

- **The National Security Agency (NSA)** is the largest and most secret of the government's clandestine agencies. Headquarters is a large complex within the confines of the Fort George Meade Army Base located between Washington and Baltimore. The prime responsibility of the NSA is monitoring communications worldwide. This means collecting electronic signals emitted from radio, telegraph, fax, and telephone transmissions as well as obtaining high altitude photographic and infra red images electronically. The agency also is much involved in researching and developing sophisticated electronic gathering and processing equipment including the first large-scale computer, the first solid state computer and many applications involving high density electronic storage. The agency is also responsible for all the nation's codes and ciphers as well as attempting to break those codes of other countries.

  When President Richard Nixon mentioned that the United States had overheard telephone conversations from the Kremlin, he neglected to disclose that those calls were monitored by secret satellites hovering several hundred miles over Moscow and transmitting the electronic signals to NSA headquarters in Fort Meade. When you read that the Department of Defense launches a secret spy satellite you know it is doing service for the NSA. For example, the NSA receives electronic photo images of the world's most sensitive areas many times a day. Sophisticated spy cameras can read the license number of a car from 250 miles in space. A missile launch pad can not be moved in Iraq without someone at NSA knowing about it within hours.

  Working for the NSA involves many disciplines including computer sciences, mathematics, political science, linguistics and languages (NSA translates thousands of pages of overheard foreign conversations every day), statistics, probability, information science, semiconductor physics, superconductivity, electromagnetic propagation, systems engineering, and of course, political science. Because of the secret nature of its work, the NSA conducts its own aptitude tests and interviews and selects its employees directly. Only U.S. citizens will be hired. Those employees assigned overseas are either based at a U.S. embassy or one of the many NSA secret satellite monitoring stations throughout the world. The average tour of foreign duty is two or three years.

The hiring process can take up to a year as various physical, mental, and aptitude tests must first be passed before the agency begins the arduous and time consuming background check that is made on all serious applicants. For additional information contact: Director, National Security Agency, Attn: M32 (Recruitment), Fort George G. Meade, MD 20755.

- **The Defense Intelligence Agency (DIA)** is the arm of the Defense Department responsible for all military intelligence activities. Each military department—Army, Navy, Marine, and Air Force—has its own intelligence division, yet all fall under the control of the Secretary of Defense and the DIA. Although many of the approximately 2,500 DIA employees are members of the military, it is certainly not an exclusive military domain. Civilians with experience in economics, security, engineering, intelligence, languages, and international relations are needed as well. For example, the DIA describes its nonmilitary people as part of "a civilian team engaged in collecting, analyzing, evaluating, interpreting and disseminating information which affects our national security."

DIA jobs abroad are almost always based with the U.S. embassy or consulate. A "military attaché" with an embassy, for example is almost certainly employed by the DIA. In most cases, however, civilians are not assigned to attaché duty. Contact: Civilian Personnel Division, Defense Intelligence Agency, The Pentagon, Washington, DC 20310 (703/695-7353).

- **Department of Defense Schools**—The Defense Department also maintains jurisdiction over 270 elementary, middle, junior high and high schools plus one community college in 20 countries around the world. More than 11,000 teachers hired by the Defense Department serve some 136,000 students who are almost exclusively the dependents of military personnel or civilian department employees stationed abroad. Teachers, librarians, school nurses and other school personnel are paid on a scale established by the Department but in a range competitive with a mid-sized U.S. city. Nationwide interviews are held every March and April for appointment the following school year. Applicants are notified of their selection and country assignment in May and June. More details of the DOD foreign teacher program is covered in the section on "Teachers."

- **Drug Enforcement Administration**—Formerly known as the Bureau of Narcotics and Dangerous Drugs, the DEA now comes under the administration of the FBI. Unlike those employed for the CIA, NEA, or DIA, Drug Enforcement Agents are civil service employees. It is considered the most dangerous of all undercover work within the government. Agents are involved in the criminal investigation of narcotics dealers and the enforcement of narcotics laws. Many of the close to 2,000 agents working for the DEA are involved in foreign work monitoring narcotics dealing and drug trafficking. A background in police work is extremely helpful. Unlike other federal intelligence agencies, no college degree is required for DEA work. Contact: Director of Personnel, Drug Enforcement Administration, International Division, 700 Army-Navy Drive, Arlington, VA 22202. (703/653-5883)

- **Department of Agriculture**—The Foreign Agricultural Service (FAS) is the agency within the government that promotes American agricultural products abroad. Representatives try to improve U.S. markets and develop new ones through contacts and negotiations with both foreign governments and private organizations. The FAS also reports back to the American farmers with specific data on developing needs and markets available to the U.S. agricultural trade. An international network of agricultural attaches stationed in more than 70 countries analyzes world agriculture production, trade and policies with particular interest in its impact on the American farmer.

Most professional positions are filled by Department of Agriculture employees with experience in agricultural marketing and economics. Secretarial positions are filled through the Office of Personnel Management. Contact: Director, Personnel Division, Foreign Agricultural Service, U.S. Department of Agriculture, Washington, DC 20250. (202) 720-3935.

- **Department of Commerce**—There are several agencies under the Commerce Department that offer opportunities to work abroad. The International Trade Administration (ITA) is the umbrella group with the charge to promote America's position in the international trade arena. Their employees should be well versed in economics, international business and trade.

- **The U.S. Travel and Tourism Administration** has offices staffed with Americans in London, Mexico City, Paris, Frankfort, Tokyo, and Toronto. The objective of this agency is to assist in the promotion of U.S. tourism. A knowledge of international economics, tourism and the ability to speak a foreign language are most helpful in fulfilling one of these positions. Contact the specific agency at: Department of Commerce, 14th Street and Constitution Avenue NW, Washington, DC 20230.

- Another agency under Commerce that hires Americans to work abroad is the **National Oceanic and Atmospheric Administration**. The agency oversees the weather stations in Puerto Rico, Mexico, Wake Island, Guam, Johnson Island, America Samoa, and the Trust Territories. A background in meteorology or electronics is essential. A few positions are also periodically available for technicians with experience in geophysics to work at observatories in Antarctica and American Samoa. Contact: Personnel Director, National Oceanic and Atmospheric Administration, Department of Commerce, 14th Street and Constitution Avenue NW, Washington, DC 20230. (202) 482-6076.

OTHER FEDERAL JOBS ABROAD

There are other governmental departments and agencies that hire Americans for foreign posts. These jobs vary, of course, with the agency and in most cases they try to place people abroad from within their current staffs. In some cases, however, they will search for an outside candidate. These jobs all fall under the Civil Service code and a job applicant is expected to place high on the appropriate Civil Service examination.

- **Department of Health and Human Services (HHS)**—is involved with many joint research projects involving foreign medical personnel. Work with underdeveloped countries attempts to share medical technology with doctors, and health care administrators. HHS searches for individuals with experience in nutrition, medicine, hospital administration, chemistry, reproductive physiology, medical technology and health. Contact: Director of Personnel, Office of International Health, Department of Health and Human Services, 5600 Fishers Lane, Rm. 1875, Rockville, MD 20857. (301) 443-1774.

- **Department of Education**—oversees an international teacher exchange program. Reciprocal arrangements are made with various countries to exchange approximately 250 elementary, secondary, and college teachers each year. (Associate and full Professors will only exchange with teachers in the United Kingdom.) Applicants must be experienced and able to spend at least two semesters abroad, although a few exchange programs are for a single semester. Contact: Teacher Exchange Section, International Education Branch, U.S. Department of Education, 7th and D Streets, S.W., Washington, DC 20202. (202) 732-6061.

Other agencies that, upon occasion, will hire outsiders for a foreign assignment include:

Bureau of International Labor Affairs
Department of Labor
200 Constitution Avenue
Washington, DC 20210
(202) 219-6043

National Science Foundation
1800 G Street NW
Washington DC 20550
(202) 357-5000

U.S. Nuclear Regulatory Commission
11555 Rockville Pike
Rockville, MD 20852
(301) 492-0347

Foreign Claims Settlement Commission of the U.S.
1111 20th Street NW
Washington, DC 20579
(202) 482-3133

Office of International Affairs
Department of Energy
1000 Independence Avenue
Washington, DC 20585
(202) 586-5493

International Division
General Accounting Office
441 G Street NW
Washington, DC 20548
(202) 275-5205

Bureau of International Aviation
Civil Aeronautics Board
1825 Connecticut Avenue
Washington, DC 20428
(202) 267-3133

Federal Maritime Commission
800 N. Capitol St. NW
Washington, DC 20428
(202) 253-5773

International Affairs Division
National Aeronautics and Space Administration
400 Maryland Avenue SW
Washington, DC 20546
(202) 477-1234

THE UNITED NATIONS AND OTHER INTERNATIONAL ORGANIZATIONS

The United Nations is the largest international organization in the world. Its membership includes representatives from each of the 159 countries that make up the UN body. Although most people know of the UN's work during times of international crises, it is, in actuality, as close to a world government that we have. Separate UN agencies, departments and commissions deal with matters ranging from international postal delivery, atomic energy, health, agriculture, aviation, economics and banking, labor, science, culture, population, international law, shipping and trade, and, of course, the rights and care of children. Although, offices of the various agencies are located throughout the world, the major cities serving UN functions (outside of New York) are Geneva, Vienna, Rome and Paris.

The largest employer within the UN is the Secretariat. It is the organization that serves the Secretary General and, in essence, is the administrative arm of the UN. The General Assembly, Security Council, Economic and Social Council, and Trusteeship Council all fall within the purview of the office of the Secretary General, thus the Secretariat. Its foreign offices include: the UN offices in Geneva and Vienna, The UN Conference on Trade and Development (UNCTAD) and the Office of the UN Disaster Relief Coordinator (UNDRO) in Geneva, the UN Center for Human Settlements (HABITAT) in Nairobi and more than 60 information centers throughout the world.

The greatest need is for personnel with a background or experience in economics, area studies, agriculture, social science, health and medicine, and administration. If you have an interdisciplinary background, so much the better. In areas of economics there is a demand for specialists in accounting, business planning, developmental planning, econometrics, and statistics. Other specialists are always needed in the fields of energy and natural resources, petroleum and mineral exploration and development, energy systems planning, water management, urban and rural planning, construction, environmental planning, and of course computer systems, processing, and information science. There is also a continuous need for additions to the secretarial and clerical staffs. It will help if you have a working knowledge of at least two of the UN's official languages: English, French, Spanish, Chinese, Arabic, and Russian.

Salaries are usually below those of a comparable position in industry but there are fringe benefits including cost of living allowances, tax advantages and generous holidays. Professional positions are graded from P-1 to P-5 depending on your experience and degree. For example a P-1 ranges from about $19,200 to $27,200; P-2 from about $25,200 to $34,800. At present the UN is making a concentrated effort to hire more women.

Since many foreign nationals are applying for jobs, the UN tries to balance national representatives within each department and agency. It also has a policy of allotting jobs on a quota system based upon each nation's financial contribution to the organization. Thus if the agency to which you apply receives 20% of it's funding from the United States, they try to hire one American for every five employees. Despite the simplicity of the quota system, it never works. If an experienced individual from an underdeveloped nation applies for the same job the chances are he or she will get priority. Yet, in many agencies you will find well over the quota for Americans. Unlike many foreign jobs, connections do make a difference at the UN. If you know a high official and that influence can be applied you have a big edge. The higher the position for which you apply, the more important the political strings become. Your ability to speak a foreign language is also a major factor in obtaining a UN position.

Another critical factor in trying to obtain a job with the UN is their continual financial problems. Many nations are years delinquent in paying their assigned dues to the UN, and it is extremely difficult managing an organization as large as the UN without being able to plan on a known source or amount of income. As a result, there are periods in which the UN simply stops hiring. Individual commissions or agencies can also be faced with a periodic hiring freeze as well. Like so many other things in life, timing is critical when applying for work with the United Nations.

For more information on UN employment opportunities abroad write for: *Opportunities Overseas in International Organizations and Opportunities with UNESCO* available at any UN Information Center or from United Nations Department of Public Information, United Nations, New York, NY 10017. Also fax or send your letter and resume to: Recruitment and Placement Division, Room S-2500, United Nations, 1 UN

Plaza, New York, NY 10017. Fax: (212) 963-3134.

To apply for a job with the Secretariat outside New York, write to Secretariat Recruitment Section, Personnel Service, International Trade Center, 54-56 Rue de Montbrillant, CH-1202, Geneva, Switzerland.

Let's take a look at other United Nations agencies and commissions:

- **United Nations Development Programs (UNDP)**—is the agency which coordinates and finances the many programs in more than 100 under developed countries. UNDP has two main goals: to assist developing nations provide their own population with more than the basics in such vital areas as health, nutrition, housing, education, jobs, and public service; and, to help these countries develop their own commodities and, where possible, raw materials. The United States alone spends about $540 million through the UN on about 8,000 UNDP projects. This agency administers about 80% of all funds that go for developmental purposes. The agency maintains over 100 field offices and expects their staff to spend most of their careers on four year tours of duty at the field bases. Their needs are for individuals experienced in agriculture, industry, transportation, economics, sociology, and public health. A graduate degree is expected as is fluency in either French or Spanish. Contact: Division of Personnel, Overseas Development Administration, United Nations Development Program, 1 UN Plaza, New York, NY 10017.

- **United Nations Department of Technical Co-operation for Development**—is one of the many development agencies financed by UNDP that rarely makes the news. This group works in many underdeveloped countries to provide assistance in areas involving energy resources, public administration, finance, transportation, economic development and social welfare. The agency looks for individuals who have had at least a decade or more experience and a high professional standing in their specific field. This is not a spot for beginners—the competition is too rough for the few openings. Contact: Recruitment Section, Division of Personnel, United Nations Development Programme, 1 UN Plaza, New York, NY 10017.

- **United Nations Industrial Development Organization (UNIDO)**—has been in existence since 1967 but since 1986 has been a specialized agency devoted to assisting nations develop their industrial capabilities. One goal of UNIDO is to "increase the developing nations' share of the world industrial production from 7 per cent to 25 per cent by the year 2000." To accomplish this goal, UNIDO looks for highly experienced individuals with a background in business management, industrial relations, labor relations, industrial technology, economics and industrial engineering. Contact: Recruitment Section, United Nations Industrial Development Organization, P.O. Box # 300, Wagrammerstrasse 5, A-1400 Vienna, Austria.

- **Food and Agriculture Organization (FAO)**—has some 2,000 people working in more than 130 countries (and another 3,000 in their Rome headquarters) helping developing nations help themselves. Most of the work is in the fields of agriculture, fisheries, and forestry. Experience in soil management, water resources, economics, statistics, nutrition, marketing and economic management is essential. Most jobs require a minimum of five years on the job experience. Contact: Personnel Officer, Food and Agriculture Organization, Via delle Terme di Caracalla, 00100 Rome, Italy.

- **International Fund for Agricultural Development (IFAD)**—is a recently established agency with an initial backing of $1 billion. IFAD works with FAO to help finance developing nations increase their agricultural production. This is not as much an in-field organization as a financing organization to provide the necessary funds to get the job done. Thus, experience in agricultural economics, banking and finance, food technology and international development is what is needed here. Contact: International Fund for Agricultural Development, Via del Serafico 107, EUR 00142 Rome, Italy.

- **International Trade Center UNCTAD/GATT**—is a permanent organ of the UN General Assembly. Its mandate is to assist in carrying out technical cooperation activities with developing nations in promoting international trade as a means to raise standards of living. There are about 250 employed in Geneva headquarters with about 600 to 700 consultants hired annually to work in marketing, trade promotion, import and export techniques, and finance. Contact: Director, Division of Programs, Finance and Personnel, International Trade Center UNCTAD/GATT, Palais des Nations, 1211 Geneva 10, Switzerland.

- **International Monetary Fund (IMF)**—is a Washington-based international organization involved in world economic problems. It provides financial assistance to nations, monitors balance-of-payments, analyzes world economic developments and assists nations develop financial policies and practices. Although most of the staff is located in Washington IMF maintains offices in Paris and Geneva. Only individuals experienced in banking, finance and accounting will be considered. A few candidates with master's degrees are hired but most have either a Ph.D. in finance or economics or a solid multi-year background in the field. Contact: Director of Personnel, International Monetary Fund, 700 19th Street NW, Washington, DC 20431. (202) 263-7000.

- **United Nations Educational, Scientific, and Cultural Organization (UNESCO)**—is very much involved in problems concerning world illiteracy, the exchange of scientific and technological knowledge through international conferences, helping developing nations create and develop local newspapers and training centers for aspiring journalists, and of course the much publicized efforts to initiate cultural rescue operations such as saving early Egyptian tombs and temples along the Nile during the construction of the Aswan Dam. Most field appointments are for a period of one to two years. UNESCO looks for individuals experienced in education (particularly with a background in science, engineering or technology). Teaching experience at the university level or at a technical school is a plus as is experience in educational training, curriculum, administration, and teacher training. Occasional jobs open up requiring a background in broadcasting, communications skills, mass media, audio-visual aids, and information science. Contact: Personnel Officer, United Nations Educational, Scientific, and Cultural Organization,

UNESCO House, 7 Place de Fontenoy, 75700 Paris, France.

- **World Health Office (WHO)**—is constantly on the look out for experienced medical personnel to work in undeveloped countries. WHO assists member nations carry out basic health care and is heavily involved in medical training. The organization also promotes health and medical research and conducts international conferences to promote the free interchange of scientific information. Most employees are stationed at one of the agencies six regional offices: Brazzaville, Washington, Alexandria, Copenhagen, New Delhi, and Manila. Openings at WHO's headquarters in Geneva are rare but there is a constant demand for doctors, nurses and qualified health care professionals to serve out of the regional offices. Fluency in the language of the region is extremely helpful. Contact: Director, World Health Organization, 20 Avenue Appia, 1211 Geneva 27, Switzerland.

- **International Labor Organization (ILO)**—is unlike most UN bodies in that its policy making board includes representatives of government, workers and management from each member country. The purpose of the agency is to improve labor conditions around the world and by doing so raise the standard of living and promote economic stability. The experts employed by the ILO are experienced in manpower planning, alleviation of rural poverty, vocational or apprentice training, labor-management relations, industrial relations, and labor economics. A knowledge of foreign languages is also most helpful as is experience in trade unionism. Contact: Personnel Department, International Labor Organization, 4 Route des Morillon, 1211 Geneva, Switzerland.

- **International Bank for Reconstruction and Development (IBRD)**—is the umbrella organization that encompasses: the World Bank, the International Development Association, the International Center for Settlement of Investment Disputes, and the International Finance Corporation. The primary mandate of these organizations is to assist developing countries secure the economic resources needed to accomplish their growth and progress. The World Bank, for example has a staff of about 1,800 experienced economists and bankers. In addition to finance specialists the IBRD searches for experienced individuals in the fields of development economics, agriculture, international trade, industrial problems, energy specialists, public administrators, etc. Applicants 30 and under with a master's degree can apply for the Young Professionals Program. You are given two or three rotating four to eight month assignments in one of the various areas of IBRD's specialization. Upon completion of these "apprentice" tours you join the organization as a full fledged member. The complete selection/interview process can take up to six months. The program is most prestigious and extremely competitive. Contact: Director of Personnel, International Bank for Reconstruction and Development, 1818 H Street NW, Washington, DC 20433 (202) 477-1234.

- **International Atomic Energy Agency (IAEA)**—works with developing nations to provide assistance and information on the use of nuclear energy for all non-military purposes. Work might involve studying and making recommendations on the use of nuclear reactors to introduce low cost energy to a region or the applications of radioisotopes in agriculture, industry or medicine. Experience in nuclear physics and engineering is important as is knowledge in areas others than science including economics, public administration and international relations. Contact: Personnel Office, International Atomic Energy Agency, Wagramerstrasse 5, P.O. Box 100, A-1400 Vienna, Austria.

Several other United Nations agencies also provide employment opportunities:

International Civil Aviation Organization (ICAO)
P.O. Box 400
1000 Sherbrooke Street W
Montreal H 3A 2R2, Canada
(514) 285-8219

United Nations Children's Fund (UNICEF)
866 UN Plaza
New York, NY 10017
(212) 326-7000

UN Conference on Trade and Development (UNCTAD)
Palais des Nations
CH-1121 Geneva 10, Switzerland

United Nations University
Toho Sheimei Building
15-1 Shibuya 2-Chome, Shibuya-ku,
Tokyo, 150, Japan

General Agreement on Tariffs and Trade (GATT)
Centre William Rappard
154 Rue de Lausanne
CH-1211 Geneva 21, Switzerland

United Nations Environment Program
P.O. Box # 30552
Nairobi, Kenya

Organization of American States (OAS) is considered a United
Nations related organization, but in fact is united only in objectives: the
maintenance of "peace, security, and prosperity for all Americans" in the
Western Hemisphere. Its network of agencies and organizations include
the Pan American Health Organization, Inter-American Institute of
Agricultural Sciences, as well as eight permanent committees. The OAS
maintains its headquarters in Washington but many of its standing groups
are located elsewhere. For example, The Inter-American Children's
Institute is in Montevideo and the Pan-American Institute of Geography
and History is in Mexico City. Much of the work is conducted abroad. A
background in Latin American studies, economic development, international relations as well as a knowledge of either Spanish or Portuguese
is most helpful. Contact: Director of Personnel Development, Organization of American States, Constitution Avenue and 17th Street NW,
Washington, DC 20006 (202) 458-3000.

Other international organizations of interest to job seekers include:

Council of Europe
67006 Strasbourg, France

The European Organization for Nuclear Research (CERN)
1211 Geneva 23, Switzerland

North Atlantic Treaty Organization (NATO)
110 Brussels, Belgium

Organization for Economic Co-operation
 and Development (OECD)
2 rue Andre-Pascal
75775 Paris, France

NON-PROFIT ORGANIZATIONS

Aside from the two largest non-profit groups, the U.S. Government and the United Nations, there are a host of groups and organizations ranging in size and dollar expenditures from the Ford Foundation to small, almost one-person operations designed to promote and enhance a specific political, social or religious point of view. For the most part, non-profit organizations don't pay the sort of salaries that you'll find with a major company doing business abroad. You'll also discover that many non-profit groups have interesting sounding names and an attractive description of their activities. However, when you start digging into the group's activities and true objectives you discover that it is a one or two person operation with no office outside this country. You'll also discover that many interesting sounding organizations that appear to promote an international interest are, in reality, a political action group established primarily to lobby congress for their private agendas. Not to suggest that there is anything wrong with these practices. They are perfectly legal and fully above board. But you won't find many groups establishing a foreign base if their prime concern is domestic policy.

In almost all cases working for a non-profit organization requires a substantial background into that organization's special interest. Obviously, if you're a petroleum engineer, you won't stand much of a chance sending a resume to the Foreign Policy Association. You'll find that many employees of the non-religious international organizations have solid backgrounds in economics, political science, sociology, business management and quite often a specific scientific discipline such as agronomy. Many non-profit organizations also rely heavily upon volunteer workers to do much of the leg work.

A detailed list of many non-profit organizations divided by specific fields and subjects can be found in most libraries. Ask for the multi-volume *Encyclopedia of Associations* published periodically by Gale Research as well as the *Foundation Directory* published by the Foundation Center in New York. These works provide names and addresses of many non-profit groups. Another important reference source containing the names of U.S. non-profit organizations (more than half are religious) as well as a description of their work is *U.S. Nonprofit Organizations in Development Assistance Abroad*, published by UNIPUB-Kraus International Publications, 1 Water Street, White Plains, NY 10601. For a listing of more than 150 agencies containing a description of their activities, addresses and phone numbers, request the report, *American Voluntary Agencies Engaged in Overseas Relief and Development*, from the Agency for International Development, Department of State, Washington, DC 20523.

Of the more important groups with strong roots in foreign countries and a history of hiring individuals to work overseas consider:

African-American Institute
833 United Nations Plaza
New York, NY 10017

Agricultural Development
 Council
1290 Avenue of the Americas
New York, NY 10020

American Council on Education
1 Dupont Circle
Washington, DC 20036

American Council on Germany;
 John J. McCoy Fund
680 Fifth Avenue
New York, NY 10019

American Field Service
313 East 43rd Street
New York, NY 10017

American Friends Service
 Committee
1501 Cherry Street
Philadelphia, PA 19102

American Jewish Committee
165 East 56th Street
New York, NY 10022

American Political Science
 Association
1527 New Hampshire Avenue
Washington, D.C. 20036

American Red Cross
2025 E Street NW
Washington DC 20006

Amnesty International USA
304 West 58th Street
New York, NY 10019

Asia Society
725 Park Avenue
New York, NY 10021

Brookings Institution
1775 Massachusetts Ave. NW
Washington, DC 20036

CARE
660 First Avenue
New York, NY 10016

Carnegie Corporation
437 Madison Avenue
New York, NY 10022

Catholic Relief Services
1011 First Avenue
New York, NY 10022

Charles Kettering Foundation
5335 Far Hills Avenue
Dayton, OH 45429

Conference Board
845 Third Avenue
New York, NY 10022

Council of the Americas
684 Park Avenue
New York, NY 10021

Council on Foreign Relations
58 East 68th Street
New York, NY 10021

Council on International
 Educational Exchange
205 East 42nd Street
New York, NY 10017

Ford Foundation
320 East 43rd Street
New York, NY 10017

Foster Parents Plan
 International
P.O. Box 400
Warwick, RI 02887

German Marshall Fund of the
 United States
11 Dupont Circle
Washington, DC 20036

Hudson Institute
Herman Khan Center
5395 Emerson Way
Indianapolis, IN 46226

Institute of Current World
 Affairs
4 West Wheelock Street
Hanover, NH 03755

Institute of Defense Analysis
1801 N. Beauregard
Arlington, VA 22202

Institute of International
 Education
809 UN Plaza
New York, NY 10017

International Human Assistance
 Programs
360 Park Avenue South
New York, NY 10010

International Research and
 Exchanges Board
1616 H Street NW
Washington, DC 20006

International Institute for
Environment and Development
27 Mortimer Street
London W1A 4QW,
ENGLAND

International Red Cross
7 Avenue de la Paix
Geneva, SWITZERLAND

International Rescue
 Committee
386 Park Avenue
New York, NY 10016

National Committee on
 American Foreign Policy
350 Fifth Avenue
New York, NY 10118

National Foreign Trade
 Council
1270 Avenue of the Americas
#300
New York, NY 20002

Near East Foundation
342 Madison Ave. #1030
New York, NY 10173

New TransCentury Foundation
1901 N. Fort Myer Drive
Suite 1017
Arlington, VA 22209

Overseas Development Council
1717 Massachusetts Ave, NW
Washington, DC 20036

Pan American Society
 of the United States
680 Park Avenue
New York, NY 10021

Pathfinders Fund
9 Galen St. #217
Watertown, MA 02172

Population Council
1 Dag Hammarskjold Plaza
New York, NY 10017

Population Institute
107 2nd St. NE
Washington, DC 20002

Project HOPE
People to People
 Health Foundation
Millwood, VA 22646

Rockefeller Foundation
1133 Avenue of the Americas
New York, NY 10020

Rockefeller Fund
1290 Avenue of the Americas
New York, NY 10020

Social Science Research
 Council
605 Third Avenue
New York, NY 10016

Twentieth Century Fund
41 East 70th Street
New York, NY 10021

World Wildlife Fund
1250 24th Street NW
Washington, DC 20002

TEACHING ABROAD

In addition to working as an employee for one of the many governmental, non-profit or industrial operations overseas, there is a growing market for individual consultants or freelance employees willing to work on a contractual basis for a period of several months to several years. Perhaps the most widely held position for the consultant or freelance worker is in teaching. Although for the majority of overseas teaching jobs you need the same basic credentials, you would need to teach in the states, there is one major exception.

If you want to teach abroad you have four options:

- Teaching as a freelancer primarily to foreign nationals who want to learn English or for one of the many foreign language schools (such as Berlitz) operating in countries throughout the world.

- Teaching in one of the 25schools operated by the Department of Defense for dependents of Defense Department personnel (including the military).

- Teaching at one of the hundred-plus American K-12 schools serviced by the Department of State and designed for the children of American dependents abroad.

- Teaching at one of the private schools established by an American business concern for their employee's dependents.

Another option for teachers is an exchange program. Although, in most cases, you are paid your normal teacher's salary and lose many of the tax advantages you might receive as a full time foreign resident, you do gain the beneficial experience of living and working abroad. For example, the U.S. Dept. of Education operates a program for teachers with at least a bachelor's degree and three years teaching experience to teach in elementary and secondary schools abroad for either a full year or a semester. Information about this program is available from:

Teacher Exchange Section
Center for International Education
U.S. Department of Education
7th and D Streets, S.W.
Washington, DC 20202
(202) 732-6061

Teachers interested in an English exchange package can contact:

The Central Bureau for Educational Visits and Exchanges
Seymour Mews House, 2nd Floor, Suite 26-37
Seymour Mews, London, W1H 9PH, ENGLAND

For employment information about the State Department's overseas program as well as other data including fact sheets on individual U.S. State Department supported schools and their 31-page publication, *Overseas American-Sponsored Elementary and Secondary Schools Assisted by the U.S. Department of State* is available from:

Office of Overseas Schools
Bureau of Administration,
Department of State, SA6, Room 234
Washington, DC 20520

Another organization involved in placing approximately 250 teachers and administrators in foreign schools is the International School Service. Their annual directory lists more than 600 schools in 124 countries complete with per cent of U.S. faculty, curriculum details, facilities, etc. Available from:

International School Service (ISS)
15 Roszel Road
PO Box 5910
Princeton, NJ 08543
(609) 452-0990

To serve as one of the 11,000 teachers at one of the 270 overseas dependent schools operated by the Defense Department, you need at least 18 semester hours of professional teacher education courses, a minimum of one year classroom teaching experience, and a valid teaching certificate.

The school year is 190 days with 175 days in the classroom. Interviews are held in March and April. It takes about six weeks to process the applications of those interested in teaching for the government. This time period can drag out if you fail to submit all the required paper work. For additional data, including their annual 44 page publication, *Overseas Employment Opportunities for Educators*, contact:

Department of Defense Dependents Schools
Department of Defense
4040 N. Fairfax Drive
Alexandria, VA 22314

American companies that operate schools abroad for their employee's dependents first try to locate locals to handle the assignment rather than sustain the expense of transporting Americans abroad. Too often, however, hiring an experienced American to handle the assignment proves far more beneficial in both terms of cost effectiveness and productivity—the kids learn more. The major employer of U.S. teachers abroad are the oil companies operating in the Middle East. For example, Exxon, Texaco, Gulf Oil Corporation, Arabian American Oil Co. all have educational operations for their overseas employees. Other U.S. companies with educational programs include: United Fruit Co., Firestone Tire and Rubber Co., and Orinoco Mining Co.

Another group that has an expanding foreign educational program is the International Friends movement. This group with roots founded in Quakerism is interested in teachers with a "world outlook on human problems" to teach college level courses in their schools located on every continent. For more information about requirements and opportunities contact:

Director of International Operations,
Friends World College
Lloyd Harbor, NY 11743

Of late there has been a growing demand for teachers of English in both Japan and several of the developing countries in the Middle East. For example, one of the largest employers of teachers in Japan is the GEOS Corporation (Simpson's Tower, 401 Bay Street, Toronto, Ontario, Canada, M5H 2Y4), a Canadian-based firm specializing in establishing language schools in Japan; they presently maintain more than 130 schools. They require a bachelor's degree but no teaching experience.

Salary is about $2,000 per month plus a furnished private apartment, a medical program and end-of-contract bonus of $4,000. Although a TEFL (Teaching English as a Foreign Language) certificate almost guarantees you placement, there are still opportunities for those with neither the certificate nor experience.

The United Nations University in Japan also has periodic openings for university professors. The university is not a traditional school; it employs a multidisciplinary approach to specific world problems such as hunger, health, international trade, human rights, etc. For further information write to: United Nations University, Toho Sheimei Building, 15-1 Shibuya 2-Chome, Shibuya-ku, Tokyo, 150, Japan.

The standard teaching contract runs from two to three years (except if you elect to become an independent contractor where you establish your own duration) with transportation, housing and bonuses part of the contractual package.

TRAVEL-RELATED JOBS ABROAD

Would you like a free airline pass? Perhaps vouchers for the world's leading resorts and hotels? The answer to everyone's dream! Unfortunately, this is all too often the picture many people have of the "exotic" travel agent or commercial air line pilot. Alas, it IS but a dream. Yes, there are many good travel-related jobs overseas but the majority of them are based in the United States with the only travel possibilities limited to periodic work-related junkets or business trips overseas. Not at all bad, but hardly a foreign-based overseas career. Yet, there are occasional needs in the travel or tourism business for individuals with a solid background in the business to work in a foreign branch. For example, several major travel agents have foreign operations to assist in the planning and organizing of overseas tours. Experience in the business is an essential element in obtaining most of these jobs.

There are about 25,000 travel agencies in the United States with about half of them owned or controlled by women. (There are about two women for every man employed in the business.) The average agency has five or six full time and one or two part time employees. The largest agency is American Express. American Express frequently hires trainees. Starting salaries are considered low, averaging less than $12,000 at entry and about $15,000 to $20,000 after five years. The business is seasonal and it is likely that layoffs will occur during slow parts of the year or during any economic downturn. It is also unlikely that you would be assigned an overseas job without working for the parent company for a period of time. For additional information contact:

American Society of Travel Agents
1101 King St. #200
Alexandria, VA 22314

Institute of Individual Travel Agents
148 Linden Street
Wellesley, MA 02181

American Express Co.
American Express Tower
World Financial Center
New York, NY 10285-4765

Ask Mr. Foster Travel Corp
7833 Haskell Avenue
Van Nuys, CA 91406

Thomas Cook Travel
2 Pennsylvania Plaza
New York, NY 10001

Many of the major U.S. hotel chains also have substantial foreign operations. Although all overseas hotels are staffed by local workers, occasionally an American is transferred to a foreign hotel to either gain additional experience, train local management, or serve as the eyes of management to learn local business methods and practices. Don't count on foreign hotels to employ an American in place of a local. Again, experience is essential if you expect to work for an American hotel chain abroad. For further information, contact the following organizations:

American Hotel & Motel Association
888 Seventh Avenue
New York, NY 10019

The Educational Institute of the
 American Hotel & Motel Association
1407 South Harrison Road
East Lansing, MI 48823

Hotel Association of Canada
804-10080 Jasper Avenue
Edmonton, Alberta CANADA T5J 1V9

Hilton International Co.
605 Third Avenue
New York, NY 10158

Holiday Inns, Inc.
3742 Lamar Avenue
Memphis, TN 38195

Hyatt International Corp.
200 West Madison Avenue
Chicago, IL 60606

Knott Hotels Corp.
840 Madison Avenue
New York, NY 10021

Ramada, Inc.
3838 East Van Buren
Phoenix, AZ 85008

Sheraton Corp.
60 State Street
Boston, MA 02109

Westin Hotel Co.
The Westin Bldg.
2001 6th Ave.
Seattle, WA 98121

The airline business is another limited opportunity for an overseas career. Although all of the U.S. based transcontinental airlines have offices in most of the cities from which they operate, these offices are staffed by locals. The ground crews abroad are almost entirely native to the country. In some of the larger foreign cities an American airline will send a trained executive to assist in operations and management, but these foreign tours are usually limited to a period of several months of a year or two at most. The airlines prefer training local management. It is

far less costly and is good public relations in the host country.
For information about airline jobs abroad, contact:

Airline Employees Association
5600 South Central Avenue
Chicago, IL 60638

American Association of Airport Executives
4224 King Street
Alexandria, VA 22302

Major U.S. airlines for foreign operations include the following:

American Airlines
P.O. Box 61616
Dallas-Fort Worth Airport, Texas 75261

Continental Airlines
2929 Allen Parkway
Houston, TX 77019

Delta Airlines
Hartsfield Atlanta International Airport
Atlanta, GA 30320

Northwest Airlines
Minnneapolis-St. Paul International Airport
St. Paul, MN 55111

Trans World Airlines
100 South Bedford Road
Mt. Kisco, NY 10549

United Airlines
Professional Employment Division
P.O. Box # 66100
Chicago, IL 60666

MONEY AND BANKING

With the constant change in the international economic scene there is a
greater need than ever for individuals with experience in international
finance, banking, accounting, investment analysis, marketing, political
risk analysis, economics and international affairs. In the past decade
many of America's major banks have been burned badly investing in the
international arena. Both Bank of America and Chase Manhattan Bank,
for example, have admitted that their losses from investments in Mexico
alone have had a severe impact on the banks' profitability.

Yet even with the inherent risks and questionable loans abroad,
American banks are more aggressive than ever in establishing a strong
foothold overseas. U.S. banks are competing actively with the major
European and Japanese banks to take advantage of the strong economic
growth potential in Europe and Asia as well as the challenge of assisting
Eastern Europe and Central Asia meet the demands of a free market.
Despite Chase's losses in Mexico, for example, earnings from their
international business have more than tripled in the last five years. Half
of the operating income of Manufacturers Hanover Corporation comes
from foreign operations with the major source of their loans centered in
industrial countries. More than 40% of Chemical's loans, for example,
are outside the United States. Citicorp, a holding company with Citibank
as its principal subsidiary, has more than 300 offices in about 100 foreign
countries. Bank of America has more than 1,000 offices around the
world. Chase has established offices in more than 100 countries while
Chemical Bank is in 26 countries abroad. Most of the U.S. banks heavily
engrossed in the foreign market establish separate divisions or subsidiaries based upon geographic region or banking function. The Bank of
America, for example, has four geographic departments: Asia Division;
Europe, Middle East, and Africa Division; Latin America Division; and
North America Division. Citibank is initially organized by function.
Their Institutional Banking Unit is further subdivided into five regional
groups; their Capitol Markets Group is divided in two regions: the
Western Hemisphere, and, the rest of the world. The Bank of New York
separates its overseas operations by bank function: International Banking
Group, International Corporate Banking Group, International Correspon-
dent Banking Division, International Operations Division, International
Investments Department, Foreign Exchange Trading Department, and,
the International Planning Department.

In addition to banking operations, many American investment firms
have also established offices abroad. Merrill, Lynch, Pierce, Fenner &

Smith, Goldman Sachs, Shearson/American Express, and Wertheim & Co. are but a few of the major Wall Street firms with foreign offices. Not to be left out, anyone with a solid background in accounting coupled with the specific knowledge of a foreign country (and the ability to speak the language fluently), is a prime candidate to work for one of the more than 25 major American accounting firms with offices abroad. Ernst & Young, for example, has offices in more than 300 cities in 70 countries. It also has representation agreements with firms in another 13 countries.

Many of the financial companies involved in foreign operations maintain active trainee programs in America prior to a foreign assignment. In most cases trainees are assigned to domestic operations for a period of from six months to several years before an international opening occurs. In all cases, those sent abroad representing their companies must be thoroughly experienced and, in most cases, also familiar with the country, culture and language. Years spent gaining an MBA with the expectation of working in the financial markets abroad may be for naught if you're unable to communicate in the language of the country. It is true that English is a universal tongue and certainly the business leaders in Europe and much of Asia are multilingual. Yet, most American companies think twice before sending a representative abroad that can not read or comprehend another language. Not only does it reflect on the parent company but in observing and understanding the business and financial conditions in a foreign country—much of which is written in the local press, business magazines, and trade publications —you better know the language of the country. (An exception to this general rule is those countries in which English is the primary language for conducting business, such as the nations of the Middle East.)

Major U.S. Banks with International Operations:

BankAmerica
201 California Street
San Francisco, CA 94111

Bank of New England
28 State Street
Boston, MA 02106

Bank of Boston Corp.
100 Federal Street
Boston, MA 02110

Bankers Trust Co.
280 Park Avenue
New York, NY 10017

Bank of New York
1 Wall Street
New York, NY 10015

Chase Manhattan Bank
1 Chase Manhattan Plaza
New York, NY 10015

Chemical Bank
277 Park Avenue
New York, NY 10172

Citibank
399 Park Avenue
New York, NY 10043

Continental Illinois National
 Bank and Trust Company
 of Chicago
231 South La Salle Street
Chicago, IL 60693

Crocker Bank International
299 Park Avenue
New York, NY 10017

Fiduciary Trust Co of NY
2 World Trade Center
New York, NY 10048

First City National Bank
1001 Main Street
Houston, TX 77002

First National Bank of Boston
100 Federal Street
Boston, MA 02110

First National Bank of Chicago
One First National Plaza
Chicago, IL 60670

Marine Midland Bank
One Marine Midland Center
Buffalo, NY 14240

Mellon Bank
One Mellon Bank Center
Pittsburgh, PA 15258

Morgan Guaranty Trust
 Company
60 Wall Street
New York, NY 10015

Philadelphia International Bank
5th and Market Streets
Philadelphia, PA 19101

Wells Fargo International
20 Montgomery Street
San Francisco, CA 90024

Major International Accounting Firms:

Anderson Consulting
69 West Washington Street
Chicago, IL 60602

Ernst & Young
277 Park Avenue
New York, NY 10172

Coopers & Lybrand
 International
1251 Avenue of the Americas
New York, NY 10020

Deloitte & Touche
1 World Trade Center #9300
New York, NY 10048

Grant Thornton International
Prudential Plaza
Chicago, IL 60601

KPMG Peat Marwick
767 Fifth Avenue
New York, NY 10153

Horwath & Horwath
 International
919 Third Avenue
New York, NY 10022

Price Waterhouse & Co.
1251 Avenue of the Americas
New York, NY 10020

Major International Investment Firms:

A.G. Becker Inc.
Two First National Plaza
Chicago, IL 60603

Kidder Peabody & Co., Inc.
10 Hanover Square
New York, NY 10005

Dominick & Dominick Inc.
90 Broad Street
New York, NY 10090

Merrill Lynch & Company
250 Veseu Street
New York, NY 10081

Donaldson Lufkin &
 Jenrette Inc.
140 Broadway
New York, NY 10005

Paine Webber Group
1285 Avenue of the Americas
New York, NY 10019

Droulia & Co.
120 Broadway
New York, NY 10005

Shearson/American Express
2 World Trade Center
New York, NY 10048

First Boston Corp.
55 East 52nd Street
New York, NY 10055

Smith Barney
1345 Avenue of the Americas
New York, NY 10019

Goldman Sachs & Co.
85 Broad Street
New York, NY 10005

Wertheim Schroder & Co., Inc.
787 Seventh Avenue
New York, NY 10019

E. F. Hutton & Co., Inc.
1 Battery Park Plaza
New York, NY 10004

MANUFACTURING

With rapidly changing economic conditions around the world, it is only natural that America's major manufacturers are keeping abreast of these fluctuating conditions as well as what they can do to take advantage of these changes. Manufacturers learned some time ago of the inexpensive labor supply in countries such as Taiwan, Hong Kong, Malaysia, and the Philippines (Will Eastern Europe be the next labor bank for American manufacturers?). Whereas using foreign labor may solve many cost problems, whenever an American manufacturer takes advantage of the overseas work force he must also be prepared to either turn over the responsibility of quality control to foreign management or supply his own executives abroad. In most cases, overseas plants are locally run. Often foreign executives are brought to the U.S. for training or in some cases an American executive is sent abroad to set up a management/employee training program. In a few cases, however, it is more cost effective to send an American company representative abroad for a period of six months to several years to oversee an operation.

Contacting major U.S. manufacturers may lead to a foreign job, but the best opportunities are either by checking the various want ads in the newspapers and trade journals covering your particular field of expertise or though an employment agency specializing in foreign jobs. *The Wall Street Journal* and the *International Herald Tribune* often carry want ads from manufacturers looking for specialists for overseas work. *The Times of London* is another good source for foreign jobs in the manufacturing sector.

Overseas manufacturers need experienced executives, not on-the-job trainees. Individuals with a solid background in business management, marketing, sales, accounting and economics, product management, and general administration are most apt to be considered. Naturally language ability is a major plus.

Several American companies maintain internship programs which can lead to work abroad. Many companies use college interns during the summer and offer them a position upon graduation. Some companies have structured intern/training programs that lead to a foreign assignment. Several of the major petroleum companies such as Mobil Oil and Exxon have internship programs for students with backgrounds in engineering and business.

Major American manufacturers with foreign interests:

3M Company
3M Center
St. Paul, MN 55144

Allen-Bradley Co.
P.O. Box 2086
Milwaukee, WI 53201

Allis-Chalmers Corp.
P.O. Box 512
Milwaukee, WI 53201

American Can Co.
75 Holly Hill Lane
Greenwich, CT 06830

American Hoist &
 Derrick Corp.
63 S Robert Street
St. Paul, MN 55107

American Optical Corp.
14 Mechanic Street
Southbridge, MA 01550

American Standard, Inc.
40 West 40th Street
New York, NY 10018

AMF, Inc.
777 Westchester Avenue
White Plains, NY 10604

Anchor Hocking Corp.
109 North Broad Street
Lancaster, OH 43132

Armstrong World
 Industries, Inc.
P.O. Box 3001
Lancaster, PA 17604

Bell & Howell Co.
6800 N. McCormick Blvd.
Chicago, IL 60645-2775

Black & Decker Mfg Co.
701 East Jappa Road
Baltimore, MD 21204-5559

Borg-Warner Corp.
701 East Joppa Road
Baltimore, MD 21204

Cabot Corp.
25 High Street
Boston, MA 02110

Caraborundum Co.
Carborundum Center
P.O. Box 156
Niagara Falls, NY 14302

Caterpillar Tractor Co.
100 North East Adams Street
Peoria, IL 61629-0001

Christensen International
P.O. Box 26135
Salt Lake City, UT 84126

Chrysler Corp.
P.O. Box 1688
Detroit, MI 48231

The Coca Cola Company
PO Box 1734
Atlanta, GA 30301

Crane Co.
757 Third Avenue
New York, NY 10017

Cummins Engine Co., Inc.
P.O. Box 3005
Columbus, IN 47202

A B Dick Co.
5700 West Touhy Avenue
Chicago, IL 60648

Fairchild Aircraft Corp.
P.O. Box 32486
San Antonio, TX 78284

Ford Motor Co.
The American Road
Dearborn, MI 48121

General Electric Co.
3135 Easton Turnpike
Fairfield, CT 06431

General Motors Corp.
3-251 GM Bldg.
3044 West Grand Blvd.
Detroit, MI 48202

Goodyear Tire & Rubber Co.
11144 East Market Street
Akron, OH 44316

Hewlett-Packard Co.
3000 Hanover Street
Palo Alto, CA 94304

IBM
Armonk, NY 10505

Ingersoll Rand Co.
200 Chestnut Ridge Road
Woodcliff Lake, NJ 07675

Kidde Inc.
9 Brighton Road
Clifton, NJ 07015

Le Tourneau Inc.
P.O. Box 2307
Longview, TX 75606

Libbey-Owens-Ford Co.
811 Madison Avenue
Toledo, OH 43695

Lockheed Martin Corp.
4500 Park Granada Blvd.
Calabasas, CA 91399

Lockheed Martin Corp.
6801 Rockledge Road
Bethesda, MD 20817

Manville Corp.
P.O. Box 5108
Denver, CO 80217

Morton Thiokol Inc.
110 North Wacker Drive
Chicago, IL 60606

Motorola Inc.
1303 East Algonquin Road
Schaumburg, IL 60196

McDonnell Douglas Corp.
P.O. Box 516
St. Louis, MO 63166

Norton Co.
1 New Bond Street
Worcester, MA 01606

Packaging Corporation
of America
1603 Orrington Avenue
Evanston, IL 60204

Parker-Hannifin Corp.
17325 Euclid Avenue
Cleveland, OH 44112

Raytheon Co.
141 Spring Street
Lexington, MA 02173

Rockwell Intl. Corp.
625 Liberty Ave.
Pittsburgh, PA 15222-3123

St. Regis Paper Co.
237 Park Avenue
New York, NY 10017

The Stanley Works
1000 Stanley Drive
New Britain, CT 06050

Sunbeam Corp.
2001 South York Avenue
Oak Brook, IL 60521

Texas Instruments Inc.
P.O. Box 655474
13500 N. Central Expressway
Dallas, TX 75265

Trane Co.
3500 Pammel Creek Road
La Cross, WI 54601

Transamerica Corp.
600 Montgomery Street
San Francisco, CA 94111

TRW, Inc.
1900 Richmond Road
Cleveland, OH 44124

Uniroyal, Inc.
World Headquarters
Middlebury, CT 06749

Unisys
PO Box 500
Blue Bell, PA 19424

United Technologies Corp.
United Technologies Bldg.
Hartford, CT 06101

Vickers, Inc.
1401 Crooks Road
Troy, MI 48084

Warnaco, Inc.
350 Lafayette Street
Bridgeport, CT 06601

Warner-Swasey Co.
11000 Cedar Avenue
Cleveland, OH 44101

Westinghouse Air Brake Co.
40 West 40th Street
New York, NY 10018

Westinghouse Electric Co.
Gateway Center
Pittsburgh, PA 15222

White Consolidated
Industries, Inc.
11770 Berea Road
Cleveland, OH 44111

Worthington Group/
 McGraw Edison Co.
233 Mt. Airy Road
Basking Ridge, NY 07920

York International Corp.
631 South Richmond Road
York, PA 17405

Xerox Corp.
P.O. Box 1600
800 Longridge Road
Stamford, CT 06904

COMMUNICATIONS

For those expecting the glamour of foreign correspondent's jobs covering a NATO meeting or the life of a broadcaster reporting from the backwaters of Moscow or London, you are in for a disappointment. Yes, there are still foreign correspondents and American broadcasters abroad, but the entire communications industry has changed significantly in the past decade. Where the major networks had significant offices in all major world cities a few years ago, today a single freelance stringer is responsible for covering an entire region. The famed "Berlin Correspondent" is no more. The reason is basically the two Cs: cost and competition. To maintain large foreign staffs amidst growing competition was just too expensive for both the print and electronic media. A single stringer or a well known local broadcaster sent abroad on assignment is far more cost effective. However, despite the reduction in American reporters, writers and correspondents abroad there is still a need for specialists in the communications business.

For example, United Press International, maintains a staff of about 600 in their 80 overseas offices. The Associated Press maintains a staff of more than 2,500 journalists in their 60 foreign and 100 American offices. News magazines such as Time and Newsweek also maintain a small international staff as do major newspapers such as the New York Times, The Chicago Tribune, The Washington Post and the Christian Science Monitor.

The world's largest news agency, Reuters Ltd., often needs replacements for their stable of some 1,000 full time journalists. They recruit about a dozen college graduates each year for on the job training as journalists. (They also recruit about 20 for management training.) With a staff of 9,500, the turnover is much higher than the American news media.

In almost all cases a newspaper, magazine or broadcast network will only send experienced staff members on overseas assignments. The chances are a long-time employee with get first crack at the assignment and even then the internal competition is rough. The possible exception is the Board for International Broadcasting which oversees the operation of both Radio Free Europe and Radio Liberty. These foreign-based broadcast services beam programs to Russia and Eastern Europe. Before the political transformation in the Soviet block countries, these stations were funded by the CIA with the purpose of broadcasting about 1,000 program hours weekly in 22 languages. The future of both these operations is now cloudy. However, if any overseas jobs become available they will require individuals experienced in foreign affairs with a fluency in an Eastern European language.

To obtain consideration with any of the international news organizations a background in journalism is a must. In addition it is helpful to have a special understanding of international affairs and some language fluency.

Although the number of foreign jobs in journalism is shrinking, the same can't be said in the fields of advertising and public relations. As business abroad continues to expand, there is a greater need for experienced personnel in both these fields. Of course, there is a solid local base for talent, but many U.S. firms have opened offices abroad to represent both American clients as well as newly developed local customers. Again, previous experience in the field is a must. An experienced individual with language fluency and knowledge of a foreign country can often be a godsend. This is one field where knowing the local customs and business practices is an absolute essential. Contacts:

- **Journalism:**

ABC News
7 West 66th Street
New York, NY 10023

Associated Press
50 Rockefeller Plaza
New York, NY 10020

Board for International
 Broadcasting
1030 15th Street NW
Washington, DC 20005

Cable News Network
100 International Blvd
Atlanta, GA 30303

Capitol Cities/ABC News
77 West 66th Street
New York, NY 10023

CBS News
51 West 52nd Street
New York, NY 10019

Christian Science
 Publishing Society
1 Norway Street
Boston, MA 02115

Dow Jones & Co., Inc.
22 Cortlandt Street
New York, NY 10007

Los Angeles Times
Times Mirror Square
Los Angeles, CA 90053

National Broadcasting
 Company (NBC)
30 Rockefeller Plaza
New York, NY 10012

New York Times
229 West 43rd Street
New York, NY 10036

Reuters, Ltd.
85 Fleet Street
London, EC4
ENGLAND

United Press International
1400 I Street NW
Washington, DC 20005

The Washington Post
1150 15th Street NW
Washington, DC 20071

- **Public Relations:**

Burston-Marsteller
 Intl.
866 Third Avenue
New York, NY 10022

Hill & Knowlton Inc.
420 Lexington Avenue
New York, NY 10017

Ruder & Finn Intl.
110 East 59th Street
New York, NY 10022

- **Advertising:**

Benton & Bowles, Inc.
909 Third Avenue
New York, NY 10022

Leo Burnett Co., Inc.
Prudential Plaza
Chicago, IL 60601

Foote Cone & Belding
401 North Michigan Avenue
Chicago, IL 60611

Grey Advertising, Inc.
777 Third Avenue
New York, NY 10017

Ketchum Communications
4 Gateway Center
Pittsburgh, PA 15222

Marsteller Intl.
1 East Wacker Drive
Chicago, IL 60690

Needham Harper & Steers, Inc.
909 Third Avenue
New York, NY 10022

Ogilvy & Mather, Inc.
2 East 48th Street
New York, NY 10017

SSC&B: Lintas Worldwide
1 Dag Hammarskjold Plaza
New York, NY 10017

J. Walter Thompson Co.
466 Lexington Avenue
New York, NY 10017

Sudler & Hennessey, Inc.
1633 Broadway
New York, NY 10019

Young & Rubicam Intl., Inc.
285 Madison Avenue
New York, NY 10017

Ted Bates Worldwide, Inc.
1515 Broadway
New York, NY 10036

ENGINEERING, CONSTRUCTION, OPERATIONS AND MAINTENANCE

Of all professions, no trade, other than the military, offers more opportunities to work abroad than the engineering, building and construction, operations and maintenance field. The Middle East, for example, has a surplus of dollars and an acute shortage of skilled personnel in engineering and construction. Laborers are plentiful; managers are scarce. In Saudi Arabia alone, there are 3 million foreign born workers. Americans with construction experience can demand and get considerably more for a basic job than they may at home in the U.S. With solid experience behind you, the salaries increase accordingly.

As a result of the increased profits made on high-priced oil, contracts for roads, power stations, water supply, sewerage, and irrigation systems, airports and even military bases are being let at a rate never before experienced. For example, Saudi Arabia is now the world's leader in desalinated water production. Plants costing millions of dollars are now under construction with dozens more in the planning stage. In 1989 the country spent more than $530 million on just power plants. In 1980 there were 10 dams in the country. Today there are 200 with more under construction.

Very often, once a major project is constructed, there is a lack of sufficient technical and supervisory personnel to maintain and operate it. Hence the increasing need for trained individuals in the growing field of maintenance, or O&M. At one time O&M was considered as limited to general "house cleaning." No more!

During my days as Managing Director of a large Saudi company, the vast majority of our work was in O&M projects. For example, we were responsible for assuring that the power plants, built to handle a city the size of Pittsburgh, were always fully functional. In addition, we were called on to oversee vehicle maintenance and supply manpower. These O&M jobs provide openings for professional, technical and supervisory personnel in a wide range of disciplines.

Keep in mind that working in the Middle East isn't all peaches and cream as many Americans discovered during the Iraq situation. Americans in Kuwait were left stranded as soon as the first Iraqi troops crossed the borders. Also, working in the Middle East does mean you must consider your family responsibilities. Americans live in modern complexes with apartments usually part of the contract. Life in American complexes built close to work sites is not unlike life at home. Recreational facilities with modern swimming pools are common. Commissaries stock many American foods. The cost of food both in the housing complexes as well as in the local markets will vary. Western foods, fruits and vegetables will be high.

ENR Magazine reported that both design and construction contracts for 1993 declined significantly over 1992 for U.S. firms both at home and abroad. Low oil prices were given as a primary reason for this decline. Many megaprojects were put on hold and with recovery in many parts of the world, these projects will be on stream again in the near future. ENR further reported that M.W. Kellogg projects that $100 billion in jobs in the international hydrocarbon (oil) market will be available over the next five years. This should liven up traditional opportunities for Americans overseas in the oil and associated industries.

In addition to the oil countries of the Middle East, there will continue to be all types of engineering and construction projects. For example, the Israeli government will continue building accommodations for its growing number of immigrants and changing political borders.

The international growth of engineering and construction jobs isn't limited to underdeveloped countries. American construction firms are rushing to bid on contracts to assist in the rebuilding and development in Eastern Europe and the former Soviet Union. Engineering projects requiring American expertise will involve not only the infrastructure of these eastern nations but petroleum exploration as well. Chevron Corporation has signed an agreement with Russia to joint venture the extraction of oil from the huge oil field on the northeast shore of the Caspian Sea. Many American petroleum engineers were sent to the area in the last two years with more needed in the years ahead.

Several U.S. contractors have already established joint venture projects with European firms to gain access to the coming building boom in Eastern Europe. One of America's largest firms, Turner International

Industries, Inc., for example, has joined forces with Karl Steiner Ltd. of Zurich, Switzerland to harvest forthcoming construction projects. The World Bank continues to loan significant amounts to developing countries, particularly for environmental projects. These are all signs that more engineers and construction personnel are needed throughout the world.

In general, the types of available positions worldwide include: project managers, superintendents, foremen, chemists, motor vehicle specialists, maintenance specialists, engineers (electrical, civil, mechanical, hydraulic, HVAC) just to name a few. Recent ads in the trade press, for example, stressed that major construction companies are constantly in need of experienced individuals for foreign projects. For example, Brown & Root, Inc. has been searching for contract managers, expediters, sub-contracts administrators, and senior buyers for their worldwide projects; Continental Controls, Inc. advertised for mechanical engineers for their projects in the Caribbean; and, Bechtel wanted design engineers, cost accountants, project managers, and estimators, for its international work.

The top ten American contractors in terms of total billings for both domestic and foreign contracts for 1993 were:

Fluor Daniel, Inc.
222 Michaelson Dr.
Irvine, CA 92730

Bechtel Group, Inc.
PO Box 3965
San Francisco, CA 94119

The Parsons Corporation
100 W. Walnut St.
Pasadena, CA 91124

Jacobs Engineering Group,
Inc.
251 S. Lake Ave.
Pasadena, CA 91101

Brown & Root, Inc.
PO Box 3
Houston, TX 77001

The M.W. Kellogg Co.
1300 Three Greenway Plaza
Houston, TX 77046-0395

Stone & Webster Engineering
Corp.
PO Box 2325
Boston, MA 02107

Black & Veach/The Prichard
Group
8400 Ward Parkway
Kansas City, MO 64114

Foster Wheeler Corp.
Perryville Corp. Park
Clinton, NJ 08809-4000

John Brown E&C
7909 Parkwood Circle Drive
Houston, TX 77036

ENR reports that while U.S. Design Company billings were off 6.5% in 1993, Executives are generally happy with business and are optimistic about the future. The top ten Design Firms for 1993 included many of the top ten contractors with the addition of:

ABB Lummus Crest, Inc.
1515 Broad St.
Bloomfield, NJ 07003

Raytheon Engineers
 & Constructors
1 Broadway
Cambridge, MA 02142

Litwin Engineers
 & Constructors
PO Box 1281
Houston, TX 77251-1281

Rust International Inc.
PO Box 101
Birmingham, AL 35201

Further information may be available from:

National Society of
 Professional Engineers
345 East 47th Street
New York, NY 10017

Other major international engineer-contractors include:

Aramco Services Co.   Guy F. Atkinson
P.O. Box 4534   10 W. Orange St.
Houston, TX   South San Francisco, CA 94080

The Austin Company
3650 Mayfield Road
Cleveland, OH 44121

The Badger Co., Inc.
1 Broadway
Cambridge, MA 02142

Bechtel Corp.
50 Beale Street
San Francisco, CA 94119

Brown & Root USA, Inc.
4100 Clinton Drive
Houston, TX 77020

Burns & Roe, Inc.
550 Kinderkamack Road
Oradell, NJ 07649

Corrpro Co., Inc.
1090 Enterprise
Medina, OH 44256

Ebasco Services, Inc.
Two World Trade Center
New York, NY 10048

Epstein & Sons Intl., Inc.
600 West Fulton Street
Chicago, IL 60606

Foster Wheeler Corp.
110 South Orange Avenue
Livingston, NJ 07039

George A. Fuller Co.
919 Third Avenue
New York, NY 10022

Harbert International
P.O. Box 1297
Birmingham, AL 35201

Holmes & Narver, Inc.
999 Town & Country Rd.
Orange, California 92668

Jacobs Engineering Group
251 South Lake Avenue
Pasadena, CA 91101

Kiewit Pacific Co.—Global
1000 Kiewit Plaza
Omaha, NE 68131

Lummus Co.
1515 Broad Street
Bloomfield, NJ 07003

McDermott, Inc.
P.O. Box 60035
New Orleans, LA 70160

Nico Construction Co.
3545 Hudson Street
New York, NY 10014

Parsons Brinckerhoff
One Penn Plaza
New York, NY 10119

Parsons Corporation
100 West Walnut Street
Pasadena, CA 91124

Raymond International, Inc.
P.O. Box 22718
Houston, TX 77027

Riedel International, Inc.
4555 North Channel Avenue
Portland, OR 97217

Schal Associates
200 West Hubbard Street
Chicago, IL 60610

Stone & Webster
 Engineering Corp.
245 Summer Street
Boston, MA 02107

Williams Brothers
 Engineering Co.
6600 South Yale Avenue
Tulsa, OK 74136

In addition to the major American firms specializing in engineering, it would also be a good idea to make contact with a few of the best of Britain. Although the salary scale in England is considerably below American standards, the money can be negotiated for many foreign assignments. The work can take you to many of the world's developing and growing areas. Kennedy & Donkin, for example, has many electric power supply and generation projects underway internationally. Sir M. MacDonald & Partners looks for new graduates in such areas as hydrology, economics, water resources, engineering and management for their overseas work. About 85 percent of the work is outside England with at least two-thirds of their staff working onsite. Ward, Ashcroft and Parkman does most of its consulting engineering in Nigeria, Kenya, Uganda, Indonesia and other countries in East Africa and Asia. Civil and mechanical engineers with knowledge or experience in water supply, public health, irrigation and highway design are high on their want list. Contact:

W.S. Atkins Group Consultants
Woodcote Grove, Ashley Road
Epsom, Surrey KT18 5BW
ENGLAND

Kennedy & Donkin
Westbrook Mills
Godalming, Surrey GU7 2AZ
ENGLAND

John Laing International Ltd.
Page Street
London, NW7 2ER
ENGLAND

Sir M. MacDonald & Partners
Dementer House, Station Road
Cambridge CB1 2RS
ENGLAND

Survey and Development Services
3 Hope Road
Bo'ness, West London EH51 OAA
ENGLAND

Ward Ashcroft and Parkman
Cunard Building
Liverpool L3 1ES
ENGLAND

In addition, you should also consider foreign firms in the engineering, architectural, and consulting business. Ten of the top companies based on billings are:

- Lavalin, Inc. Montreal, Canada

- NEDECO, The Hague, Netherlands

- Nethconsult, The Hague, Netherlands

- Jaakko Poyty Oy, Helsinki, Finland

- Tractebel, Brussels, Belgium

- Simons Intl. Corp., Vancouver, B.C. Canada

- Nippon Koel Co. Ltd., Tokyo, Japan

- Dar Al-Handasah Consultants, (Shair & Partners)
  Cairo, Egypt

- Fugro-McClelland BV, Leidschendam, Netherlands

- Energoprojekt Consulting & Engineering Co.
  Belgrade, Yugoslavia

PETROLEUM AND MINING

With the constant demand for new sources of energy and greater natural mineral resources, it is not surprising that individuals with experience in the petroleum and mining field will have little problem locating work abroad. Although the location of jobs may not always be where the days are cool and the evenings balmy, if you have solid experience in this field you can be reasonably sure that you have a salable profession.

Oil and gas companies, for example, have an on going need for experienced field workers as well as other types of personnel from the exploration phase of an operation (geologists, petrologists, chemists, cartographers) through the actual mining and refining of a finished product. In addition, a total on-site petroleum operation will also incorporate computer experts, accountants, project managers, administrators, drivers and mechanics, and other base personnel including doctors, nurses, and maintenance people.

The major opportunities abroad are within the Third World and underdeveloped nations. The Middle East is the largest employer of Americans in the petroleum business. Other prime areas include: Venezuela, Ecuador, North Africa, and Australia. Even opportunities within the former Soviet Union exist now where a few years ago it would have been folly to even consider working there. Work with non-petroleum minerals and you could be in the hills of Chile or along the jungle waters in South East Asia. The work is hard, the salaries high and the jobs very competitive.

The number of petroleum companies is finite enough to allow you to send your resume to every major one. Keep in mind that when an oil company needs an experienced engineer, geologist, foreman or electrician, they usually turn first to their personnel officer who places ads and does the interviewing. Write to the major oil companies and be sure your resume is up to date with an accurate current address. However, also send a copy of your resume to the various fee-paid employment agencies that may advertise overseas jobs. It never hurts to have an extra line in the water.

There is always some work available on one of the many pipelines being constructed worldwide. One of the fastest ways to keep abreast of the needs of pipeline contractors is to subscribe to the publication Pipeline Digest available from the publisher at P.O. Box #55225, Houston, TX 77255. (A single issue costs $5.00. A better buy is 24 issues for $45.) The booklet lists all the major contracts planned throughout the world with the name and address of the prime contractor, start-up date, and completion date. With this data, it is easy to obtain lists of sub-contractors and start sending your resume about.

For a free list of the major mining operations in Canada, write to the British Columbia and Yukon Chamber of Mines, 840 West Hustings Street, Vancouver BC, CANADA V6C 1C8. A worldwide listing of mining companies is also found in the Mining International Yearbook, available in any major library.

In addition to the petroleum companies also consider whether your particular expertise may also be of value to one or more of the many secondary companies that work hand in hand in the oil fields: oil tools and drilling equipment, pipeline maintenance, transportation equipment for mining, and electrical equipment used in mining. Contacts:

■ **Petroleum:**

Amerada Hess Corp.
1185 Avenue of the Americas
New York, NY 10036

Buttes Gas & Oil Co.
3040 Post Oak Blvd. #300
Houston, TX 77056

Conoco, Inc.
600 N. Dairy Ashford
Houston, TX 77079

Consolidated Oil & Gas, Inc.
410 17th St. #440
Denver, CO 80202

Dorchester Gas Corp.
5735 Pineland Drive
Dallas, TX 75231

Exxon Corp.
225 E. John W. Carpenter Fwy.
Irving, TX 75062-2298

Getty Oil, Co.
3810 Wilshire Blvd.
Los Angeles, CA 90010

Chevron Corporation
225 Bush St.
San Francisco, CA 94104-4289

Hunt Oil Co.
2900 InterFirst One Bldg.
Dallas, TX 75202

Loffland Brothers
515 W. Greens Road
Houston, TX 77067-4524

Louisiana Land &
 Exploration Co.
PO Box 60350
New Orleans, LA 70160

Mobil Corp.
3225 Gallows Road
Fairfax, VA 22037

Occidental Petroleum Corp.
10889 Wilshire Blvd.
Los Angeles, CA 90024

Ocean Drilling and
 Exploration Co., Inc.
P.O. Box 61780
New Orleans, LA 70161

Offshore Co.
P.O. Box # 2765
Houston, TX 77001

Penrod Drilling Co.
2200 Thanksgiving Tower
Dallas, TX 75201

Phillips Petroleum Co.
Phillips Bldg.
Bartlesville, OK 74004

Quaker State Oil Refining
 Corp.
255 Elm Street
Oil City, PA 16301

Santa Fe International Corp.
P.O. Box 4000
Alhambra, CA 91802

Standard Oil of California
225 Bush Street
San Francisco, CA 94101

Sun Exploration and
 Production Co.
P.O. Box 2880
Dallas, TX 75221

Tenneco, Inc.
P.O. Box 2511
Houston, TX 77001

Tesoro Petroleum Corp.
8700 Tesoro Drive
San Antonio, TX 78286

Texaco, Inc.
2000 Westchester Avenue
White Plains, NY 10650

Unocal Corp.
1201 West 5th Street
Los Angeles, CA 90051

- **Oil Field Equipment:**

A-Z International Tool Co.
P.O. Box # 7108
Houston, TX 77248

Anglo Energy Co.
233 Broadway
New York, NY 10279

Guy F. Atkinson Co. of
 California, Inc.
10 West Orange Avenue
South San Francisco, CA 94080

Bowen Tools, Inc.
P.O. Box 3186
Houston, TX 77253

Camco, Inc.
7010 Ardmore Street
Houston, TX 77021

Christensen International
P.O. Box 26135
Salt Lake City, UT 84126

Galveston-Houston Co.
4900 Woodway
Houston, TX 77056

Gearhart Industries, Inc.
1100 Everman Street
Fort Worth, TX 76140

Halliburton Co.
3600 Lincoln Plaza
Dallas, TX 75201-3391

Hughes Tool Co.
P.O. Box 2539
Houston, TX 77001

Mid-Continent Supply Co.
P.O. Box # 189
Fort Worth, TX 76101

Milchem, Inc.
3900 Essex Lane
Houston, TX 77027

Muskegon Tool Industries, Inc.
1000 East Barney Avenue
Muskegon, MI 49443

National Supply Co.
P.O. Box # 4638
Houston, TX 77210

Otis Engineering Corp.
P.O. Box # 819052
Dallas, TX 75381

Schlumberger Ltd.
277 Park Avenue
New York, NY 10172

Texas Gas Transmission Corp.
3800 Frederica Street
Owensboro, KY 42301

Tidewater, Inc.
P.O. Box 61117
New Orleans, LA 70161

Vetco-Gray, Inc.
250 West Stanley
Ventura, CA 93001

- **Mining:**

Anaconda Co.
555 17th Street
Denver, CO 80202

Englehard Corp.
Menlo Park, C.N. 40
Edison, NJ 08818

Kennecott Corp.
1717 Midland Bldg.
Cleveland, OH 44115

St. Joe Minerals Corp.
250 Park Avenue
New York, NY 10017

- **Foreign Companies:**

British Petroleum Co.
Britannic House, Moor Lane
London EC2 9BU
ENGLAND

Shell International   Pan-Canadian Petroleum Ltd.
 Petroleum Co.   Pan Canadian Plaza
Shell Centre   Calgary, Alberta T2P 2S5
London SE1 7NA   CANADA
ENGLAND

Petro-Canada
P.O. Box # 2844
Calgary, Alberta T2P 3E3
CANADA

MEDICINE, NURSING & PHARMACOLOGY

If you have a background or experience in the health care professions you
will be able to find work abroad, not necessarily in the country of your
choice but certainly in one or more of the many Third World or underdeveloped nations desperate for medical assistance. Pick up any of the
dozens of medical journals and the chances are good that you will find
at least one ad searching for doctors or nurses overseas. For a period of
several years the Saudis were spending millions of dollars building their
hospitals and medical schools. Their problem was that they constructed
beautiful, modern structures but lacked the human portion of the
equation. As a result, any Western-trained doctor could almost write his
own ticket.

In addition to the need for medical practitioners there is also a
potential market for those skilled in pharmacology, medical marketing
and product managers dealing with hospital products. Most major
American pharmacological companies have sales and marketing offices
throughout the world. Although most foreign employees are well trained
in the corporate product before being sent abroad there are occasions
when an American company will hire an experienced individual and train
that person in the home office for six months to a year prior to beginning
the foreign assignment. There is also a constant need for experienced
public health workers with the large non-profit organizations. The UN
alone maintains a sizable staff of public health specialists within the
World Health Organization.

One of the largest employers of medical personnel abroad is the
Hospital Corporation of America (One Park Plaza, Nashville, TN 37202).
HCA has offices in London, Sao Paulo, Sydney, Panama City, and
Riyadh. They own more than 4,000 hospitals around the world. Their
King Faisal Specialist Hospital and Research Center in Saudi Arabia is

one of the most modern medical facilities in the world staffed with a respected, well-paid international staff. HCA is constantly looking for qualified medical, nursing, and para-medical personnel. Contracts can be negotiated for one or two years. Charter Medical Corp (577 Mulberry Street, Macon, GA 31298) also manages medical facilities in many countries throughout the world.

In England, the International Hospitals Group (Stoke Park, Stoke Poges, Slough, Berkshire SL2 4HS) is similar to HCA but much smaller. They specialize in consultancy, management and hospital operation throughout the world. Allied Medical (12-18 Grosvenor Gardens London SW1W 0DZ) also requires a wide variety of medical personnel for their health care projects in the Middle East. BNA International (443 Oxford Street, London W1R 2NA specializes in placing nurses throughout the world on both short and long term contracts. Appointments are usually available in the Middle East, South Africa and much of Europe. Additional contacts:

- **Pharmaceuticals:**

Abbott Laboratories
Abbott Park
North Chicago, IL 60064

Allegran Pharmaceuticals
International, Inc.
2525 DuPont Drive
Irvine, CA 92713

American Home Products Corp.
685 Third Avenue
New York, NY 10017

Ayerst Laboratories
685 Third Avenue
New York, NY 10017

Baxter Travenol
Laboratories, Inc.
1 Baxter Parkway
Deerfield, IL 60015

Forest Laboratories, Inc.
150 East 58th Street
New York, NY 10155

Eli Lilly Co.
307 East McCarty Street
Indianapolis, IN 46285

Mallinckrodt, Inc.
675 McDonnell Blvd.
St. Louis, MO 63134

Merck Sharp & Dohme Intl.
P.O. Box 2000
Rahway, NJ 07065

Norwich-Eaton
Pharmaceuticals
17 Eaton Avenue
Norwich, NY 13815

Warner-Lambert Co.
Parke Davis Group
201 Tabor Road
Morris Plains, NJ 07950

Pfizer, Inc.
235 East 42nd Street
New York, NY 10017

Riker Laboratories, Inc.
Bldg 225-1N-07, 3M Center
St. Paul, MN 55144

A.H. Robins Co., Inc.
1407 Cummings Drive
Richmond, VA 23220

Rorer Group, Inc.
500 Virginia Drive
Ft. Washington, PA 19034

G.D. Searle & Co.
P.O. Box 1045
Skokie, IL 60076

Smithkline Corp.
P.O. Box # 7929
Philadelphia, PA 19101

E.R. Squibb & Sons, Inc.
P.O. Box # 4000
Princeton, NJ 08540

Sterling Drug. Inc.
90 Park Avenue
New York, NY 10016

Warner-Lambert Co.
201 Tabor Road
Morris Plains, NJ 07950

■ Medical & Hospital Supplies:

American Cystoscope
Makers, Inc.
300 Stillwater Avenue
Stamford, CT 06902

C.R. Bard, Inc.
731 Central Avenue
Murray Hill, NJ 07974

Bentley Laboratories, Inc.
17502 Armstrong Avenue
Irvine, CA 92714

Camp International Co.
P.O. Box # 89
Jackson, MI 49204

CIBA-Corning Diag Corp.
63 North Street
Medfield, MA 02052

Cutter Laboratories, Inc.
2200 Powell Street
Emeryville, CA 94608

Gelman Sciences, Inc.
600 South Wagner Street
Ann Arbor, MI 48106

Gilford Instrument Labs, Inc.
132 Artino Street
Oberlin, OH 44074

Instrumentation Laboratory
113 Hartwell Avenue
Lexington, MA 02173

Johnson & Johnson
501 George Street
New Brunswick, NJ 08903

Milton Roy Co.
P.O. Box # 12169
St. Petersburg, FL 33733

The Kendall Co.
P.O. Box # 10
Boston, MA 02101

Technicon Instruments Corp.
511 Benedict Avenue
Tarrytown, NY 10591

FOOD AND AGRICULTURE

With the world's population constantly growing, it is only natural that there is a constant demand for experts in the field of food and agriculture. In actuality the types of food and agricultural jobs break down into two different and rather distinct areas: direct agricultural work, consultation, planning and marketing, and the manufacture, packaging, marketing, and distribution of food and food by-products. Keep in mind that consultation and field work is not along the banks of the Seine or the green fields of Tuscany. The underdeveloped nations often offer hardship, crude living conditions, inadequate pay, and a lot of hard work. The rewards are almost always in the knowledge that your work matters rather than in a fat bank account. Work for a food processor and you just may be fortunate enough to find yourself in a major city. Keep in mind that what attracts a General Foods to France is not access to a central European country but, in most cases, access to those specialized food products that will contribute to the company's bottom line.

Few American food companies maintain a large American staff abroad. Rather, they tend to rely upon local experts and those familiar with the provincial scene: able to speak the language, know the customs, deal with the local producers as a native rather than an outsider. Occasionally, an American expert will be asked to evaluate a local market or spend some time in a country preparing business plans based on his knowledge of the parent company. Again, those asked to spend a year or two abroad are most often well experienced with the home company's operation and ways of doing business. Yet, exceptions do exist and it isn't totally out of the question for an individual with experience in the food business to find a foreign job.

The prime source of agricultural jobs with Third World governments is through one of the several non-profit organizations devoted to one of the myriad assistance programs. The UN alone, for example, provides agricultural aid through several of its agencies although the Food and Agricultural Organization (FAO) is its primary organ "to improve the efficiency of production and distribution of food and agricultural products." FAO, which also oversees the World Food Programme—a voluntary program to collect commodities, cash and services for victims of natural disasters, refugees and displaced persons—is headquartered in Italy. It maintains regional offices in Ghana, Ethiopia, Thailand, Chile, Egypt, and the United States. The needs of FAO are for individuals experienced in agricultural economics, economic development, world resources, and the nutritional sciences. Contact: Food and Agricultural Organization (FAO), Via delle Terme di Caracalla, 00100 Rome, Italy. The liaison office for North America is located at 1776 F Street NW, Washington, DC 20437.

Several non-profit organizations assist underdeveloped nations with their food and agricultural programs. The Agricultural Development Council (1290 Avenue of the Americas, New York, NY 10020), for example, is heavily involved in research and training to provide experienced people to help many Asian countries help themselves. In essence, ADC looks for trained agronomists as well as experts in agricultural economics to work directly with Third World countries so they may use their own agricultural resources more effectively.

The International Agricultural Development Service (1133 Avenue of the Americas, New York, NY 10036) has a data bank of specialists in the field of agriculture, administration, food economics, management, and nutrition. They like academics and those who have had previous experience dealing with Third World areas. IADS works with underdeveloped countries to help nations and regions within nations accelerate agriculture and rural development. Be expected to accept both short-term as well as long-term assignments.

Other non-profit organizations such as the New TransCentury Foundation (1901 N. Fort Myer Drive, Suite 107, Arlington, VA 22204); the Rockefeller Foundation (1133 Avenue of the Americas, New York, NY 10020); Food First (2588 Mission Street, San Francisco, CA); Meals for Millions (815 Second Avenue, New York, NY 10017); OXFAM-America (302 Columbus Avenue, Boston, MA 02116); Carnegie Corporation (437 Madison Avenue, New York, 10022); and the Ford Foundation (320 East 43rd Street, New York, NY 10017) all maintain some involvement in assisting underdeveloped countries improve their agricultural position. Jobs with foundations are hard to come by and, when available, are usually for a short term, consultation, basis. In all cases experience is essential. This is no spot for a first-time crack at a job abroad.

There are a few foreign agencies that are worth noting: Hendrikson

Associierte Consultants GmbH, Mergenthalerallee 51-59, Postfach 5480, 6236 Eschborn 1, Germany is constantly looking for well qualified and experienced individuals in the areas of livestock management, range management, agricultural economics and banking, and, financial controllers. They mainly service African and Asian countries.

Minster Agriculture, Belmont, 13 Upper High Street, Thames, Oxfordshire OX9 3HL England also specializes in locating agricultural specialists for projects in the Middle East, Far East and Africa. They cover basic agronomy and areas as refined as arid zone development and peanut development.

In addition to the agencies and not for profit groups, it often pays to send a resume to the home offices of the food companies that maintain foreign offices. The odds are slim but you never know when your particular talent is the need on the top of an executive's want list. Contact:

American Home Products Corp.
685 Third Avenue
New York, NY 10017

Campbell Soup Co.
Campbell Place
Camden, NJ 08101

Archer-Daniels-Midland Co.
P.O. Box 129
Decatur, IL 62525

The Coca Cola Co.
PO Drawer 1734
Atlanta, GA 30301-1734

Baker Perkins, Inc.
100 Hess Avenue
Saginaw, MI 484601

DCA Food Industries, Inc.
919 Third Avenue
New York, NY 10022

Beatrice Companies, Inc.
2 North La Salle Street
Chicago, IL 60602

Del Monte Corp.
1 Market Plaza
San Francisco, CA 94119

Beatrice Meats, Inc. Intl.
1919 Swift Drive
Oak Brook, IL 60522

General Foods Corp.
250 North Avenue
White Plains, NY 10625

Borden, Inc.
420 Lexington Avenue
New York, NY 10170

General Mills, Inc.
P.O. Box 1113
Minneapolis, MN 55440

H J Heinz Co.
P.O. Box 57
Pittsburgh, PA 15230

Henningsen Foods, Inc.
2 Corporate Park Drive
White Plains, NY 10604

Heublein, Inc.
16 Munson Road
Farmington, CT 06032

Hobart Intl., Inc.
World Headquarters Avenue
Troy, OH 45374

Hubbard Farms, Inc.
P.O. Box 415
Walpole, NH 03608

Hygrade Food Products Corp.
P.O. Box 4771
Detroit, MI 48219

Ibec, Inc.
1230 Avenue of the Americas
New York, NY 10020

Kellogg Co.
235 Porter Street
Battle Creek, MI 49016

Kraft, Inc.
Kraft Court
Glenview, IL 60025

A J Mills & Co., Inc.
745 Fifth Avenue
New York, NY 10022

Nabisco Brands, Inc.
195 River Road
East Hanover, NJ 07936

Namolco Co., Inc.
506 Prudential Road
Willow Grove, PA 19090

Pepsico, Inc.
700 Anderson Hill Road
Purchase, NY 10577

Pet, Inc.
400 South Street
St. Louis, MO 63101

Quaker Oats Co.
345 Merchandise Mart Plaza
Chicago, IL 60654

Swift & Co.
115 West Jackson Avenue
Chicago, IL 60604

United Brands Intl.
1271 Avenue of the Americas
New York, NY 10020

COMPUTER SCIENCES

Although there are positions for experienced programmers and computer
specialists abroad, keep in mind that Americans do not have a monopoly
in this field. Europeans and Japanese are well versed in this area and

have already made serious inroads in their own countries as well as in the Third World. The need for Americans with a computer background is, therefore, not nearly as great abroad as positions are not easily available throughout the world. This is not to say that it isn't possible for computer specialists to find a job overseas. Very often American companies doing business abroad require those experienced with their product line to assist in marketing, servicing, and designing special product application software to compliment their hardware line or customer service needs.

Fortunately, there are now serious computer applications in every country of the world. Even the most backward underdeveloped nation is relying heavily on the input of computer experts to assist in everything from economic planning to forecasting river flow to determine planting and irrigation schedules.

Locating a job abroad can be accomplished in several ways: through one or more of the established foreign agencies; by directly contacting the electronic companies in one or more of the countries of your choice; or, by contacting one or more of the American companies listed below that have solid operations in several foreign countries. In all cases only experienced personnel in the following key specialities will be considered: systems design and analysis, programming, operations, servicing and teaching, hardware design, and sales and marketing.

The following foreign agencies recruit computer and electronics specialists.

- **I.C. Software A.G.:** Artherstrasse 5, 6300 Zug Switzerland. This well established European agency assigns experienced individuals to specific software development projects depending upon the needs of a client. The range of areas of specialization is extremely varied as is their client base. Assignments can range from a period of several months to several years in countries primarily within Europe. Applicants with three years or more experience are at an advantage. EDP Systems Ltd, 31 Palace Street, London SW1E 5HW England. Established a quarter of a century ago, this is one of the oldest computer agencies in Europe. Most of their client contracts are extended—from a year to multi-year—which enables their hired consultants to establish a long term relationship with the client. Most assignments are in continental Europe.

- **Ingineur Ltd.:** Pendicke Street, Southam, Warks. CV33 0PN England. An agency well known among Europe's electronic professionals. They look for design engineers, managers, and electronic specialists experienced in hardware, telecommunications, aerospace, and semiconductor applications. Assignments rarely extend beyond two years. Knowledge of a foreign language is helpful.

U.S. electronic companies with offices abroad include the following:

Advanced Micro Devices, Inc.
P.O. Box 3453
Sunnyvale, CA 94088

Computer Sciences Corp.
2100 East Grand Street
El Segundo, CA 90245

Aeromaritime, Inc.
6733 Curren Street
McLean, VA 22101

Computervision Corp.
201 Burlington Road
Bedford, MA 01730

Amdahl Corp.
Newburgh Road
Hackettstown, NJ 07840

Datagraphix, Inc.
P.O. Box 82449
San Diego, CA 92138

Analog Devices, Inc.
Route One, Industrial Park
Norwood, MA 02062

Digital Equipment Corp.
29 Parker Street
Maynard, MA 01754

Anderson Jacobson, Inc.
521 Charcot Avenue
San Jose, CA 95131

Ferranti Electric, Inc.
87 Modular Avenue
Commack, NY 117725

Apple Computer, Inc.
20525 Mariani Avenue
Cupertino, CA 95014

General Automation, Inc.
1055 South East Street
Anaheim, CA 92806

Burr-Brown Research Corp.
P.O. Box 11400
Tucson, AZ 85734

General Instrument Corp.
767 Fifth Avenue
New York, NY 10153

Compucorp
1901 South Bundy Drive
Los Angeles, CA 90025

Hewlett-Packard Co.
3000 Hanover Street
Palo Alto, CA 94304

Infotron Systems Corp.
Cherry Hill Industrial Center-9
Cherry Hill, NJ 08003

International Business
 Machines Corp.
Old Orchard Road
Armonk, NY 10540

International Telephone
& Telegraph Corp.
320 Park Avenue
New York, NY 10022

Leach Corp.
6900 Orangethorpe Avenue
Buena Vista, CA 90620

Measurex Corp.
One Results Way
Cupertino, CA 95014

Mostek Corp.
1215 West Crosby Road
Carrollton, TX 75006

National Semiconductor Corp.
2900 Semiconductor Drive
Santa Clara, CA 95051

NCR Corp.
1700 South Patterson Blvd.
Dayton, OH 45479

Omni-Spectra, Inc.
21 Continental Blvd.
Merrimack, NH 03054

Perkin-Elmer Corp.
761 Main Avenue
Norwalk, CT 06859

Prime Computer, Inc.
Prime Park
Natick, MA 01760

Pulse Engineering, Inc.
7250 Convoy Court
San Diego, CA 92111

Recognition Equipment, Inc.
PO Box 222307
Dallas, TX 75222

Shure Brothers, Inc.
222 Hartrey Avenue
Evanston, IL 60204

Storage Technology Corp.
2270 South 88th Street
Louisville, CO 80027

System Industries, Inc
560 Cottonwood Drive
Milpitas, CA 95035

Systems Engineering Labs, Inc.
6901 West Sunrise Blvd.
Fort Lauderdale, FL 33313

Tally Corp.
8301 Southeast 180th Street
Kent, WA 98031

Tandem Computers
19333 Valico Parkway
Cupertino, CA 95014

Tandy Corp.
1800 One Tandy Center
Fort Worth, TX 76102

Tech/Ops, Inc.
1 Beacon Street
Boston, MA 02108

Texas Instruments, Inc.
P.O. Box 655474
Dallas, TX 75265

Teknis, Inc.
PO Box 1687
Plainville, PA 02762

TRW, Inc.
1900 Richmond Road
Cleveland, OH 44124

Tektronix, Inc.
PO Box 500
Beaverton, OR 97077

Universal Computing Co.
UUC Tower Exchange Park
Dallas, TX 75235

Teledyne, Inc.
1901 Avenue of the Stars
Los Angeles, CA 90067

Varian Associates, Inc.
18 Hansen Way
Palo Alto, CA 94303

Teledyne Semiconductor
1300 Terra Bella Avenue
Mountain View, CA 94043

Wang Laboratories, Inc.
One Ind Avenue
Lowell, MA 01851

Telex Computer Products, Inc.
6422 East 41st Street
Tulsa, OK 74135

Western Digital Corp.
2445 McCabe Way
Irvine, CA 92714

CONSULTING

It seems that everyone is in search of the so-called expert. Call yourself a consultant and you can double your hourly fee and expect the red carpet treatment. American consulting firms have discovered that a business card with the title "Consultant" earns respect, an entry to the upper echelons of business leaders, and a nice living. This is observed to no greater extent than overseas where growing businesses and governments search out U.S. consulting firms to help them solve problems in every imaginable area.

In 1990, one of America's largest consulting firms signed contracts to assist the government of Poland evaluate their economy; develop a sales and marketing plan for a highly successful Japanese electronics company interested in crashing the American market; and establish a method to increase productivity for a mid-sized producer of Italian wine. The obvious question is where does a single consulting organization develop the in-house talent to solve problems in such a diverse range of economic and technical areas. The answer is simply, they don't! What so many of the consulting firms do possess is the skill and know-how to find the best outside people to do a specific job. Universities are often the knowledge-well of talent for many companies. Place a Ph.D. and a college affiliation after your name and you automatically become an expert. As a result many college professors have discovered that they can earn significant consultant fees working for consulting firms. However, university professors aren't the only "experts" hired by outside firms. Often business leaders with a proven background in their specific field, frequently retired individuals, are asked to spend a month or a year handling an assignment. America's consulting firms are already well established abroad competing fiercely with local consultants for a share of the growing business.

U.S. consultinig firms maintain extensive talent banks of men and women with special skills that may be called upon to fill an assignment. Keep in mind that whereas many consulting firms hire individuals for a specific assignment or specific period of time, they are neither head hunters (executive search agencies) nor employment agencies. Executive employment services are an entirely different entity covered elsewhere in this book. Consultants don't like to be confused with head hunters—undoubtedly a question of propriety, experiences and capability. There is no reason why you can't submit your resume to one of the many American firms doing business abroad. The odds are obviously against your being flooded with offers, but remember it's a number game and if a firm needs your specific talent in the future at least you are a known item. Keep in mind when addressing these firms that they want a proven commodity to sell to their foreign clients. Any knowledge you may have of foreign customs, language skills, business or labor methods and practices are strong pluses. Emphasize them!

Major American consulting firms doing business abroad include the following:

Booz Allen & Hamilton, Inc.
101 Park Avenue
New York, NY 10178

Brown & Root, Inc.
4100 Clinton Avenue
Houston, TX 77020

Boyden Associates, Inc.
260 Madison Avenue
New York, NY 10016

Canny Bowen, Inc.
425 Park Avenue
New York, NY 10022

Handy Associates, Inc.
245 Park Avenue
New York, NY 10167

Harbridge House, Inc.
11 Arlington Street
Boston, MA 02116

Harris PRC, Inc.
300 East 42nd Street
New York, NY 10017

Ingersoll Engineers, Inc.
707 Fulton Street
Rockford, IL 61103

A.T. Kearney, Inc.
222 South Riverside Plaza
Chicago, IL 60606

Keene Corp.
200 Park Avenue
New York, NY

Arthur D Little, Inc.
25 Acorn Park
Cambridge, MA 02140

McKinsey & Co., Inc.
55 East 52nd Street
New York, NY 10022

Bruce Payne Consultants, Inc.
666 5th Avenue
New York, NY 10019

Science Management Corp.
1011 Rte # 22
Bridgewater, NJ 08807

Spencer Stuart &
 Associates, Inc.
55 East 52nd Street
New York, NY 10055

SRI International
333 Ravenswood Avenue
Menlo Park, CA 94025

Strategic Planning
 Associates, Inc.
600 New Hampshire
 Avenue NW
Washington, DC 20037

Towers, Perrin, Forster
 & Crosby, Inc.
600 Third Avenue
New York, NY 10016

4

FINDING AND
LANDING YOUR JOB

*B*efore embarking upon your job search, do a little homework. Consider what part of the world you'd like to spend the next several years of your life. If you have a family, by all means discuss it with them. There are always advantages and disadvantages with every job and location. Make a list of both the good and the bad. A job in the Middle East, for example, will often pay substantially more than an equivalent job in Europe. Yet the Middle East is far more isolated with fewer cultural advantages than Europe. Do you speak a foreign language? Will being in a country whose language is totally unfamiliar be a problem for you?

If you have children, what are the educational facilities like in the countries you are considering? In many parts of the world there are American and English schools established for expatriates. Also, in many places there are special schools established by large American companies abroad just for their employees. In some countries you can send an older child to college at no cost. Is this a major advantage for you, worthy of considering a job search there?

What are your religious requirements? Will locating in a Muslim country be a problem for you? If you are Jewish, it is more than a major consideration; it may be a job barrier. Many Arab countries won't grant you a visa if they know you are Jewish.

Also remember that it is always easier to find a job while employed. If you have a job, keep it until you have the new job offer you want. If you're unemployed, you may be better off getting a job in the States rather than searching only for that perfect job overseas. Getting a foreign job can be a time consuming task lasting up to six months or even a year. An interesting and valuable guide to evaluating various potential job sites is a computerized world atlas. The atlas, produced by the Software Toolworks, (60 Leveroni Court, Novato, CA 94949 (800 231-3088), is an almanac, fact book and colorful atlas all in one. With a specific country on your screen, you can obtain data covering education, communications, government, people, geography, economy, travel, entrance requirements, health and travel.

Once you've decided to obtain a job abroad and narrowed down the countries of your choice, your "work" begins! You must undertake a careful, deliberate campaign to find what foreign jobs are available to you and do everything you can to get the best one attainable.

Be objective about your chances! This book will help you analyze your talents and capabilities in relationship to the job demands abroad. Think of a job search as a separate task unto itself. Prepare to undertake painstaking, time consuming research; make telephone calls; keep careful records; wear out your fax and copy machine; and, in the end, do something you may have considered totally foreign to you—be a darn good salesman! In actuality that's what it really takes to land the job: selling. You are about to sell the most important commodity you have—**you and your skills!!**

In actuality there are four basic steps you will follow in landing an overseas job:

- Find where the jobs are.

- Make sure the right person within the companies of your choice is aware of you and your abilities.

- Sell yourself to the decision makers.

- Negotiate the best deal possible for you and your family.

STEP ONE—LOCATING THE JOBS ABROAD

The initial step, obviously, is locating or identifying the companies that are hiring overseas workers. This book is the first place to start! Not only will you find specific company names and address but also the addresses of other potential job sources such as local American Chambers of Commerce abroad, employment agencies and professional headhunters. Other basic sources are those lists of companies doing business in the country or countries of your choosing. (Note: Although this book doesn't list major British firms abroad, they too are potential employers. A list of British companies in a specific country may be obtained through a local British Chamber of Commerce in a country. The address can be obtained by contacting the British embassy in that country.) The lists supplied by local American Chambers' of Commerce overseas are not only the most up to date but, in most cases, also provide the names and addresses of specific contacts within a foreign company.

Another excellent listing of U.S. companies doing business abroad is the book, *Directory of American Firms Operating in Foreign Countries,* 13th Edition (1994), Published by World Trade Academy Press, New York, NY. ($195). If you are a professional you probably have already discovered that advertisements in your trade publications often are keyed to foreign employment. Other publications such as the Wall Street Journal, New York Times, The Economist, Christian Science Monitor, and International Herald Tribune, also list foreign jobs. It pays to make friends with the local reference librarian at your public library. He or she will know of current materials and possible job sources.

In addition to the general reference listings there are several sources of foreign jobs and new of overseas employment conditions that are well worth evaluating: the *International Employment Gazette,* the *Fischer Report* and the *Overseas Craftsman's Association.* The *International Employment Gazette* is a newspaper published bi-weekly. An annual subscription is $95; single issue, $8.00. Their address: 1525 Wade Hampton Blvd., Greenville, SC 29609. In addition to the paper listing about 400 foreign jobs by country and profession, the paper also maintains an international placement network. For $45.00 they will send you a "personalized" report of current openings geared to your occupational and geographical interests. You can either write to the above address or call them at 1-800 882-9188.

In addition, *The International Employment News,* 70 Chartres, Montreal., Quebec, Canada H9A 1J7 (Fax: 514 421-6831) is a bi-monthly listing of foreign jobs. $95 a year or $65 for six months; $35 for three months (in U.S. dollars). Another bi-monthly publication is the *Overseas Employment Services*, 1255 Laird Blvd., Suite 208, Town of Mount Royal, Quebec, Canada H3P 2T1 (tel: 514 739-1108; Fax: 514 739-0795).

The *Fischer Report* is a bi-monthly newsletter that lists contracts and awards on a country-by-country basis as well as news and data about employment conditions abroad. If you are interested in the foreign engineering and construction business, this is the bible. A three month subscription is $200; six months, $300, a year subscription is $400 which also includes a computer matching service. Contact: Group Fischer, 160 Newport Center Dr., #200, Newport Beach, CA 92660. (714) 759-3374; Fax: (714) 760-1792.

The Overseas Craftsman's Association, (714) 827-5800, is a non-profit organization designed to "promote the betterment of overseas employment, to provide information and education about overseas employment, and to provide professional and networking services to overseas professionals." They publish a quarterly directory of foreign contractors. In addition to listing foreign companies they will also accept your "Position Wanted" ad.

When you have accumulated a substantial list of potential employers abroad, you are ready to start your sales campaign. It's a very good idea to keep detailed records of your job search in a notebook, index cards, or using your computer. Keep track of the individual or individuals you contact and record the substance of all conversations. Also maintain a tickler file recording the dates that you should return an individual's call, and follow up on a previous conversation. Remember, it's a numbers game! The more contacts you make or resumes you mail, the better your chances for success. So, with your list complete and your record-keeping system in order you're ready to commence the next stage in your conquest of that best foreign job.

Many job hunters prefer to submit their names to a professional employment agency and allow the agency to earn their commission by doing all the legwork and finding them a job. Relying on an agency may work when you're looking for a domestic position, but even then foolish to rely upon. Overseas employers rely less on agencies and more on their internal recruiting staffs. These are the jobs that this book is designed to help you find! We hope this book will also help you avoid having to pay up-front fees to agencies for their help. Do the work yourself and you will not only save a considerable amount of money but make a better impression on the potential employer as well. Remember, getting that job is **work**! It will not be an easy task; but few things are that are truly worthwhile!

In some cases a good agency will find you a job, but remember that most agencies are paid by the employer and therefore work for the employer. That means they will submit the candidate that will most likely succeed in order to collect their fee (often 10 to 30% of your first year's salary). Also, if a company has a choice of hiring you without such a large agency fee or a slightly better applicant with a fee they will more often than not choose you.

There are not many employment agencies that specialize in foreign employment. For those that do, your careful evaluation of their business record, will be important. Carefully evaluate their qualifications as personnel professionals and their professional standing within the employment industry. Don't be afraid to contact your local Better Business Bureau and query them about the agency. If the BBB talks of complaints—beware!

The recruiter you talk with should be a personnel professional. Expect a qualifying interview (by phone if the agency isn't local) to determine the viability of your being listed with the agency. After you submit your resume (and one is expected), don't be surprised to be asked to supply additional information about yourself or your employment history. The more an agency knows about you the better they can represent your interests.

A good agency will turn down most applicants they feel are not good candidates. Why waste their time and yours as well? An agency that is an EPF (Employer Paid Fee) agency will accept many applications for the same job. These agencies' obligation is to the company—not to you. Thus, it is in their interest to garner as many resumes as they can. Don't be afraid to submit you resume to as many EPF agencies as you can. It is in your best interest to have as much exposure as you can get.

STEP TWO—INITIAL CONTACT

With a list of potential employers and, if possible, the names of the individual within a company best able to make the hiring decision it is time to commence your self-selling marketing campaign. The cover letter which must accompany your resume should be a grabber. You want to indicate several things to a potential employer immediately: You have the experience and qualifications to do the job; and, you have the ability to communicate. Don't overlook the latter. Few people, from CEOs to shop foremen, know how to write a good letter, report or memo. Just look at some you have recently received! Your letter should be typed on quality stationary. If you don't have personal stationary, use the same paper on which your resume is printed. The continuity will be noticed by the reader. There are many different ways to design a cover letter. (Your library has books on preparing a resume. Writing the cover letter will be included. Check one out.) Essentially, include a brief description of your skills, job background and desire to work with the recipient's company. Get your message across directly and strongly. Use active words. Never let your cover letter run more than a single page. Here's an example:

[Your address]
[Telephone number]
[Date]

Mr. John D. Day
Director of Foreign Operations
XYZ Company
Anytown, USA 12345

Dear Mr. Day:

As a Project Manager in the petrochemical field, I am seeking a
position abroad that would use my extensive experience managing
quality projects. After speaking with colleagues in the field, I've learned
your company is one of the best in the business.

I am an experienced project manager and a specialist in managing
complex, high budget operations. I am familiar with your operations in
the Middle East and would be interested in meeting with you about how
my talents could be best put to use with your company. I am a person of
unusual efficiency, dedication and drive.

My achievements include:

- Managing a $1.7 million construction project from inception
  to completion—on schedule, on budget.
- Managing all operation and maintenance aspects of a large
  international chemical production facility.
- Total budgetary responsibility for planning a chemical
  distribution facility scheduled for operation in 18 months.

I enclose a copy of my resume and look forward to discussing with
you how my background and skills might best benefit XYZ Company.
While I prefer not taking personal calls at work, with discretion you can
reach me at 515-555-1234 during the day or the above number in the
evenings.

Sincerely,

[Signature]
[If your name isn't on your letterhead
type it here.]

Note that your letter is addressed to an individual. This is not always possible but it is important. The quicker you can establish any form of personal contact with a decision-maker, the faster you get a decision. It also allows you to follow-up with a personal phone call about a week later. Your follow up call isn't to "bug" your new contact but to ascertain that he or she did receive your letter and resume. No more than that. Just ask if the letter was received. It shows not only that you know how to follow-up on a project but also allows a voice-to-voice relationship to begin. You are no longer a name on a file. Also, it is unlikely that your contact will simply acknowledge that your letter was received. The chances are he or she will also impart some information about the company's needs or lack of them. It is all data you should record in your notebook or index card.

The most important tool in your campaign to get that overseas job is your resume. It is the only tangible article your potential employer has that represents you! Although we make a point of describing the best way to prepare a cover letter, in all honesty, most people do not pay much attention to it. When a prospective employer opens his or her mail, the resume must tell the story. It's the resume that either sells you or doesn't.

Your resume must be as detailed as possible without mixing the chaff with the wheat. In other words, facts not fluff. The easier your resume is to read the better. Keep in mind that the first person to read your resume is rarely the person who is the final decision maker. However, he or she is the person that often makes the most important decision as far as your potential future with the company is concerned—does your resume get passed along to the next level or do you get that tell-tale form letter: "blah, blah, blah—but we would like to keep your resume in our active file."

There are basically two types of resumes, the chronological and the functional, as well as different methods of presenting yourself in the best and most complete manner. There are also different points of view as to which type of resume works best. We like the chronological as it is easier to see where an individual is at all steps up the career ladder. The functional resume is fine if you've been out of work for a period of time served in the military.

There are dozens of resume formats. Pick up a good resume book and choose which best suits you. The actual format is most subjective. Some managers prefer one, some another. Regardless, the basic essentials don't change. You must present yourself strongly and in an easy-to-read fashion. This doesn't imply that your resume should read like a novel. Creative writing has no place here. The people in personnel spend their lives reading resumes. And believe it when you hear that for the most part a resume is a very boring read. Yet, it is all the employer has to make that initial judgement—to request a personal interview with you or slide your resume in a dead file.

Fortunately, to help you plan and write your resume, modern technology has entered the field. Several computerized resume production kits are now available on either disk or CD-ROM. Most of these programs allow you to simply fill in the blanks, make a few basic decisions about type style and size, format, and your resume is complete. Many of the programs also include follow-up modules and interview scenarios.

Check your local software store for current programs several companies now market these computerized resume kits. They are relatively inexpensive and just ask you to fill in the blanks, make a few decisions about type, style and format and the program does the rest!

As for the resume itself, here are a few do's and don'ts to assist you in preparing your resume and placing you and your achievements in the best light:

DO:

- **Begin your resume with a job summary.** However, be sure you are concise and only include your years of experience and major job titles or descriptions. This is helpful if resumes are being reviewed in volume and will get yours shifted to the stack marked "qualified."

- **Emphasize your education.** If resumes are being screened before being passed on to a decision maker, education may be one of the major requirements being looked for. Include your education simply and concisely early in your resume and before your job history. If you are applying for a job that requires a specific degree and you don't have one, then list your education at the end of the resume. Individuals often try and compensate for that missing degree by listing training courses and seminars. Managers will spot this gambit in a minute. Make up for your lack of a degree by emphasizing your job experience.

- **Keep your resume simple.** Flowery writing and colorful words is a waste of your literary efforts and will not impress anyone. Make every word count but be careful not to be too sketchy. If your job title doesn't explain your job, you have omitted important information.

- **Start off by listing your work experience going back from your current job.** This is the easiest resume to read as well as to write. Your present job is the most important and should have the most space devoted to it. After all, if a former job was so impressive, why did you leave it? Put yourself in the personnel manager's place.

- **Keep your resume to two pages if possible.** Obviously, some individuals just can't boil a career down to two pages. If you can do the job on a single sheet that is even better.

- **Customize your resume to the job to which you're applying.** This is impossible to do if you plan to Xerox a batch and mass mail. But if you have access to a word processor, you are better off designing each resume to a specific job. Thus, you can emphasize those particular aspects of your work experience that are applicable to the position you seek.

- **Emphasize the positive, but don't brag.** By all means highlight your achievements, but if your success is part of a team effort, say so. The person who reads your resume is able to read between the lines. Besides it is in your interest to show that you are a good team player.

- **Proof read...proof read..then...proof read again!** There is nothing worse than a sloppy, mistake-filled resume. It shows you to be an individual who is also sloppy. A common mistake many people make when re-reading their creative work is to assume that by reading and re-reading they have caught all the errors. No matter how talented the writer, we all fail to catch our own word blips no matter how many times we proof. When you're sure all is in order, ask your spouse, relative or friend to double-check your work.

DON'T:

- **Don't start your resume with a self-centered objective:** Your employer is only interested in what you can do for the company—how hiring you will improve the bottom line. The emphasis in your resume is on selling yourself. Not on what you want but on what you can offer the employer. Any objective should always be employer-centered.

- **Don't be negative:** Always emphasize the positive! Such statements as, "As a result of an automobile accident, I have been out of work for a period of time..." or, "Although I've never managed people before, I feel fully qualified." Believe it or not statements such as these are very common in resumes. Also believe that they rarely are read to their conclusion. Omit data on your health, religion or race, and reasons for leaving a previous job. These are all questions which may be covered during an interview.

- **Don't deal with salary:** Many want ads ask you to "specify your salary requirements." Don't do it in a resume. If the question is raised, you can always say that your salary is a matter for negotiation. Once you put a figure in a resume, you are locked in. Besides, you should be as free to be as flexible as your employer regarding your salary and benefits.

- **Don't list references:** All employers will require references. However, by including them in a resume, you not only take valuable space with data which has no bearing whatsoever on your skills, but this prevents you from selecting those particular references you may want to use for a particular job. Some firms may even call your listed references before calling you in for an interview. If your references keep receiving calls about you they may wonder what is happening. To be safe, request permission from those you want to use as a reference so that calls from a stranger are expected. Add the tag line: "References upon request."

- **Don't send a photograph:** You should be evaluated on your skills. Allowing a possible employer to make judgements without meeting you is a mistake.

- **Don't overemphasize your military experience:** Unless your work in the service has a direct bearing on the position you seek, it has little bearing on your skills. The simple word, "veteran" or "1st Lt. US Navy" is enough. The most important part of your resume is your education and current job. Your next employer wants to know what you are doing now and what direction your career is heading. If you are recently retired from the military seek a position that ties in closely with your MOS. In this situation, a functional resume works best as it simplifies the many stations and assignments common to the military.

EXAMPLE OF CHRONOLOGICAL RESUME:

John Doe
123 Fourth Street
Anytown, CA 12345
(415) 555-1234

EDUCATION

University of Wisconsin. M.S. in Engineering—1982
Kenyon College. B.S.—1980

EXPERIENCE

Senior Project Engineer, Acme Corporation, 1988—Present

Responsible for managing conception team, design and construction of
mechanically controlled feed system internationally sold by agricultural
client. Full system design, all budgetary, scheduling and procurement aspects
relating to project. Marketing and promotion consultant on product. Manage
staff of 12.

Production Engineer, Digby, Cates Co, 1985—1988

Responsible for machine and system design, procurement and production
scheduling, and quality control for automated conveyor system. Initiated
computerized system to assure quality control standards. Managed staff of 4.

Assistant Engineer, Dallas Corporation, 1982—1985

Served on project team to design bearing races and high speed gear chains
for dental equipment manufacturer. Team awarded corporate commendation
and bonus.

PROFESSIONAL ORGANIZATIONS

American Society of Professional Engineers
Society of Mechanical Engineers

PERSONAL

Single, excellent health, willing to travel and relocate.
References available upon request.

EXAMPLE OF FUNCTIONAL RESUME:

John Doe
123 Fourth Street
Anytown, CA 12345
(415) 555-1234

EDUCATION:

University of Wisconsin. M.S. in Engineering—1982
Kenyon College. B.S.—1980

ENGINEERING:

Nine years experience in the design and construction of mechanical and electromechanical equipment for the OEM market. Experienced in hydraulics, pneumatics, structural engineering, materials, and quality control.

MANAGEMENT:

Directed as many as 12 engineers and support staff. Responsibilities cover staff selection and financial review. Served on corporate Executive Committee. Prepared quarterly and annual forecast and review.

SALES:

Consulted with Sales and Marketing departments on all product lines from engineering department. Provided monthly and quarterly data on products during development stage.

FINANCIAL:

Prepared monthly, quarterly and annual forecasts. Presented, reviewed and defended those data to corporate management. Department under my direction has never run over budget!

RECRUITMENT:

Responsible for the selection of more than a dozen engineers and ancillary personnel. Addressed engineering conferences and college audiences searching for qualified engineers.

PRODUCTION:

Handled all aspects of component selection, acquisition and quality control. Final approval of all engineered products during production phase. Developed method to cut rejects by more than 15% during final production process.

WORK EXPERIENCE:

Sr. Project Engineer, 1988—Present
Acme Corporation.
Los Angeles, CA

Production Engineer, 1985—1988
Digby, Cates Co.
Long Beach, CA

Assistant Engineer, 1982—1985
Dallas Corporation
Midland, TX

PROFESSIONAL ORGANIZATIONS:

American Society of Professional Engineers
Society of Mechanical Engineers

PERSONAL:

Single, Excellent health, willing to travel and relocate.

REFERENCES:

Available upon request

STEP THREE—SELLING YOURSELF TO DECISION MAKERS—THE INTERVIEW!

After you've done all your homework, searched for the companies that have jobs abroad, and prepared and mailed your resumes, you reach the mark you have aimed for getting a person-to-person meeting with someone in the company who might offer you the position. All your previous work is for naught if you fail to make the right impression. And sadly, so many well qualified, highly experienced workers wash out during the interview. It never fails to amaze us that so few people actually know how to be interviewed. What seems like such an simple process is constantly misunderstood.

The interview is not designed as a confrontational encounter but a basic exchange of views regarding the open position. Of course it is a stressful situation; the employer is well aware that you're under pressure and takes that into consideration. It also gives the employer a chance to observe you under tension. After all, your job is often pressure packed as well. You are being observed on how you relate. Do you show self confidence or are you a follower? What is your knowledge of the job? You'll be asked how your skills can help the company? Keep in mind that the company really isn't interested in your career goals unless they directly benefit the company. Your school days are behind you; from now on, it's strictly dollars and cents.

Don't be surprised to arrive for your interview only to be "pre-interviewed" by someone from the personnel department. They want to welcome you to the company, explain a few of the basic benefits and allow you to familiarize yourself with the company's business before escorting you to the decision maker. Be yourself! Don't try and be what you believe is expected of you. It never works. Work towards a healthy give and take. Not only are you expected to solicit company views but the company wants to know yours as well. Above all—relax!

There are a few basics that everyone being interviewed should follow. And much can be accomplished before you drive up to the company door:

- **Know the company's business.** As soon as you know you're in the running for a job begin to bone up on the company. Obviously you'll have a very good idea as to what you'll do for them, but what about other aspects of the company's operations. Are they independent or part of a conglomerate?

What portion of the company's business centers around the areas in which you'll be involved? Again, your library will have annual reports, financial statements, perhaps a newspaper clipping file if it is a local company.

- **Make a list of the questions you have about both the company and the specific job.** The number of times we have asked a prospective employee if he or she has any questions only to be told "no" is shocking. We can also state that of the hundreds of people hired, we have never employed anyone who could sit through a complete interview and not have a single question about the job or the company. Ask about company products, or your divisions expectations, goals and future. Cover areas of responsibility. To whom would you report and who reports to you? There is nothing wrong with taking notes during an interview or having your preconceived questions before you. Actually, it impresses a potential boss that you have foresight. Avoid questions about company benefits, vacations, or pensions plan. These areas can be covered later. If the question of salary comes up, it should be raised by the employer, not you. If you're asked how much money you want, explain that it is a negotiable factor. If pressed, never name a number—always state a salary range. This gives you plenty of room to maneuver.

- **Be prepared for the basic questions.** You know well in advance that certain questions will be asked of you. For example, you know you will be asked about your previous job experiences. Although the interviewer will have your resume before him, he will pursue those aspects of your work that appealed to him and led him to want to know you better. He will also ask why you want to work abroad. Why did you select the particular firm? Know the answers before you leave home.

- **Expect the unexpected.** It's a common technique to try and shock you with a question out of the blue. For example, one Air Force captain always asks men applying to flight school how they feel about being a hired killer? You may be asked such things as: What are your weakest characteristics? Where would you like to see your career in five years from now? (If your potential boss is asking this question, there is nothing wrong with saying, "To sit where you are now.") What will you do if you don't get this job? etc. Remember also that just as there are poor interviewees, there are also poor interviewers. Just because a person is in a position of authority doesn't make him a good interviewer. Interviewing is a talent. You may face an interview in which you're lectured to the entire time.

- **Always highlight your accomplishments rather than just your responsibilities.** Modesty doesn't become you in an interview. Although there is a broad line between self confidence and bragging, be sure your potential employer sees you as one proud of your accomplishments and totally confident that you can handle the job under discussion.

- **Tell the truth. Don't play word games.** There is nothing worse or more obvious than one who skirts the issue rather than confront it. Besides, a lie is too easily caught.

- **Conclude the interview with an awareness of the next step.** There is nothing wrong with asking the direct question, "when may I expect to hear from you?" If you're told in a week and there is no response from the company, call the individual with whom you met and follow-up. Know how to spell the name of the individual interviewing you as well as his or her title. When you return home, write a brief letter thanking the individual for meeting with you. If there were any questions you were unable to answer fully, you can use this thank-you letter as the place to do it. Far too few people respond with a note. It makes a big impression.

STEP FOUR—NEGOTIATING THE BEST DEAL

With a job offer in your pocket, now is the time to consider how you can influence you prospective boss to provide you with the best deal possible. Remember that a finiancial figure is just part of your total compensation package. Obviously by the time you have a firm offer and the question of dollars is out on the table there are still a few points to consider.

Your job offer and total financial package should include more than just an annual salary figure. It should also cover such considerations as:

- Bonuses—including any bonuses for meeting a pre-determined sales, construction, or productivity targets; contract completion bonus; annual bonus.

- Allowances—including: housing, moving, cost of living equalization, schooling, costs of moving, furniture or appliances, transportation (will you have a company car or an allowance towards your own?), costs of vacations or home leave.

- Tax equalization or protection considerations.

- Profit sharing and stock options.

- Medical and dental coverage.

- Pension plans.

- Social security payments.

Obviously most contracts will not give you the entire package unless they are desperate for your talents, but at least you should be aware of the range of possible negotiating points in the general salary and compensation arena. Once you know what your total offer is, take a work sheet and compare numbers. How does the total income and expense picture abroad compare with your income and costs during the same period of time at home?

Add up all costs and expenses that you will incur by living abroad and compare them with the identical costs at home. It is important to be as fair and objective as possible. For example, if you normally spend about $1,000 a year for vacations, don't budget $3,000 abroad. Even if you want to use the opportunity to see the world, and you should, it is an unfair comparison to load the equation.

Use this basic worksheet to compare the numbers:

NET DISPOSAL INCOME WORKSHEET

ITEM	HOME			ABROAD		
	YEARS			YEARS		
	1	2	3	1	2	3

INCOME

Salary
Bonuses
     Allowances:
Housing
Moving
Cost of Living
Transportation
Medical
Vacations/Home Leave
Misc allowances:

TOTAL INCOME:

EXPENSES

Taxes
    U.S., State, Local
    Foreign

Living:
    Automobile
    Clothing
    Education
    Entertainment
    Food
    Furniture and appliances
    Housing
    Language school
    Loan repayment
    Medical
    Misc.
    Social Security
    Telephone
    Utilities
    Vacation

TOTAL EXPENSES:

NET DISPOSAL INCOME:

In discussing salary with your potential employer it is essential to learn up front whether or not the money you are paid will be taxed in the United States. In other words, does your future employer have an independent foreign company from which your salary will be paid. Remember, to qualify for that $70,000 tax exemption, your income must be earned from "foreign sources." Quite often your employer will give you the option to have your salary paid to you on site or deposited in your U.S. bank. He may also offer you the option to receive your salary in U.S. dollars or in the local currency. If you elect the local currency, you are gambling that the value of the dollar will decline against the local currency during the period you are abroad. If the dollar becomes stronger while you're overseas, you may see yourself taking a pay cut with every pay check. On the other hand, should the dollar weaken, as it has in the 1990s, you can actually maintain or possibly increase your buying power abroad. Sometime you can hedge by having part of your salary deposited in a local bank and part in a U.S. bank. Where you are paid has no bearing on U.S. taxes and does not effect your $70,000 tax exemption.

Another aspect to consider is the local tax rules. Some countries tax only money paid within the country. If this is the case, you are probably better off having your entire salary deposited in a U.S. bank at home and having your American bank transfer money to a local bank on a periodic basis at the current exchange rate.

It is a good idea to consult with your accountant or financial planner to assist you in working out the money and taxation pros and cons of living overseas. There are often steps that can be taken to save money depending on the state in which you reside, the country in which you plan to live and, of course, changes in the tax laws. Remember that in working with your $70,000 tax exclusion, your taxable income is more than just your salary. It also includes your overtime, bonuses, and allowances. Again an accountant will be able to determine your bottom-line income for tax purposes.

Another factor in your salary discussion is the value of your take home pay compared to the buying power that money represents. In other words, what is the impact of local inflation on your lifestyle? Work in a country with a huge rate of inflation and your buying power is constantly being eroded. The answer, of course, is to have an escalation or cost of living clause in your contract. As previously discussed, the U.S. State department issues a periodic report on the relationship between the buying power of the dollar as measured against the cost of living in every major world city.

Other important areas for contractual discussion include:

- **Housing.** If you work in the Middle East, you can expect that housing will be part of your total package. Americans live in modern, well situated complexes complete with local schools, markets and general shops. For those who would rather live on their own it is often possible to rent a house or apartment. If you become involved in a house purchase, you'll require a local lawyer. Will your contract also cover legal services? Again, find out before you sign an agreement. Off-site living may or may not be part of your compensation plan however. If you do elect to live off-site, be sure to determine who pays for it. In some countries housing may be considerably more expensive than your present home. You could end up paying a third to half of your income on housing. Even if your agreement states that your employer will pay a ceiling towards your housing, find out the difference you pay. Also ask if maid service is either provided or allowed for in your agreement? It never hurts to ask!

- **Furnishing your house or apartment.** If you move into an American complex you may discover your new home fully equipped with all the furnishings and appliances common to your lifestyle. On the other hand you may end up in an empty apartment. Who pays to furnish it? Your contract may provide an allowance towards your furnishings or may allow you to ship your possessions (including car?) from America to your new job at company expense. Work for many government agencies and transporting your furnishings abroad is part of the deal.

- **Education.** English-speaking schools are everywhere. But are they any good? In some parts of the world you may be better off sending your children to the local schools; in others you are limited only to English-speaking or company schools. What if there are no schools available for your children near your new job site? You may have to make other arrangements for their education. This costs money. Find out what educational facilities exist and if you're not satisfied what it will cost to provide the best education for your children? Will the company pick up the tab? Besides your children, will the company provide an allowance to enable you to learn the language at a local language school? Intensive language programs for you and your wife can run into the thousands of dollars. Will your new employer foot the bill?

- **Vacations.** Most contracts specify not only the amount of time allotted for your vacation but a statement that transportation to and from the United States is paid for by the company. Usually you are allowed one round trip a year. The more liberal contracts also pick up the costs for members of your family as well. If not, consider it as another bargaining chip.

- **Health Care.** Medical coverage is an essential aspect when considering an overseas job. In many countries you qualify for full coverage within the country's socialized health program regardless of your citizenship. In countries that don't have a socialized program, you must rely on your employer to provide medical services. By all means maintain some insurance coverage in effect that provides stateside coverage in the event of a serious accident or illness and you are repatriated. If you currently are covered by a company health care program but plan to leave your job to take another with a new company overseas, you can usually continue your policy if you pick up the premiums on your medical insurance. If you elect this option, be sure your policy covers you abroad. Many of the large companies in the Middle East have their own health care facilities complete with well equipped hospital facilities. And, don't forget that the American Embassy has a list of English-speaking doctors should the need arise.

- **Profit sharing and pension plans.** Many U.S. companies have some form of bonus programs for executives. If you're working abroad, do you qualify for whatever company programs exist? Are you part of an executive stock option plan, for example? Although most companies do not distinguish between stateside and expatriate employees, you should be clear about your employer's policies. The same holds true for a company's pension plan. Can you participate as an American abroad?

- **Social Security.** If you're working for an American firm abroad, be sure your company continues to fund your social security; it's not compulsory. You also will have monies taken from your paycheck, but unless you want to jeopardize your social security status, it's a good idea. Again, social security payments is a matter to bring up with your financial or tax consultant. Obviously, if you're working for a foreign company, you will not have money deducted from your pay check for Uncle Sam. You may, however, be required to pay into your resident country's social security or retirement program. From your point of view, this is just another tax as it is unlikely that you'll be a resident long enough (usually fifteen years) to reap any benefits.

The actual contract document or letter of agreement is a legal document and is usually prepared by a lawyer. It's probably not negotiable but still, if you have your own attorney, it is a good idea to get his or her opinion. You and your family may have to live under the terms of the contract for several years. Be sure you understand it. If questions arise or you have any problems with the clauses, don't be afraid to discuss them with your future employer. Get the best starting salary you can and be sure the deal is fair!

5

WORKING AND LIVING ABROAD

Your general living conditions abroad will depend not only on the country but on the specific region within the country where you will be working and living. Consider two petroleum geologists working in Saudi Arabia. One is stationed at the oil fields at Al-Hasa, the other works in a modern, air conditioned office in Riyadh. Life in the oil fields is a far cry from life in a modern city, yet the same can be said for work in America as well. The only difference is that it is far easier to obtain information about living and working conditions here than abroad. What other aspects of life abroad should you consider?

COST OF LIVING

As every traveler quickly discovers, the cost of a hotel, dinner, taxi, or movie varies tremendously from country to country. You can find a moderate hotel in London for about $200 a night. The equivalent room would cost about $180 in Paris, $160 in Sydney and $140 in New York City. Travel to Johannesburg and the equivalent room would be about

103

$90. The same cost-ratio holds for most other items as well. As a result of these varied costs, it is essential to compare your take home pay with what your actual out of pocket expenses may be.

The U.S. Department of Labor, Bureau of Labor Statistics periodically issues a listing of living costs abroad. (U.S. Department of State Index of Living Costs Abroad, Quarters Allowances, and Hardship Differentials.) It is this data which appears in the statistical data on each country listed in this book. The indexes of living costs abroad are used to compute allowances for government employees stationed overseas. They are based on a comparison of costs of goods and services (excluding housing and education) abroad with comparable goods and services in Washington, D.C.

As an example of the wide divergence of allowances compare the following based on the *U.S. Department of State Index of Living Costs Abroad* issued in the summer of 1994:

Caracas (Venezuela)	74
Ascuncion (Paraguay)	93
Rangoon (Burma)	80
Riyadh (Saudi Arabia)	112
Washington, D.C.	100
Accra (Ghana)	98
Rome	145
Brussels	167
London	142
Vienna	167
Copenhagen	166
Sapporo (Japan)	196

Very often U.S. companies also provide a cost of living adjustment, or COLA, which is usually based upon the above government index. However, it is important to determine this fact before heading abroad. A large salary may sound great based on your known costs in America but it might not be as impressive if you're working in Japan. Conversely, a high salary in Caracas will go much further than in the U.S. It's hard to believe but the cost of just a gallon of gasoline can vary from as much as $0.65 a gallon in Caracas to more than $4.00 in many parts of Europe.

When you sign on with a foreign company, your cost of living adjustment should be spelled out in detail in your contract or letter of agreement. Be sure the index upon which your COLA is based is a standard one such as the U.S. government's index. Don't be mislead by some arbitrary standard generated by a foreign company.

In addition to your COLA, also consider what additional benefits a company is offering which must be considered as a rebate against your true cost of living. For example, many companies provide you with housing facilities at either no cost or a substantially reduced cost. This policy is most common in the Middle East, but it holds true in other parts of the world as well. Obviously if you consider your housing expenses as about a quarter of your income, low or no-cost housing is actually money in the bank!

Other possible benefits that are offered as incentives include a car, servants, free or low-cost travel, medical care, and education. These items are nothing to look down upon. If you had to pay for your own medical costs or a complete medical insurance package for you or your family, you are talking about several thousand dollars annually. Although you pay nothing for elementary school through high school in America, a college education can cost thousands. Work in a country with free education (most of European and some Middle Eastern countries) and, if your children pass the basic exams taken by all local residents, they go to college at no cost to you. Most other foreign countries provide free education through high school and low cost university programs. America stands alone as the most expensive for a private university education.

HOUSING

If you elect to work in the Middle East or one of the underdeveloped countries, you'll find that housing is usually provided by your employer. In most cases, housing complexes, mobile home parks, or apartments are built specifically for Americans. Families usually have standard homes with two to four bedrooms, an American-style kitchen and at least one bath.

Housing for singles may be shared apartments, dorms or even barracks depending on the country and location within the country. If you're assigned to a new location, you could well be housed in a local hotel. Fortunately, most companies have learned through too many bad experiences not to keep secrets when it comes to housing. They learned the hard way: surprised candidates quit! My policy was to present a worse picture than actually existed. Then I had a psychological advantage when the new employee found conditions better than expected. Some companies don't do this, however, so it's best to expect the worse and you won't be disappointed! You'll be sent a very detailed description, often with pictures, of your living quarters before you leave the states. Spouses especially want to know what conditions to expect and how to plan. Company representatives are often available and knowledgeable as far as housing, shopping, schools, churches and medical facilities.

If you are working for a major foreign employer in either the Middle East or several of the developing nations, your housing is part of your employment package. In other areas you can negotiate a specific allowance towards housing. Obviously, to buy a home abroad raises several risks and is generally not recommended. In some countries it is against local law to sell land to foreigners; in many others the bureaucracy and red tape just aren't worth the hassle.

Keep in mind that electric power in most parts of the world is 220 volts (in the U.S. it is 110 volts). None of your appliances will work without both an adapter to alter 220 volts to 110 as well as an adapter plug to fit into the wall socket. Your American plug will not fit in sockets in most countries. Unfortunately, although many countries have 220 volts, there are as many as five different plug designs. Even throughout Europe a plug that fits into an Italian wall socket won't work in neighboring France. Your best bet is to buy a simple adapter kit containing a standard 220/110 volt converter and several plug adapters. Most companies will advise you as to the type of adaptor, if any, you may need.

Another serious consideration is the fact that many American-made appliances are designed only for 110 volts, and using a higher voltage can lead to serious damage. This is particularly true of shavers, hair dryers, toasters, radios and stereos. Be sure and consult with the manufacturer before toting an appliance abroad only to have it go up in smoke. Also, leave your TV set at home. Not only will the voltage be different but the television signals we receive in the United States are not compatible with those in the rest of the world. Obviously the same holds true if you buy a new TV set abroad. Leave it there; it won't work here!

Fortunately, your foreign employer is a few steps ahead of you. If you move into an American housing complex or rent a house formerly used by an American heading back to the states, you're most likely to discover your new home equipped with the basic appliances. If not, there is rarely a problem finding someone moving back home ready and willing to sell you his used appliances.

Remember that before you rush out and buy a local TV set in a foreign city check with someone to find the sort of programming offered. Obviously the local language is predominant. And, if you can't speak the language, watching TV will be most frustrating. Imagine American sitcoms and soap operas in Urdu or Chinese. Although some returnees claim that watching local TV is a good way to learn the language, most find the frustration factor overwhelming. As for sports, if you like soccer (called football abroad), you'll see a lot. It is the true international sport.

If you're working for an American company in one of the major world cities or regions, you most likely will have to select your own housing. Again, local company reps will assist you by providing names of known realtors, and lists of available apartments or houses. The cost of local housing depends, of course, on the city or region. Here is where your COLA comes in handy. In general, unless you're working in a back region of an underdeveloped country, expect to find conditions equal to or better than the states. The general commissaries in the Middle East, for example, are fully stocked with most items requested by Americans.

American-style food is generally provided for you. Everything from corn flakes to catsup; from Ding Dongs to Cheez Whiz (and even grits for us Southerners) is shipped from America to the job site. American food service professionals are normally hired to inspect the local supply of meat and fresh produce. They try to maintain quality and assure the well being of workers and their families. If there are many families on the job site, food is provided through the company supported commissary in which you have an account or allowance. If the site has many single workers, it usually establishes company dining facilities. If the local food is reasonably priced and conforms to U.S. standards, the company may give you a food allowance and let you shop and cook for yourself.

Whether or not to buy a car abroad is a question that comes up regularly. Believe it or not, the price of a car in America is cheaper than almost anywhere else in the world. A Japanese car, for example, is far cheaper to buy in America than in Japan. A Saab or Volvo, which is manufactured in Sweden, costs more than twice as much to buy in Sweden than in America. The reason: extremely high local taxes. In a case of carrying coals to Newcastle, many Scandinavians come to America to work then buy a car as part of their income package. If they are out of their home country for at least one year, they can return home with a car that is then considered "used." There is no local tax on imported used cars, only new ones. They will buy a new top-of-the-line Saab for $25,000, use it a year and are able to resell it back home for more than $50,000.

In many cases on-site transportation is provided for by your foreign employer. Sometimes you are housed so close to the job site you only need access to a vehicle for shopping or recreational purposes. Many large foreign sites have excellent, reliable, comfortable mass transit. If you are living some distance from the job site or your job requires you to travel, your employer not only supplies the car but also handles gas, maintenance, insurance and sees to it that you obtain a local driver's license. Keep in mind that in some Middle East countries, driving a car is for men only. It may not be fair but it's fact! If a woman is in a car, she must be accompanied by a man. Women employees, usually teachers and nurses in these countries, are provided transportation with a driver.

PETS

A final note on living abroad. If you're planning to bring Fido, by all means check with your employer or local immigration officials at your ultimate destination before you leave to find out if there is a local quarantine for pets. Although some countries have no regulations regarding the importation of pets, many do. Take a dog to Australia, for example, and he must remain in quarantine at your expense for a full year; England's quarantine is six months. Tiffany, our miniature poodle, went to Saudi Arabia as a certified watch dog! So, it pays to check out the local country rules. Returning to the states with a pet bought overseas can also impose problems. Again, check with both foreign and local authorities. Most living things brought into the United States require a U.S. permit. Some living objects (both plants and animals) are forbidden altogether. Also, some foreign countries forbid the export of local animals. Do your homework before leaving America.

RECREATION

Living overseas must not be all work. Even the most regressive company manager now recognizes this. If you have an employment contract, it will clearly specify the amount of time that is required of you on the job site. Overtime is covered and there will also be a clause covering vacations and holidays.

However, don't expect work rules abroad to be the same as in the United States. Remember, the labor laws in the country of residence apply, not U.S. rules. For example, in the Middle East the standard work week is usually five days, eight hours per day. However, you work Saturday through Wednesday. Friday is their holy day and Thursday equates to our Saturday. Many contracts specify six day work weeks in order to maximize efficiency. Overtime is either built in to the salary or shown as an overtime addition. Your contract will also specify whether or not you have time off at company expense to return to America (home leave) after a specified period of time. Rarely will you be granted home leave during your first year on the job. Airfare is usually paid for by your employer as well. Choose extra stops or layovers in exotic spots and you pay the tab.

If you are on a single status and located in a developing country or hardship location, you may receive am interim rest and recreation (R & R) trip. These trips are normally of a shorter duration and a lot closer than your home leave.

If you're in an American complex, you'll find a variety of activities can be planned for you and your family. These may include local sightseeing trips, beach or mountain trips, organized sports such as softball, volleyball, or touch football (American style). Low cost trips to neighboring countries are also available.

Our children went to elementary and junior high school in an American school in the Middle East. As a result, they enjoyed superior training by an excellent teaching staff and a much earlier start in languages than traditional U.S. schools. In addition, they participated in Brownies, Boy Scouts, drama, varsity sports, and Halloween carnivals. Not bad for a "hardship" location! There were 1,400 other students at the school located at the U.S. consulate.

Situations may differ for locations other than the large job complexes where we lived. In other places you may live "on the economy" or more like the locals. This too can be a rewarding experience as you will gain a great insight into other people and their culture. Regardless of where you make your new home, take advantage of the local terrain if you enjoy hiking and picnics. Visit the nearby towns and cities. Sporting events are popular in every country. Here is a wonderful opportunities to experience a different lifestyle. Take advantage of it.

MEDICAL FACILITIES

No matter where you'll be working be assured that your employer has already considered the fact that you and your family want information on the cost and quality of the local medical facilities. In the large job sites in the Middle East and a few of the underdeveloped countries, you'll find a Western educated doctor and at least one nurse as an integral part of the overall complex. In other countries the quality of medical care is solely dependent upon location. However, don't make the mistake of assuming that medical care abroad is inferior to that in America. To the contrary, in many countries you'll actually discover superior care. (Keep in mind that in some areas, such as child fatalities following birth, we're not even in the top ten.)

Generally speaking, the best medical facilities are in countries with a high standard of living—most European countries, Japan, Israel, Australia, and Canada. In the Middle Eastern countries you'll discover that health care in the major cities is quite good. Major new hospitals have been build recently in cities like Riyadh, Saudi Arabia and Muscat, Oman. They are often staffed with American doctors that most likely are spending their time overseas for the very same reason you have elected to go abroad. Equipment is usually modern and top of the line.

Now that many of the Eastern European countries are providing limited employment opportunities, keep in mind that medical facilities may be quite meager compared to U.S. standards. Hospitals in Russia, for example, are considered even below some Third World standards.

In some developing countries, you will find a lack of top quality health care. This is not to say that no doctors are available; rather, they are few and not easily accessible in remote regions. Hospitals may be old, overcrowded and poorly stocked with both equipment and modern medicines. If you work in a remote region, your employer should assist you as to the proper procedures to follow to locate the best care available. Be sure to bring with you those basic medicines and health aids that you'll need. It's a good idea to contact your own physician before leaving for his council on specific medical aids you should take with you. Remember that in some parts of the world, particularly the under-developed countries, you'll need to be immunized against diseases such as yellow fever, tetanus, typhoid and polio. Malaria suppressants and gamma globulin are also recommended. The embassy representing the country or countries you plan to visit can provide you with information on local health conditions.

Also keep in mind that in many parts of the world you will not find potable drinking water. Bottled water is available in most places. There are also many commercial water purification products you can buy in the states. Again, let your physician recommend a specific agent for you.

Fortunately, you'll find that in most foreign countries you will pay little of nothing for your medical care. Most countries have some form of socialized medical care. Even as a temporary resident you should qualify for this care. Your employment contract might cover a full medical and dental insurance package as well.

If you have any medical problems, be sure to bring specific medical data with you to assist the local doctors. Unlike the states, it is hard to obtain your U.S. medical records from abroad. Xerox copies of certain records may be worth including with your personal documents. Carry a card in your wallet or with your passport containing such information as your blood type, chemical or drug allergies, name, address and phone number of your primary physician in America, and the individual to contact in an emergency. It's also a good idea to record any prescription information if it becomes necessary to replace your eyeglasses overseas.

6

REGIONS AND COUNTRIES

*H*ere's a breakdown of the countries, region by region, for your job search. The data is acquired from both U.S. State Department sources as well as public material made available by the Central Intelligence Agency. Unfortunately, in some cases economic and statistical data issued by one source varies considerably from that issued by the other. In all cases of statistical discrepancy, we have accepted the CIA data to assure consistency as well as the fact that it is most recent. A few comments on the statistical material. GDP or Gross Domestic Product is the value of all goods and services produced domestically. GNP or Gross National Product is the value of all goods and services produced domestically, plus income earned abroad, minus income earned by foreigners from domestic production. The Official Exchange Rate is the amount of foreign currency you would receive for one U.S. dollar in the Spring of 1994. Obviously, this number fluctuates on a daily basis. The Cost of Living data is based on information provided by the U.S. State Department in the Spring of 1994. Current statistics are published quarterly in the *U.S. Department of State Indexes of Living Costs Abroad, Quarters Allowances, and Hardship Differentials*. These data are used in the following country by country analysis and are provided for comparative purposes.

THE AMERICAS AND THE CARIBBEAN

The Bahamas

GEOGRAPHY:
AREA: 5,380 sq. mi.
CAPITAL: Nassau
PRINCIPAL CITIES: Freeport, New Providence
TERRAIN: Long, flat coral islands
CLIMATE: Tropical marine with summer temperatures ranging from 70 to 94° F in the summer and 60 to 75° in the winter.

PEOPLE:
POPULATION: 273,055
ANNUAL GROWTH RATE: 1.7%
RELIGION: Baptist 29%; Anglican 23%; Roman Catholic 22%
LANGUAGE: English
EDUCATION: Attendance in primary school 96%; Literacy 93%
LIFE EXPECTANCY: Men 67; women 75 years.

GOVERNMENT: Independent British Commonwealth. Bicameral parliament with executive authority vested in British monarch. Governor General is head of State; Prime Minister head of government. Elections at least every five years. Government budget: $582 million.

ECONOMY:
GNP: $4.4 billion
ANNUAL GROWTH RATE: 2.0%
PER CAPITA GNP $16,500.
AVERAGE RATE OF INFLATION: 6.5%
WORK FORCE: Of the 110,900 employed, the majority work in the government, hotel & restaurant, and financial sectors. The unemployment rate is about 5.7%.
OFFICIAL EXCHANGE RATE: 1 Bahamian Dollar = US$
COST OF LIVING INDEX: 133

The Bahamas have been known as a tax haven, way station for the drug trade and a tourist's delight. Perhaps a little bit of all three is closer to reality. Certainly tourism is the mainstay of the economy, accounting for an estimated 50% of the gross national product and employing about half of the local work force. Four of every five tourists are American.

Finance is the economy's second most important sector. Of the 387 banks and trust companies licensed in The Bahamas, most are involved in managing assets for individual and offshore companies and trusts. The Bahamas' status as a tax haven and its system of banking regulations that guarantee secrecy of financial transactions have led to its growth as an international banking center.

Other industries include a cement plant, several pharmaceutical plants, and rum & liqueur distilleries. Sun dried sea salt is produced in Inagua, and aragonite, a type of limestone with several industrial uses, is extracted from the sea floor at Ocean Cay. The government has been attempting todiversify the economy and attract new industries with little success. The Industries Encouragement Act offers manufacturers relief from import duties and taxes.

The best areas for Americans interested in working in The Bahamas are either in specialized financial areas, education, or tourism. Of course it is easier to secure a position with one of the 85 U.S. companies located here than try and compete directly with the local talent. A work permit is required from the government and before one is granted it must be shown that no qualified Bahamians are available for the position. The application for a job permit asks you to provide evidence that an attempt has been made to advertise for the position in a local newspaper and that no qualified locals have applied for the job. It is the responsibility of the Ministry of Labor to confirm that you or your potential employer have made every attempt to fill the position locally. When the government is convinced that you are indeed unique you'll be charged a fee for your permit and can then finalize your employment deal. This process can be most time consuming and expensive but it is the only way to secure a permit.

Occasionally there are positions in teaching but the government controls most schools. Of the 225 schools, 187 are fully maintained by the government; the rest are private. Several college programs are offered in cooperation with the University of Miami and of the West Indies. Information of possible teaching jobs with the government can be obtained by contacting the Commissioner of Education, Department of Education, Nassau.

The Bahamas has an embassy at 600 New Hampshire Avenue NW, Washington, DC 20037 (202-338 3940) with a consulate in Miami. The U.S. Embassy is located in the Mosmar Building, Queen Street, Nassau. Contacts:

Banking:

Allied Bank International
Beaumont House, P.O. Box # N 3944
Nassau

Bank America Trust
  and Banking Corp., Ltd.
King and George Streets,
P.O. Box # N 9100
Nassau

Fidelity Bank
50 Shirley St., P.O. Box N 100
Nassau

Tourism:

Holiday Inn
Freeport-Lucaya G.B.,
Lucaya Beach

Sheraton British Colonial Hotel
Number One Bay Street,
P.O. Box # N 7148
Nassau

Bahamas Development Ltd.
P.O. Box # F 160
Freeport, Grand Island

Petroleum:

Esso Standard Oil S.A. Ltd.
Bay & Armstrong
P.O. Box # N 3237
Nassau

Texaco Bahamas Ltd.
P.O. Box # N 4807
Nassau

Accountants:

Arthur Young & Co.
Sassoon House, Shirley
  & Victoria
P.O. Box N 1348
Nassau

Deloitte, Haskins & Sells
Centerville House
Collins Avenue
P.O. Box # N 3739
Nassau

CENTRAL AMERICA

Costa Rica

GEOGRAPHY:
AREA: 19,652 sq. mi.
CAPITAL: San Jose
PRINCIPAL CITIES: Alajuela, Limon, Golfido
TERRAIN: Coastal plains separated by rugged mountains.

CLIMATE: Tropical. Dry season December to April; rainy season May through November.

PEOPLE:
POPULATION: 3,342,154
ANNUAL GROWTH RATE: 2.7%
RELIGION: 95% Roman Catholic
LANGUAGE: Spanish
EDUCATION: Attendance in primary school 98%; Literacy 93%
LIFE EXPECTANCY: Men 75; women, 79 years.

GOVERNMENT: Democratic republic. Unicameral legislature elected at four year intervals. President is both head of state and head of government. Government budget: $792 million.

ECONOMY:
GDP: $19.3 billion
ANNUAL GROWTH RATE: 6.5%
PER CAPITA GDP $5,900.
AVERAGE RATE OF INFLATION: 9%
WORK FORCE: Of the 965,000 in the work force, 38% are employed by services and the government; 32% agriculture; 25% industry and commerce; and, 5% banking and finance. The unemployment rate hovers about 4%.
OFFICIAL EXCHANGE RATE: 150.67 colones = US$
COST OF LIVING INDEX: 085

Traditionally, Costa Rica has been one of the region's strongest and most stable nations, both economically and politically. The economic future, however, rests heavily on the price of two commodities, coffee to export and oil to import. These commodities have a major impact on the country's balance of payments and thus its economic development and growth. The nation continues its efforts to industrialize and shift labor out of traditional and import-substitution industries into more productive and profitable activities. These changes may provide job opportunities for Americans with experience in light industry and agribusiness.

The U.S. has responded to Costa Rica's economic problems with developmental assistance programs. Many of these (i.e. agriculture, health, nutrition, education, natural resources development, etc.) may provide an opportunity for those with skills in these fields to obtain consultation assignments. Write:

International Development Cooperation Agency
320 21st Street
Washington, DC 20523.

Foreign Agriculture Section
U.S. Department of Agriculture
Washington, DC 20250

International Trade Administration
Department of Commerce
14th Street and Constitution Avenue, NW
Washington, DC 20230

Office of International Health
Department of Health and Human Services
200 Independence Avenue
Washington, DC 20201

Both the Peace Corps (with some 200 volunteers) and the U.S. agency for International Development are quite visible here. Other U.S. agencies, including the U.S. Information Service and the Department of Agriculture are active. More than 20,000 Americans, mostly retirees, live in Costa Rica.

Working for a U.S. company is the most financially lucrative but these jobs require specialized skills and, in most cases, a knowledge of Spanish. A work permit and visa is required and will be issued by the Costa Rican government upon application by a prospective employer indicating that your job can not be filled by a native. Although this is a tourists haven, not many jobs exist in the tourist industry. Additional information about American companies located here can be obtained from the American Chamber of Commerce of Costa Rica, Apartado 4946, Calle 3, Avenidas 1 y 3, San Jose, 1000.

Life here is comfortable and rarely rushed. Medical services are good with the most serious health problems—intestinal disorders, malaria, and typhoid—occurring outside the capital. Drinking water in the major San Jose hotels and restaurants is purified; outside the capital drinking water should be boiled.

Costa Rica has an embassy at 1825 Connecticut Avenue NW, Suite 213, Washington, DC 20009 (202/234-2945). The U.S. Embassy is located at Calle 1, Avenida 3, San Jose 1000. Contacts:

Engineering:

Reifi S.A.
Aptdo. 3156
San Jose

Sam P. Wallace
 de Centroamerica S.A.
Aptdo. 7-3380
San Jose

Food Processing:

Pan American Standard
 Brands Inc.
Aptdo. 1436
San Jose

Standard Fruit Co.
Puerto Limon

United Fruit Group
Aptdo. 30
San Jose

Petroleum:

Sardimar S.A.
Aptdo. 8-4430
San Jose

Exxon Corp. S.A.
Aptdo 23
San Jose

Chemicals:

Union Carbide Centro America
S.A.
Aptdo. 10160
San Jose

FMC Intl..
Aptdo. 2847
Correo Central 1000
San Jose

Dominican Republic

GEOGRAPHY:
AREA: 18,704 sq. mi.
CAPITAL: Santo Domingo
PRINCIPAL CITIES: Puerto Plata, Santiago, Haina
TERRAIN: Rugged highlands and mountains with fertile valleys interspersed.
CLIMATE: Tropical maritime; little seasonal variations.

PEOPLE:
POPULATION: 7,826,075
ANNUAL GROWTH RATE: 1.8%
RELIGION: 95% Roman Catholic
LANGUAGE: Spanish

EDUCATION: Attendance in primary school 70%; Literacy 88%
LIFE EXPECTANCY: 68 years.

GOVERNMENT: Republic. President is chief of state. Bicameral legislature with elections every four years. Government budget: $938 million of which 5% is for the military.

ECONOMY:
GDP: $23 billion
ANNUAL GROWTH RATE: 3%
PER CAPITA GDP $3,000.
AVERAGE RATE OF INFLATION: 8%
WORK FORCE: 35% of the work force are employed in agriculture; 13% industry and commerce; 23% government; and, 14% services. The unemployment rate is about a quarter of the work force.
OFFICIAL EXCHANGE RATE: 12.8 pesos = US$
COST OF LIVING INDEX: 093

Like it's adjacent neighbor, Haiti, the Dominican Republic is an extremely poor nation. The economy is largely dependent on the agricultural sector, which employs about half the labor force and provides about half of export revenues. Industry is based on the processing of agricultural products, durable consumer goods, and chemicals. Rapid growth of free trade zones has established a significant expansion of manufacturing for export, especially clothing apparel. Over the past decade tourism has also increased in importance and is a significant source of new jobs. Most of these jobs, however, are grabbed by locals willing to work long hours for low pay. Administrative and executive jobs in the tourist industry may occasionally become available through U.S. companies.

A list of U.S. companies located here as well as up to date data on the labor situation is available from the American Chamber of Commerce in the Dominican Republic, P.O. Box 95-2, Hotel Santo Domingo, Avenida Independencia, Santo Domingo.

There are American trained doctors in Santo Domingo but medical facilities outside the capital are not readily available. Tap water is not potable anywhere on the island.

The Dominican Republic has an embassy at 1712 22nd Street NW, Washington, DC 20008 (202/332-6280) with consulates in Boston, Chicago, Los Angeles, New York, Miami, New Orleans, Philadelphia, Detroit, San Juan, and Charlotte Amalie. The U.S. Embassy is located at

Calle Cesar Nicolas Penson and Calle Leopoldo Navarro, Santo Domingo. Contacts:

Engineering:

Burns & Roe
Santo Domingo

Calmest S.A.
Abraham Lincoln
Esquina Modesto Diaz
Aptdo. 1693
Santo Domingo

Manufacturing:

3M Santo Domingo S.A.
Aptdo. 103-2, Ave. Luperon,
Zona Industrial de Herrera,
Santo Domingo

American Can Co.
Envases Antillanos C. por A.
Santiago

Tourism:

Holiday Inn
Avenida Anacaona
Santo Domingo

Santo Domingo Sheraton
 Hotels & Casino
Ave. George Washington 365
Aptdo. 1493
Santo Domingo

Food Products:

Exportadora Dominicana
 de Guneos C. por A
Calle Beler No. 98
Santiago

Nabisco Inc.
Tamara C. por A.
Aptdo. Postal No. 1146
Santo Domingo

Honduras

GEOGRAPHY:
AREA: 68,000 sq. mi.
CAPITAL: Tegucigalpa
PRINCIPAL CITIES: Puerto Cortes, Juticalpa, San Pedro Suia
TERRAIN: Mostly mountainous in the interior; narrow coastal plain.
CLIMATE: Subtropical in the lowlands; becomes more temperate with elevation.

PEOPLE:
POPULATION: 5,314,794
ANNUAL GROWTH RATE: 2.73%

RELIGION: 97% Roman Catholic
LANGUAGE: Spanish
EDUCATION: Attendance in primary school 70%; Literacy 56%
LIFE EXPECTANCY: Men 65; women 70 years.

GOVERNMENT: Democratic constitutional republic. Unicameral legislature with president directly elected for a four year term. Government budget: $1.1 billion with 16% devoted to the military.

ECONOMY:
GDP: $10 billion
ANNUAL GROWTH RATE: 3.7%
PER CAPITA GDP $1,950.
AVERAGE RATE OF INFLATION: 13%
WORK FORCE: 62% of the work force are employed in agriculture; 20% in services; 9% in manufacturing; and, 3% in construction. The unemployment rate hovers 10% (30-40% underemployed).
OFFICIAL EXCHANGE RATE: 7.26 lempiras = US$

Honduras is one of the poorest and the least developed countries in Latin America. The economy is based primarily on agriculture, but there are extensive forest, marine, and mineral resources. Although unemployment is officially estimated at 10% to 15%, under employment is much higher, perhaps as high as 40% of the work force. The last years of the 1980s, however, did show an economic growth of about 3 to 4%, sparked by strong growth in the mining, construction, and service sectors. Employment opportunities here are obviously not widespread.

The United States accounts for about 85% of total direct foreign investment worth about $230 million. The largest American interests are in fruit (particularly banana and citrus) production, petroleum refining and marketing, and mining. In addition, American corporations have invested in tobacco, shrimp culture, beef, poultry and animal feed production, insurance, leasing, food processing, brewing, and furniture manufacturing.

The primary opportunities are with U.S. companies needing a special expertise, government employees working directly with the Honduran people, and international agencies. AID and the U.S. Information Agency are active. The Peace Corp has some 340 volunteers with programs primarily in health, education, and forestry.

Americans must have a passport to either work or visit in Honduras. Although visas aren't necessary to visit, you'll need one to obtain a work permit. As an underdeveloped nation be aware of health conditions. Water is not potable and must be boiled and filtered, and is often in short supply. The main health hazards include rabies and various intestinal diseases, including typhoid, hepatitis, parasites, and dysentery. When traveling outside the capital take malaria precautions.

For information about American companies located in Honduras as well as possible employment opportunities write to the Honduras-American Chamber of Commerce, Hotel Honduras Maya, Apartado Postal 1838, Tegucigalpa.

Honduras has an embassy at 4301 Connecticut Ave. NW, Washington, DC 20008 (202/966-7700) with consulates in Chicago, Los Angeles, Miami, New Orleans, New York, Boston, Detroit, and San Francisco. The U.S. Embassy is located on Avenida La Paz, Tegucigalpa. Contacts:

Manufacturing:

Compania Hulera S.A.
P.O. Box # 164
San Pedro Suia

Otis Elevator Co.
9 Avenida 12 y 13 Calles
Comayaguela # 1216
Tegucigalpa

Food Products:

Alimentos Concentrados, S.A.
la Avenida entre la y 2A,
Calles N.E. Calle 6
San Pedro Suia

Aimidones del Istmo SA de CV
Aptdo. 234
San Pedro Suia

Petroleum:

Exxon Corp.
La Burrera
Camayagula

Lloyd Petroleum Co.
Aptdo. 38,
Tegucigalpa

Texaco Inc.
Aptdo. Postal # 112
San Pedro Suia

Engineering:

Brown & Root Inc.
Tegucigalpa

Calmaquip Ingenieros
 de Honduras S.A.
Aptdo. 845
Boulevard Morazan # 1518
Barrio de Guacerique
Comayaguela

Clothing:

Novelty Honduras S.A.
12th Avenue # 5
San Pedro Suia

Jazmin S. de R.L. Barrio
el Jasmin
Tegucigalpa

Jamaica

GEOGRAPHY:
AREA: 4,244 sq. mi.
CAPITAL: Kingston
PRINCIPAL CITIES: Montego Bay, Spanish Town
TERRAIN: Mountainous island
CLIMATE: Tropical. Hot and humid with a temperate interior.

PEOPLE:
POPULATION: 2,555,064
ANNUAL GROWTH RATE: 1.1%
RELIGION: Predominantly Protestant (including Anglican and Baptist),
some Roman Catholic, some cults.
LANGUAGE: English
EDUCATION: Attendance in primary school 98%; Literacy 74%
LIFE EXPECTANCY: Men 75; women 78 years.
GOVERNMENT: Independent state within British Commonwealth.
Bicameral legislature. Cabinet headed by prime minister. Government
budget: $973 million.

ECONOMY:
GDP: $8 billion
ANNUAL GROWTH RATE: 1.2%
PER CAPITA GDP $3,200.
AVERAGE RATE OF INFLATION: 30%
WORK FORCE: Of the 781,000 in the work force, 36% work in
agriculture; 13% in manufacturing; 19% in services; and, 10% for the
government. The unemployment rate is about 15.4%.
OFFICIAL EXCHANGE RATE: -32.7 Jamaican dollar = US$
COST OF LIVING INDEX: 092

This island paradise is too often considered solely a vacation retreat
when in reality it has a great deal more. More than 120 American firms

have established a base here to take advantage of both the island's natural resources but the inexpensive labor pool as well. More than $1 billion have been invested in the country. Most jobs, therefore, are limited to local workers but the need for experienced technical people is always there. The Jamaican economy traditionally was based on plantation agriculture, primarily sugar and bananas. Although agriculture remains basic to Jamaican life, the discovery of bauxite in the 1950s and the subsequent establishment of the bauxite-alumina industries became the dominant factor in the island's economic growth.

During the 1960s, the expansion of tourism and establishment of local manufacturing industries were emphasized. Today, the Jamaican government provides a wide range of incentives to investors, including remittance facilities, tax holidays, and duty free access for machinery imported for approved enterprises. Garment manufacturing, light manufacturing and data entry are some of the activities being undertaken by Jamaican and foreign-owned firms. A recently announced new program guarantees access in the United States for garments made in Jamaica from textiles woven and cut in America.

No passport or visa is required to visit but a work permit issued by the Jamaican government is necessary to work here. Your prospective employer is responsible for the paperwork and assuring local officials that no local resident can handle the job. The American Chamber of Commerce was set up in 1986 to enhance trade opportunities between Jamaica and the U.S. The organization also publishes a list of their members complete with the names and addresses of the managing directors of U.S. companies here. This list is an excellent starting point in any job search. Write to: The American Chamber of Commerce of Jamaica, The Wyndham Hotel, 77 Knutsford Blvd., Kingston, 5. Another potential contact is Industrial Commercial Developments Limited, 3-9 Harbour Street, Kingston. This organization comprises 23 companies involved in manufacturing, marketing, services and finance. Although their key priority is assisting new business development they may also be aware of changing job trends, needs, etc.

Jamaica has an embassy at Suite 355, 1850 K Street NW, Washington, DC 20008 (202/452-0660) with consulates in New York and Miami. The U.S. maintains its Embassy at 2 Oxford Road, Jamaica Mutual Center, Kingston. Contacts:

Mining:

Alcoa Minerals of Jamaica Inc.
13 Waterloo Road
Kingston 6

Alkali Ltd.
Spanish Town

Petroleum:

Esso West Indies Ltd.
95 Marcus Garvey Dr.
Kingston 11

Texaco Caribbean Inc.
Mutual Life Centre
2 Oxford Street
Kingston 5

Food Products:

Pan American Standard Brands
P.O. Box # 82
Spanish Town

Cremo Ltd.
284 Spanish Town Road
Kingston

Clothing:

Colonial International Ltd.
4 Fairchild Ave.
Kingston 11

Colonial Shirts of Jamaica Ltd.
110 Bay Farm Road
Kingston 11

Manufacturing:

Gillette Caribbean Ltd.
21 Gordon Town Road
Kingston 6

Singer Sewing Machine Co.
6 Oxford Road
Kingston 5

NORTH AMERICA

Canada

GEOGRAPHY:
AREA: 3.8 million sq. mi.
CAPITAL: Ottawa
PRINCIPAL CITIES: Toronto, Montreal, Vancouver
TERRAIN: Mostly plains with mountains in the west and lowlands in the southeast.
CLIMATE: Varies from temperate in the south to subarctic and Arctic in the north.

PEOPLE:
POPULATION: 28,113,997
ANNUAL GROWTH RATE: 1%
RELIGION: 46% Roman Catholic; 16% United Church; 10% Anglican
LANGUAGE: English and French (both are official)
EDUCATION: Attendance in primary school: 98%
LITERACY: 99%
LIFE EXPECTANCY: Men 73; Women 81
GOVERNMENT: Confederation with parliamentary (bicameral) democracy. Elizabeth II is recognized as sovereign. Federal executive power is vested in cabinet collectively responsible to House of Commons and headed by prime minister. Government budget: $127 billion of which about 9% is for the military.

ECONOMY:
GDNP: $617.7 billion
ANNUAL GROWTH RATE: 2.4%
PER CAPITA GNP: $22,200
AVERAGE RATE OF INFLATION: 1.9%
WORK FORCE: Of the 13.3 million in the work force, 31% were involved in community, business, or personal services; 16% in manufacturing; 16% in trade; 6% public administration and, 1% in agriculture. The unemployment rate is about 11%.
OFFICIAL EXCHANGE RATE: 1.31 Canadian dollars = US$
COST OF LIVING INDEX: 122

Americans often look to Canada as our 51st state. But don't ever say that to a Canadian. The usually unspoken—but occasionally quite vociferous—rivalry between our two countries is actually one of the great examples of peaceful coexistence between neighbors. (Yet one of the underlying reasons behind the drive for the French separatist movement within Canada is to assure a greater division between Canadian interests and those of the United States—specifically language.) The years of sharing a common border has not only allowed for a normal and tranquil trade relationship but also the easy exchange of peoples across the border for business, tourism, and in many cases jobs.

Four out of every five of Canada's 26.3 million people live within 100 miles of the U.S. border. Yet, Canadians and Americans are not as similar as casual observers frequently assume. The Canadian character and outlook have been forged from a distinctive historical and social background. Canada's more than 6 million French-speaking citizens are primarily descendants of colonists who settled the country three centuries ago; the English speaking community has been built up mostly by immigration from the United Kingdom. The flow of immigrants into Canada has had a significant impact on jobs. Since World War II, more than 4 million immigrants have flooded the country; more than a quarter from Britain and Ireland. Most immigrants have settled in the province of Ontario. Since 1967, unacceptably high unemployment levels (close to 10%) have led to strict controls. Today, it is necessary to have the skills and qualifications required by Canada's growing economy before you're granted a work permit. Fortunately for skilled Americans, there are still ample job opportunities in a wide range of areas.

The mineral industry has been a major factor in Canada's economic development. Canada's lakes have more than half of the world's fresh water and three quarters of the country's needs are met by hydroelectric energy. The United States is the largest foreign investor in Canada at over $70 billion, or about 80% of all foreign investment. America's investments are primarily in the mining and smelting industries, petroleum, chemicals, the manufacturing of machinery and transportation equipment, and finance. More than 1,300 American companies have set up shop across the border.

Entry into Canada is regulated by the federal government but immigration programs are undertaken in full cooperation with the provincial governments as well. Thus, the location of a particular job may be impacted by local labor policies of the province in which you want to work.

There are two ways to obtain a work permit (or immigration status): sponsorship by a Canadian dependent relative (spouse, retired parent, or unmarried child); or, by independent application. The latter, obviously the most common for Americans, means finding a job which no Canadian is "qualified to fill." Although this sounds like an impossibility there are still a great number of jobs in this still developing nation that are begging for applicants. Once you have located a position your potential employer presents your accepted job offer to the nearest Canadian Employment Manpower Center. If your application is accepted by the CEMC, your employer is notified and sends you confirmation that your request is approved. A medical exam (at your expense) may be required before the Employment Authorization is finally issued.

Another far easier way to work in Canada is to start your own business. The country is encouraging business persons willing to invest in a going concern or establish a new business "which will be of significant economic benefit to Canada" to cross the border and start a new life. Detailed information on investing in or starting a new business is available from the Trade Office at the Canadian Embassy or any consulate.

There are several ways in which to obtain data on specific job opportunities. If you are a professional person contact the Canadian professional association representing your field and ask them of specific needs and possible job openings. A list of Canada's professional associations is published in the Canadian Almanac and Directory available in most U.S. libraries. The Directory also gives the names and address of many potential employers including: colleges and universities, libraries, law firms, insurance companies, publishers, broadcasters, etc.

If you are job hunting in Canada stop at any of the county's 400 Manpower Centers (addresses listed in local phone directories). Their computerized job bank lists vacancies in a wide variety of fields including many blue collar openings. As for specific fields:

- **Teachers:** Obtain the book, *Teaching in Canada*, published by the Canadian Teacher's Federation, 110 Argyle Avenue, Ottawa, Ontario K2P 1B4. Although the CTF won't get you a job their publication does provide valuable data on requirements, provincial authorities, etc. The Canadian Education Association, 252 Bloor Street W, 8th Floor, Toronto, Ontario M5S 1V5 issues the brochure Information for Teachers Thinking of Coming to Canada. Other important job sources include the Computerized Teacher Registry, British Columbia School Trustees' Association, 1155 West 8th Avenue, Vancouver, British Columbia V6H 1C5; Department of Education, P.O. Box 6000, Fredericton, New Brunswick E3B 5HI. If you want data on appointments in Canada's private schools and academies write to the Executive Secretary, Canadian Association of Independent Schools, Stanstead College, Stanstead, Quebec J0B 3E0.

  To teach at the college level subscribe to both the CAUT Bulletin published by the Canadian Association of University Teachers (75 Albert Street, Suite 1001, Ottawa, Ontario K1P 5E7 (cost—$30.00 a year; Canadian money only); and, University Affairs published by the Association of Universities and Colleges in Canada, 151 Slater Street, Ottawa, Ontario K1P 5N1 (cost—$20.00 a year; Canadian money only). If you are interested in a listing of specific university departments and their addresses contact AUCC Information office at the above address.

- **Engineering:**The best sources of information for job opportunities are the Canadian Council of Professional Engineers, 116 Albert Street, Suite 401, Ottawa, Ontario; and, the Ordre des Ingenieurs du Quebec, 2020 University, Montreal, Quebec H3A 2A5. Although neither will serve as an employment service, both can advise you as to possible companies with specific job needs as well as procedures for obtaining work within the profession.

- **Medical:** There are always openings here for qualified medical specialists. The Canadian Medical Association Journal (CMAJ) is published by the Canadian Medical Association (P.O. Box #8650, Ottawa, Ontario K1G 0G8) and lists openings in every issue. The Association also will send you their free brochure, Medical Practices in Canada, which has the address of the various provincial medical associations and outlines their specific requirements. A private medical concern, the Grenfell Regional Health Service (Charles Curtis Memorial Hospital, St. Anthony, Newfoundland), operates several Canadian hospitals and is responsible for staffing several dozen health centers. They are often on the look out for qualified dentists, doctors, nurses, and therapists. Employment can range from a two year period to a multi-year contract.

  Pharmacists are licensed by the various provinces. Data on jobs and licensing requirements is available from either the Pharmacy Examining Board of Canada, Suite 603, 123 Edward Street, Toronto, Ontario M5G 1E2; or, Pharmaciens du Quebec, 266 Notre Dame Ouest, Montreal, Quebec H2Y 1T5.

- **Mining & Petroleum Industry:** Your best bet is to contact the various companies involved in exploration, drilling, pumping, refining, and mining. The Canadian Department of Mining, Ottawa, Ontario K1P 5K7 can provide a listing of the various Canadian companies in the field. American companies are available from the U.S. Embassy in Ottawa.

  The Canadian pay scale is less than that in the United States with income taxes about the same or slightly higher. For example, a single tax payer earning $25,000 would pay a tax (in two parts: federal and provincial) of about $5,600. A married man with the same income would be assessed about $4,100. Social benefits, including free medical care, are about the same as Great Britain.

There is no American Chamber of Commerce in Canada. Canada has an embassy at 501 Pennsylvania Avenue NW, Washington, DC 20001, (202/682-1740) with consulates in Atlanta, Boston, Buffalo, Chicago, Cleveland, Dallas, Detroit, Los Angeles, Minneapolis, New York, San Francisco, and, Seattle. The United States Embassy is located at 100 Wellington Street, Ottawa. Contacts:

Manufacturing:

Allen-Bradley (Canada) Ltd.
Cambridge, Ontario
Black & Decker Canada, Inc.
100 Central Avenue
Brockville, Ontario K6V 5W6

Ford Motors Co. of
 Canada, Ltd.
Canadian Road
Oakville, Ontario

Canadian General Electric
 Co., Ltd.
P.O. Box 417
Toronto, Ontario M5L 1J2

General Motors of Canada, Ltd.
215 William Street East
Oshawa, Ontario L1G 1K7

A.O. Smith Corp.
768 Erie Street
Stratford, Ontario

Financial:

Bank of America Canada
20 Queen Street
West P.O. Box 38
Toronto M5H 3R3

Chemical Bank of Canada
181 University Avenue
Toronto, Ontario M5H 3M7

The Mercantile Bank of Canada
625 Dorchester West
Montreal, Ontario

Mellon Bank Canada
One First Canadian Plaza
Toronto, Ontario M5X 1A4

Chemical:

Dow Chemical of Canada, Ltd.
P.O. Box 1012
Sarnia, Ontario N7T 7K7

DuPont Chemicals of
 Canada, Inc.
Montreal, Quebec

W.R. Grace & Co of
Canada, Ltd.
294 Elements Road West
Ajax, Ontario L1S 3C6

Monsanto Canada, Inc.
P.O. Box 787
Streetsville Postal Station
Mississauga, Ontario L5M 2G4

Electronics:

NCR Canada, Ltd.
6865 Century Avenue
Mississauga, Ontario L5M 2E2

Tandom Computers
Canada, Ltd.
Edmonton, Alberta

Varian Associates of
Canada, Ltd.
45 River Drive
Georgetown, Ontario L7G 22J4

Wang Laboratories
(Canada), Ltd.
180 Duncan Mill Road
Don Mills, Ontario M3C 1K5

Engineering/Construction:

Bechtel Canada, Ltd.
10123 99th Street
Edmonton, Alberta T5J 2P4

Brown & Root, Ltd.
P.O. Box 5588
Edmonton, Alberta T6C 4E9

Foster Wheeler, Ltd.
P.O. Box 3007
St Catherines, Ontario L2R 7B7

Phillips Barratt
Kaiser Engineers, Ltd.
2150 West Broadway
Vancouver, British Columbia
V6K 4L9

Stone Webster Canada, Ltd.
2300 Yange Street
Toronto, Ontario M4P 2W6

Petroleum:

Andex Oil Co., Ltd.
1300 700 Ninth Avenue SW
Calgary, Alberta T2P 3V4

Geosource-SIE
5513 Third Street SE
Calgary, Alberta T2H 1K1

Gulf Canada Products, Ltd.
800 Bay Street
Toronto, Ontario M5S 1Y8

Chevron Standard, Ltd.
400 5th Street
Calgary, Alberta T2P 0L7

Texaco Canada, Inc.
90 Wynford Drive
Don Mills, Ontario M3C 1K5

Mexico

GEOGRAPHY:
AREA: 764,000 sq. mi.
CAPITAL: Mexico City
PRINCIPAL CITIES: Guadalajara, Monterrey, Ciudad Juarez
TERRAIN: Mostly high rugged mountains with low coastal plains and
high plateaus.
CLIMATE: Varies from tropical to desert.

PEOPLE:
POPULATION: 92,202,199
ANNUAL GROWTH RATE: 2%
RELIGION: 97% Roman Catholic
LANGUAGE: Spanish
EDUCATION: Attendance in primary school 98%; Literacy 90%
LIFE EXPECTANCY: Men 68; women 76 years.
GOVERNMENT: Federal republic. President, elected for a four year
term, is both chief of state and head of government. Bicameral legisla-
ture. Government budget: $106 billion.

ECONOMY: GDP: $740 billion
ANNUAL GROWTH RATE: 0.4%
PER CAPITA GDP $8,200.
AVERAGE RATE OF INFLATION: 8%
WORK FORCE: Of the 30 million in the work force, 30% are involved
in services; 19% manufacturing; 13% commerce; 24% agriculture; 7%
construction; and 4% transportation and communication. The unemploy-
ment rate is about 10.7%.
OFFICIAL EXCHANGE RATE: 3.35 pesos = US$
COST OF LIVING INDEX: 105

Although Mexico has long been recognized as a Mecca for American
tourists it has never achieved much of a reputation as a job haven. More
than 675 American companies have opened facilities south of the border
to take advantage of the country's cheap labor and accessibility to rail,
road and water. Mexico's high rate of inflation has raised havoc with the
foreign exchange rate and thus made it difficult to maintain an economic
structure. For example, in 1987 inflation reached 159% and the following
year was only reduced to 105%. Although the Salinas government has
taken measures to control the economy there are still major problems for

both foreign corporations located in the country as well as for Americans interested in working here. Fortunately, with the revised standard of exchange in 1993 and the NAFTA Agreement, Mexico is making major economic advances. Total foreign investment in 1993 reached $34 billion. The Salinas government announced major changes in his country's foreign investment regulations. These regulations coupled with the NAFTA Agreement has opened the door to huge American investments. Drug and automobile companies are now heavily involved in the country.

Mexico is rich in mineral and energy resources. The country is a leading producer of silver, sulfur, lead, zinc, gold, copper, coal and iron ore. The discovery of extensive oil fields along the Gulf of Mexico enabled Mexico to become self-sufficient in crude oil and to export significant amounts of petroleum. Job opportunities in the energy field, mining and mineral exploitation may be available through U.S. companies under contract to local authorities. A growing automobile industry has become one of Mexico's most important industrial segments. Those with expertise in the manufacturing sector may find opportunities here as well.

To obtain a work permit it is necessary to satisfy the Central Immigration Office that there is no Mexican national available to handle the job. Those who possess special skills or professions will be given priority. The Mexican employer usually handles the application to the Immigration Office.

Life in the capital can be most pleasant. The pace is slow; the climate pleasurable. With an exception of a few areas along the tourist track much of the country reflects its underdeveloped nature. Medical facilities are good in the larger cities. Tap water is questionable in most of the country. It's safer to boil the water than to gamble with intestinal disorders.

Information about U.S. companies and possible job opportunities is available from the American Chamber of Commerce of Mexico, Lucerna 78-4, Mexico City 6. Branch offices are also located in Guadalajara and Monterrey.

Mexico has an embassy at 2829 16th Street NW, Washington, DC 20009 (202/234-6000) with consulates in Chicago, El Paso, Los Angeles, New Orleans, New York, San Francisco, Miami, Boston, San Antonio, Dallas, Detroit and St. Louis. The U.S. Embassy is located at Paseo de la Reforma 305, Mexico City 06500. Contacts:

Manufacturing:

Productos Corning de
 Mexico SA de CV
Kelvin 10
111590 Mexico DF

General Motors de
 Mexico SA de CV
Aptdo. Postal 1-7-bix
Mexico 1 DF

ITT de Mexico SA
Bosque de Duraznos 127
Mexico 10 DF

Pharmaceuticals:

Cutter Laboratories de
 Mexico SA de CV
Postal 17-508
Deig. Miguel Hidalgo
11230 Mexico DF

Rorer de Mexico SA de CV
Avenue Insurgentes Sur 1991
Mexico 20 DF

Petroleum/Mining:

Cla. Minera de Cananea
 SA de CV.
Avenue Insurgentes Sur 1377
Mexico 12, DF

Mobil Atlas SA
146 Poniente 700
Col. Industrial Valiejo
Mexico 16 DF

Clothing:

Arrow de Mexico SA
Aptdo. Postal 1395
Mexico 1 DF

Levi Strauss de
 Mexico SA de CV
Atomo #3
Parque Industrial Naucaplan
Naucaplan de Juarez
Edo. de Mexico

Chemicals:

Cyanamid de Mexico SA de CV
Aptdo. Postal 283,
Mexico 1 DF

Dow Quimica Mexicana
 SA de CV
Paseo de las Palmas 555-1
Mexico 10 DF

Panama

GEOGRAPHY:
AREA: 29,762 sq. mi.
CAPITAL: Panama City

PRINCIPAL CITIES: Colon, David
TERRAIN: Interior mostly rugged, steep mountains and dissected upland plains; coastal areas largely plains and rolling hills.
CLIMATE: Tropical, hot and humid. Prolonged rainy season May to January; short dry season January to May.

PEOPLE:
POPULATION: 2.6 million
ANNUAL GROWTH RATE: 1.94%
RELIGION: 93% Roman Catholic; 6% Protestant.
LANGUAGE: Spanish
EDUCATION: Attendance in primary school 95%; Literacy 87%
LIFE EXPECTANCY: Men 72; women 77 years.

GOVERNMENT: Formerly a military dictatorship. Today a constitutional democracy. Government budget: $900 million with about 4% going to national defense.
ECONOMY: GDP: $11.6 billion
ANNUAL GROWTH RATE: 5.9%
PER CAPITA GDP $24,500.
AVERAGE RATE OF INFLATION: 1.0%
WORK FORCE: Of the 820,000 in the work force, 27% are employed by the government or for service organizations; 25% agriculture; 15% tourism (hotels, restaurants, etc.); 11% manufacturing and mining; 10% finance; 2% canal area.
OFFICIAL EXCHANGE RATE: 1 balboa = US$
COST OF LIVING INDEX: 093

Following the U.S. invasion and overthrow of the Noriega government, Panama has been in controlled chaos. However, with the return of a democratically elected civilian government the United States lifted all sanctions and in 1993, provided more than $450 million in grant aid and more than $500 million in credits and guarantees. The country's future, therefore, depends on a continued confidence in its economic recovery and political reform.

Economic development is concentrated in the urban areas, making them a magnet for the rural population. (Currently more than half the population lives in the Panama-Colon metropolitan corridor around the Canal.) Panama was in a serious economic decline before Noriega, the country was in a deep recession well before the overthrow of Noriega.

- Causes—Economic mismanagement and continuing repression.
  The GDP in 1988, for example, shrank approximately 20%.
  Today, however, the picture is far brighter. Panama has long
  been a major international financial center. Its location and well
  educated labor force make it attractive for foreign investment.
  Since the economy is dollar based, the country maintains no
  foreign exchange controls. The U.S. dollar circulates as legal
  tender.

Employment of non-Panamanians is highly limited. Employment is
limited almost exclusively to government and working for an American
company, volunteer work with the many agencies here to help the
Panamanians and educational work.

There are some American companies located here and the number is
growing as confidence develops. Information about them is available
from the American Chamber of Commerce and Industry in Panama,
Aptdo, 168, Estafeta Balboa, Panama City.

Panama has an embassy at 2862 McGill Terrace NW, Washington,
DC 20008 (202/483-1407) with consulates in New York, Atlanta,
Baltimore, Boston, Houston, Dallas, Chicago, Detroit, Los Angeles, San
Diego, San Francisco, Miami, Philadelphia, New Orleans, and San Juan.
The U.S. maintains an embassy at Avenida Balboa y Calle 38, Panama
City. Contacts:

Pharmaceuticals:

Pfizer Corp.
P.O. Box # 840
Zona Libra
Colon

Upjohn Co. S.A.
P.O. Box # 536
Colon

Financial:

American Life Insurance Co.
P.O. Box # 5306
Panama City 5
 Bank of America

Calle 50 y Calle 53
Aptdo. Aereo 7282
Panama City 5

Chemicals:

Sun Chemical de Panama S.A.
Aptdo. 6-896
El Dorado
Panama City 6

Union Carbide Interamerica
P.O. Box # 7504
Panama City 4

Engineering:

Calmaquip Panama
Aptdo. 6-3001
El Dorado
Panama City 6

Intl. Morrison-Knudsen Co.
Constructora Em Kay S.A.
Aptdo. 7300
Panama City 5

SOUTH AMERICA

Argentina

GEOGRAPHY: AREA: 1,100,000 sq. mi.
CAPITAL: Buenos Aires (plans to move to Viedma in the 1990s)
PRINCIPAL CITIES: Cordoba, Rosario, La Plata
TERRAIN: Rich plains of the Pampas in northern half; flat to rolling plateau of Patagonia in south; rugged Andes along western border.
CLIMATE: Mostly temperate; arid in the southeast; subantarctic in southwest.

PEOPLE: POPULATION: 33,912,994
ANNUAL GROWTH RATE: 1.12%
RELIGION: 92% Roman Catholic
LANGUAGE: Spanish
EDUCATION: Attendance in primary school 98%; Literacy 95%
LIFE EXPECTANCY: Men 68; women 74 years.

GOVERNMENT: Republic with president head of state. Bicameral congress. Government budget: $11.5 billion

ECONOMY: GDP: $185 billion
ANNUAL GROWTH RATE: 6.5%
PER CAPITA GNP $5,500.
AVERAGE RATE OF INFLATION: 7.4%
WORK FORCE: Industry and commerce 36%; services 20%; agriculture 19%; Transportation and communication 6%.
OFFICIAL EXCHANGE RATE: .99 pesos = US$
COST OF LIVING INDEX: 138

In Argentina, a country about four times the size of the United States east of the Mississippi, the big question is how can a nation with such rich natural resources and such a literate and advanced population have so mismanaged its economy. Economic growth almost stopped following the debacle over the Falkland Islands. The widening public sector deficit and a triple-digit inflation rate dominated the economy in the late 1980s. Since 1978, for example, Argentina's external debt has nearly doubled to more than $58 billion, creating severe debt servicing problems and hurting the country's credit worthiness with international lenders.

The country has a rich labor pool, the lowest population growth rate in Latin America, with more than a third of the population living in the metropolitan Buenos Aires area. Unemployment is low but so are the wages. The basic monthly minimum wage is about $165.00. With the initiation of the Menim government in 1989 the economic mess began to straighten. Economic reform under Minister Domingo Cavall reversed decades of economic decline. Today, Argentina is becoming one of the most important and economically vital nations in the Western hemisphere.

Because of Argentina's relatively advanced economy, the United States phased out its bilateral economic assistance program in 1971. For example, there are no peace corps volunteers here. More than 315 U.S. firms have established a base here. Licensing agreements with local companies are common. U.S. private investment totals more than $3 billion, primarily in manufacturing, chemicals, agricultural manufacturing, and banking. Several thousand Americans now live in the capital region.

Everyone needs a visa to work or visit Argentina. If you do obtain employment it is simply a matter of acquiring a temporary visa which represents a work permit. Your temporary visa is renewable twice for the identical term as the original. Following the expiration of your third temporary visa you automatically qualify for a permanent visa. If all this sounds like a confusing bureaucratic maze you now have a better idea why the economy is in such an untenable state.

The temporary visa, or work permit, is obtained by completing identity papers and a good conduct certificate. Both are issued by any Argentine consulate in America. With these forms your potential employer sends a formal petition to the Argentina immigration office with an explanation as to why you should be hired rather than a local worker. Obviously, the greater the skill, the easier it is to obtain work here.

Like any major world city Buenos Aires is advanced, quite modern and, as many expatriates have discovered, an unpublicized Mecca of good living. There are no unusual health risks, the water is safe and more than one American has decided to retreat here rather than return to the

States following a job tour. The major problem according to many expatriates is the totally unpredictable inflation rate. The only answer is to keep your funds in dollars and convert only when necessary.

The best source of employment is with an American company located here. A current list is available from the American Chamber of Commerce in Argentina, Av. Pte. Roque Saenz Pena 567, P. 6, 1352 Buenos Aires.

Argentina has an embassy at 1600 New Hampshire Avenue NW, Washington, DC 20009 (202-939 6400) with consulates in Houston, Miami, New York, New Orleans, San Francisco, Baltimore, Chicago, Los Angeles, and San Juan. The U.S. Embassy is located at 4300 Columbia, Buenos Aires. Contacts:

Finance:

Bank of America NT & SA
Castilla Postal 5393/779
1038 Buenos Aires

Marine Midland Bank NA
Avenida Corroentes 311
1043 Buenos Aires

Manufacturing:

Uniroyal S.A.C.I.
25 de Mayo 444
Buenos Aires

Clark Argentina S.A.I.C.I.F.
San Martin 345
Buenos Aires

Cummins Americas, Inc.
Lovalle 421, 6 Piso
1047 Buenos Aires

Abrasivos Norton S.A.
Los Patos 2175
1283 Buenos Aires

Chemicals:

Indoquim S.A.
Ave. L. N. Alem 896
1001 Buenos Aires

Monsanto Argentine S.A.I.C.
Avda. E. Modero 1020
1106 Buenos Aires

Petroleum:

Esso, S.A., Petrolero Argentina
PJE Della Paolera 297
1001 Buenos Aires

Hughes Services
Esmeralda 130—Piso 132
1035 Buenos Aires

Food Products:

Coca-Cola S.A.I.C. y F.
Uruguay 1134
1016 Buenos Aires

CPC International
Avenue Eduardo Madero 940,
Pisos 23 y 24
1106 Buenos Aires

Bolivia

GEOGRAPHY:
AREA: 424,162 sq. mi.
CAPITAL: La Paz (administrative); Sucre (judicial) PRINCIPAL
CITIES: Santa Cruz, Cochabamba
TERRAIN: Mountains, high plateaus, valleys, and tropical lowlands.
CLIMATE: Varies with altitude. From humid and tropical to cold and
semi-arid.

PEOPLE:
POPULATION: 7,719,455
ANNUAL GROWTH RATE: 2.28%
RELIGION: 95% Roman Catholic
LANGUAGE: Spanish
EDUCATION: Attendance in primary school 82%; Literacy 70%
LIFE EXPECTANCY: Men 60; women 65 years.

GOVERNMENT: Republic with a bicameral legislature. President and
cabinet represent the executive. Judicial based on Spanish law and Code
of Napoleon. Government budget: $1.62 billion a third of which is spent
on the military.

ECONOMY:
GDP: $15.8 billion
ANNUAL GROWTH RATE: 2.2%
PER CAPITA GNP $2,100.
AVERAGE RATE OF INFLATION: 9.3%
WORK FORCE: Of the 1.8 million in the labor pool, 47% are involved
in agriculture; 23% in services; 19% in industry and commerce; and,
11% in the government. The unemployment rate is about 5.8%.
OFFICIAL EXCHANGE RATE: 4.5 boliviano = US$
COST OF LIVING INDEX: 093

Bolivia is one of the most interesting countries in South America. Its topography— -thick jungles in the east, arid Andean plains in the west—coupled with an Indian population unlike any in the world makes it a tourist's joy and a resident's pleasure. The pace is slow, primitivism is obvious; it's almost like living in a place time ignored. Until the 1950s most Bolivians worked their farms and economic advances were not considered on a national level. During the 1950s an interest was initiated among the Indian villages to establish small factories, mostly textile plants, which supply inexpensive alternatives to imported clothes. However, industry has never taken hold here. Even the power plants that were built by the government have failed to provide the necessary impetus for any large scale development.

Today, Bolivia is among the poorest countries in Latin America, its per capita gross national product is the lowest in South America. During the period 1983-86, the government financed growing budget deficits through expansion of the money supply, which caused a spiraling inflation—peaking at an unbelievable 11,700% in 1985—and a steady economic decline. Strong austerity measures were then adopted that helped bring down the rate of inflation to between 15% and 20% during the end of the 1980s. However, Bolivia continues to face substantial problems, such as relatively weaker prices for its major exports, including natural gas and tin. Tin alone represents three-fifths of the value of the nation's total mineral exports although agriculture, including forestry, is the most important sector of the economy in terms of employment (47%) and has tremendous potential for future growth.

Oil exploration in the mid 1990s should spur the economy especially if oil, as opposed to natural gas, is discovered. Exploration of the country's large salt flats of the Altiplano should also help the economy and serve as an incentive to foreign employment.

One of the major problems facing the country in terms of its relationship with America is the drug trade. Nearly half of the raw materials utilized in producing the cocaine consumed in the United States originates in Bolivia. The corruption and disregard for the law that accompanies the growth of the illegal drug have made narcotics trafficking not only a major domestic but international problem for Bolivia.

If you plan to visit or work here plan to rest for the first days upon arrival to adjust to the altitude. Avoid alcohol and cigarettes for the first week. Drink plenty of water in La Paz where the humidity is low—but only bottled water. Sanitation is poor in most parts of the country. Yellow fever inoculation is recommended.

You need a visa to visit or work here. A tourist visa good for a 90 day stay can be obtained at the airport. A work visa must be issued before arrival. You or your potential employer must show that your job can't be handled by a local resident. The need for high-tech personnel, specialists in agriculture, mining, and energy are welcome.

Employment possibilities are best found with American firms already established. The American Chamber of Commerce of Bolivia with 150 active member companies publishes a bi-annual directory. They can be contacted at Av. 6 de Agosto 2570, La Paz.

Bolivia has an embassy at 3014 Massachusetts NW, Washington, DC 20008 (202/483-4410) with consulates in San Francisco, Houston, Los Angeles, Miami, New York and New Orleans. The U.S. Embassy is located in the Banco Popular del Peru building at the corner of Calles Mercado and Colon in La Paz. Contacts:

Mining:

Berisford Bolivia, Ltd.
C. Montevideo 152, 1st Floor
20239, La Paz

Cargill Bolivia S.A.
C. Colon 12th floor
2657, La Paz

Compania Minera Del Sur
 S.A. "Comsur"
Av. 16 de Julio, Edif. Petrolero
4326 La Paz

Textiles:

Fabrica Textil Universaltex Ltd.
C. Jose Maria Perez
 de Urdininea 590
6065, La Paz

Fabrica de Camisas La Modelo
C. San Salvador 1333,
6348, La Paz

Manufacturing:

IBM de Bolivia S.A.
Av. Mcal. Santa Cruz
1061, La Paz

Fabrica de Productos de Goma
"Gomatex" LTDA
Av. 15 de Avril 568
980, La Paz

Industrias Bolivianas
 Philips S.A.
C. Mercado
2964, La Paz

Fabrica Boliviana de
 Envases "Fabe"
Cruce Taquina
1103, Cochabamba

Brazil

GEOGRAPHY:
AREA: 3,290 sq. mi.
CAPITAL: Brasilia
PRINCIPAL CITIES: Rio de Janeiro, Belo Horizonte, Sao Paulo.
TERRAIN: Dense forests; semi-arid scrub land; rugged hills and mountains; rolling plains; and coastal strip.
CLIMATE: Mostly tropical or semitropical with temperate zone in the south.

PEOPLE:
POPULATION: 158,739,257
RELIGION: 90% Roman Catholic
LANGUAGE: Portuguese
EDUCATION: Attendance in primary school 85%; Literacy 78%;
LIFE EXPECTANCY: 62.2 years

GOVERNMENT: Federal Republic. President is elected to a single 6 year term. Strong executive and a bicameral legislature. Government budget: $50 billion with 2.6% devoted to the military.

ECONOMY:
GDP: $785 billion
ANNUAL GROWTH RATE: 5%
PER CAPITA GDP: $5,000
WORK FORCE: Of the 50 million in the work force, 40% are in services; 35% in agriculture; and 25% in industry. The unemployment rate is about 4.9%.
OFFICIAL EXCHANGE RATE: 390.845 Cruzados = US$
COST OF LIVING INDEX: 107

It is hard to picture what this country, a bit smaller than the United States, will be like a few decades from now. The dense jungles which cover about half the nation are slowly being carved away to create more farms and cities while the slow systematic destruction of the great rain forests is causing environmental havoc worldwide. Brazil is the world's fifth largest country and the sixth most populated. Its economy ranks it in the world's top ten (in terms of GDP). Brazil's economy ranges in complexity from the hustle and bustle of Sao Paulo, Latin America's largest and most modern industrial complex, to trading posts along the

Amazon River. Industrial development has been concentrated in the southeastern states of Rio de Janeiro, Sao Paulo, Parana, and Rio Grande do Sul, but is now expanding to include the northeast and far west.

Throughout the country the visitor is confronted with the modern against the ancient. Tribesmen row carved wooden canoes along a river graced by a modern nuclear power plant. Actually, nuclear power has reduced Brazil's dependence on foreign oil by a considerable amount. Whereas in the early 1980s almost two-thirds of the country's imports were oil, now they consist of only about half. Brazilian auto manufacturers began large scale production of alcohol-powered cars in 1979. Today more than 1.5 million are on the road. More than 80% of all vehicles (93% of all passenger cars) are alcohol powered.

One of the major economic problems facing the country is the inflationary spiral which increased from 40% at the end of 1978 to a record 900% in 1989. The primary causes are large public sector deficits at the state and municipal level, as well as the deficits of the state enterprises, the government owned companies, and large federal subsidies.

For the past several decades, successive governments have been successful in exploiting the country's agricultural and mineral resources. As a result Brazil is today the most powerful industrial force in Latin America. The government of President Collor has been able to reverse the economic decline, so that by 1993 the country recorded a substantial trade surplus.

Although there are employment needs, particularly in the high-tech areas, the best opportunities for working here are with one of the 675 American firms. All who come to Brazil need a visa. If you work here you will also need a work permit. There are three ways to obtain working papers: through a contract of employment with a Brazilian employer, certified by the Brazilian Ministry of Justice; through an application by a prospective employer in Brazil to the Brazilians Ministry of Labor for permanent stay in the country; or, through a capital transfer of $100,000 to establish commercial or industrial activities. Obviously, unless you're planning to set up your own company here it is easier to obtain a job first and then allow your prospective employer to grease the skids and secure the necessary documents for you. As a rule most companies are obliged to maintain a staff of at least 66% Brazilians among their total personnel. However, there are always exceptions for the specially skilled.

Living conditions in the major cities are similar to any modern city in the U.S. or Europe. Sanitary facilities in the country are being expanded and, depending on where you are, can be considered acceptable.

Unfortunately tap water in most parts of the country is not potable. Precautions against the major tropical diseases are also suggested if you plan to leave the major metropolitan areas.

The best information about U.S. companies located here is through the American Chamber of Commerce for Brazil. They maintain three offices: Caixa Postal 916, Praca Pio X-15, 20.040 Rio de Janeiro; Rua de Espanha, 2 Salas 604-606, 40.000 Salvador, Bahia; and, Rua Alexandra Dumas, 2372, 04717 Sao Paulo.

Brazil has an embassy at 3006 Massachusetts Avenue NW, Washington DC 20008 (202/797-0200) with consulates in New Orleans, New York, Chicago, Los Angeles, Miami, Houston, Dallas, San Francisco and Atlanta. The U.S. Embassy is located at Lote 3, Avenida das Nacoes, Brasilia, D.F. Contacts:

Manufacturing:

Dresser Industria e Com., Ltda.
Caixa Postal 2191
01039 Sao Paulo

FMC do Brazil S.A.
Alameda Campinas 463
01404 Sao Paulo

Ford Motor do Brazil S.A.
Av. Henry Ford 1787
Postal 8062
Caixa Sao Paulo

Construction:

Rimi Equipamentos Ltda.
Franklin Roosevelt 238
Rio de Janeiro

Kaiser Engenharia
e Construcores Ltda.
Baia do Flamengo No. 284
Conj. 101 CP
16.211-AG, Largo do Machade
20000 Rio de Janeiro

Pharmaceutical:

A. H. Robins & Cia. Ltda.
Rua Jeronimo de Lemos 92
ZC-11
Rio de Janeiro, RJ

Searle Farmaceutica do
Brazil Ltda.
Rua Pamplona 512
Sao Paulo

Chemicals:

Stauffer Productos
Quimicas Ltda.
Av. Faria Lima 2003
Caixa Postal 12.654
01451 Sao Paulo

Union Carbide do Brazil S.A.
Ind. e Com.
Av. Paulista 2073, andar 24
Caixa Postal 30362
Sao Paulo

Management Consultants:

Spencer Stuart
 Consultores Gerenciais
Av. Paulista 1499
01311 Sao Paulo, SP

Arthur D. Little Ltda.
Rua Macedo Sobrinho, 48
Caixa Postal 9041
02114 Sao Paulo

Chile

GEOGRAPHY:
AREA: 302,778 sq. mi.
CAPITAL: Santiago
PRINCIPAL CITIES: Vina del Mar, Concepcion, Arica
TERRAIN: Desert in north; fertile central valley; volcanos and lakes toward the south, giving way to fjords, inlets and islands; Andes Mountains on the eastern border.
CLIMATE: Desert in north, Mediterranean in center, cool and damp in south.

PEOPLE:
POPULATION: 13,950,557
ANNUAL GROWTH RATE: 1.5%
RELIGION: 89% Roman Catholic; 11% Protestant
LANGUAGE: Spanish
EDUCATION: Attendance in primary school 97%; Literacy 96%
LIFE EXPECTANCY: Men 71; women 77 years.

GOVERNMENT: The constitution of 1981 established a president and legislature. A military junta ruled the country from 1974 until late 1989 when the Chilean people elected Patricio Aylwin president. Government budget: $7.1 billion of which 13% is for the military.

ECONOMY:
GDP: $96 billion
ANNUAL GROWTH RATE: 6%
PER CAPITA GDP $7,000.
AVERAGE RATE OF INFLATION: 12.3%
WORK FORCE: Of the 4.8 million in the work force, 34% work in industry and commerce; 30% services and government; 19% agriculture; 7% construction; and 2% mining. The unemployment rate is 5.1%.

OFFICIAL EXCHANGE RATE: 430 Chilean pesos = US$
COST OF LIVING INDEX: 100

Another country of great contrasts. More than 300,000 Indians live in southern Chile in much the same fashion they have for centuries. Yet in the capital you can ride one of the world's most efficient subway systems. The education system is one of the most advanced in South America. The northern desert offers isolated beaches as well as access to the Andean highland Indian culture and numerous but hard-to-reach archaeological sites. Visit the famous mountain resorts and enjoy the best summer skiing in the world.

The country's economy is based on minerals. Chile supplies a tenth of the world's copper. In northern Chile rich veins of iron, gold and silver provide jobs for the locals and important exports for a country trying to recover from the economic mismanagement of former dictator, General Augusto Pinochet. From 1925 to 1975 Chile experimented with various economic philosophies, but the general trend was toward increasing state intervention in the economy and protecting or isolating the Chilean economy from outside competition. When Pinochet seized power he introduced the economic model championed by economist Milton Friedman stressing freedom of capital, free competition and reduced import duties. The system failed and as a result inflation soared and international credit almost dissolved. The country is still struggling to overcome the Pinochet disaster but initial results under the newly elected president appear promising.

Mining is still a mainstay of the economy with minerals accounting for more than half of the country's exports. It has the world's largest nitrate deposits in the Atacama Desert as well as a third of the world's known lithium reserves.

When the Chilean economy was exposed to foreign competition by the progressive lowering of tariffs, the manufacturing sector was one of the most seriously affected. Fixing the peso to the dollar from 1979 to 1982 hurt manufacturing even more. During the 1982-83 recession capacity utilization fell dramatically and many industries collapsed. With the adoption of a more realistic exchange rate in 1984-85 the manufacturing sector has become one of the engines of Chile's export-led growth. The Chilean Interoceanic Navigation Company, for example, introduced the first full container shipping system. Thus the company took the lead as an international shipper.

What this means is jobs—more employment for Chileans and the need for foreign expertise. Many U.S. companies are working directly with

Chilean interests to serve the needs of both countries. More than 160 American companies have established operations here. The Chilean company, Compania Continental Agricola S.A., was formed when America's Continental Grain Co. joined forces with Chile's O'Shea de Comercio S.A. to assist small and midsized Chilean producers import products directly. To provide engineering, procurement, project management and construction services to Chile's mining and metallurgy industry the U.S. company Fluor Mining and Metals Inc., formed a Chilean subsidiary, Fluor-Chile Ltda.

There are still needs for Americans with a background in computer programming, data processing, mining and petroleum engineers and project managers, experts in solar energy, those with financial and accounting expertise. Although a tourist card is required to visit here it is usually issued aboard your plane prior to arrival. A work permit is also required but it is easily available through any Chilean consulate. Chile is one of the very few country's that will issue a work permit from within the country. Come as a tourist and get a job without having to cross borders and wait endless weeks for the bureaucratic wheels to turn.

Living conditions are quite modern. Of course if you wander off the beaten track you will experience off beat conditions. In Santiago the only problems you're likely to face are those associated with living in a high altitude and occasional periods of heavy smog. The water is potable in almost all regions of the country. Parts of Chile may experience winter floods. If so, boil the water.

The best source of job information is through the Chamber of Commerce of the U.S.A. in the Republic of Chile, Av. Americo Vespucio Sur 80, 90, P.O. Box # 4131, Santiago. Chile has an embassy at 1732 Massachusetts Avenue NW, Washington, DC 20036 (202/785-1746) with consulates in Chicago, Houston, Los Angeles, Miami, New York and San Francisco. The U.S. Embassy is located at Augustinas 1343, Santiago. Contacts:

Mining:

3M Chile S.A.
Casilla 3068, Las Hortensias
650 Maipo
Santiago

Cobre Cerrilios S.A.
Camini a Melipilla 6307,
Casilla 100
Correo 21
Santiago

Compania Minera San Jose
 Ltda.
Clasificador # 45, Correo 9
Santiago

Minera Utah de Chile Inc.
Isidora Goyenechea 2925
Santiago

Petroleum:

Geotec Boyles Bros. S.A.
La Violetas 5931
Santiago

Geosource Exploration Co.
Compania 1085,
Santiago

Computers:

Data General Chile Ltda.
Suecia 392, Providencia
Santiago

NCR S.A.
McLyer 370
Santiago

Manufacturing:

Kodak Chilena S.A.F.
Alonso Ovalie 1180
Casilla 2979
Santiago

Jacuzzi Chile
Casillia 46
Cerillos

Construction:

Combustion Engineering
c/o Dimtel Ltda.
Matias Cousino 82
Santiago

Kaiser Ingeniero de Chile Ltda.
Las Urbinas 53, Providencia
Santiago

Columbia

GEOGRAPHY:
AREA: 440,000 sq. mi.
CAPITAL: Bogata
PRINCIPAL CITIES: Medellin, Cali, Cartagena
TERRAIN: Flat coastal areas, central highlands, mountains, and eastern plains.
CLIMATE: Tropical on coast and eastern plain, cooler in highlands.

PEOPLE:
POPULATION: 35,577,556
ANNUAL GROWTH RATE: 1.77%
RELIGION: 95% Roman Catholic

LANGUAGE: Spanish
EDUCATION: Attendance in primary school 77%; Literacy 80%
LIFE EXPECTANCY: Men 69; women 64 years.

GOVERNMENT: Republic with a strong president as both head of state
and head of the government. Bicameral legislature. Elections every four
years. Government budget: $3.7 billion with 15% going for the military.

ECONOMY:
GDP: $192 billion
ANNUAL GROWTH RATE: 5.4%
PER CAPITA GDP $5,500.
AVERAGE RATE OF INFLATION: 23%
WORK FORCE: Of the 14 million in the work force, 58% are employed
in the service field; 21% by industry; and, 26% in agriculture. The
unemployment rate is about 7.9%.
OFFICIAL EXCHANGE RATE: 921.20 Comoran francs = US$
COST OF LIVING INDEX: 078

Columbia's reputation as a major narcotics center doesn't do justice
to the fourth most populous country in Latin America. True, the drug
cartel plays an important role in current governmental activities but this
most attractive and livable country has a lot more to it than the unfortu-
nate press centered on the drug trade. Columbia is now one of the most
economically viable nations in Latin America. It is in the process of
emerging from a serious decline that started in the early 1980s resulting
from many factors including low prices for many exported goods,
depressed domestic demand and high interest rates. These elements
coupled with a reduced harvest, guerrilla disruption of petroleum
production, and the government's tight money policy designed to control
inflation cut the nation's growth rate considerably. Although inflation
continues to be a serious problem newly initiated governmental policies
have increased the growth rate to a respectable 5.4%.

Although coffee is still Columbia's most important export (15% of the
world's consumption), mining and energy resources are rapidly becoming
important both to the Columbian economy and to Americans interested
in employment in these fields. Exports are expected to grow from 11
million metric tons in 1988 to 20 million in 1993. In addition, Columbia
has an estimated 4% of the world's nickel; 15 % of the world's
ferronickle plus iron ore, gold, platinum, phosphate rock, gypsum, and
limestone. Nine of ten emeralds that end up in the world's finest jewelry

shops were mined here.

The most important manufacturing industries are: textiles and clothing, food processing, paper and paper products, chemicals and petrochemicals, iron and steel products, and metalworking. Of the $3 billion invested here by foreign interests $2.5 was American. More than 230 U.S. companies have are located in Columbia.

Americans working in Columbia must have a work visa. It usually takes about three months to obtain the visa and requires more than the normal bureaucratic hassles. For example, in addition to supplying the Ministry of Labor with the original plus three copies of your employment contract (stating among other things that your employer will guarantee a paid passage to your home residence when your contract expires), you must also supply a birth certificate, a statement from one or more U.S. police departments vouching for your status as a good citizen over the past ten years, a medical certificate issued by a Columbian doctor, copies of all your diplomas notarized in the country they were issued, and, just to prove that you do exist, six photographs. Little wonder that Columbia is not high on the work list of Latin American countries for Americans with the high tech, managerial, computer, mining and petroleum skills needed in this nation.

For those working here the U.S. State Department has issued warnings of sporadic guerilla activity in certain areas. For the most part, however, Americans have not been involved in local incidents. It is recommended that you check with the nearest U.S. consulate or the State Department's Bureau of Consular Affairs in Washington.

Columbia has an unofficial division of the chamber of commerce in Bogata with branches in Valle, Medellin and Cartagena. For information on U.S. companies located in Columbia write to the Columbia-American Chamber of Commerce, Apartado Aereo 8008, Calle 35, No. 616, Bogata. Pamphlets on Columbia, including a monthly newsletter, *Columbia Today* are available without charge from the Columbia Information Service, 140 East 57th Street, New York, NY 10022 (212/421-8270).

Columbia has an embassy at 2118 Leroy Place NW, Washington, DC 20008 (202/387-8338) with consulates in Atlanta, Boston, Chicago, Detroit, Houston, Ft. Lauderdale, Los Angeles, Miami, Minneapolis, New Orleans, New York, Philadelphia, San Diego, San Juan, St. Louis, Tampa, and Wheeling. Contacts:

Petroleum:

Chevron Petroleum Co.
of Columbia
Carrera 7, 32-33, Edif. Fenix
Bogata

Occidental de Columbia, Inc.
Calle 79, No. 8-70
Bogata

Management. Consulting:

Boyden/Consultores
Ejecutivax Ltd.
Calle 71, No. 3-74
Bogata

Food Processing:

American Coffee Corp.
Edif. Coltabaco 406
Cali

Productos Quaker S.A.
Aptdo. Aereo 2074
Cali

Mining:

LL & E Columbia Inc.
Aptdo. Aereo 91001
Bogata 8

Geophysical Co. of America
Edif. Interamerica de Seguros
Calle 78, No. 9-57
Aptdo Aereo 91014
Bogata

Manufacturing:

Cummins de Columbia S.A.
Aptdo. Aereo 90988
Bogata

General Electric Columbia S.A.
Aptdo. Aereo 3644
Bogata

Construction:

Combustion Engineering
c/o Sudamerica de
 Perforaciones y Servicos S.A.
Aptdo. Aereo 7940
Bogata

Ecuador

GEOGRAPHY:
AREA: 109,483 sq. mi.
CAPITAL: Quito
PRINCIPAL CITIES: Guayaquil, Machala, Loja
TERRAIN: Coastal plain (Costa); inter-Andean central highlands
(Sierra); and flat to rolling eastern jungle (Oriente).
CLIMATE: Tropical along the coast becoming cooler inland.
Temperature varies with altitude not season.

PEOPLE:
POPULATION: 11,000,000
ANNUAL GROWTH RATE: 2.4%
RELIGION: 95% Roman Catholic
LANGUAGE: Spanish
EDUCATION: Attendance in primary school 52%; Literacy 88%
LIFE EXPECTANCY: 66 years.

GOVERNMENT: Republic with the executive made up of an president elected every four years and 12 cabinet members. Unicameral congress elected every two years. Government budget: $1.4 billion.

ECONOMY:
GDP: $41.8 billion
ANNUAL GROWTH RATE: 2%
PER CAPITA GDP $4,000.
AVERAGE RATE OF INFLATION: 31%
WORK FORCE: Of the 2.9 million in the work force, 39% are engaged in agriculture; 42% services; 11% industry; 12% sales.
OFFICIAL EXCHANGE RATE: 1,947 sucres = US$
COST OF LIVING INDEX: 072

Ecuador is the smallest of the South American countries. It has also been dubbed, the "most innocent." by travel writer Michael Shichor who observes that Ecuador "exudes an unmistakable calm and tranquility—so different from the tension which reigns across the borders." The Ecuadoreans are hearty, unprejudiced, genuine and guileless. The economy is basically agrarian with a constant need for experts in this field. Oil, however, is an important part of the future economic picture. It accounts for about 15% of the country's GDP but more than two thirds of foreign exchange earnings. The government receives half of its revenues from the sale of Ecuadorian oil.

The bulk of Ecuador's oil is produced in the Oriente, the Amazon jungle region, and carried to the export terminal through the 310 mile-long TransEcuadorean pipeline. In the mid-1980s the government began signing contracts with foreign oil companies to develop Ecuador's untapped oil reserves. To date contracts have been signed with Occidental, Belco, Esso/Hispanoil, Conoco, British Petroleum, and Texaco/Pecten. Exploration of oil and natural gas is now being conducted in the Gulf of Guayaquil. With the growth of the country's petroleum industry there is a constant need for foreign expertise.

The manufacturing sector (excluding petroleum refining) represents about 17% of the country's GDP and is oriented primarily to the domestic market. Food processing represents the largest component of the sector, although textiles and pharmaceuticals are also important. Throughout the industrial sector there is a shortage of qualified upper management personnel and project managers. As a result, both middle and upper management salaries are considerably higher than many countries in the region, about $1,000 a month for a middle manager; twice that for upper management. A local office worker can easily earn as much as four times the basic minimum salary. Certainly not high by U.S. standards but considering that three fifths of the work force in the country earns less that $900 it is an impressive financial picture for skilled and semi-skilled personnel. The minimum wage for unskilled workers is $150 a month with white collar workers earning from $225 to $600 a month. More than 120 American corporations have operations in the country.

Inoculations against typhoid, polio, tetanus, and hepatitis are recommended throughout the country. If you work away from the major cities you should also take precautions against amoebas and parasites. The tap water is not potable in any area.

To visit the country you need a visa. You can either obtain the 90 day visa from any Ecuadorian consulate or from the immigration authorities upon arrival. A working visa can only be obtained from the Immigration Department at an embassy or consulate. Prior to granting the visa your Ecuadorian company must first obtain approval from the Director of Human Resources at the Labor Ministry. The best source of data on U.S. companies is through the Ecuadorean-American Chamber of Commerce, Apartado 2432, Quito. The Chamber also has a branch in Guayaquil.

Ecuador has an embassy at 2535 15th Street NW, Washington, DC 20009 (202/234-7200) with consulates in Chicago, Dallas, Houston, Los Angeles, Miami, New Orleans, New York and San Francisco. The U.S. Embassy is located at Avenida Patria 120, Quito. Contacts:

Petroleum:

Belco Petroleum Ecuador, Inc.
Cordova 808 y V.M. Rendon,
Edif.
Torres de la Merced,
Guayaquil

Mobil Oil Co. del Ecuador
P.O. Box # 169
Quito

Parker Drilling Co.
Avda Amazonas 648, P.O. Box
3544
Quito

Texaco Petroleum Co.
Edif. Perez Guerrero
Calle Jorge Washington 715
Esq. de Amazona, P.O. Box #
1006
Quito

Food Processing:

Bebidasy Refrescos de Quito,
Cia. Ltd.
Villa Lengua y San Francisco
Casilla 260
Quito

Fleischmann Ecuatoriana S.A.
Costanera 504 & Ave. de las
Manjas
Urdesa Central, Aptdo. 340
Guayaquil

Textiles:

Industrios Artectum S.A.
Jorge Washington No. 718 y
Amazonas
Quito

Pharmaceuticals:

Abbott Labs del Ecuador S.A.
1 de Mayo 610
P.O. Box # 3423
Guayaquil

Sterling Products Intl.. Inc.
9 de Octobre 1503
P.O. Box # 3738
Guayaquil

Engineering:

Caimaquip Engineering
 del Ecuador S.A.
Aptdo. 56, Edif.
 Torres de Colon
Av. Colon # 1345
Quito

Construction:

Raymond Corp. S.A.
Casilia 9272
Guayaquil

Peru

GEOGRAPHY:
AREA: 496,222 sq. mi.
CAPITAL: Lima
PRINCIPAL CITIES: Aerequipa, Chiciayo, Cuzco
TERRAIN: Western coastal plains, central rugged mountains (Andes),
eastern lowlands with tropical jungle forests.
CLIMATE: Varies from tropical in east to dry desert in west.

PEOPLE:
POPULATION: 23,650,671

ANNUAL GROWTH RATE: 1.86%
RELIGION: Mostly Roman Catholic
LANGUAGE: Spanish and Quechua
EDUCATION: Attendance in primary school 82%; Literacy 79%
LIFE EXPECTANCY: Men 61; women 66 years.

GOVERNMENT: Constitutional republic. President and two vice presidents as well as bicameral legislature elected every five years. Government budget: $3.9 billion.

ECONOMY:
GDP: $70 billion
ANNUAL GROWTH RATE: 6%
PER CAPITA GDP $3,000.
AVERAGE RATE OF INFLATION: 39%
WORK FORCE: Of the 5.2 million in the work force, 45% are involved in the government or other services; agriculture 38%; industry and mining 17%. The unemployment rate is about 1.5%.
OFFICIAL EXCHANGE RATE: 2.180 sols = US$
COST OF LIVING INDEX: 091

Another country of contrasts. Indians and mestizos living the lifestyle they lived for centuries and trying to integrate into a society heavily influenced by Spanish conquest and the need to be an active partner in the 21st century. Don't be surprised to visit a market in Lima operated by Indians displaying handicraft goods, fish and vegetables in the same fashion they have for centuries. Adjacent to the market you'll note modern hotels and the bustle of an active 20th century city. This is a fascinating country and those expatriates that have returned do so eagerly. Most Americans live in modern apartments or houses complete with gardens and swimming pools. The residential suburbs of San Isidro, Chacarilla and Monterrico offer all the appointments of modern living complete with beautiful beaches within walking distance.

However, despite the beauty of the country and the easy pace there is a serious negative element to life here. Crime! A Maoist underground group that calls itself Sendero Luminoso (The Glittering Path) operates in Lima, Callao, and the mountains. Both cities have experienced a 1:00 AM to 5:00 AM curfew. Unfortunately, terrorism is unpredictable. It is advisable to check with the U.S. State Department before leaving for Peru for the latest information. In addition, street thugs are common in the major cities and will steal anything they can get their hands on. Be extremely careful with your valuables at all times.

Peru's economy has also been an exercise in contrast. The economy has moved erratically in recent years, the result of shifts in government orientation and policies, fluctuating international prices for the nation's major exports, and to a lesser extent, weather patterns that have seriously damaged both farms and the fishing industry. For example, prior to the mid-1980s Peru was one of the world's largest fish producers. The climatic effects associated with the El Niño phenomenon killed schools of fishes and forced them offshore into deeper waters. Although fishing is still an important aspect of the total economic picture the harvests of yesteryear have yet to be repeated.

Mines and minerals are the major economic asset. Peru is one of the world's leading producers of silver, lead, zinc, copper, gold, and iron ore. Although the country's crude oil reserves are not great—only 500 to 550 million barrels—Occidental Petroleum has recently made several substantial discoveries both in the eastern jungle and on the northern part of the continental shelf. More importantly, Royal Dutch Shell has uncovered a major gas deposit near the Brazilian border; the initial report indicates that the find contains 7 trillion cubic feet of gas.

Most of the U.S. investment in Peru is concentrated in the mining and petroleum sectors; many other American subsidiaries manufacture consumer products r provide services. Current book value of U.S. investment in the country is estimated at $3 billion. The largest single U.S. investors are the Southern Peru Copper Corporation—primarily owned by ASARCO—and Occidental Petroleum, which has important concessions and operations in the northern jungle areas.

Work permits are not difficult to obtain in Peru, but there is a strict regulation against tourists conducting any form of business without proper credentials. Your Peruvian employer is responsible for your working visa. He will submit your application together with a signed contract guaranteeing the job to the Director General of Immigration.

The best opportunities for employment here are with American companies engaged in the mining business. Expertise is always needed whether as a project supervisor or in the management end. A more complete listing of the 170 U.S. American companies in Peru is available from the American Chamber of Commerce of Peru, Av. Ricardo Palma 836, Lima 18.

Peru has an embassy at 1700 Massachusetts Avenue NW, Washington, DC 20036 (202/833-9860) with consulates in Miami, New York, Chicago, Houston, Los Angeles and San Francisco. The U.S. Embassy is located at Avenidas Garcilaso de la Vega and Espana, Lima. Contacts:

Mining:

Compania Minera del Madrigal
Jiron de la Union 264, Aptdo.
5979
Lima

Huber del Peru, S.A.
Avenida Mariscal Benavides
1225
Aptdo 3744
Lima

Compania Minero Mercantil del
 Peru S.A.
Minerco, Avenida Republica de
 Chile 295
Aptdo. 3633
Lima

Compania Minerales
 Santander, Inc.
Castilla 1 171
Lima

Construction:

Gray Tool Intl.. Inc.
c/o General Well Service S.A.
Castilla Postal 657
Lima

Kaiser Engineers, Inc.
Castilla 321, Miraflores
Lima 18

Petroleum:

International Petroleum
 Co., Ltd.
Jiron Zepita 423
Lima

Peruvian Gulf Oil Co.
Jiron A. Miro Quesada 376
Of. 407
Aptdo. 1012
Lima

Occidental Petroleum
 Corp. of Peru
Occidental Peruana, Inc.
Los Nardos 1018, San Isidro
Lima 27

Manufacturing:

Joy Mfg. Co. (Peru) S.A.
Martin de Murua 187
Edif. Banco Wiese
Lima

Sunbeam del Peru, S.A.
Avenida Faucett Km. 32000
Callas. Aptdo. 5673
Lima 100

Paraguay

GEOGRAPHY:
AREA: 157,047 sq. mi.
CAPITAL: Asuncion

PRINCIPAL CITIES: Caaguazu, Coronel Oviedo, Pedro Juan
TERRAIN: Grassy plains, wooden hills, and tropical forests east of Paraguay River; low flat marshy plains west of river.
CLIMATE: Temperate East of Paraguay River; semiarid to the west.

PEOPLE:
POPULATION: 5,213,772
ANNUAL GROWTH RATE: 2.76%
RELIGION: 97% Roman Catholic
LANGUAGE: Spanish and Guarani
EDUCATION: Attendance in primary school 83%; Literacy 81
LIFE EXPECTANCY: Men 71; women 74 years.

GOVERNMENT: Republic under authoritarian rule. New government under Gen. Andres Rodriguez has ruled since a coup in 1989 overthrew the 34 year old government of dictator Gen. Alfredo Stroessner. Government budget: $655 million of which a tenth goes to the military.

ECONOMY: GDP: $15.2 billion
ANNUAL GROWTH RATE: 3.5%
PER CAPITA GDP $3,000.
AVERAGE RATE OF INFLATION: 20.4%
WORK FORCE: Of the 1.6 million in the work force, 44% are involved in agriculture, 34% in industry and commerce, 18% in services, and 4% with the government. The unemployment rate is about 11%.
OFFICIAL EXCHANGE RATE: 1,861 guaranies = US$
COST OF LIVING INDEX: 093

This relatively little known country can actually be considered two distinct regions within a common boundary. One of the world's few totally landlocked countries, Paraguay is divided by the Paraguay river. To the east is a pretty region with gently rolling hills, tropical forests and fertile grasslands. To the west is the region known as the Chaco—a low semi-arid marshy plain covered with dense scrub forests. The Chaco accounts for about 60% of the country but less than 4% of the population live here. The vast majority live in the east, most of them within 100 miles of the capital. A number of foreign groups, primarily German, Japanese, Koreans, Brazilian, and Argentines have settled in Paraguay. About 1,500 Americans reside here. Certainly not a large number of expatriates but those who have settled here have developed a unique community on the outskirts of Asuncion. Although few American companies have located here, compared to the rest of South and Latin America, there are jobs for those with certain skills: electrical engineering, economics, business management, project directors, land development or agronomists.

Paraguay is predominantly an agricultural country with no known significant mineral or petroleum resources, although petroleum exploration is intensifying. Agricultural commodities normally account for a major share of the country's exports. Particular obstacles to Paraguay's development include fluctuating prices for major export items, the long and expensive river or land routes that foreign trade must traverse, a small domestic market, and internal and external trade barriers.

The nation has exceptional hydroelectric potential and within the next decade should become the world's largest exporter of hydroelectric energy. The country is looking for foreign expertise in developing its economy. Thus, it is one of the few countries that encourages immigration. The requirements for establishing residence are minimal. All you need is a passport, health certificate and character references. An offer of work is not essential. The Consular Section at the Paraguay Embassy can provide the forms and basic information.

In the past few Americans have attempted to obtain jobs here. The former dictatorial regime, human rights situation and lack of American corporate interest has dissuaded many. Whether the political situation will change under the new government is still to be determined. The U.S. government does provide modest funding for AID development and both the U.S. Information Service programs and the Peace Corps are active.

A list of American companies is available from the Paraguay-American Chamber of Commerce, Ntra. Senora de la Asuncion 719, Haedo-8 piso, "A", Asuncion. Paraguay has an embassy at 2400 Massachusetts Avenue NW, Washington, DC 20008 (202/483-6960) with consulates in New York, New Orleans, Chicago, Detroit, and Los Angeles. The U.S. Embassy is located at 1776 Avenida Mariscal Lopez, Asuncion. Contacts:

Finance:

Bank of America
Chile & Oliva St.
Casilla de Correo 1321
Asuncion

Chase Manhattan Bank N.A.
Vitor Haeda 103
Esquina Ind. Nacional
Casilla de Correo 317
Asuncion

Peat, Marwick, Mitchell Inc.
Independencia Nacional 7
Azara
Asuncion

Price Waterhouse & Co.
Azara 197 Esquina Yegros
Casilla de Correo 975
Asuncion

Construction:

Brown & Root Inc.
Asuncion

Cia. Internacional de Ingeniera
S.A.
Casilla Correo 1691
B. Constant 977
Asuncion

Technical Services:

SGS Paraguay S.A.
Colon 517, Esquina Oliva
Edificio Nauar 114/115
Casilla de Correo 497
Asuncion

Uruguay

GEOGRAPHY:
AREA: 68,037 sq. mi.
CAPITAL: Montevideo
PRINCIPAL CITIES: Melo, Tacuarembo, Mercedes
TERRAIN: Mostly rolling plains and low hills; fertile coastal lowland.
CLIMATE: Warm temperate; freezing temperatures almost unknown.

PEOPLE:
POPULATION: 3,198,910
ANNUAL GROWTH RATE: 0.6%
RELIGION: 66% Roman Catholic; 30% nonprofessing or other.
LANGUAGE: Spanish
EDUCATION: Attendance in primary school 98%; Literacy 96%
LIFE EXPECTANCY: Men 70; women 77 years.

GOVERNMENT: Republic with president both chief of state and head
of government. Bicameral National Congress. Elections every five years.
Government budget: $2.0 billion

ECONOMY:
GDP: $19 billion
ANNUAL GROWTH RATE: 2%
PER CAPITA GDP $3,600.

AVERAGE RATE OF INFLATION: 50%
WORK FORCE: Of the 1,305,000 in the work force 22% are involved
in manufacturing; 17% in commerce; 12% in utilities, construction,
transportation and communications; and 13% in agriculture. The
unemployment rate is about 9%.
OFFICIAL EXCHANGE RATE: 4.4710 new Uruguayan pesos = US$
COST OF LIVING INDEX: 126

Although one of the smallest countries in South America, Uruguay has
one of the highest standards of living. A strong European influence is felt
throughout the population. There is a high literacy rate (the highest in all
of Latin America) and a large urban middle class population. Metropolitan Montevideo, with an estimated 1.3 million inhabitants, is the only
large city. Most of the rest of the population (80% to be exact) live in
about 20 towns. As a result of the low birth rate and relatively high rate
of emigration of younger people, Uruguay's population is quite mature.

The country's economy is in transition and has slowly showed signs
of recovering from serious economic difficulties that gripped the nation
in the late 1970s and early 1980s. The present democratic government is
trying to make structural changes to break the general pattern of
stagnation that has marked the economy for more than three decades.
(For example, an inflation rate of 9,000% between 1955 and 1970.)
President Sanguinetti has tried to improve conditions since taking over
from an incompetent military regime in 1985 but has not experienced
great success. The lack of natural resources such as coal and petroleum
coupled with no developed industrial infrastructure place a heavy burden
on the economy.

A significant portion of the economy is in the hands of state enterprises, which dominate banking, insurance, aviation, petroleum refining,
railroads, power, and other areas. However, the government is proceed-
ing cautiously with a number of projects to privatize, scale down, shut
down, or otherwise reform state corporations.

There is a growing need for experienced personnel in such areas as
finance, business management, engineering, computer technology and
data processing, marketing and sales, food processing, to name but a few.
To encourage foreigners to consider settling here the government has one
of the most lax rules for obtaining a work or residence visa of any
country. All it takes is proof of "mental, physical, political and financial
soundness." No proof of employment is required. In other words: come
to Uruguay, make yourself at home, find a job and stay awhile. The only
restrictions upon the hiring of foreigners are:

- At least half the employees of Uruguayan banks must be Uruguayan.
- The captain of a Uruguayan fishing boat must be Uruguayan as must half his crew.
- The crew aboard all Uruguayan airlines must be Uruguayan. More complete details are spelled out in the circular, Formalities to be Compiled by Applicants for Permanent Residence in Uruguay available from the Consular Section of any Uruguay Embassy or consulate.

The names and address of more than 150 U.S. companies in Uruguay are published in the Membership Directory (Lista de Socios) available from the Chamber of Commerce of the U.S.A. in Uruguay, Calle Bartolome Mitre 1337, Casilla de Correo 809, Montevideo. Uruguay has an embassy at 1919 F Street NW, Washington, DC 20006 (202/331-1313) with consulates in Miami, Los Angeles and New York. The U.S. Embassy is located at Lauro Muller 1776, Montevideo. Contacts:

Manufacturing:

3M Uruguay
Camino Carrasco 4683
Montevideo

General Electric S.A.
Calle Defensa 1926,
Casilla de Correo 360
Montevideo

General Motors Uruguaya S.A.
Avenida Sayago 1385
Montevideo

Food Processing:

Fleischmann Uruguaya, Inc.
Juan Paullier 2373
Montevideo

Pepsi-Cola Interamericana S.A.
Avenida Millan 4284
Casilla de Correo 947
Montevideo

Financial:

First Nat'l City Bank of NY
Calle Cerrito 445
P.O. Box 690
Montevideo

Coopers & Lybrand
Casilla de Correo
1396, Yaguaron 1231
Montevideo

Petroleum:

Esso Standard Oil Co.
(Uruguay) S.A.
Calle Cerrito 461, P.2
Montevideo

Texaco Uruguay S.A.
18 de Julio 985 P.4
Montevideo

Pharmaceutical:

Abbott Labs Uruguay Ltd.
Calle 31 de Marzo 4496
Montevideo

Johnson & Johnson
 del Uruguay S.A.
Cno Carrasco 5436
Casilla de Correo 273
Montevideo

Venezuela

GEOGRAPHY:
AREA: 352,143 sq. mi.
CAPITAL: Caracas
PRINCIPAL CITIES: Maracaibo, San Cristobal, Cumana
TERRAIN: Andes mountains and Maracaibo lowlands in northwest;
central plains (llanos); Guyana highlands in southeast.
.CLIMATE: Varies from tropical to temperate depending on altitude.

PEOPLE:
POPULATION: 20,562,405
ANNUAL GROWTH RATE: 2.16%
RELIGION: 96% Roman Catholic
LANGUAGE: Spanish
EDUCATION: Attendance in primary school 95%; Literacy 89%
LIFE EXPECTANCY: Men 70; women 76 years.

GOVERNMENT: Republic with a president and bicameral National
Congress elected every five years. Government budget: $17 billion.

ECONOMY:
GDP: $161 billion
ANNUAL GROWTH RATE: -1%
PER CAPITA GDP $8,000.
AVERAGE RATE OF INFLATION: 46%
WORK FORCE: Of the 6.8 million in the work force, industry and
commerce employs 35%; services 26%; and agriculture 15%. The
unemployment rate is about 8.2%.
OFFICIAL EXCHANGE RATE: 107.260 Bolivares = US$

COST OF LIVING INDEX: 074

Venezuela is one of the Western Hemisphere's least densely populated countries. Most of the population is concentrated in the Andes and along the coast. One out of every five Venezuelans lives in Caracas. These are hard working, industrious people. Their economic present and future can be summed up in one word—oil. Venezuela is a major producer and exporter of oil. A founding member of the Organization of Petroleum Exporting Countries (OPEC), it plays a key role in the world oil market. At the end of the 1980s, oil accounted for about 90% of Venezuela's total merchandise exports income, 61% of the government's revenues and some 22% of the gross national domestic product. The government nationalized the industry in 1976. Since then, employment has doubled, income has quadrupled, and production of crude oil has declined.

In addition to petroleum, the country produces about 15 metric tons of iron ore a year. Iron, steel and aluminum are all major industries. Of the major services, only the telephone, telegraph and water supply are wholly government owned. The government also owns a steel mill, the iron ore and petrochemical industries, most of the aluminum industries, one of the two domestic airlines and a chain of hotels.

More than 400 American firms have established operations here; U.S. investment in Venezuela is about $1.8 billion. Until recently, Venezuela's

major employment problem was a shortage of skilled workers and managers to operate what had been a burgeoning and increasingly technological economy. To fill the gap, Venezuela recruited many skilled foreign technicians, expanded its technical education facilities, and sent Venezuelans abroad for training. With the economic decline of the past few years, rising unemployment has displaced the lack of technically qualified personnel—though still a significant factor—as the primary manpower concern. Still, industrial wages, benefits and working conditions remain relatively high, an achievement of Venezuela's large, disciplined multiparty labor movement.

Americans with certain high tech and specialized skills can still find a welcome here although there may be quotas in certain industries. To obtain employment you must first obtain a transient visa valid for a period of 45 days to a year. Obtain your visa through any Venezuelan consulate (not the embassy). The visa is renewable once you enter the country. When in the country you are also required to stop by the national Identification Office and acquire an identity card. There is a basic rule that requires that three-quarters of all employees of a company be

Venezuelan. The only exceptions are for certain positions such as foremen, those in charge of industrial relations personnel, ship and airline captains. These positions must be filled by Venezuelans. Unlike many of the nations in the Middle East who have flooded their employment roles with Western petroleum experts, the Venezuelans are extremely cautious of allowing too many non-Venezuelans into the industry. Yes, many jobs are available and being filled with experienced Americans but don't expect the oil business here to mirror the industry in Saudi Arabia.

The best listing of U.S. companies operating here is available from the Venezuela-American Chamber of Commerce & Industry, Centro Plaza, Torre A. Nivel 15, Los Palos Grandes, Apartado 5181, Caracas, 1010. Venezuela has an embassy at 2445 Massachusetts Avenue NW, Washington, DC 20008 (202/797-3800) with consulates in Baltimore, Boston, Chicago, Houston, Los Angeles, Miami, New Orleans, New York, Philadelphia, Portland, and San Francisco. Contacts:

Petroleum:

Creole Petroleum Corp.
Aptdo. 889, Edif. Centro
 Industrial No. 1
Los Chaguaramos
Caracas

Mobil Oil Co. de Venezuela
Aptdo. 60167
Caracas 106

Occidental de
 Hidrocarburos Inc.
Centro Plaza Torrea
Avda. Francisco
Miranda Torre A
Los Palos, Grandes
Caracas 1206

Chemicals:

Cyanamid de Venezuela S.A.
Edif. Principal N. 1
Avda. Principal
Los Ruices
Caracas

Dow Quimica de
 Venezuela C.A.
Edif. Feran, Ofic. 32, Piso 3
Las Mercedes
Caracas 1060

Executive Search:

Korn/Ferry. de Venezuela C.A.
Multicentro Empresarial
 del Este
Torre Libertador A
Avda. Libertador
Caracas 1060

Manufacturing:

Black & Decker de
 Venezuela C.A.
Aptdo. 61860, Chacao
Caracas 1060A

Ford Motor Co. Venezuela S.A.
Aptdo. 611131 del Este
Caracas

General Motors de
 Venezuela C.A.
Aptdo. 666
Caracas 1100

Construction:

C.A. Armco Venezolana
Calle Norte-Sur No. 1
Los Cortijos de Lourdes
Aptdo. 368
Caracas 107

Brown & Root S.A.
Calle 80 No. 3-G-43
Maracaibo, Edo. Edo.
Caracas

Lummus Co. Venezuela C.A.
Centro Plaza Torrea
Avda. Fco. Miranda
Los Palos Grandes
Caracas 1206

EUROPE

Austria

GEOGRAPHY:
AREA: 32,369 sq. mi.
CAPITAL: Vienna
PRINCIPAL CITIES: Graz, Salzburg, Innsbruck.
TERRAIN: Mostly mountainous with Alps in west and south; flat with
gently rolling hills along eastern and northern sectors.
CLIMATE: Temperate. Cold winters with frequent rain in lowlands;
snow in the mountains. Cool summers with occasional showers.

PEOPLE:
POPULATION: 7,954,974
RELIGION: Roman Catholic 85%; Protestant 6%.
LANGUAGE: German
EDUCATION: Attendance in primary school 95%; Literacy 98%
LIFE EXPECTANCY: Men 73; women 80 years.

GOVERNMENT: Parliamentary democracy. President is chief of state
Chancellor is head of government. Bicameral legislature. President is
elected every 6 years; parliament every 4 years. Government budget: $38
billion; 3.6 % is for military.

ECONOMY:
GDP: $134.4 billion
ANNUAL GROWTH RATE: -0.5%
PER CAPITA GDP $17,000.
AVERAGE. RATE OF INFLATION: 3.7%
WORK FORCE: Most workers (56%) are employed in the service
industry with but 8% involved in agriculture. 36% work in commerce
and industry. Unemployment is about 5.5%.
OFFICIAL EXCHANGE RATE: 12 schillings = US$
COST OF LIVING INDEX: 167

This small (slightly smaller than Maine) but beautiful country is very
much impacted by the growth and economic pangs of Eastern Europe as
well as by developments and Post-World War II changes throughout
Western Europe. Its neighbors to the East are just experiencing the
beginnings of an economic rebirth while its western neighbors (Germany,

Italy, and Switzerland) are leading Europe's dynamic economic rampage.

Austria has a social market economy in which the government plays an important role. Many of the country's largest firms were nationalized in the early postwar period to protect them from Soviet takeover as war reparations. Today these state-owned corporations are intended to operate largely as private businesses. The government operates various state monopolies, utilities, and services. Austrian industry, banking, transportation, services and commercial facilities are well developed.

Although the nationalized industries, which include several large iron and steel works and chemical plants, are large industrial enterprises employing thousands of people, most industrial and commercial enterprises are smaller.

With a slight increase in the unemployment rate (about 4.5% in the early 80s; about 5.5% in the late 80s) the number of foreign workers has declined to about 140,000 or 5% of the work force. The Austrian government, however, is hard-nosed concerning non-Austrian citizens working in their country. U.S. citizens living or working in Austria, for example, are subject to Austrian taxes on all income regardless of its source. Thus, you may be subject to taxation on money earned in Austria as well as any income you also receive from non-Austrian sources.

All employees require a work permit issued by the Austrian Ministry of Labor. Fortunately these permits are almost always secured by the employer rather than the employee after a job has been secured. A permit is issued before you come to Austria and won't be issued once you're in the country. For certain special trades or skills either a license or proof of qualifications is required.

A knowledge of German is essential for any job. The Teutonic imperative is very much in evidence here. All senior level executives speak English but won't accept many foreign employees that aren't fluent in German. The best opportunity for employment in Austria is with a foreign company doing business in the country. There are about 225 American corporations in Austria. Exceptions may be considered in computer services, banking and accounting, and medical services. Teachers have difficulty working in Austrian schools as the State School System employs only those with civil service status. To be an Austrian civil servant you must be an Austrian citizen. There are, however, possibilities of teaching in private schools. The Central Bureau for Educational Visits and Exchanges (Seymour Mews House, Seymour Mews, London W1H 9PE) often arranges programs for qualified teachers and some advanced students.

Ads for foreign workers can be found in the Austrian papers including

Die Presse, available in the U.S. at major libraries that receive foreign newspapers. Regional employment offices (Landesarbeitsamt) have current data on job vacancies. The Vienna Landesarbeitsamt is located at Weihburggasse 30, 1010 Vienna for example. Other locations are available at:

- Bergenland, Permayerstrasse 10, 7001 Eisenstadt
- Carinthia, Kumpfgasse 25, 9010 Klagenfurt
- Lower Austria, Hohenstaufengasse 1, 1013 Vienna
- Upper Austria, Gruberstrasse 67-69, 4010 Linz
- Salzburg, Auerspergstrasse 67-69, 5020 Salzburg
- Styria, Bahnhofgurtel 95, 8010 Graz
- Tyrol, Schoepfstrasse 5, 6010 Innsbruck
- Voralberg, Rheinstrasse 32, 6901 Bregenz

A list of U.S. companies operating in Austria is available from the American Chamber of Commerce in Austria and is the first place to start in any comprehensive job search. Data on temporary job situations may be obtained through Manpower, Lugeck 1/33, A-1010 Vienna.

Austria has an embassy at 2343 Massachusetts Avenue NW, Washington, DC 20008 (202/483-4474). There are Austrian consulates in New York, Los Angeles and Chicago. The U.S. Embassy is at Bolzmanngasse 16, Vienna. Contacts:

American Chamber of
 Commerce in Austria
Tuerkenstrasse 9
A-1090 Vienna

Manufacturing:

3M Osterreich GmbH
Postfach 611, A-1011 Vienna

Black & Decker Werkzeuge
Vertreibs GmbH
Eriaaerstrasse 165,
Postfach 47, 1233 Vienna

Worthington GmbH,
Industries Trave B, Nr.6
2345 Brunn Am Gebierge

Electronics/Computers:

Digital Equipment Corp.
Mariahilferstr. 136
1150 Vienna

ITT Austria Intl.
 Telephone Telegraphen
75 Fresdner Strasse,
A-1200 Vienna

NCR Osterreich GmbH
Heitzingerkai 101
A-1130 Vienna

Advertising:

Team Austria
Heutteieort Strasse 65
1150 Vienna

McCann-Erickson GmbH
Regor Mendel-Strasse 50,
Postfach 57,
A-1191 Vienna

Accountants:

IPW Interaudit Prufungs-und
Wirtschaftsberatungs GmbH,
Traungasse 12,
A-1030 Vienna

Touche Ross & Co., GmbH
Postfach 178, Vienna

Belgium

GEOGRAPHY:
AREA: 11,799 sq. mi.
CAPITAL: Brussels
PRINCIPAL CITIES: Antwerp, Ghent, Liege
TERRAIN: Varies from coastal plains in the northwest, through gently rolling countryside in the center, to the Ardennes Mountains in the southwest.
CLIMATE: Cool, temperate and rainy. Summer temperatures average 60°. Temperatures rarely reach as low as 10° or as high as 90°.

PEOPLE:
POPULATION: 10,062,836
ANNUAL GROWTH RATE: 0.2%
RELIGION: 75% Roman Catholic
LANGUAGE: 56% Flemish (Dutch); 32% French; 1% German. Legally bilingual; divided along ethnic lines.
EDUCATION: Attendance in primary school 100%; Literacy 98%.
LIFE EXPECTANCY: Men 73; women 80 years.

GOVERNMENT: Parliamentary democracy under a constitutional monarch. The king is chief of state; the prime minister is head of government. Bicameral parliament. Elections held at least every four

years. Government budget: $51 billion with approximately 6% devoted
to the military.

ECONOMY:
GNP: $153 billion
ANNUAL GROWTH RATE: -1.5%
PER CAPITA GNP $17,700.
AVERAGE RATE OF INFLATION: 2.8%
WORK FORCE: Of the 4.2 million employed 37% are employed in
services and transportation; 26% are employed in industry and com-
merce; 23% in public service; and, 2% in agriculture. The unemployment
rate is about 13.5%.
OFFICIAL EXCHANGE RATE: 36.2 Belgian francs (BF) = US$
COST OF LIVING INDEX: 167

Belgium is a densely populated, highly industrialized country in the
middle of one of the world's foremost industrial regions. It lies within
100 miles of London, the Ruhr Valley, and most of the Netherlands.
Following an economic period of stagnation concluding with the 1980-82
recession the country augmented an austerity program that began to show
results in 1983. In 1984, industrial activity gained further momentum and
exceeded an annual growth rate of 5%. Production in the steel and
metalworking industries increased due to greater investments.

The expansion of high-tech industry, particularly in Flanders, and the
service sector continued at a steady pace. Residential construction also
picked up when preferential value-added tax rates on construction were
phased out. Belgium is one of the few European countries to have solved
their housing problem. More than 30,000 new homes are built each year
which leaves a constant vacancy rate of about 4%. It is possible to obtain
a nice two-bedroom unfurnished apartment in Brussels for about $425 to
$650 a month. However, be prepared to pay a three-month advance
deposit.

Unfortunately, average real wages have declined about 12% since
1982. Unemployment leveled off in 1984 at 12.3% and has been
declining gradually since that time. Although conditions have not shown
improvement for the average worker, there exists widespread acceptance
that the austerity program will lead to better economic health as
economic activity picks up during the rest of the decade.

Foreign investment plays an important part in the Belgium economy.
The total U.S. direct investment of more than 900 American companies
operating in Belgium is estimated at $5.15 billion. The American

Chamber of Commerce has calculated that U.S. companies provide about 1 of every 11 jobs in Belgium. Because of their strong export orientation, these jobs were more resilient in the economic crisis than was employment geared to the domestic market.

This is a unionized country with about two-thirds of all workers belonging to a union; 90% of the country's unions are affiliated with one of the three major political parties. Membership is voluntary. Although there are no legal minimum wages, unions have been able to establish "guidelines" for white-collar workers according to age and skill. For example, the average monthly salary for clerical workers is about $1,060. The average weekly wage for an industrial worker is about $275.

All workers are subject to Belgium income tax which is deducted from your salary. The initial BF 100,000 (about $3,100) is passed through tax free with a progressive rate beyond that. Depending on number of dependents, the tax rate ranges from a minimum of 25% to a maximum of 72%.

Aside from work with an American company, the most significant employers of foreigners are the many international agencies located in the country. Belgium is headquarters to NATO, the European Common Market and more than 300 other international organizations which are always on the look out for English speaking personnel. A solid knowledge of French or Dutch is a major plus.

Although there is a job market for certain English-speaking personnel with the international organizations, the high unemployment rate makes it difficult to compete for non-specialized or low-skill jobs. The best source for job information and possible openings is the national employment service: Office National de l'Emploi (ONEM), 65 Boulevard Anspach, 1000 Brussels. The service maintains 30 regional offices throughout the country. Addresses of these regional offices is available from ONEM's central administration office at Boulevard de 'Empereur 7, 1000 Brussels.

Private employment services are also located in Brussels as well as a few other major cities. For example, ACT Careers, Avenue des Arts 50, Box 3, 1040 Brussels handles jobs in middle management and office staff personnel. Secretarial jobs and mid-level administrative positions are handled by Career Secretaries, Avenue des Arts 50, 1040 Brussels and International Secretaries, Avenue de Tervuren, 1040 Brussels. Teaching positions are handled directly through the many language schools in the country. Addresses of these schools as well as those of universities is available from the Belgium Embassy.

Names and addresses of U.S. companies located in Belgium as well as other helpful information about employment is available from the American Chamber of Commerce in Belgium, Avenue des Arts 50, Bte 5, 1040 Brussels.

If you plan to work in Belgium or reside in the country for longer than three months you do need permission. The Belgium Embassy or a local consulate general will grant a visa once a work permit is obtained. The work permit is issued by the Ministry of Labor in Brussels and must be obtained prior to entry. The permit is usually handled by the prospective employer but the applicant must supply the employer with a medical certificate written in either Dutch or French on a physician's letterhead; three recent passport-size photographs; and, personal data including name, place and date of birth, and U.S. residence.

Belgium has an embassy at 3330 Garfield Street NW, Washington, DC 20008 (202/333-6900) with consulates in Atlanta, Chicago, Houston, Los Angeles, and New York. The U.S. Embassy is located at 27 Boulevard du Regent, 1000 Brussels. Contacts:

Banking:

Bankers Trust Co.
Banque du Benelux S.A.
Rue des Colonies 40
1000 Brussels

Bank of America N.T. & S.A.
34 Van Eycklei
B-2018 Antwerp

Engineering:

Bechtel Intl. Co.
Postbus 269
9000 Ghent

Frederic R. Harris S.A.
71 Rue de la Loi
1040 Brussels

Pharmaceuticals:

Cooper Laboratories S.A.N.V.
Avenue Leopold 66,
B-1330 R. Xensart
Eli Lilly Benelux S.A.
Rue de L'Etuve 52
1000 Brussels

Manufacturing:

Navistar Intl Overseas
 Service Co.
6 Avenue Lloyd George
BTE 2
1050 Brussels

Stanley Works Belgium N.V.
Dickstraat 9 P.B. 34
9100 Lokeren

Societe Trane S.A.
Chausse de Watermael 38
B-1160 Brussels

Management Consultants:

Science Management Intl. S.A.
Siege et Bureaux,
Administrarifs 66
Rue de Livourne
1050 Brussels

Arthur D. Little Intl.
Boulevard de la Woluwe 2
B-1150 Brussels

Denmark

GEOGRAPHY:
AREA: 16,631 sq. mi.
CAPITAL: Copenhagen
PRINCIPAL CITIES: Aarhus, Odense, Aalborg
TERRAIN: Low and flat to gently rolling plains.
CLIMATE: Temperate; humid and often overcast. Windy, mild winters
and cool summers. Strong prevailing westerly winds.

PEOPLE:
POPULATION: 5,187,821
ANNUAL GROWTH RATE: 0.23%
RELIGION: 97% Evangelical Lutheran
LANGUAGE: Danish
EDUCATION: Attendance in primary school 100%; Literacy 99%
LIFE EXPECTANCY: Men 72; women 78 years.

GOVERNMENT: Constitutional monarchy (the oldest in Europe) with
the queen head of state; prime minister, head of government. Unicameral
parliament. Elections on call of prime minister but at least every four
years. Government budget: $34 billion of which 7.3% is for the military.

ECONOMY:
GDP: $95.6 billion
ANNUAL GROWTH RATE: 0.5%
PER CAPITA GDP $18,500.
AVERAGE RATE OF INFLATION: 1.8%
WORK FORCE: Of the 2.8 million employed 51% work in industry and
commerce; 30% in government; 12% in services; and 6% in agriculture
and fisheries. The unemployment rate is about 11.8%.
OFFICIAL EXCHANGE RATE: 6.7 Danish kroner (DKr) = US$

COST OF LIVING INDEX: 166

For several decades, the Danish economy has been characterized by industrial expansion and diversification as well as a continued dependence on foreign trade, which accounts for more than half of gross domestic product. The major problem with both the Danish economy and the interest of foreigners desirous of working here is the growing unemployment rate. Following the economic upswing in the early 1980s, unemployment declined to about 8% of the total labor force in 1987. However, with the flow of both western and eastern Europeans into the country and the labor market's inability to absorb new entrants the unemployment rate currently hovers about a tenth of all eligible workers.

With about 10% of all Danish out of work, it is extremely difficult for foreigners to get jobs here. Unless you possess a skill not available within the country or are hired by a non-Danish company, you will have a difficult time working in Denmark. American citizens can apply for a work permit at the Danish Embassy or consulate before leaving the United States but they had better be prepared to assure an issuing officer that they possess a trade or special skill that is unavailable in Denmark. Even then the Danish government may limit a permit to the time it takes to train and educate a Danish citizen in that particular skill. Ironically, the Danish government places no restrictions on the number of foreign employees a Danish company can hire. Just claim a skill not available in the motherland. No foreigner, regardless of nationality, can obtain a job in the Danish Civil Service. These posts are exclusive to the natives. Obviously, if you're employed by an American company in Denmark you won't be hampered by many of the Danish restrictions.

If you should be fortunate enough to get through the bureaucratic hurdles you will usually have the benefit of a trade union to battle for both your wages and continued employment. Taxes are deducted directly from your salary and vary between 25 and 70% depending on gross earnings. A personal allowance of 22,000 DKr ($3,800) is tax free. Further details on the Danish tax system as well as other extremely useful information is detailed in the brochure Worth Knowing When You Come to Work in Denmark issued by any Danish Embassy.

The best source of potential job information is from Arbejds-direktoratet, the Danish state employment service, Adelgade 13, Dk-1304, Copenhagen. Two private employment services in Copenhagen may also provide information about specific jobs and employment possibilities: Adia, N. Volgade 82, Copenhagen and Western Services, Kobmagergade 54, Copenhagen. Being in Denmark and visiting these offices in person is by far the best way to get hot job leads. The Catch-22, of course, is that the only way you can obtain your work permit is to then leave the country and go through the bureaucratic maze in quest of official sanction. The Danish Embassy suggested to the authors that a qualified worker place an ad in one of the leading Danish newspapers such as: Berlingske Tidende, Pilestraede 34, DK-1112 Copenhagen K; Politiken, Raadhuspladsen, DK-1550 Copenhagen V; or Jyllands-Posten, Groenendalsvej 3, 8260 Viby J.

Occasionally there are openings in Danish hospitals for doctors. Since all vacancies are advertised in the weekly journal of the Danish Medical Association (Trondhjemsage 9, 2100 Copenhagen) a doctor interested in job in Denmark can start his or her search by contacting the DMA. Also, request their free brochure, Information for Doctors Migrating to Denmark.

Seasonal employment is also available on Danish farms as well as with the tourist industry. A knowledge of the Danish language is essential. Students interested in spending a summer in this beautiful Scandinavian country can find temporary work around Copenhagen. Contact the Studenternes Arbejdsformidling, Tondergade 14, Dk-1752, Copenhagen, (a branch of the national employment service).

About 225 U.S. firms have offices, affiliates or subsidiaries in Copenhagen alone. Although there is no American Chamber of Commerce, the American Club attracts members from the American business community and Danes interested in closer ties with Americans.

Denmark has an embassy at 3200 Whitehaven Street NW, Washington, DC 20008 (202/234-4300). Consulates are located in Chicago, Los Angeles, New York and Houston. The U.S. Embassy is located at Dag Hammarskjolds Alle 24, 2100 Copenhagen. Contacts:

Chemicals:

Cyanamid Denmark
St. Kongensgade 68,
2 DK-1264, Copenhagen K

Kobenhavens Pektinfabrik A/S
DK 4623
Lille Skensved

Electronics:

Control Data A/S
35 Sonder Blvd.
1720 Copenhagen V

Digital Equipment Corp. A/S
Sandtofften 9,
2820 Gentoffte

Petroleum:

Gulf Oil A/S
6A Kvaesthusgade
1251 Copenhagen

Dansk Esso A/S
13 Skt. Annae Plods,
1298 Copenhagen K

Construction:

Norton B.V. Holland
Fynsvej 73,
6000 Kolding

Gray Tool. Ltd.
6700 Esbjerg
Andorp

Food Products:

Nordisk Kellog's A/S
Ostre Havnevej 25
5700 Svenborg

Kraft Foods A/S
Vasbyqade 45,
DK 2450 Copenhagen

Finland

GEOGRAPHY:
AREA: 130,160 sq. mi.
CAPITAL: Helsinki
PRINCIPAL CITIES: Tampere, Turku
TERRAIN: Low, flat rolling plains. 70% forested and more than 60,000 lakes.
CLIMATE: Cool temperate. Potentially subarctic but mild because of influence of water currents.

PEOPLE:
POPULATION: 5,068,931
ANNUAL GROWTH RATE: 0.4%
RELIGION: 97% Evangelical Lutheran
LANGUAGE: 94% Finnish; 6% Swedish (both are official)
EDUCATION: Attendance in primary school 100%; Literacy 99%.
LIFE EXPECTANCY: Men 71; women 79 years.

GOVERNMENT: Constitutional republic. President is chief of state; prime minister, head of government. Unicameral parliament elected every four years; president every six years. Government budget: $28.9 billion of which 5% is for the military.

ECONOMY:
GDP: $114.9 billion
ANNUAL GROWTH RATE: 5%
PER CAPITA GNP $23,153.
AVERAGE RATE OF INFLATION: 6.6%
WORK FORCE: Of the 2.6 million employed, 53% work in industry, commerce or finance; 25% in either public or personal services; 9% agriculture; 8% transportation and communications; and, 5% government. The unemployment rate is about 5%.
OFFICIAL EXCHANGE RATE: 4.9 Finnmarks (FMk) = US$
COST OF LIVING INDEX: 144

Finland has a dynamic industrial economy based on capital investment and new technology. During the first half of the 1980s Finland's economic growth rate was one of the highest in Western Europe. Wood and steel are the main industries. However a wide range of other industries produce everything from electronics to motor vehicles. The manufacturer of machines, ship building and textiles are important industries. The most important export is lumber or lumber products. Finnish-designed consumer products are internationally known and respected. The country's architecture and product design are considered among the most innovative and creative in the world.

Finns work hard but also know how to enjoy the benefits of their land. Their northern location means that the summer months are almost in total sunlight while the winter is grey and dark much of the day. As a result the most important holiday is mid-summer night (June 23rd) when the sun doesn't set in the northern part of the country. Many Finns have both a winter residence as well as a summer house on one of the 60,000 lakes or thousands of islands off the coast.

Americans working here must first secure both a work and residence permit from a Finnish Embassy or consulate prior to arrival. It takes at least a month to process an application as the work permit is issued by the Ministry of Labor and the residency permit by the Ministry of Interior Affairs. Your employer is required to notify the local police of your work status within 24 hours of your date of employment.

The best potential source of employment is with one of the 100 U.S. companies with offices in Finland. Most Finnish companies will hire locals unless there is a clear need not too. The government does have a stated policy that no foreigner should be hired for a job that a Finn can accomplish. The language is extremely difficult and may be required for many jobs. Fortunately, most Finns at the executive level also speak

Swedish (a language not at all similar to Finnish), but if you expect to work or live away from Helsinki you had better learn Finnish.

There are some opportunities for short term work particularly for young people aged 18—23 whose mother tongue is English, French or German. The Ministry of Labor has a program called the Finnish Family Program in which young people are hired to spend a summer with a Finnish family and teach them a "foreign" language.

Finland has an embassy at 3216 New Mexico Avenue NW, Washington, DC 20016 (202/363-2430). The U.S. Embassy is located at Itainen Puistotie 14B, Helsinki 14. Contacts:

Electronics:

OY International Business
Machines AB
P. Roobertinkatu 8B
00100 Helsinki 10

Mathematica Scandinavia
Fredrikinkatu 33-B
00120 Helsinki

Petroleum:

Exxon Corp. OY, Esso AB
Etelaranta 12
28100 Helsinki 10

OY Mobil Oil AB
Keeskuskatu B
00100 Helsinki 10

Management Consulting:

OY Rastor AB
Kiviaidank 11,
00210 Helsinki 21

OY Mec-Rasto AB
Satamakatu 4
00160 Helsinki 10

Paper:

Beloit Corp.
Vaitameri OY
Pakilantic 61
00660 Helsinki 66

Accuray Finland OY
Helsinki

France

GEOGRAPHY:
AREA: 220,668 sq. mi.
CAPITAL: Paris
PRINCIPAL CITIES: Marseille, Lyon, Nice, Bordeaux
TERRAIN: Mostly flat rolling hills in the north and west; mountains in south (Pyrenees) and east (Alps).

CLIMATE: Generally cool winters and mild summers except along the Mediterranean where it can be mild in the winter and hot during the summer.

PEOPLE:
POPULATION: 57,840,445
ANNUAL GROWTH RATE: 0.5%
RELIGION: 90% Roman Catholic; 2% Protestant; 1% Jewish; 1% Muslim.
LANGUAGE: French
EDUCATION: Attendance in primary school 100%; Literacy 99%
LIFE EXPECTANCY: Men 74; women 82 years.

GOVERNMENT: Republic. President is head of state; prime minister is head of government. Bicameral parliament. Government budget: $318 billion of which 16% is for the military.

ECONOMY:
GDP: $1.05 trillion
ANNUAL GROWTH RATE: -0.7%
PER CAPITA GNP $18,200.
AVERAGE RATE OF INFLATION: 2.1%.
WORK FORCE: Of the 24 million employed 47% worked in services; 45% in industry and commerce, and 8% in agriculture. The unemployment rate is about 12.2%.
OFFICIAL EXCHANGE RATE: 5.9 French francs = US$
COST OF LIVING INDEX: 174

France is one of the world's foremost industrial and agricultural countries. It has substantial agricultural resources, a diversified modern industrial system, and a highly skilled labor force. The government exerts considerable control over the industrial sector both through planning and regulatory activities as well as through direct state ownership. The most important areas of industrial production include steel and related products, aluminum, chemicals, and mechanical and electrical goods.

The government has been notably successful in developing dynamic telecommunications, aerospace, and weapons. With virtually no domestic oil production the country has banked heavily on the development of nuclear power which now produces about 70% of France's electrical energy. The primary industries are steel, automobile manufacturing, chemicals, and textiles. Of course you can't think of France without thinking wine. And, indeed French wines are an important source of both revenue and employment. France remains the largest food producer and food exporter in Western Europe.

With the growth of the economy the French have also increased their standard of living by more than 80% since 1975. Although the overall housing situation has remained poor—70% of all French homes were built prior to 1948—there are still some inexpensive living situations in areas away from Paris and the Cote d'Azur. The increase in domestic spending is also quite evident in the numbers of cars, television sets, and phones purchased over the past decade.

The glamour that once was France still is! Paris remains a city of high fashion, good living, art and culture. The towns and villages along the Mediterranean coast still attract both Frenchmen and tourists eager to enjoy the bon vivre. It is only natural therefore that working in France can be a major plus for Americans interested in enjoying the best of Europe.

Unfortunately, the French government has not made it easy for non-EC residents to work here. French companies are restricted from hiring foreigners unless they possess skills not available from their own nationals. However, once a French employer satisfies the requirements that no local is available for a specific job a declaration d'engagement signed by the employer is forwarded to the local police department and a carte de sejour (residence permit) is issued. A formal work permit is next obtained from the Ministry of Labor. This means bureaucracy and paperwork, but in this area the French excel.

The high unemployment rate has also made it difficult for foreigners to secure jobs. The government maintains a retraining program for French workers to assure that the labor pool in high-tech positions will be filled by Frenchmen.

The government has set the 40 hour work week as a standard and any time beyond that is paid at a higher rate. The average annual income is about FFr 44,000 ($8,150) with salaries in Paris a good 25% above the rest of the country. Benefits are usually better than in the United States with 10 public holidays a year plus a five week annual vacation. Taxes used to be considered a joke here with considerably less than half of all French households contributing. Now, a wage earner is expected to declare his previous year's annual salary then pay an income tax in a single settlement. The single wage earner can earn about FFr 14,000 tax free. Rates above that vary from 5 to 65%. Considering the various deductions and allowances, the average tax bite rarely goes beyond 20%. The French government doesn't have much confidence in the income tax.

As a result value added taxes and other indirect forms of taxation are a far more important source of national revenues.

If you are captivated by the French lifestyle and believe you can beat the system your best chance for obtaining work—assuming you don't work for one of the 925 American companies located in France—is through the Agence Nationale pour l'Emploi (national labor exchange). The agency has more than 600 offices throughout the country. Although all offices are supposed to handle most available jobs, the offices in the major cities (Paris, Marseille, and Lyon, for example) have special engineering departments. For additional information contact the main office at 53 Rue General Leclerc F92136, Issy-les-Moulineaux. Another potential job-source is through the private employment agencies. For example: Manpower France S.A.R.L. deals with office workers. It is one of the nation's largest agencies with branches throughout France). Address: 9 Rue Jacques Bingen, 75017 Paris. Select France handles workers with computer skills, industrial talent, and those with experience in engineering particularly in the fields of aeronautics and petrochemicals. Address: 34 Boulevard de Picpus, 75012 Paris. Needless to say: be prepared to speak fluent French.

Seasonal work is available in some areas. Grape pickers, general farm workers, and harvesters are always wanted. French farms employ over 100,000 foreigners during the summer. Most of these workers are from Spain, Portugal and Morocco who return every year, However, many American students have obtained work over the summer in the tourist industry and with farms. Unfortunately, you can't obtain these jobs unless you're on-site and ready to work. This means gambling with your time, resources and the hope you won't be asked to produce a work permit. Brochures issued by the Centre d'Information et de Documentation Jeunesse, IOI Quai Branly, 75740 Paris cover much seasonal work available to students and other young people.

The best source of data concerning American companies located in France is through the American Chamber of Commerce in France, 21 Avenue George V, F-75008 Paris.

France has an embassy at 4101 Reservoir Road NW, Washington, DC 20007 (202/944-6000) with consulates in Boston, Chicago, Detroit, Houston, Los Angeles, New Orleans, New York, San Francisco, and San Juan. The U.S. Embassy is located at 2 Avenue Gabriel, Paris 8. Contacts:

Pharmaceuticals:

Abbott Laboratories
127 Ave. Charles de Gaulle
92201 Neuilly

Eli Lilly France SA
203 Bureaux de la Colline
92-213 Saint Cloud

Manufacturing:

Wabco Westinghouse SA
2 Blvd. Westinghouse,
B.P. 2, F.
93270 Freinville Sevaran

Reims Aviation
B.P. 2745
51062 Reims

Case France SA
10 Rue Pierre Semard
18101 Vierzon

Textiles:

Ames France
3 Chemin Departemental
Falleres, St. Nabord
88200 Remiremont

Societe Francaise
 des Frabrications Riby
51 Faub des Bosges
68800 Thann

Construction:

Badger France SA
Tour Manhattan Cedex 21
92025 Paris de la Defense
Combustion Engineering
 France Europe,
SARL, F.
92085 Paris, La Defense Tour,
Winterthur Cedex 18

Management Consultants:

Boyden International SARL
13 Rue Madeleine Michelis
92522 Neuilly Diebold France
SA
56 Rue de Loudres
75008 Paris

Executive Search:

Heidrick & Struggles Intl. Inc.
6 Rand Point des Champes
 Elysees
75008 Paris

Germany

In late 1990 the Federal Republic of Germany (West Germany) was unified with the German Democratic Republic (East Germany). Economic data for the "reunified Germany" is not yet available.

GEOGRAPHY:
AREA: 137,602 sq. mi.

CAPITAL: Bonn
PRINCIPAL CITIES: Berlin, Hamburg, Munich, Leipzig, Dresden, Cologne, Frankfurt
TERRAIN: Low plain in the north; high plains, hills in the center, mountainous Alpine region in the south.
CLIMATE: Temperate and maritime; cool, cloudy, wet winters and summers, occasional warm, tropical foehn wind; high relative humidity.

PEOPLE:
POPULATION: 81,087,506
ANNUAL GROWTH RATE: 0.36%
RELIGION: 45% Roman Catholic; 44% Protestant.
LANGUAGE: German
EDUCATION: Attendance in primary school 100%; Literacy 99%
LIFE EXPECTANCY: Men 73; women 79 years.

GOVERNMENT: Federal republic. Bicameral parliament. President is titular head of state; chancellor is executive head of government. Elections held every four years. Government budget: $245,000,000 of which 10% went to the military.

ECONOMY:
GNP: $1.2 trillion
ANNUAL GROWTH RATE: 4%
PER CAPITA GNP $19,000
AVERAGE RATE OF INFLATION: 2.8%
WORK FORCE: Of the 39 million employed Germans, approximately 54% work in government and service industries; 41% industry; 5% agriculture. The unemployment rate is about 8.5%.
OFFICIAL EXCHANGE RATE: 1.5 deutsche marks = US$
COST OF LIVING INDEX: 143

With the reunification of the country in 1989 the country has undergone major social and economic changes. The immediate influx of some 11 million former East Germans to a unified nation added immediate problems as well as the hope and expectations that the country will be the most important economic, political and potential military power in Europe, if not the world.

Even prior to reunification the Federal Republic of Germany (F.R.G.) ranked among the world's most important powers. From the 1948 currency reform until the 1970s it experienced almost continuous expansion. Today the economy operates mainly on a free market basis. Competition and free enterprise are fostered as a matter of government policy. However, the state participates in the ownership and management of major segments of the economy, including such public services as railroad, airline, and telephone systems.

Exports have been a key element in economic expansion and foreign investment has been a key to economic growth. Total U.S. assets in the F.R.G. amount to about $19 billion (with F.R.G. investment in the U.S. around $27 billion); with 65% devoted to manufacturing and 25% in the petroleum industry. More than 1,100 American companies have operations in the F.R.G.

Since the end of World War II, the number of German youths entering universities has nearly tripled. The F.R.G.'s trade and technical schools are among the world's best. With per capita income approaching $20,000. Germany is today a broadly middle class society. A generous welfare system provides for the needy German citizens. The nation's social welfare philosophy is to assure that any individual will receive help when in need through no fault of his own (i.e. though sickness, accident or old age), but not to allow any able-bodied worker to rely on the state for subsistence. Modern Germans are also mobile; millions travel abroad each year.

All those earning income in Germany are subject to German taxes. There are six income tax classes based upon age, marital status and number of dependents. Single wage earners under 50 pay the highest tax rate; low income groups pay no taxes at all. The rates range from 22% to 56%.

With the continuing growth of the German economy the need for skilled workers is ever present. Unfortunately, with the incorporation of the two Germany's into a single state it will be some time before the true employment picture can be evaluated. One thing not needed in Germany is manual labor or unskilled workers. Prior to reunification, about 7.2% of the country's population (about 4.3 million) was represented by foreign workers and their families. Now with the extensive labor pool of East German workers searching for work many foreign workers will join the country's unemployment list.

The best avenue of employment in the new Germany is through one of the many American companies doing business here. However, for those skilled workers interested in working for a German company the most important office is the Zentralstelle fur Arbeitsvermittlung, Feuerbachstr. 42-46, D-6000 Frankfurt/Main 1. This is the central German labor exchange office that handles inquiries for all types of work from students interested in a summer jobs to professionals searching for permanent work. When contacting this office tag your letter "International Department" and be sure to include detailed information about you and the job you seek. Include: date and place of birth, marital status, number of family members accompanying you, education, qualifications and experience, knowledge of the German language, and length of stay. Also include an international postal coupon to assure a reply.

If you want to isolate your job search to a specific city or town you can send a letter similar to the above to the Arbeitsant (Labor Exchange) in that town. Addresses for the various arbeitsants are available from the central headquarters (Zentralstelle fur Arbeitsvermittlung) in Frankfurt.

Another important source of job data is the Bundesanstalt fur Arbeit (Federal Employment Institute), Frauentorgraben 33-35, Nurnberg. Although you can obtain job leads from the States it improves your chances to apply directly while in Germany. This, of course, presents a Catch-22 situation since you must have a work permit (Arbeitserlaubnis) to obtain a job and stay in the country more than three months. And to obtain a work permit you must apply directly to any German Embassy or consulate before entering the country. The German Embassy in Washington may also provide information on industries and areas of potential need. The Embassy does not, however, help directly in finding employment.

Doctors and those in the medical profession interested in working in Germany must apply through the Zentralstelle fur Arbeitsvermittlung in Frankfurt. Legal restrictions single out this organization as the only source of medical employment. Teachers, on the other hand, can contact German universities who often have semester or full-year appointments for foreign lecturers. English teachers at private schools or the state school system are also in periodic demand. Contact Linguarama, an English language school, at Deichmannhaus IV, Bahnhofsvorplatz 1, 5000 Koln 1. Also, Schiller College, Friedrich-Ebert Anlage 4, 6900 Heidelberg hires foreign teachers. For qualified specialists in agriculture contact Hendrikson Associierte Consultants GmbH, Mergenthalerallee 51-59, Postfach 5480, 6236 Eschborn 1.

Other sources of job information are the many German newspapers published abroad and available in the United States. The English language International Herald Tribune lists job openings, particularly on an executive level. The major German daily papers include: Die Welt, Welt am Sonntag, Bild, Munchner Merkur, and, Frankfurter Allgemein Zeitung.

Detailed lists of American companies in German are available from the American Chamber of Commerce in Germany, Rossmarkt 12, Postfach 2123, 6000 Frankfurt/Main 1. Branch offices of the chamber of commerce are located at: Kurfurstenstrasse 114, 1000 Berlin 30; Fallstrasse 40, P.O. Box 70 14 29, D-8000 Munich 70; Brauweiler Weg 88, 5000 Koln 41; and, Leiblweg 28, 7000 Stuttgart 1.

The Federal Republic of Germany has an embassy at 4645 Reservoir Road NW, Washington, DC 20007 (202/298-4000) with consulates in Atlanta, Boston, Chicago, Detroit, Houston, Los Angeles, San Francisco, Seattle, and New York. The U.S. Embassy is located at Deichmannsaue, 5300 Bonn 2. Contacts:

Language Schools:

Berlitz School of Languages
Dusseldorferstr. 1-7
Postfach 110261
6000 Frankfurt/Main 2

Management Consultants:

Booz, Allen & Hamilton
 International
Steinstr. 2,
4 Dusseldorf

Boyden Intl. GmbH
Postfach 1724
D-6370 Bad Hamburg
Arthur D. Little International
 Inc.
Abraham Lincolnstr. 34,
6200 Wiesbadan

Accountants:

Coopers & Lybrand GmbH
Postfach 270 507
D 5000 Cologne 1

Deloitte Haskins & Sells GmbH
Postfach 2324,
Stresemannstr. 15
4000 Dusseldorf

Technical Construction:

Kohlenscheigungs GmbH
Postfach 395
Stuttgart

Holmes & Narver
Burton Cohen GmbH
Nordenstr 2, 6082 Moerfeiden
Waldorf

Manufacturing:

EMCO Wheaton GmbH
Emcostr. 2-4,
Postfach 25 35 75
Kerchain 1

IBM Deutschland GmbH
Pascalstr. 100, Stuttgart,
Bad-Wuertt 7000

Chronos Richardson GmbH
Frankfurter Str. 89-95
D-5202 Hennel 1

Chemicals:

GAF (Deutschland) GmbH
Postfach 1380
5020 Frechen

Velsicol Chemical GmbH
Vordenbergstr. 16
D-7000 Stuttgart

Greece

GEOGRAPHY:
AREA: 50,949 sq. mi.
CAPITAL: Athens
PRINCIPAL CITIES: Salonika, Pireaus, Patras
TERRAIN: Mostly mountains with ranges extending into the sea as peninsulas or chains of islands.
CLIMATE: Temperate; mild, wet winters; hot dry summers.

PEOPLE:
POPULATION: 10,564,630
ANNUAL GROWTH RATE: 0.84%
RELIGION: 98% Greek Orthodox; 1% Muslim
LANGUAGE: Greek
EDUCATION: Attendance in primary school 96%; Literacy 95%
LIFE EXPECTANCY: Men 75; women 80 years.

GOVERNMENT: Presidential parliamentary. Unicameral legislature with both presidential and parliamentary elections every four years. Government budget: $25.3 billion of which 11% is for the military.

ECONOMY:
GDP: $93.2 billion
ANNUAL GROWTH RATE: 1%
PER CAPITA GNP $8,900.
AVERAGE RATE OF INFLATION: 14.8%
WORK FORCE: Of the 3.86 million employed, 43% are in services; 27% in agriculture, 20% in manufacturing and mining. About half of the labor force is self employed.
OFFICIAL EXCHANGE RATE: 250 drachmas = US$
COST OF LIVING INDEX: 118

Overall the economy of Greece is in a bind. Since 1981 it has shown little growth with the GNP actually stagnating since 1986. The economy is characterized by a strong service sector that accounts for more than half of the GDP, and a relatively large but inefficient agricultural sector that contributes but 14% to GDP yet employs 27% of the country's labor force. The industrial sector accounts for a quarter of GDP and employs 20% of the work force. The catch is that 9 out of 10 Greek businesses employ less than 10 workers and half of the country's labor force is self employed. The major industrial output is manufacture of textiles, production of chemicals, mining of metals, and the processing of food and wine.

As a result of the tight economic situation and lack of any major industrial drive, Greece may be the cradle of Democracy but it's Hell on earth if you're an American looking for work here. The government has all but enacted an edict preventing foreigners from working in Greece. However, if you possess a special skill required by a local industry you can receive a temporary work permit. Your prospective employer is responsible for the paperwork and acting as your sponsor.

In some cases a company operating under special arrangements with the Greek government is allowed to hire a specified number of non-Greek employees. Find one of these companies and your permit will be issued readily. As an incentive to American companies to invest in Greece the government will allow the company to hire an agreed upon number of expatriates for administrative and technical positions. Slightly fewer than 200 U.S. companies have branches here.

Many Americans have obtained jobs teaching English in one of the many growing language schools. In most cases they work "off the books" and no work permits are discussed. If you hold a Teaching of English as a Foreign Language (TOEFL) certificate you will find obtaining a teaching job much easier. Also, you need not speak Greek to teach English but it helps. The best way to locate a job is to be in the country at the right time—the end of August—and simply knock on any and every door that hangs a plaque stating it is a language school, (front-istiria). Classes run from mid-September through May. Ads for teaching jobs are often placed in the daily Athens News (an English language paper available at 23-25 Lekka Street in Athens) as well as the British Guardian and the Times Educational Supplement. (The latter are available in the United States.) You can also supplement your income by serving as a private tutor. When in Athens the Hellenic American Union or the British Council can put you in contact with perspective students. Going rate is about $12 per hour.

Part time work is hard to obtain in the tourist industry as these positions are almost all filled by Greeks. English speaking au pairs are in great demand however. Check the ads in the Athens News as well as through one of the specialist agencies: International Staff, Th. N. Camenos, Botasa 12, Athens or Working Holidays, Nikis 11, Athens.

Names of U.S. companies in Greece are available from the American Hellenic Chamber of Commerce, 17 Valaoritou Street, Athens 134.

Greece has an embassy at 2221 Massachusetts Avenue NW, Washington, DC 20008 (202/667-3168) with consulates in Atlanta, Boston, Chicago, Los Angeles, New Orleans, New York, and San Francisco. The U.S. Embassy is located at 91 Vasilissis Sophias Blvd, 10160 Athens. Contacts:

Manufacturing:

General Motors Hellas ABEE
P.O. Box 610-20
Amaroussian 151 10
Attica

General Electric Intl.
 Operations Co.
Athens Tower,
P.O. Box # 3075, Ambelokipi
Athens

Cummings Corp.
P.O. Box # 66042
15510 Halandri
Athens

Pharmaceuticals:

Abbott Laboratories
 (Hellas) S.A.
194 Syngrou Avenue
Athens

Eaton Laboratories
(Hellas)
28 Kapodistriou Street
Athens 147

Upjohn ABEE
16th Km. Marathonos Avenue
Palllini
Attikis

Chemicals:

Ethyl Hellas Chemical Co. S.A.
P.O. Box # 260
Thessaloniki

Dow Corning Europe S.A.
9 Dousmani, Glyfada
Athens

Food Products:

Carnation Hellas AEBE
Marathonos &
 Anthoussis Avenue
Pallini, Attikis

Knorr (Hellas) ABEE
282 Kifissias, Halandri
Athens

Ireland

GEOGRAPHY:
AREA: 26,593 sq. mi.
CAPITAL: Dublin
PRINCIPAL CITIES: Cork, Limerick, Galway, Waterford
TERRAIN: Mostly level to rolling interior surrounded by rugged hills and low mountains.
CLIMATE: Temperate maritime. Mild winters, cool summers; consistently humid, overcast much of the time.

PEOPLE:
POPULATION: 3,551,000
ANNUAL GROWTH RATE: 0.02%
RELIGION: 94% Roman Catholic; 4% Anglican
LANGUAGE: English (Gaelic is spoken in a few areas).
EDUCATION: Attendance in primary school 100%; Literacy 99%
LIFE EXPECTANCY: Men 72; women 78 years.

GOVERNMENT: Republic. Bicameral parliament. President elected every seven years, members of parliament every five years. Government budget: $16 billion with 4% going to the military.

ECONOMY:
GNP: $46.3 billion
ANNUAL GROWTH RATE: 2.7%
PER CAPITA GNP $13,100.
AVERAGE RATE OF INFLATION: 3.4%
WORK FORCE: Of the 11.6 million employed, 51% are employed in services; 29% in manufacturing and construction; and 15% in agriculture and fishing. The unemployment rate is about 16%.
OFFICIAL EXCHANGE RATE: .64 Irish pounds = US$
COST OF LIVING INDEX: 154

Ireland is a wonderful country to visit but it's hard to find a job here unless you are hired by an American firm. The country's unemployment rate places a severe restriction on most job seekers. The government of Charles Haughey, elected in 1987, faces severe economic problems that impact heavily on jobs. Ireland has a high tax rate, growing inflation, and a high public debt, not to mention the unsolvable sectarian problems in the North. As a result, Haughey's party lost ground in the `89 general elections and a coalition government has been able to make few inroads into the nation's problems.

If you have one parent of Irish birth or are a resident of any EC country you'll have first crack at any jobs in Ireland. The government has a stated policy of "protecting job opportunities for EC citizens in determining whether or not work permits are issued." If you have special skills, particularly high tech skills, experience in banking and accountancy, or teaching you'll stand a far better chance of obtaining a job here. For information on the current employment needs write to the Training and Employment Authority (FAS), 27-33 Upper Baggot Street, Dublin 4. Ask for their booklet, Working in Ireland. Those interested in summer seasonal work may stand a chance working for one of the many tourist hotels. The largest demand is in the south western counties of Cork and Kerry. A list of the hotels is available from the Irish Tourist Board, 757 Third Avenue, New York, NY 10017 (212/418-0800).

Although the hundreds of American firms with facilities in Ireland hire local residents for all but the most highly skilled jobs they will, of course, hire Americans with skills to fit the right slot. The largest U.S. employer is Digital Electronic Corporation. They opened a manufacturing plant in Galway with 100 workers. Today, they employ almost 2,000. Their Galway Ballybrit plant concentrates on the manufacturer of their VAX family of components for the European market. General Motors employs over 1,000 employees at its Packard Electric Plant in Tallaght. Merck Sharp & Dohme has a work force of 260 and is led by an all-Irish management team. A detailed listing of U.S. companies in Ireland is available from the U.S. Chamber of Commerce in Ireland, 20 College Green, Dublin 2.

Ireland has an embassy at 2234 Massachusetts Avenue NW, Washington, DC 20008 (202/262-3939) with consulates in Boston, Chicago, New York, and San Francisco. The U.S. Embassy is located at 42 Elgin Road, Ballsbridge, Dublin. Contacts:

Electronics:

Analog Devices B.V.
Raheen Industrial Estate
Limerick

Apple Computer Ltd.
Warrington House
Mount Street Crescent
Dublin 2

Digital Equipment
International B.V.
Ballybrit Industrial Estate
Galway

Pharmaceuticals:

Allergan Pharmaceuticals
(Ireland)
Carrowberg, Westport
County Mayo

Becton, Dickinson &
 Company Ltd.
Kill o' the Grange
Dun Laoghaire
County Dublin

Merck Sharp &
 Dohme (Ireland) Ltd.
Ballydine, Kilsheelan
Clanmel
County Tipperary

Manufacturing:

General Motors Corporation
Belgard Road, Tallaght
Dublin 24

Dollinger Ireland Ltd.
Ballycasheen, Kilarney
County Kerry

Howmedica International Inc.
Raheen Industrial Estate
Limerick

Engineering:

Jacobs International Ltd. Inc.
Merrion House, Merrion Road
Dublin 4

Petroleum:

Gulf Oil Terminals (Ireland)
Whiddy Island, Bantry
County Cork

Marathon Petroleum
Ireland, Ltd.
Mahon Industrial Estate
Blackrock
County Cork

Italy

GEOGRAPHY:
AREA: 116,303 sq. mi.
CAPITAL: Rome
PRINCIPAL CITIES: Milan, Naples, Venice, Bologna, Turin
TERRAIN: Mostly rugged and mountainous. Some plains and coastal
lowlands.
CLIMATE: Mediterranean. Alpine in the north; hot and dry in the south.

PEOPLE:
POPULATION: 58,138,394
ANNUAL GROWTH RATE: 0.2%
RELIGION: Roman Catholic

LANGUAGE: Italian
EDUCATION: Attendance in primary school 100%; Literacy 98%
LIFE EXPECTANCY: Men 73; women 80 years.

GOVERNMENT: Republic. Bicameral parliament. President is chief of state; prime minister is head of government. Elections every five years. Government budget: $311 billion of which 4.5% is for the military.

ECONOMY:
GDP: $967 billion
ANNUAL GROWTH RATE: -0.7%
PER CAPITA GDP $16,700
AVERAGE RATE OF INFLATION: 4.2%
WORK FORCE: Of the 21 million employed, 58% Services; 32% Industry and commerce; 10% Agriculture.
OFFICIAL EXCHANGE RATE: 1,700 lire = US$
COST OF LIVING INDEX: 146

Like the rest of Western Europe, Italy's economy is booming. Since the end of World War II the nation has evolved from an agriculturally based economy to one of the top six industrial countries in the free world. The economy is largely in private hands, but the government runs many large enterprises and services including the railroads, airlines, electricity, telephones, and large portions of the telecommunications industry. The government is also a large employer accounting for about 15% of employment.

Italy's economic strength is in the processing and the manufacturing of goods, primarily in small, family-owned firms. Its major industries are precision machinery, motor vehicles, chemicals, pharmaceuticals, electrical goods, and fashion and clothing.

Despite the growing economy Italy is still faced with an unemployment rate of about 12% (persons under the age of 30 account for some 70% of the unemployed). As a result it is extremely difficult for non-Italians to find employment here with Italian companies. The situation reached the point that the U.S. Embassy in Rome released a statement warning: "There are more job seekers than there are jobs. The competition for available openings is consequently intense. Preference for nearly all jobs is naturally given to Italians. The Italian Government employment service will not register nonresidents of Italy on its rolls of job seekers." Yet despite these dire warnings Americans have found jobs in Italy. Most work for one of the 500 plus U.S. companies located in the country. However, a few have found both full-time and seasonal work. The local Italian newspapers and the International Herald Tribune do carry want ads for specialized talents possessed by many Americans.

The bureaucracy in Italy is almost comical. A simple procedure of stepping into a state bank and changing a travelers check from dollars to lire may take 30 minutes, require the official stamp of approval from three or four "bankers", and leave you totally frustrated. Forget to bring your passport and you're out of luck—to say nothing of lire.

The advantage of this outlandish bureaucracy does have its benefits. Many Americans seeking temporary jobs as secretaries and English teachers (one of the few areas where non-Italians can obtain work fairly easily) ignore the residency requirements or lack of official permission. Their theory is that so much bureaucratic effort is involved in clearing an alien for a temporary job, the paper-chasers are more interested in headier matters than to be concerned with a part-time worker.

Officially if you plan to either work or live in Italy you must apply to the ufficio stranieri at the local police headquarters. After more bureaucratic paper shuffling in which the local police contact the Provincial Labor Office, who are empowered to grant or deny your status, you may or may not receive an official stamp on your visa enabling you to work or live here.

Generally, wages are lower here than other parts of Europe for comparable work. Fringe benefits (more paid holidays—between 20 and 30 days a year—vacations, bonuses, etc.) often make up for the lower salaries. Women doing the identical job as men can count on lower wages. This is one European country in which career women are looked down upon. Italians pay an income tax which ranges from on to 65%. The first 360,000 lire is tax free; the top tax bracket is 500 million lire.

Aside from working for an American company based in Italy, the best area for potential employment is in teaching. Although jobs with the Italian State schools are not open to foreigners (except in conjunction with teacher-exchange programs or other State-sponsored educational visits) there are many private schools throughout the country on the lookout for bilingual Americans. A host of English and American international institutes are located throughout the country. For example, the American Overseas School of Rome, Via Cassia, 811 Rome and the NATO School, Via Della Liberazione, 80100 Bagnoli are potential teacher contacts. Also consider The International School of Milan, Via Caccialepori 22, Milan, The American Junior High School in Italy, Ravello, Costiera Amalfitana, and St. Stephen's School, Via Lungro 1, 00178 Rome. There are also four British colleges in southern Italy.

Contact is made through the Director of Studies, British College, Via Luigi Rizzo 18, 95131 Catania.

A list of American companies located in Italy is available from the American Chamber of Commerce in Italy, Via Cantu 1, 20123 Milan. Italy has an embassy at 1601 Fuller Street NW, Washington, DC 20009 (202/328-5500). The U.S. Embassy is located at Via Veneto 119, Rome. Contacts:

U.S. International
 Marketing Center
Via Gattamelata 5
20149 Milan

Electronic:

Apple Computer S.p.A.
Via Bovio 5, Zona Ind.
 di Mancasaie
42100 Reggio Emilia

Anilam Electronica S.R.L.
Via G. Gallilei 36
10040 Borgaretto
Turin

Manufacturing:

Erico Italia S.p.A.
Via Mencci 16
20093 Settimo, Milan

Panduit S.R.P.
Via Brunone 21
20156 Milan

Pulse Engineering Inc.
Viale Regina Giovanna 20
20129 Milan

Management Consultants:

A.T. Kearney Inc. S.p.A.
Via Durini 18
20122 Milan

McKinsey & Co.
Piazza del Duomo
22-20122 Milan

Sippican Consultants Intl Inc.
 (Engineering)
Via Gregoriana 40
Rome

Secretarial:

Astra Secretarial Services
Via XX Settembre 1
Rome

Rome Secretarial Bureau
Via Torino 40
Rome

Luxembourg

GEOGRAPHY:
AREA: 1,034 sq. mi.
CAPITAL: Luxembourg City
PRINCIPAL CITIES: Esch/Alzette, Dudelange
TERRAIN: Mostly gently rolling hills uplands with broad, shallow valleys; uplands to slightly mountainous in the north; steep slope down to Moselle floodplain in the southeast.
CLIMATE: Cool, temperate, rainy like the Pacific northwest. Mild winters; cool summers.

PEOPLE:
POPULATION: 401,900
ANNUAL GROWTH RATE: 0.8%
RELIGION: 97% Roman Catholic; 3% Protestant and Jewish. LANGUAGE: Luxembourgish, German, French
EDUCATION: Attendance in primary school 100%; Literacy 100%
LIFE EXPECTANCY: Men 73; women 80 years.

GOVERNMENT: Constitutional monarchy. Bicameral parliament. Grand Duke is chief of state. Elections every five years for Chamber of Deputies. Government budget: $2.2 billion with 2.1% going to the military.

ECONOMY:
GNP: $8.7 billion
ANNUAL GROWTH RATE: 1%
PER CAPITA GDP $22,600
AVERAGE RATE OF INFLATION: 3.6%
WORK FORCE: Of the 162,500 employed 49% work in services; 36% industry and commerce; 11% government; and, 5% agriculture. The unemployment rate hovers around 5.1%.
OFFICIAL EXCHANGE RATE: 36.2 Luxembourg francs (LuxF) = US$
COST OF LIVING INDEX: 144

Read the tourist literature and you'll find Luxembourg described as the "green heart of Europe." Green heart yes but bring a raincoat. This beautiful country doesn't remain green without water. Damp weather prevails and rain gear is needed year round. Despite its pastoral scenery, however, Luxembourg is a highly industrialized and export-intensive country. Its main industry, steel, is produced along the border with France. The country enjoys a degree of economic health and prosperity unique among industrialized democracies.

In 1876, English metallurgist Sidney Thomas invented a refining process that led to the development of the steel industry in Luxembourg and the founding of the ARBED company in 1911—now the fourth largest producer in Europe. Steel now accounts for 36% of the nation's exports. One out of every employee in Luxembourg is involved in steel. Unfortunately, steel has been in the decline of late which has led Luxembourg to develop a major financial center. Today there are more than 120 banks in Luxembourg employing more than 10,000.

The government has also been most successful in attracting new investment in medium and light industry. Incentives cover taxes, construction and plant equipment. U.S. firms among the most prominent include: Goodyear (tires), DuPont (chemicals), Guardian Industries (glass), and National Intergroup (aluminum foil). The U.S. investment of some $1 billion represents, on a per capita basis, the highest level of U.S. direct investment outside of North America.

Despite its size, about as large as Rhode Island, Luxembourg makes it much easier for foreign nationals to live and work here than most European countries. You do need an Identity Card for Foreign Nationals which is available from any municipal office. This residence permit is good for five years and is easily renewable.

The official language is French but German and English are also commonly used in business. The local language, or dialect, is known as Letzeburgesch or Luxembourgeois. Aside from trained technicians the best areas for job possibilities in Luxembourg are in the fields of banking and accountancy, computer services, and secretarial, translating and interpreting. The first place to start a local job search is the national employment office, Administration de l'Emploi, 34 Avenue de la Porte-Neuve, Luxembourg City. Several private employment firms also are worth noting: Manpower-Aide Temporaire, SARL, 19 Rue Glesenar, Luxembourg handles all forms of temporary work. Bureau-Service, SARL, 2 Alle Leopold Goebel, Luxembourg City specializes in various office jobs. For a multilingual secretary it may be easier to make direct contact with the many multi-national companies in the country. An up-to-date listing is available from the Luxembourg Embassy.

Seasonal jobs are also available at the various hotels. There are about 260 in the country. A list of these is also available from the Luxembourg Embassy, located at 2200 Massachusetts Avenue NW, Washington, DC

20008 (202/265-4171). The U.S. Embassy is located at 22 Boulevard Emmanuel Servais, Luxembourg. Contacts:

Banking:

First National City Bank S.A.
16 Avenue Marie-Theresa
P.O. Box # 263
Luxembourg City

Manufacturers Hanover Bank
39 Blvd.Prince Henri
P.O. Box # 807
Luxembourg City

Accountants:

Touche Ross & Co.
21 Rue Glesener
Luxembourg City

Coopers & Lybrand
P.O. Box # 215
6 Rue de l'Ancien
Athenee, 2012 Luxembourg

Deloitte Haskins & Sells Intl.
16 Rue Notre Dame
Luxembourg City

Chemicals:

A.P.E. Administration
 de Participations
Etrangeres S.A.
Blvd. Royal 13, L-2449
Luxembourg City

Rubber:

Rub-Kor Benelux SARL
Case Postale 2032
Luxembourg City

Luxembourgwire S.A.
Colmar-Berg
Luxembourg City

Uniroyal Luxembourg S.A.
Steinfort

Netherlands

GEOGRAPHY:
AREA: 16,464 sq. mi.
CAPITAL: Amsterdam
PRINCIPAL CITIES: The Hague, Rotterdam, Utrect
TERRAIN: Mostly coastal lowland and reclaimed land; some hills in southeast.
CLIMATE: Temperate marine with cool summers and mild winters. Temperatures rarely exceed 74°; winters can be long and damp.

PEOPLE:
POPULATION: 15,000,000
ANNUAL GROWTH RATE: 0.5%
RELIGION: 40% Roman Catholic; 31% Protestant; 24% unaffiliated.
LANGUAGE: Dutch
EDUCATION: Attendance in primary school 100%; Literacy 98%
LIFE EXPECTANCY: Men 76; women 79 years.

GOVERNMENT: Parliamentary democracy under a constitutional monarch. Queen is head of state; prime minister is head of government. Bicameral parliament located in The Hague. Elections at least every four years. Government budget: $98 billion with 3% of GNP going to the military.

ECONOMY:
GNP: $262 billion
ANNUAL GROWTH RATE: -0.2%
PER CAPITA GNP $17,200
AVERAGE RATE OF INFLATION: 3.5%
WORK FORCE: Of the 6 million employed approximately 45% work in services (of which 23% are employed by the government); 30% work in industry; and, 2% agriculture. The unemployment rate is 9.1%.
OFFICIAL EXCHANGE RATE: 1.95 guilders or florin (fl) = US$
COST OF LIVING INDEX: 120

The Dutch economy is based on private enterprise. The government has little direct ownership or participation, but it heavily influences the economy with more than 45% of gross national product (GNP) involved in its operations and social programs. Government at all levels makes its presence felt through the many regulations and permit requirements pertaining to almost every aspect of economic activity.

Services, which account for half of the national income, are primarily in the transport and financial areas, such as banking and insurance. Industrial activities provide about 19% of the national income and are dominated by metalworking, oil refining, chemical and food processing industries. Construction amounts to about 6% of the national income.

One of the major problems in seeking employment here is the growing unemployment rate. Those with unique skills will always find a job opportunity but when it comes to competing with a Dutchman, there is no affirmative action program here. Actually, there is a note in the circular describing Dutch visa requirements. In capital letters it reads: "In view of considerable unemployment, a seemingly permanent housing problem and the increasing density of the population, immigration is not encouraged and permanent residence is only rarely granted." A note to the author from the Royal Netherlands Embassy (dated summer 1994) goes even further: "The high rate of unemployment makes it virtually impossible for a foreigner to obtain a work permit."

With these negative caveats there are jobs in the Netherlands; some 200,000 foreigners are currently working here. The best opportunity is with one of the 670 American companies doing business in the Netherlands. Qualified personnel in such fields as oil refining, machinery production and aerospace may find opportunities. For example, several U.S. companies, including Chevron, Exxon, Mobil, Gulf, and Shell maintain refineries in the Netherlands. New policies of the Lubbers government will boost public spending on the environment by $3 billion and education, housing, social security, and health by $1 billion by 1996. Opportunities for foreign consultants may be available in these areas as well.

A complete listing entitled: "American Firms In The Netherlands" is available from World Trade Academy Press, Inc., 50 East 42nd St., Suite 509, New York, NY 10017, 212/697-4999. A less detailed listing is also available from the American Chamber of Commerce in the Netherlands, Carnegieplein 5, 2517 KJ, The Hague.

A labor permit is required but is obtainable once it is established that no Dutch person is available to fill the slot. A prospective employer will handle the paperwork. Local taxes are high and everyone is taxed. There is a personal tax allowance of fl 7,392 (about $4,500). Beyond that you are taxed on a sliding scale from 14% on the first fl 9,652 ($5,885) to 72% on fl 108,764 ($66,320) and above.

There are regional employment offices in most cities. For an up to date listing as well as current data on the job situation contact Directoraat-Generaal voor de Arbeidsvoorziening (DG-ARBVO), (the Dutch National Employment Office), Visseringlaan 26, Postbus 5814, 2280 HV Rijswijk (2-H).

An employment service in London recruits nurses for hospitals in the Netherlands. For more information contact: BNA International, 443 Oxford Street, London W1R 2NA. For medical personal interested in vacancies in Dutch hospitals contact: Geneeskundige Vereniging tot Bevordering van het Ziehenhuiswezen, Postbus 9696, 3506 GR Utrect.

A list of U.S. companies located in the Netherlands is available from the American Chamber of Commerce in The Netherlands, Carnegieplein 5, 2517 KJ The Hague.

The Netherlands has an embassy at 4200 Linnean Avenue NW, Washington, DC 20008 (202/244-5300) with consulates in Chicago, Houston, Los Angeles, New York,and San Francisco. The U.S. Embassy is located at Lange Voorhout 102, 2514 EJ The Hague. Contacts:

Chemical:

Cyanamid BV
Botlekweg 175
Rozenburg, P.O. Box # 7085
Rotterdam

Dow Chemical (Nederland) BV
Herbert H. Dowweg
P.O. Box 48
Terneuzen

Metalworking:

Abex-Div. Denison NV
Kamerlingh Onnesweg 22
3316 GI Dordrecht

Mueller Europa BV
Postbus 20
Lichtenvoorde

Petroleum:

Esso Beleggingsmaatschappij
 NV
Zuid Holiandlaan 7
P.O. Box # 110
The Hague

Gulf Oil (Nederland) BV
Boompjes 55, P.O. Box # 1137
Rotterdam

Food Processing:

Borden (Nederland) BV
Nijverheidsweg 16
P.O. Box # 44
Mijdrecht

Heinz BV HJ
Stationsstraat 50, P.O. Box # 6
Elst (Gld.)

Construction:

Badger BV
P.O. Box # 91
Binckhorstiaan 117
2501 AK
The Hague

Bechtel Inc.
Bezuidenhoutseweg 187-189
P.O. # 2188
The Hague

Norway

GEOGRAPHY:
AREA: 150,000 sq. mi.
CAPITAL: Oslo

PRINCIPAL CITIES: Bergen, Trondheim, Stavanger
TERRAIN: Rugged, with steep fjords, mountains and fertile valleys.
CLIMATE: Temperate along the coast, modified by the North Atlantic current. Colder interior; rainy near year round on west coast.

PEOPLE:
POPULATION: 4,314,604
ANNUAL GROWTH RATE: 0.39%
RELIGION: 94% Evangelical Lutheran (state church); 4% other protestant and Roman Catholic.
LANGUAGE: Norwegian
EDUCATION: Attendance in primary school 100%; Literacy 100%
LIFE EXPECTANCY: Men 74; women 80 years.

GOVERNMENT: Constitutional monarchy. King is chief of state; prime minister is head of the government; modified unicameral parliament. Elections held every four years. Government budget: $52 billion of which 8% is for military expenditures.

ECONOMY:
GDP: $89.5 billion
ANNUAL GROWTH RATE: 1.6%
PER CAPITA GDP $20,800.
AVERAGE RATE OF INFLATION: 2.3%
WORK FORCE: Of the 2.1 million employed; Government, social, personal services 37%; Manufacturing 15%; Wholesale, retail trade, hotels, restaurants 18%; Construction 6%; Agriculture, forestry, fishing 8%; Oil extraction, gas and water supply 2%
OFFICIAL EXCHANGE RATE: 7.4 kroner = US$
COST OF LIVING INDEX: 194

When oil was discovered off the coast of Norway in the 1970s Norway was changed overnight. The country's emergence as a major oil and gas producer transformed the economy. Today, Norway is one of the world's richest countries. Its large shipping fleet is one of the most modern among maritime nations. Metals, pulp and paper products, chemicals, shipbuilding, and fishing are among the significant traditional industries.

The influx of oil revenue also permitted Norway to expand an already advanced social welfare system. Education is free through the university level and is compulsory from ages 7 through 16. Norway's health system includes free hospital care, physician compensation, cash benefits during illness and pregnancy and other medical and dental plans. A "people's pension plan" guarantees a standard of living during retirement close to that achieved during an individual's working life.

These advanced life-benefits undoubtedly has impacted the lifestyle of all Norwegians. For example, Norway is among the top rank of nations in the number of books printed per capita, even though Norwegian is one of the world's smallest language groups.

In recent years Norway became home to an increasing number of immigrant workers and asylum-seekers from various parts of the world, now totaling about 130,000 with more than 2,000 obtaining Norwegian citizenship every year.

Except for summer work or jobs considered "part-time" everyone, including foreigners, pays taxes. The income tax is progressive from 6 to 48 percent depending on total earned income. The top level is for income above 253,000 kroner per year (about $36,000).

Unfortunately for Americans interested in working here, the Norwegian government has recognized that their swelling immigrant population poses potential labor problems not to mention an additional burden on the bountiful social system. Thus the government imposed a ban on certain aliens seeking work or residence in Norway. There are exceptions of course but unless you obtain a position with a U.S. company already located in the country the ban does make it extremely hard to obtain a job. Even an American employed by a U.S. company requires a work permit. And, unless your company can show why no Norwegian can fill the position, you could well be denied. Each application is evaluated on its own and the rules can bend but won't break.

The major exemption is for workers on the mobile drilling rigs on the Norwegian continental shelf. Others exempt include Norwegian-born aliens, certain exchange workers, part-time workers, and certain seasonal jobs.

Private employment agencies are not legal in Norway. The best way to obtain data about job possibilities is through the official government Directorate of Labor (Arbeidsdirektoratet), Holbergs Plass 7, Postboks 8127, Oslo 1. The Arbeidsdirektoratet publishes several useful brochures: *Summer Employment in Norway* and *Employment in Norway* explain the employment possibilities and the exemptions to the law banning certain aliens from holding jobs. Tourist hotels, particularly along the south coast around Kristiansand and along the inland fjords north of Bergen need a constant supply of English-speaking help over the summer.

Although a long shot, teachers interested in bucking the system should send for the free brochure, *Information for Foreign Teachers Seeking Positions in the Norwegian School System* issued by the Norwegian Ministry of Church and Education, Postboks 8119, Dep 0032, Oslo 1. American teachers have been hired here despite the ban. If you have an area of expertise that is unique you have a good chance to pass the ban. Many Americans have found a year or two lecturing at a Norwegian university a most rewarding experience. More than a dozen Americans and Canadians have established their own "community" in Trondheim, for example. These can often be considered "part time jobs" and may be exempt from the alien-work ban.

Norway has an embassy at 2720 34th Street NW, Washington, DC 20008 (202/333-6000) with consulates in Los Angeles, Minneapolis, New York and San Francisco. The U.S. Embassy is located at Drammensveien 18, Oslo. Contacts:

Petroleum:

Amerada Petroleum Corp. of
 Norway
Kronprinsesse Marthas Plass 1,
Oslo 1

A/S Norske Esso
Haakan VII's Gate 9
Oslo 1

Phillips Petroleum Co.
Akersgaten 45
Oslo 1

Construction:

Motordrift S/A
P.O. Box 868 Bryn
Oslo 6

Gray Tool Co. (Norway)
A/S. P.O. Box 4
4033 Forus

Mining Supplies:

Dresser Norway A/S
Dresser Atlas Div.
P.O. Box 55, Kvernevik Rings
4042 Hafrsfjord

Midco Norway
P.O. Box 688
4001 Stavanger

Chemicals:

Dow Chemical International
 Inc. A/S/
Fridtjof Nansens Vei 2
Oslo 3

W.R. Grace A/S
Ostreaker Vei 210
Oslo 9

Portugal

GEOGRAPHY:
AREA: 36,390 sq. mi.
CAPITAL: Lisbon
PRINCIPAL CITIES: Oportom Coimbra, Faro, Setubal
TERRAIN: Mountainous in the north; rolling plains in the south.
CLIMATE: Maritime temperate. Cool and rainy in the north; warmer and drier in the south. Less rainfall in the interior.

PEOPLE:
POPULATION: 10,524,210
ANNUAL GROWTH RATE: 0.36%
RELIGION: 97% Roman Catholic; 1% Protestant.
LANGUAGE: Portuguese
EDUCATION: Attendance in primary school 60%; Literacy 83%
LIFE EXPECTANCY: Men 71; women 78 years.

GOVERNMENT: Parliamentary democracy. Unicameral legislature. President is head of state; prime minister is head of government. Elections for assembly at least once every four years; for president, five years. Government budget: $23.3 billion of which 4.2% is for the military.

ECONOMY: GDP: $91.5 billion
ANNUAL GROWTH RATE: -0.4%
PER CAPITA GDP $8,700
AVERAGE RATE OF INFLATION: 7%
WORK FORCE: Of the 4.7 million employed 46% work for government, commerce and services; 35% for industry; and 21% in agriculture. The unemployment rate is about 8%.
OFFICIAL EXCHANGE RATE: 176.16 escudo (Esc) = US$
COST OF LIVING INDEX: 120

After nearly a decade of rapid growth, Portugal's economy declined in the mid-1970s due to disruption after their 1974 revolution and the large influx of refugees from Portugal's former colonies in Africa. The second period of recovery started in the mid-1980s after two years of recession. The economy is currently on the upswing partly as a result of improved governmental planning and the country's joining of the European Community (EC) in 1986.

Where Portugal was once heavily dependent upon agriculture today industry has now taken hold. For example, in the past three decades the proportion of the labor force engaged in agriculture has dropped from 42% to 21%. Industrial employment has increased from 21% to 35%. In addition, since the revolution, financial and commercial relations with former colonies have declined in importance. The large industrial-financial groups that once controlled much of the economy have been dismantled. Six foreign banks, including three from the United States, have begun operation.

The country's leading products include: textiles, clothing, cork and cork products, pottery, glassware, electronic equipment, machinery, steel, woodpulp and paper, cement, tomato paste, canned seafood, olive oil, assembled automobiles, refined petroleum, and chemical products. Portugal also has large shipbuilding and repair yards.

Unless you can obtain a job with one of the 95 American firms doing business here (or 40 British companies) your prospects for work are not very bright. The nation's relatively high rate of unemployment as well as its standing as an under-developed country means that there is a surplus of unskilled, cheap labor in all parts of the country. Skilled workers are always welcomed but salaries are usually considered better in other parts of Europe for identical positions.

Teachers of English are always welcome if you are willing to sacrifice money for a low pressured life style in one of the more beautiful and interesting nations. A list of English-speaking schools is available from the Portuguese Embassy or any consulate general. In addition to teaching positions there is also a need for skilled personnel in the fields of banking and accountancy, computer sciences, medicine and nursing.

Although there are too many farm hands looking for unskilled work, those with special agricultural skills might obtain information on the country's current agricultural job needs from one of the regional agricultural services in the provincial capitals. (For example: Dir. Regional de Agricultura Beira Interior, Rua Dr. Francisco Prazeres, Guarda; or, Dir. Regional de Agricultura do Alentejo, Rua Cicioso 18-20, Evora.)

The best source of job information with U.S. firms as well as a listing of American companies in the country is the American Chamber of Commerce in Portugal, Rua de D. Estefania, 155, 5 ESQ, Lisbon 1000. Portugal has an embassy at 2125 Kalorama Road NW, Washington, DC 20008 (202/328-8610) with consulates in New York, Boston, San Francisco, Providence, Newark, and New Bedford, MA. The U.S. Embassy is located at Avenida Forcas Armadas, Lisbon. Contacts:

Pharmaceuticals

Abbott Laboratorios, Ltd.
Rua Nove, Jore 40
Algragide

Sterling Farmaceutica
 Portuguesa Ltd.
Apartado 4
Carcazelos

Banking:

MDM-Estudos Tecnicos &
 Financeriros Ltd.
Rua Rodriques Sampaio
50-2 Esq.
1100 Lisbon

Bankers Trust Co.
Edif. Aviz, Bloco 3A,
Rua Latino Coelho-1-12DT,
Lisbon 1000

Textiles:

DHJ Lusitana Textil Ltda.
Estrada da Luz 114-B
1600 Lisbon

Reeves Portuguesa—
 Revestimentos, SARL
Rua da Constituicao 797
Oporto

Chemicals:

Rohm & Haas Portugal Ltd.
Columbano Bordalo Pinheiro
97-70 Dto.
Lisbon 1

Gamlen Chemical
Consuinave, 37B
Rua do Giestal
Lisbon 3

Manufacturing:

Black & Decker Ltda.
Aptdo 19
P-2768 Estoril, Codex

General Electric
 Portuguesa, S.A.R.L.
Apartado 2316, Rua da Nortes
1108 Lisbon

Spain

GEOGRAPHY:
AREA: 195,988 sq. mi.
CAPITAL: Madrid
PRINCIPAL CITIES: Barcelona, Seville, Valencia
TERRAIN: Large, flat to dissected plateau surrounded by rugged hills;
Pyrenees in the north.
CLIMATE: Temperate. Clear, hot summers in interior, more moderate
and cloudy along the coast. Cloudy and cold winters in the interior with

less than 20 inches of rainfall annually.

PEOPLE:
POPULATION: 39,302,665
ANNUAL GROWTH RATE: 0.25%
RELIGION: 99% Roman Catholic
LANGUAGE: Spanish. 17% speak Catalan.
EDUCATION: Attendance in primary school 100%; Literacy 97%
LIFE EXPECTANCY: Men 74; women 81 years.

GOVERNMENT: Parliamentary monarchy. Bicameral legislature. Prime minister is nominated by monarch subject to approval by Congress of Deputies. Members of Parliament are elected for 4 year term. Government budget: $75 billion of which 9% is for the military.

ECONOMY:
GNP: $498 billion
ANNUAL GROWTH RATE: -1%
PER CAPITA GNP $12,700
AVERAGE RATE OF INFLATION: 4.5%
WORK FORCE: Of the 14.8 million workers 51% are employed in services; 25% industry and commerce; 17% agriculture, and 7% construction. The unemployment rate is 23%.
OFFICIAL EXCHANGE RATE: 136 pesetas = US$
COST OF LIVING INDEX: 150

Return to Spain today after an absence of a few years and you are amazed at what has happened to the economy. Your first shock is that the four dollar cab ride into Madrid now costs $18.00. It's not the inflation that hurts it's the strength of the peseta coupled with the decline of the dollar. For a period in the early 80s Spain was considered, next to Portugal, the bargain spot of Europe. A night at the Ritz, one of the world's best hotels, was about $125; now it's close to $400.

From 1965 to 1974, Spain was the second fastest growing industrialized country in the world, averaging a real annual growth rate of 7%. The continued economic expansion led to improved income distribution and helped develop a large middle class similar to that of other European countries. From 1975 to the mid-80s, Spain had nine years of double digit inflation, an average growth rate of 1.6% in real terms, and an increase in unemployment from about 4.7% to 18.4%. In fact the decline in employment has been a long standing trend, and in 1984, fewer people were employed than in 1952.

Spain's economic outlook depends, first and foremost, on the impact of joining the European Economic Community (EC). Initially it appears to have been a good move. Accession to the EC has generated increased foreign investment but has also turned Spain's former trade surplus with the Community into a deficit. The current outlook is mixed. Inflation is down to 5.3% but unemployment remains the highest in western Europe, a major factor in considering this country as a worker's haven.

Ironically, despite the bulging number of Spaniards out of work, the country does need skilled workers in certain industries. Modern technology is making significant inroads in the chemical, cement, steel, and automobile industries and workers with high-tech experience can often find a place that can't be filled by a Spaniard. The automobile industry, for example, has expanded rapidly, largely because of a Ford factory in Valencia and General Motors facilities in the provinces of Zaragoza and Cadiz. These two firms and IBM are among Spain's largest exporters.

Americans wishing to work for a Spanish company must apply to a Spanish Embassy or consulate prior to entering Spain for a 90-day extendable visa. After the visa is granted the Spanish employer then requests a work and residence permit from the offices of the Provincial Commissioner of Police to the Civil Governor of the province where the work is to be carried out. There are five basic permits:

- Permit A—For seasonal and temporary workers. Issued for a maximum of nine months.
- Permit B—For work that is fixed in a geographic boundary. Maximum duration of a year.
- Permit C—Self employed workers. Maximum duration of five years.
- Permit D—Like permit B with a maximum of five years.
- Permit E—Any work in any area. Issued for five years.

Keep in mind that work permits are not easily granted for jobs which a Spanish citizen can fill.

The Spanish Embassy will offer no help in obtaining jobs but will send you more detailed data in one or more brochures: *Work Permits for Spain; Foreigners in Spain;* and *Settling in Spain.* (Prior to the decline of the dollar, Spain's Mediterranean coast, Costa del Sol, became a haven for American retirees, particularly retired teachers. Although there remains a large and active community the influx of new seniors has declined sharply.)

In your job search, in addition to making contact with specific potential U.S. employers, it is a good idea to write to the Spanish employment service querying about industries or companies in need of your talents. Write: Ministerio de Trabajo, Departamento de Extranjeros, Agustin Bethencourt 4, Madrid. To query about specific job openings write the Centro Nacional de Colocacion, General Pardinas 5, Madrid or to the Delegacion Provincial de Trabajo in the various provincial capitals.

There are also some good employment services in Madrid that handle positions throughout the country. The Human Resources Management, Jose Abascal 45, 28003 Madrid is an executive head hunter looking for Spanish speaking executives for a wide variety of corporations in Spain, Portugal and Latin America. Two American executive search agencies are Korn/Ferry Espano, Calle Felipe IV, Madrid 14 and Russell Reynolds Associates Inc., Castellana 51, Madrid.

The best agency for teachers of all subjects is English Educational Services, Alceda 30, 28014 Madrid. Many of the private schools throughout Spain rely on EES to interview, assess and recommend specific individuals who are then hired directly by the school. They cover all subject areas in both primary and secondary schools.

There is a constant demand for teachers of English. A few schools worth contacting: Centro de Idiomas Oxford, San Miguel 16, Zaragoza. A private institution that is on the constant look-out for qualified teachers of English as a foreign language. The Briam Instituto SA, Calle Tetuan 5, 28013 Madrid looks for teachers of any subject. The English American College at Calle Obispo Hurtado 21-1A, 18002 Granada is usually open to those willing to sign a one year contract to teach English at the college level. For short-term teaching assignments try the Mangold Institute, Marques de Sotelo 5, Pasaje Rex-2, 46002 Valencia or Relaciones Cultuales, Ferraj 82, 28008 Madrid. In all cases be sure to write your letter of inquiry in Spanish. There is also the opportunity to obtain seasonal work in Spain but again, Spaniards get first crack. The best seasonal industry for young Americans is tourism. Agriculture is greatly in demand by unskilled Spanish workers and impossible for Americans to crack. To work for a hotel legally you must write to them before you enter Spain and secure a permit. Names and address of tourist hotels are available from any local Spanish Information Office and the Spanish Embassy. Many young American secure illegal jobs simply by being at the right place at the right time—before the start of the tourist influx in mid-May. Best areas: Costa Brava and Costa Blanca.

The American Chamber of Commerce in Spain, Avenida Diagonal

447, 08036 Barcelona 36 or the Chamber's branch office, American Chamber of Commerce in Spain, Hotel Eurobuilding, Padre Damian 23, Madrid 16 can provide a listing of the more than 400 American companies located here. A long shot but one worth considering is a British firm in Spain. The British Chamber of Commerce at Plaza Santa Barbra, 10-1, 28004 Madrid publishes a list of British Firms in Spain and Spanish Firms with British Capital. It sells for L-30 (about $60.00).

Spain has an embassy at 2700 Fifteenth Street NW, Washington, DC 20009 (202/265-0190) with consulates in Boston, Chicago, New York, Houston, Los Angeles, Miami, New Orleans, San Francisco, and San Juan. The U.S. Embassy is located at Serrano 75, Madrid 6. Contacts:

Chemical:

Cyanamid Iberica S.A.
Aptdo 471
Madrid

Industrias Quimicas
 Serpiol S.A.
Jativa 15
Valencia 2

Automotive:

General Motors Espana S.A.
Poligono de Enterrios
Figuerucias

Garlock S.A., Stemco Div.
Torre del Pardals 23
Barcelona 26

Electronics:

Apple Computer Espana S.A.
Valencia 87-89, Aptdo 35148
Barcelona 08029

International Business
  Machines S.A.E.
Paseo de la Castellana 4
Madrid 1

Management Consultants:

Tandem/DDB,
 Campmany-Guasch, S.A.
Calatrava 25
Barcelona 25

Arthur D. Little, Inc.
Jose Abascal 57
Madrid 3

Food Products:

Ibarra Beatrice S.A.
Las Cruces S/N Dos Hermanos
Seville

Gallina Blanca S.A.
Campezo S/N
Madrid

Sweden

GEOGRAPHY:
AREA: 173,731 sq. mi.
CAPITAL: Stockholm
PRINCIPAL CITIES: Goteburg, Malmo, Uppsala
TERRAIN: Mostly flat or gently rolling lowlands; mountains in the west.

CLIMATE: Temperate in the south with cold, cloudy winters and cool, partly cloudy summers. Subarctic in the north.

PEOPLE:
POPULATION: 8,778,461
ANNUAL GROWTH RATE: 0.6%
RELIGION: 93.5% Lutheran; 1% Roman Catholic.
LANGUAGE: Swedish
EDUCATION: Attendance in primary school 100%; Literacy 99%
LIFE EXPECTANCY: Men 75; women 81 years.

GOVERNMENT: Constitutional monarchy. Unicameral legislature. Executive power vested in the Cabinet which is responsible to Parliament (Riksdag). Elections every three years. Governement budget: $60 billion; about 8% is for military.

ECONOMY:
GNP: $153.7 billion
ANNUAL GROWTH RATE: -2.7%
PER CAPITA GNP $17,600.
AVERAGE RATE OF INFLATION: 4.4%
WORK FORCE: Of the 4.4 million workers: community, social services 37%; mining and manufacturing 24%; commerce, hotels and restaurants 14%; banking and insurance 7%; communications 7%; construction 6%; agriculture, fishing & forestry 5%
OFFICIAL EXCHANGE RATE: 8.12 krona = US$
COST OF LIVING INDEX : 161

One of the growing mysteries is why does Sweden, with the highest standard of living in Europe if not the world, have such a high rate of alcoholism and suicide. The country has lived through two major wars this century and, as a neutral nation, emerged without a scar. Unemployment is extremely low and the many social benefits are extremely high.

As a result, people here live well, enjoy a bountiful, beautiful country with time for a variety of recreational activities.

This is an industrial country. Agriculture, forestry and fishing contribute less than 4% to the gross domestic product. And, as an industrial nation Sweden is heavily unionized. Of the 4.4 million people in the labor force, 3.8 million (88%) are unionized. Some 90% of all Swedish employees are represented by white or blue collar unions. About 213,000 aliens work in Sweden. Most of these are from other Nordic countries. However, of late, with the reduced emigration procedures of eastern block countries, Sweden has experienced an influx of semi-skilled and unskilled workers, who reap financial rewards for a brief period then return to their families having earned as much in a few months as they could in a year at home. As a result, the country's unemployment rate has almost doubled to 10% in 1994 excluding an equal number of unemployed youths under the age of 25.

Swedes pay high taxes. Income taxes range from 30 to 85%; the value added tax, VAT, on a store item can be as high as 25%. Under Swedish law all workers, regardless of nationality, share the same rights and benefits as Swedish nationals including most of Sweden's liberal social benefits. Swedish schools, for example, are free to foreigners. And, there are American schools in Stockholm operated at no cost to the student.

Yet despite the liberal social regulations this is one of Europe's most conservative countries in dress and manner. Male executives wear ties at all times and expect formality in business dealings. In other words you must make an appointment whenever you want to discuss any matter. Work for a company for years and you still feel it necessary to make a formal appointment with your boss. No informal meetings or after work casual drinks. Post-work drinking, and there is quite a bit of it, can be as formal as an office meeting.

During a business meeting come to the point quickly. Don't waste time with the banal it just irritates the natives. And, never ask about family matters. The Swedes make a point of separating business from pleasure. The late travel writer Temple Fielding once wrote that the Swedes are: "efficient and reliable. But they're inclined to a heaviness of spirit. They tend to plod rather than jump, to walk rather than run."

A U.S. citizen can visit for up to three months without a visa but to establish residency you must apply in advance of your visit. A work permit is issued by the National Labour Markets Board (AMS) in conjunction with the associations of employers and workers. A work permit is usually valid for a year and is renewed by the police not the AMS. Reside in the country for five years and you automatically qualify for Swedish citizenship.

It is not legal to obtain work in the country without a prior permit. Thus, for almost all skilled and professional jobs you must secure a firm job offer before coming to Sweden. This is a nation where craftsmanship is held in high regard and the local unions demand proof of professional status before they will agree to open their doors. If you obtain work for a Swedish company expect to speak the language. Although most Swedes are fluent in English (as well as several other languages) they do expect fluency in Swedish as well. On the other hand, Swedes are very gracious about speaking English, etc. to their visitors, unlike some European nations, France for example.

The Swedes welcome foreign workers to staff their hotels, harvest their crops and do many of the menial tasks that seem to attract so many eastern block workers. Summer work in a tourist hotel is obtainable to many young Americans who would like the opportunity to spend a few months in a beautiful country. Just pick up any travel guide listing hotels and send a resume. Legally these jobs require the same work permits as all other work but the government seems to look the other way with seasonal employees, much like the U.S. has for migrant workers in the past.

Swedes are not job-hoppers. Most begin work with a company expecting to spend their entire working career with the same organization. There are no private employment agencies in Sweden. Jobs are obtained through local government employment offices or the Labor Market Board (Arbetsmarknadsstyrelsen, S-171 99, Solna, Sweden). For jobs in the health field, the Swedish Board of Health and Welfare (FAP 1, 106 30 Stockholm) has data on needs and requirements. The best avenue, however, is through one of the near 300 existing American companies operating in Sweden. A list of American subsidiaries and affiliates in Sweden is available from the Commercial Counselor at the U.S. Embassy in Stockholm. When we received the list, Counselor Robert S. Connan told us "there are no jobs for Americans in Sweden or for Europeans or other Scandinavians for that matter." We assume he means most if not all jobs with American companies here are held by Swedes.

Sweden has an Embassy at 600 New Hampshire Avenue NW, Suite 1200, Washington, D.C. 20037 202/944-5600 with consulates in New York, Chicago, San Francisco and Los Angeles. The U.S. Embassy is located at Strandvagen 101, S-115 27, Stockholm. Specific data about Sweden is readily available through the Swedish Information Service, 825 Third Avenue, New York, NY 10022 212/751-5900. Contacts:

Manufacturing:

3M Svenska AB
S-191 89 Sollentuna 2

AMF (Skandinaviska) AB
S-56 30 Granna

Abex Industries AB
Sporregatan 13
S-213 77 Malmo

Chemical:

GAF (Norden) AB
S-121 08, Johanneshov

AB Houghton Produkter
5 Sturegatan 46 Fack 5146
102 43 Stockholm

Electronics:

Control Data AB
Vastmannagatan 40
Stockholm VA

Tandem Computers
S-171 48 Solna

Pulse Engineering, Inc.
Ankdammsgatan 21
Box # 1226
S-171 24 Solna

Food Products:

Kraft Foods Svenska AB
Sallerupesvagen 1
S-212 18 Malmo

AB Estrella
PO Box 2101
S-42402 Angered
Sweden

Management Consultants:

McKinsey & Co., Inc.
Hamngatan 13, 6th Floor
111 47 Stockholm
Sweden

AB Knight Consulterande
Ingenjorer
Kolvaten 7
S-65341 Karlstad
Sweden

Switzerland

GEOGRAPHY:
AREA: 15,941 sq. mi.
CAPITAL: Bern
PRINCIPAL CITIES: Zurich, Basel, Geneva, Lausanne
TERRAIN: Mostly mountainous with the Alps in the south and the Jura in the northwest. Central plateau consists of rolling hills, plains and large lakes.
CLIMATE: Temperate but varies with altitude. Cold, cloudy, rainy/

snowy winters. Humid summers with occasional showers.

PEOPLE:
POPULATION: 7,040,119
ANNUAL GROWTH RATE: 0.7%
RELIGION: 49% Roman Catholic; 48% Protestant.
LANGUAGE: Very mixed. 65% German; 18% French; 12% Italian.
EDUCATION: Attendance in primary school 100%; Literacy 100%
LIFE EXPECTANCY: Men 74; women 81 years.

GOVERNMENT: Federal republic. Bicameral legislature. Executive is
represented by a Federal Council of seven members. Elections every four
years. The country consists of 26 cantons (or states). Government budget:
$16.1 billion of which 19% goes to the military.

ECONOMY:
GNP: $149.1 billion
ANNUAL GROWTH RATE: -0.6%
PER CAPITA GNP: $21,300.
AVERAGE RATE OF INFLATION: 3.3%
WORK FORCE: 3.5 million employed. Services 59%; Industry and
commerce 38%; Agriculture 3%; Government 4%.
OFFICIAL EXCHANGE RATE: 1.7 Swiss franc = US$
COST OF LIVING INDEX: 171

Switzerland is one of the few Western European countries to have
emerged from World War II with its economic structure virtually
unimpaired. Although almost totally lacking in raw materials, Switzerland is a well developed manufacturing country. Its highly skilled labor
force forms the backbone of the economy, and the Swiss transportation
and communications networks are efficient.

Typical Swiss manufacturing and export products are those containing
high labor value, such as watches and precision instruments; special
quality products such as chemicals, cheese, and chocolate; and, items that
do not lend themselves to mass production methods such as generators
and turbines.

After World War II Switzerland experienced practically uninterrupted
economic growth for more than 25 years and now maintains one of the
highest standards of living in the world. The influx of foreign workers
—about 24% of the work force—did not hamper this prosperity but, by
easing chronic labor shortages, supported it.

This is a civilized country. The shops are efficiently run, banking is world famous. The Swiss have no tolerance for any but the hard working. Employment is booming; the unemployment rate (0.7%) is one of the lowest in the world. Crime is not looked upon kindly and a jail term (without bail) is handed out for offences which in America would hardly be considered an infraction. Trains run on time and it isn't uncommon to see a Swiss check his watch when a train passes not to see if the train is on time but to assure that his watch is accurate.

Business is taken very seriously. The Swiss are punctual, polite and extremely efficient. After hours business meetings are not common. Offices close at 5:00 P.M. and that hour is the end of the business day. No drinks at a local restaurant to seal the deal. Although there is some business type entertaining in private homes, it is not commonplace. (Several good brochures detailing Swiss business methods are issued by Chase Manhattan Bank, Chase Manhattan Plaza, New York, NY 10081 and Citibank, 399 Park Avenue, New York, NY 10022.) All those living here are subject to Swiss income taxes which range from 9 to 20 percent depending on income.

Because this is a small country the Swiss guard their citizenship and residency permits like a king his virgin daughter. Aliens wishing to work or reside in Switzerland face an almost impossible barrier. A numerical quota is set each year and applicants are approved on the basis of their skills and qualifications. The main criterion is whether the position is important to the overall Swiss economy not that of a specific employer.

If you are fortunate enough to secure the offer of a job with a Swiss company your future employer must submit your application, complete with reasons why your employment will benefit the national good, to the Aliens Police in the canton where you will be based. The cantonal authorities then decide each case on its merits. If approved you receive an assurance d'autorisation de sejour which, together with a valid passport and the passage of a medical examination allow you to work and live in the country.

The government also issues seasonal permits for those interested in working in the hotel and tourist trade, agriculture, au pairing, etc. The wages are low, the work is hard and a knowledge of German, French or Italian is essential so few Americans are found in these fields. You must have a permit before you enter the country.

Those Americans who do spend their summers engaged in hotel work report that they work longer hours than expected, are asked to do work not originally specified and have too little time to enjoy the promised benefits. However, on the positive side, the Swiss tourist industry is one of the best paying in Europe and many students have found that they have been able to save most of their wages and have enjoyed considerable "social" benefits. The average net pay (after deductions for taxes and accommodations during the summer of 1990 ranged between SFr 1200 ($2,040) and SFr 1700 ($2,890). Those interested in working in the Swiss hotel industry can obtain data plus a listing of members from the Swiss Hotel Association, Monbijourstrasse 130, Bern.

Even those interested in self-employment must have a permit. And again you must receive cantonal permission. U.S. doctors must pass a Swiss state examination. If you want to practice law go elsewhere. Only Swiss citizens can become lawyers. The largest employer of Americans (some 12,000) are the various UN agencies in Geneva.

Qualified nurses with a working knowledge of French or German can apply to work in Swiss hospitals through the Swiss Employment Office for Qualified Foreign Hospital Personnel (Schweizerische Vermittlungsstelle fur Spitalpersonal, Weinbergstrasse 29, CH-8006 Zurich.) For those interested in management and professional appointments the employment agency Personal Sigma AG (Gotthardstr 14, 6300 Zug) is worth contacting. Other agencies worthy of contact: CBA Computer Brainware Advisors (Beethovenstr. 47, 8039 Zurich), Mobility Executive Services (Dersbachstr. 69, 6330 Cham, Zurich).

For banking and accountancy jobs your best shot is through an American company. However, it must be hard explaining why an American working for a Swiss bank is of any benefit to the Swiss national interest.

Teachers should contact the American School in Switzerland (CH-6926, Lugano Montagnola) or the American International School (8802 Kilchberg, Zurich). A listing of American firms doing business in Switzerland is available from the Swiss American Chamber of Commerce (Talacker 4, 8001 Zurich.)

Switzerland has an embassy at 2900 Cathedral Avenue N.W, Washington, DC 20008 202/745-7900 with consulates in Atlanta, Chicago, Houston, Los Angeles, New York and San Francisco. The U.S. Embassy is located at 93/95 Jubilaeumsstrasse, 3005 Bern. Contacts:

Financial:

American Express Bank
Bahnhofstr. 20
CH-8022 Zurich

Bank of America
40 Rue du Marche
P.O. Box # 56
CH-1211 Geneva 3

Bankers Trust AG
Dreikonigstr. 6
CH-8022 Zurich

Chase Manhattan Bank N A
63 Rue du Rhone
1204 Geneva

Accountants:

Coopers & Lybrand AG
St. Jakobs-Strasse 25
LH-4052 Basel

Deloitte Haskins Sells
Zolkikerstr. 228
8008 Zurich

Price Waterhouse & Co.
Borenstr/26
8022 Zurich

Electronics:

Servo Corp of America
Chemin du Cap 1-3
1006 Lausanne

TRW Intl. S. A.
Rue de Lyon 75
CH-1211 Geneva 13

Management Consultants:

Kepner-Tregoe S.A.
Rue de la Porcelaine 13
Case Postal 90
CH-1260 Nyon

Spencer Stuart Intl. S.A.
Breitingerstr. 35
8002 Zurich

Executive Recruiting:

Russell Reynolds Assoc. Inc.
Rue du Marche 40
1204 Geneva

Turkey

GEOGRAPHY:
AREA: 296,000 sq. mi.
CAPITAL: Ankara
PRINCIPAL CITIES: Istanbul, Izmir, Adana
TERRAIN: Narrow coastal plain surrounds Anatolia; an inland plateau
which becomes increasingly rugged as it progresses eastward.
CLIMATE: Temperate. Hot and dry summers with mild, wet winters.
Harsher in the interior.

PEOPLE:
POPULATION: 62,153,898
ANNUAL GROWTH RATE: 2.02%
RELIGION: 98% Muslim; 2% Christian and Jewish
LANGUAGE: Turkish
EDUCATION: Attendance in primary school 95%; Literacy 89%
LIFE EXPECTANCY: Men 68; women 73 years.

GOVERNMENT: Republican parliamentary democracy. Unicameral parliament with elections held every five years. Government budget: $15.5 billion with 13% devoted to the military.

ECONOMY:
GDP: $312.4 billion
ANNUAL GROWTH RATE: 7.3%
PER CAPITA GDP : $5,100.
AVERAGE RATE OF INFLATION: 65%
WORK FORCE: Of the 18.7 million employed, 58% are in agriculture; 29% in services; and, 21% in commerce. The unemployment rate is about 12.2%.
OFFICIAL EXCHANGE RATE: 15.196 Turkish lire (TL) = US$
COST OF LIVING INDEX: 103

Turkey is one of those countries that truly bridges both the new and old world. A strong Arab country that has its feet deep in Oriental ways but is still strongly influenced by Europe. Its strategic geo-position makes it one of the most important western allies. Its armed forces are the second largest in NATO.

Although the economy is developing structurally, the agricultural sector remains significant, producing cotton, tobacco, grains, fruits, and vegetables. More than half the labor force are farmers. This sector contributes more than one-fifth of the gross domestic product. In addition, a significant portion of industry is involved in processing agricultural products. An important feature of the Turkish economy is the public sector, in which state-owned or controlled enterprises account for about half of all aggregate industry production.

In 1987, Turkey applied for full membership in the European Economic Community. Its application is being reviewed by the EEC, but an early accession to the community is not expected since the EEC has various internal problems (i.e. Common Agricultural Policy, unemployment, payments to its less developed members, etc.) which

Turkey's membership would only exacerbate. Furthermore, Turkey's GNP is less than half the poorest EEC member. However, the EEC considers Turkey an "associate" and continues to draw it toward the Western world.

Although the economic reforms launched in 1980 continue to bring a steady growth, jobs in Turkey are almost always limited to American companies located here. Those with top level management skill, high tech personnel, medical personnel and teachers may find work with non-U.S. companies but it isn't easy. The pay scale is less than its European neighbors and Turks with similar skills will always be chosen over foreigners. For nonskilled jobs you're in the wrong country. Both Western and Eastern Europe are flooded with unskilled Turks who are seeking jobs unavailable in their homeland.

Public health standards in the larger cities approach those in the U.S. but care must be taken, especially in rural areas. Tap water is generally potable in Istanbul. Turkish law requires that at least one pharmacy be open in a neighborhood at all times. Note also that Turkey is subject to severe earthquakes, especially along the major river valleys in the west.

There are jobs for skilled workers, particularly during the start-up of a new foreign operation. Permission must be acquired from the General Directorate of Foreign Investment (GBFI) for a work permit beyond a six month period. Contact: Basbakanlik; Hazine Mustesarligi; Yabanci Sermaye Genel Mudurlugu; Eskisehir Karayolu Balgat-Ankara, Turkey.

As a rule there are no problems for U.S. administrative or technical personnel. However, some professions such as medical personnel, lawyers, etc. may find that the government may impose the "Turkish nationality requirement" law and restrict a work permit. Educators interested in teaching in Turkey may receive additional data and potential job openings from the Ministry of Education in Ankara.

An up to date listing of U.S. companies is available from the American Chamber of Commerce in Turkey, c/o Pfizer Ilaclari A.S. Ortakoy, Istanbul. Turkey has an embassy at 1606 23rd Street NW, Washington, DC 20008 (202/387-3200) with consulates in Chicago, Los Angeles, New York, and Houston. The U.S. Embassy is located at 110 Ataturk Blvd., Ankara. Contacts:

Construction:

Gizbill Consulting Engineers
Necatibey Caddesi
Sezenier Sokak 2/21, Yenishir
Ankara

Sanitayesi
Soguksu, Cekmece
Istanbul

Pharmaceuticals:

Wyeth Laboratuarier A.S.
P.K. 67, Aksaray
Merkez Efendi
Yapi Yolu 5, Topkapi
Istanbul

Abbott Labs C.A.
Firin Sakak 61, Bomonti
Istanbul

Chemicals:

Cyanamid Overseas Corp.
Cumhuriyet Caddesi 295/9
Harbiye
Istanbul

UC Turkey
Inonu Caddesi 22
Akar Palas Kat 6, Ayazpasa
Istanbul

Petroleum:

Turkish Gulf Oil Co.
Tunali Hilmi Caddesi 112/2
Havaklidere
Ankara

Mobil Companies in Turkey
Pegasus Evl
Cumhuriyet Caddesi 26
Harbiye, P.K. 660
Istanbul

Tobacco:

British-American Tobacco Co.
Guney Mahalesi, 1140 Sakak
Zeytinlik,
Izmir

American Tobacco Co.
of the Orient
Pasta Kutusu 222
Izmir

United Kingdom

GEOGRAPHY:
AREA: 94,251 sq. mi.
CAPITAL: London
PRINCIPAL CITIES: Birmingham, Glasgow, Liverpool, Manchester
TERRAIN: Mostly rugged hills and low mountains; level to rolling
plains in east and southeast.
CLIMATE: Temperate. Subject to frequent changes but to few extremes
in temperature.

PEOPLE:
POPULATION: 58,135,110
ANNUAL GROWTH RATE: 0.28%
RELIGION: 47% Anglican; 10% Roman Catholic; 4% Presbyterian
LANGUAGE: English (About 26% of Wales speak Welsh).
EDUCATION: Attendance in primary school 100%; Literacy 99%.
LIFE EXPECTANCY: Men 73; women 79 years.

GOVERNMENT: Constitutional monarchy. The monarch is the head of
state; the prime minister, head of government. Bicameral parliament with
elections held at the discretion of the prime minister but before the end
of a five year electoral mandate. Government budget: $320.3 billion of
which 16% is spent on the military.

ECONOMY: GNP: $980.2 billion
ANNUAL GROWTH RATE: 2.1%
PER CAPITA GNP: $16,900.
AVERAGE RATE OF INFLATION: 2.6%
WORK FORCE: Of the 28.12 million employed, 63% were employed in
services; 26% in manufacturing and engineering, 5% in construction; 5%
in mining and energy; and, 2% in agriculture. The unemployment rate is
about 10.3%.
OFFICIAL EXCHANGE RATE: .66 pounds = US$
COST OF LIVING INDEX: 142

England has always been one of the most popular countries both for
American tourists and those seeking work abroad. No wonder then that
almost 1,500 American multinational corporations have a base in
England alone. Obviously a common language and a familiar cultural
tradition means a great deal when hauling one's family to a distant land.
Assimilation into British life is much easier for most Americans than in
other foreign countries. The schools are comparable to those in the states,
shopping for a home or tonight's dinner is not unlike an American
experience. However, the quality of both the food and an English
education is quite subjective and the subject of another book.

Suffice that working in the United Kingdom can be a valuable
experience if you're fortunate enough to locate the right job. Salaries are
considerably lower than those in America for comparable jobs with
prices at a par or higher depending on the value of the dollar vs the
pound. You often wonder how the Englishman can survive on his salary.
The fact that he may own but one good suit and entertain far less than his

American counterpart is part of the answer. Basically, the Englishman has always managed to "muddle through."

Although economic growth increased markedly in the 25 years following the end of World War II, the rate of growth was much slower than most other European countries. Between 1950 and 1970, the United Kingdom dropped from having the highest per capita income in Europe to being ahead of only Ireland and Italy among the countries that became the EC-Nine when the United Kingdom joined in 1973. During the 1970s the economic growth slowed even more, as did the growth rates of most industrial countries. Nevertheless, the United Kingdom remains one of the largest European economies, and one of the world's great trading powers. As an international financial center London is unrivaled.

The unemployment rate, which stood at just over 5% in 1979, grew to more than 13% in 1986. By about 1990 it had declined to about 7%. British industry is a mixture of publicly and privately owned firms. Several important industries are publicly owned—steel, railroads, coal mining, shipbuilding, and certain utilities. However, since 1979 the British Government has sold off a number of companies as part of its privatization program.

In 1994, the United Kingdom had an employed work force of 29 million plus 3 million self employed. The major change in the British labor market in the 1990s has been the growth of female employment, particularly part-time. Such employment grew by more than a million between 1983 and 1990, and self employment for women grew by a further 250,000. In contrast, total male employment increased by just 2,000 during the same period. Of the new jobs taken by women, 650,000 involved part-time work, and the majority were created in the service industry. Although women make up 46% of the workforce, they are predominantly employed in industries with a low level of trade union activity.

Like most other foreign countries, the best opportunities for work are with one of the 1,500 U.S. companies located here. Of course if you have a unique skill not readily available in England you stand a good chance to work for an English concern. One of the better agencies that can provide solid advice on jobs in the UK as well as other foreign countries is Employment Conditions Abroad Ltd., Anchor House, 15 Britten Road, London SW3 3TY.

Other agencies worth contacting:

- Angel ASB International Recruitment 70-71 New Bond Street, London W1Y 9DE (Specializes in accountancy, banking, sales, marketing, media, teaching and lecturing).

- Campbell Brich Executive Recruitment, Parr House, 52 Broadway, Bracknell, Berks. RG12 1AG (Specializes in electronics, engineering, technical and sales support, technology.)

- Eagle Recruitment, Eagle Place, 210-212, Piccadilly, London W1V 9LD (Specializes in multilingual management, secretarial and technical.)

- Executive Search International Ltd., 8A Symons Street, Sloan Square, London SW3 2TJ (Specializes in senior executive and middle management positions worldwide.)

- J. Watson Sanderson Ltd., Moorings House, Heathfield Road, Woking, Surrey GU22 7JG (Specializes in civil and chemical engineering, building and building service, mining, petrochemical, soil mechanics.)

- ASA International, 69 St. Vincent Street, Glasgow G2 5JU. (Specializes in accountancy and financial management.)

For a listing of more than 300 recruitment agencies and search consultants write to the Centre for Professional Employment Counseling, Sundrige Park Management Centre, Plaistow Lane, Bromley BR1 3JW. Ask for their CEPEC Recruitment Guide. Additional information on job availability can be obtained from the Federation of Recruitment and Employment Services, Ltd., 10 Belgrave Square, London, SW1X 8PH.

There are also a few American executive search firms in England including: Boyden Intl. Ltd., 148 Buckingham Palace Road, London SW1W 9TR., and Korn/Ferry Intl. Ltd., Norfolk House, 31 St. James Square, London SW1Y 4JL. More specific fields:

Banking:

Barclays Bank Pic.
54 Lombard Street
London EC3A 3AH.

Lloyds Bank Pic.
71 Lombard Street
London EC3P 3BS

Midland Bank Plc.
110-114 Cannon St.
London EC4N 6AA

Accounting:

Arthur Anderson & Co.
Surrey St.
London WC2R 2PS

Coopers & Lybrand
Plumtree Court
London EC4A 4HT

Peat Marwick McLintock
1 Puddle Dock
London EC4V 3PD

Computers:

Abraxas Computer Services
Ltd.
357 Euston Road
London NW1 3AL

Benny Electronics Ltd.
1A Telford Road
Ferndown Industry Estate
Wimborne, Dorset BH21 7QN

James Duncan & Associates
8 St. John's Road
Tunbridge Wells
Kent TN4 9NP

Medicine:

HCA International Ltd.
49 Wigmore St.
London W1H 9LE

International Hospitals Group
Stoke Park
Stoke Pages
Slough, Berkshire SL2 4HS

Oil & Gas:

Technical Engineering
Administration & Management
  Services
Macklin Avenue
Cowpen Lane Industrial Estate
Billingham,
Cleveland TS23 4BZ

Engineering:

W.S. Atkins Group
  Consultants
Woodcote Grove
Ashley Road
Epsom, Surrey KT18 5BW

Kennedy & Donkin
Westbrook Mills
Godalming, Surrey GU7 2AZ

Inter Engineering Ltd.
22/24 Buckingham Palace Road
London W8 5EH

Teaching:

British Council
65 Davis Street
London W1Y 2AA

Centre for British Teachers
Quality House
Quality Court
Chancery Lane
London WC2A 1HP

English Teaching Information
 Center
10 Spring Gardens
London SW1A 2BN

Because of several of new school openings in England there has been an increased demand for teachers at all levels. If you're a qualified teacher send your resume to the following:

- The American School in London
  2-8 Loudon Road
  London NW8 ONP
  (This is the oldest American school in England).

- Center Academy
  Napier Hall
  Hide Place
  Vincent Sq., London SW1P 4NJ
  (Specializes in under achievers).

- Marymount School
  George Road
  Kingston-upon-Thames
  Surrey KT2 7PE

- TASIS England
  Coldharbour Lane
  Thorpe
  Surrey KT2 7PE

- The American College in London
  100 Marleybone Land
  London W1M 5FP

- New England College
  Arundel
  West Sussex BN18 0DA

- Schiller University
  51 Waterloo Road
  London SE1 8TX

- U.S. International University
  The Avenue
  Bushey, Herts WD2 2LN

Of course the many U.S. firms are probably your best opportunity to work in the UK. A listing of firms as well as more specific data about possible job openings may be obtained from the American Chamber of Commerce (United Kingdom), 75 Brook Street, London W1Y 2EB.

The United Kingdom has an embassy at 3100 Massachusetts Avenue NW, Washington, DC 20008 (202/462-1340) with consulates in Atlanta, Boston, Chicago, Cleveland, Dallas, Detroit, Houston, Los Angeles, New York, Philadelphia, St. Louis, San Francisco, San Juan, and Seattle. The U.S. Embassy is located at 24/31 Grosvenor Square, London W1A 1AE. Contacts:

Pharmaceuticals:

Abbott Laboratories Ltd.
Queenborough
Kent ME11 5EL

Pharmax Ltd.
5 Bourne Road, Bexley
Kent DA5 1NX

Manufacturing:

Allis-Chalmers Great Britain
  Ltd.
Allis-Chalmers House
Girling Way
Great Southwest Road
Bedford Feltham
Middlesex TW1 40PH

Cincinnati Milacron Ltd.
P.O. Box # 505
Birmingham B4 0QU

Ford Motor Co.
Eagleway, Brentwood
Essex CM13 3BW

Electronics:

AMI Microsystems
Princes House, Princes Street
Swindon SN1 2HU

Apple Computer (UK) Ltd.
Eastman Way, Helem
Hempstead Herts HP2 7HQ

IBM United Kingdom Holdings
  Ltd.
North Harbour
Portsmouth, Hants PO6 3A4

Engineering:

CDI Techniscope Ltd.
Hanover House 73/74
High Holborn
London WC1V 6LS

Ingersoll Engineers Inc.
Bourton Hall
Bourton on Dunsmore
Rugby
Warwickshire DV23 9SD.

Kellogg Co. (UK) Ltd.
Stretford
Manchester M17 1QH

Kraft Foods Ltd.
St. George's House
Bay Hill Road
Cheltenham
Gloucester GL20 8NA

Food:

H.J. Heinz Co. Ltd.
Hayes Park
Hayes
Middlesex W34 8AL

RUSSIA AND THE NIS

Prior to the collapse of the Communist state, the only jobs available for non-Soviet citizens were limited to foreign governments or companies invited by the state. Since 1990, the Russian Federation and the fourteen former soviet republics—known today as the Newly Independent States or the NIS—are looking for Western dollars. The welcome mat is out for businesses to establish a working partnership with an NIS counterpart. In the first 36 months following the death of Communism, more than 10,000 joint ventures or other investments were initiated. Today that number has increased significantly.

For the first time since the Revolution it is possible for Americans to find work in the private sector. Yes, there are jobs for the businessperson, technician, medical professional, or teacher in the NIS. They are not easy to come by, but there are jobs. Don't travel to one of the new independent states and expect to see a local newspaper soliciting your talents, however. The vast majority of openings are with American or other non-NIS businesses looking for experienced people. Also, keep in mind that these new states are experiencing their own revolution; a revolution with capitalism. Making the adjustment to self-rule and learning an entirely new way of life is causing turmoil in many regions. This is not a stable area. Read your daily paper and you can't avoid noting some of the problems.

If you're serious about working in either Russia or any of the NIS states it is best to study the economic and social conditions both before either applying for a position and before accepting. Remember that you'll need a visa to work or visit and that conditions in these states is akin to experiencing a Third World lifestyle.

The largest and most populated of the new states is Russia itself. Let's examine mother Russia and a few of the NIS where job openings for Americans may exist:

Russia

GEOGRAPHY:
AREA: 26,995,800 sq. km.
CAPITAL: Moscow
PRINCIPAL CITIES: St. Petersburg, Vladivostok, Kaliningrad
TERRAIN: Broad plain with low hills west of the Urals; vast coniferous forest and tundra in Siberia; uplands and mountains along the southern border regions.
CLIMATE: Ranges from steppes in the south through humid continental Eastern Russia; subarctic in Siberia to tundra climate of the polar north; winters vary from cool along the Black Sea to frigid in Siberia; summers vary from warm in the steppes to cool along the Arctic coast.

PEOPLE:
POPULATION: 150,000,000
ANNUAL GROWTH RATE: 0.2%
RELIGION: Varies from Russian Orthodox and Muslim to other religions depending upon region.
LANGUAGE: Mostly Russian with other local languages and dialects depending upon location.
EDUCATION: Attendance in primary school 100%; Literacy 99%.
LIFE EXPECTANCY: Men 64; women 74 years.

GOVERNMENT: Under the new constitution of 1991, the federation is headed by the president or chief of state. In December of 1991, the Commonwealth of Independent States was established to operate as a working union composed of Russia and many of the former soviets. The president of Russia is elected by the people; the next election is scheduled for 1996. There is also an elected bicameral federal assembly representing Russia's 89 territorial units.

ECONOMY:
GNP: $776 billion
ANNUAL GROWTH RATE: -12%
PER CAPITA INCOME: $5,190.
AVERAGE RATE OF INFLATION: 21% per month (average 1993)
WORK FORCE: Of the 78 million employed 84% are employed in production and economic services; 16% are employed by the government. The unemployment rate is about 2%.
OFFICIAL EXCHANGE RATE: Approximately 5,000 rubles = US$
COST OF LIVING INDEX: 156.

Yes, there are jobs in Russia but only for those who can offer a trade or skills not available in the motherland. Under President Yeltsin, the country is doing its best to emulate capitalism and not doing a good job of it. In the areas of banking and finance, food and agriculture, computer technology, chemical and petroleum technology, and business management they need all the help they can get.

As of mid-1995, Russia had approximately 2,500 licensed commercial banks and 600 investment funds with about 40 million shareholders. Since the fall of Communism, more than 15,000 medium sized and large businesses have been privatized. By the beginning of 1994, roughly 35% of Russia's medium and large state enterprises had been auctioned while the number of private farms in Russia increased to about 170,000 representing about 6% of the agricultural land. More than 95% of Russia's shops are not privately owned. According to research by Boston Consulting Group, a management consultancy, Russia now has 200 supermarkets on the western model, with an average annual turnover of between $2 and $5 million. Not a great number when you consider the size of the country, but at the turn of the decade there were none at all.

Yet owning a business and understanding how to operate it successfully in a growing world market are two different matters. Thus, the need for experienced consultants and experienced personnel. For most individuals interested in working here the best bet is to link up with one of the many international corporations hired to assist this resource-rich giant get on track.

Life in Russia is a far cry from a western European country. Although many now speak English, it is hardly the language of choice. Once outside the major cities you could easily be the first American seen by the locals. Prices are high and there is still a scarcity of many of life's basic essentials. Contacts:

Russian Agency for
 International Cooperation and
 Development
Vozdvizhenka 18
Moscow

Moscow Chamber of Commerce
Ulitsa Chexoba 13
Moscow

Ukraine

GEOGRAPHY:
AREA: 16,995,800 sq. km.
CAPTIAL: Kiev
PRINCIPAL CITIES: Simferopol, Odessa, Dnipropetrovs'k, L'viv.
TERRAIN: Fertile plains (steppes) and plateaus with some mountains in the west and extreme south.
CLIMATE: Temperate continental. Winters vary from cool along the Black Sea to cold further inland. Summers are warm across the greater part of the country; hot in the south.

PEOPLE:
POPULATION: 51,900,000
ANNUAL GROWTH RATE: 0.05%
RELIGION: Ukrainian Orthodox primarily. Some Catholic, Protestant and Jewish.
LANGUAGE: Ukrainian, Russian, Romanian with other local languages and dialects depending upon location.
EDUCATION: Attendance in primary school 100%; Literacy 99.9%.
LIFE EXPECTANCY: Men 65; women 75 years.

GOVERNMENT: Currently a republic under a pre-independence constitution. The president is head of state with the prime minister serving as head of the government. A unicameral legislative branch representing 24 autonomous republics called "*oblasti*." Political parties are legal and are active.

ECOMONY:
GNP: $205 billion (est)
ANNUAL GROWH RATE: -6%
PER CAPITA INCOME: $3,960.
AVERAGE RATE OF INFLATION: 45% per month (average 1993)
WORK FORCE: The vast majority of employed workers are involved in agriculture, which accounts for a quarter of the country's GNP. Industrial workers are employed in the coal, electric power, machinery, mining, chemical, and food processing businesses. The unemployment rate is less than 1%.
OFFICIAL EXCHANGE RATE: The hryvnya is the current legal tender. Exchange rate is in flux.
COST OF LIVING INDEX: NA.

After Russia, the Ukrainian republic is far and away the most important economic component of the former Soviet Union producing three times the output of the next ranking republic. In 1992 the Ukrainian government liberalized most prices and erected a legal framework for privatizing state enterprises while retaining many central economic controls and continuing subsidies to state production enterprises. One of the republic's prime problems, however, is oil. In the past it received its vital energy supply from the great Soviet oil fields. Those fields are now held and controlled by Russia who controls the prices and quantities of oil and gas shipped to the Ukraine. Needless to say this breeds bad blood between neighbors.

There are some Western companies and consulting groups trying to assist the Ukrainian government adapt to a market economy. An increasing number of Ukrainians are developing small, private businesses and exploiting opportunities in non-official markets. Although there are some who speak English, a knowledge of either Russian or Ukrainian is essential if you plan to work here. Contact:

U.S. & Foreign Commercial Service—Ukraine
7 Kudriavsky Uzviz
2nd Floor
Kiev 252053

Uzbekistan

GEOGRAPHY:
AREA: 447,400 sq. km.
CAPITAL: Tashkent
PRINCIPAL CITIES: Bukhoro, Nukus, Oarshi, Termiz
TERRAIN: Mostly flat-to-rolling sandy desert with dunes, broad, flat intensely irrigated river valleys along course of Amu Darya and Sidaryo Rivers. Mountains in the east.
CLIMATE: Mostly mid-latitude desert. Long, hot summers, mild winters, semi-arid grassland in the east.

PEOPLE:
POPULATION: 22,610,000
ANNUAL GROWTH RATE: 2.13%
RELIGION: Muslim 88% (mostly Sunni), Eastern Orthodox 9%.
LANGUAGE: Uzbek 74%, Russian 14%, Tajik 4%.
EDUCATION: Attendance in primary school 100%; Literacy 99.9%.
LIFE EXPECTANCY: Men 67; women 72 years.

GOVERNMENT: The Republic of Uzbekistan adopted a new constitution in December, 1992. Under the constitution, the president is head of state with the prime minister serving as head of the government. A unicameral legislative branch representing 12 autonomous divisions. Political parties are legal and are active with the Communist Party holding the largest number of seats in the government.

ECONOMY:
GNP: $54 billion (est)
ANNUAL GROWTH RATE: -3%
PER CAPITA INCOME: $2,430.
AVERAGE RATE OF INFLATION: 18% per month (average 1993)
WORK FORCE: Of the 8.2 million workers, 43% are employed in agriculture and forestry, 22% in industry and construction and 35% in government and miscellaneous jobs. The unemployment rate is less than 1%.
OFFICIAL EXCHANGE RATE: The som is the current legal tender. Exchange rate is in flux.
COST OF LIVING INDEX: NA

This landlocked country is one of the poorest states of the former

Soviet Union with 60% of its population living in overpopulated rural areas. Nevertheless, Uzbekistan is the world's third largest cotton exporter, a major producer of gold and natural gas and a regionally significant producer of chemicals and machinery. Since independence, the government has sought to prop up the Soviet-style command economy with subsidies and tight controls on prices and production. With an economic uncertainty the government has recently increased its cooperation with international financial institutions, announced an acceleration of privatization, and stepped up efforts to attract foreign investors. Yet full-fledged market reform is still in the future.

Employment opportunities here are primarily as a consultant to the growing small business owners or with existing agricultural producers. Contact with a western company doing business here is a necessity as is a knowledge of the local language. English is not spoken here! For more date and current conditions write to the Uzbekistan Mission, 122 West 27th Street, 8th Floor, New York, NY 10001, 202/675-3922.

Tajikistan

GEOGRAPHY:
AREA: 143,000 sq. km.
CAPITAL: Dushanbe
PRINCIPAL CITIES: Kulob, Khorugh, Murghob.
TERRAIN: Pamir and Alay Mountains dominate the landscape; western Fergana Valley in north, Kofarnihon and Vakhsh Valleys in southwest.
CLIMATE: Mid-latitude continental. Hot summers, mild winters.

PEOPLE:
POPULATIONS: 6,000,000
ANNUAL GROWTH RATE: 2.67%
RELIGION: Muslim 80% (mostly Sunnis), Shi'a Muslim 5%.
LANGUAGE: Tajik.
EDUCATION: Attendance in primary school 100%; Literacy 99.9%.
LIFE EXPECTANCY: Men 67; women 72 years.

GOVERNMENT: The Republic of Tajikistan adopted a new constitution in 1994. Under the constitution, the president is head of state and chairman of the national assembly with the prime minister serving as head of the government. A unicameral legislative branch represents 2 autonomous divisions. Political parties are legal and are active with the

Communist Party holding the largest number of seats in the government.

ECOMONY:
GNP: $7 billion (est)
ANNUAL GROWTH RATE: -21%
PER CAPITA INCOME: $1,180.
AVERAGE RATE OF INFLATION: 38% per month (average 1993)
OFFICIAL EXCHANGE RATE: The som is the current legal tender.
Exchange rate is in flux.
COST OF LIVING INDEX: NA.

Tajikistan has the lowest per capita GDP in the former USSR, the highest rate of population growth, and the lowest standard of living. Tajikistan's economy was severely disrupted with the breakup of the Soviet economy, which provided guaranteed trade relations and heavy subsidies. Close to half the work force is involved in some form of agriculture and nearly all petroleum products must be imported. Are there jobs here? Yes, but for non-Tajikistanies they are limited to the consulting field. Best bet, if you want to experience a third-world nation in the heart of central Asia, is to work for one of the few Western companies assisting in the re-building of the country's economy. This means in banking, industrial development, management, and land development.

For an up-to-date picture of jobs and living conditions write to the American Embassy, 105A Rudaki Prospecy, Dushanbe, Tajikstan.

Georgia

GEOGRAPHY:
AREA: 69,700 sq. km.
CAPITAL: T'Bilisi
PRINCIPAL CITIES: Sokhumi, K'ut'aisi, Rust'avi.
TERRAIN: Largely mountainous with the Great Caucasus Mountains in the north and the Lesser Caucasus Mountains in the south.
CLIMATE: Warm and pleasant; Mediterranean-like on the Black Sea.

PEOPLE:
POPULATION: 6,700,000
ANNUAL GROWTH RATE: 0.81%

RELIGION: Greek Orthodox 65%, Russian Orthodox 10%, Muslim 11%.
LANGUAGE: Georgian
EDUCATION: Attendance in primary school 100%; Literacy 99.9%.
LIFE EXPECTANCY: Men 69; women 77 years.

GOVERNMENT: The Republic of Georgia is trying to adopt a new constitution but internal strife and uncertainty has slowed the effort. At present the country is government by the chief of state, Eduard Shevardnadze, who was elected in 1992 by 95% of the electorate.

ECONOMY:
GNP: $7.8 billion (est)
ANNUAL GROWTH RATE: -35%
PER CAPITA INCOME: $1,390.
AVERAGE RATE OF INFLATION: 40% per month (average 1993)
WORK FORCE: Of the 2.76 million workers, 31% are in industry and construction, 25% are employed in agriculture and forestry. The unemployment rate is listed officially at less than 5%, but is actually close to 20%.
OFFICIAL EXCHANGE RATE: The lari is the current legal tender. Exchange rate is in flux.
COST OF LIVING INDEX: NA.

Georgia, birthplace of Joseph Stalin and the site of the famed Yalta Conference, used to be Russia's playground. The beaches and resort towns on the Black Sea were the equivalent of Russia's Riviera. Today the young nation is besieged by inter-ethnic strife in its Abkhazian and South Ossetian enclaves. The country's economy has traditionally revolved around Black Sea Tourism; cultivation of citrus fruits, tea, and grapes; mining of manganese and copper. With the inner ethnic turmoil, coupled with the painful transformation from Communism to a market economy, the nation's industry and agriculture were badly hurt. Tourism has all but ceased. Georgia is also suffering from an acute energy crisis, as it is having problems paying for even minimal imports. The country is betting that re-establishing trade ties with Russia and developing international transportation through the Black Sea ports will bring the economy back. Of course, much depends on a solution to the internal ethnic problems.

As a result of the internal strife and economic uncertainty, job opportunities are limited. Western organizations and companies have made inroads here and there are employment opportunities with those groups attempting to assist the nation's economic and industrial re-birth. In time tourism will also provide jobs. For a list of Western companies located in Georgia or a clearer, up-to-the-minute picture of job opportunities write to the Georgian Chamber or Commerce and Industry, I. Chavchavadze Prospect 1, Tbilisi, GEORGIA.

Estonia

GEOGRAPHY:
AREA: 45,100 sq. km.
CAPITAL: Tallinn
PRINCIPAL CITIES: Vohma, Tartu, Valga, Parnu
TERRAIN: Marshy lowlands.
CLIMATE: Maritime, wet, moderate winters, cool summers.

PEOPLE:
POPULATION: 1,620,000
ANNUAL GROWTH RATE: 0.52%
RELIGION: Lutheran
LANGUAGE: Estonian
EDUCATION: Attendance in primary school 100%; Literacy 99.9%.
LIFE EXPECTANCY: Men 65; women 75 years.

GOVERNMENT: The Republic of Estonia adopted its new constitution in 1992. It has a unicameral legislature. The elected president is chief of state while the prime minister is head of the government. Political parties are legal and extremely active.

ECONOMY:
GDP: $8.8 billion (est)
ANNUAL GROWTH RATE: -5%
PER CAPITA INCOME: $5,480.
AVERAGE RATE OF INFLATION: 2.6% per mont (average 1993)
WORK FORCE: Of the 750,000 million workers, 42% are involved in industry and construction, 20% are employed in agriculture and forestry. The unemployment rate is about 3.5%.
OFFICIAL EXCHANGE RATE: The kroon is closely tied to the German Deutschmark with a fixed rate of 8 to 1.
COST OF LIVING INDEX: NA.

Bolstered by a widespread national desire to reintegrate into Western Europe, the Estonian government has pursued a program of market reforms and rough stabilization measures, which is rapidly transforming the economy. Two years after independence, and one year after the introduction of the kroon, Estonians are beginning to reap tangible benefits. Inflation is much lower than for other members of the federation, production declines have reversed and living standards are on the upswing.

The private sector is growing rapidly and more than 70,000 new jobs have been created as a result of new business openings. Estonia's foreign trade has shifted rapidly from East to West with the Western industrialized countries now accounting for two-thirds of foreign trade. As a result, there are job opportunities for those who can assist the nation continue its upward strides. In particular, the welcome mat is out for Western business interests to take advantage of the country's trained workers. Western management personnel are needed as are those familiar with western know-how in banking, marketing, industrial development, etc. Of course, the first place to look for work here is with existing companies or those looking to expand. Contact the Estonian Chamber of Commerce at: Toom-Koolo 17, Tallin, ESTONIA for names of companies doing business here.

The other two Baltic republics, Latvia and Lithuania are much like Estonia. For detailed employment information contact either the U.S. Embassy, Raina Boulevard 7, Riga, LATVIA and the U.S. Embassy, Akmenu 6, Vilnuis, LITHUANIA or the Latvian Chamber of Commerce, 21 Bribas Boulevard, Riga, LATVIA and the Lithuanian Chamber of Commerce and Industry, Algirdo Strasse 31, Vilnius, LITHUANIA.

Belarus

GEOGRAPHY:
AREA: 207,600 sq. km.
CAPITAL: Minsk
PRINCIPAL CITIES: Brest, Pinsk, Orsha, Mahilyow
TERRAIN: Generally flat and contains much marshland.
CLIMATE: Cold winter, cool and moist summers.

PEOPLE:
POPULATION: 10,450,000
ANNUAL GROWTH RATE: 0.32%

RELIGION: Eastern Orthodox
LANGUAGE: Byelorussian, Russian
EDUCATION: Attendence in primary school 100%; Literacy 99.9%.
LIFE EXPECTANCY: Men 66; women 76 years.

GOVERNMENT: Bylarus is a republic. It has a unicameral legislature. The elected president is chief of state while the prime minister is head of the government. Political parties are legal and extremely active. The last election was in 1990 with none scheduled in the near future.

ECOMONY:
GDP: $61 million (est)
ANNUAL GROWTH RATE: -9%
PER CAPITA INCOME: $5,890
AVERAGE RATE OF INFLATION: 30% per month (average 1993).
WORK FORCE: Of the 4,887 million workers, 40% are involved in industry and construction, 21% are employed in agriculture and forestry. The unemployment rate is about 2% with far more "under employed" workers.
OFFICIAL EXCHANGE RATE: The Bylarusian rubel is the official currency. It is tied to the value of the Russian ruble.
COST OF LIVING INDEX: NA.

Belarus ranks among the most developed of the former Soviet states, with a relatively modern (by Soviet standards) and diverse machine building sector and a robust agricultural sector. It also serves as a transport link for Russian oil exports to the Baltic states and both Eastern and Western Europe. The breakup of the Soviet Union and its command economy has resulted in a sharp economic contraction as traditional trade ties collapsed. At the same time, the Byelorussian government has lagged behind most other former Soviet states in economic reform; privatization has barely begun; the agricultural sector remains highly subsidized; the state retains control over many prices and the system of state orders and distribution persists.

Until a true economic reform is embraced, the country will remain in its economic morass. And, until a more realistic market economy is initiated it will be hard to find jobs in Belarus. Western companies are attempting to make inroads here and there are serious employment possibilities with them. However, their needs are often met internally and there hasn't been a major attempt to locate outside consultants and workers. For a more current picture of local job possibilities contact either the US Embassy at #46 Starovilenskya, Minsk or the Belarus Chamber of Commerce at 65 Ya. Kolasa, Minsk.

If you speak Russian or the local language and are interested in finance and banking you may want to contact the following:

Inkombank
14 Manetkina Street
117420 Moscow

Menatep Bank
4 Kolpachny Lane
101980 Moscow

American International Group
Andrei Sazonov
Moscow

Bank of America
P.O. Box #37000
San Francisco, CA 94137

Russian Investment Board
101 Federal Street
Boston, MA 02110

SA Holdings, Inc.
1912 Avenue K
Plano, TX 75074

Advertising and Public Relation

BBDO Marketing
437 Madison Avenue
New York, NY 10022

Interpublic Group of Companies
Novosti-McCann
1271 Avenue of the Americas
New York, NY 10020

Young & Rubicam
285 Madison Avenue
New York, NY 10017

Ogilvy & Mather
309 West 49th Street
New York, NY 10019

Aerospace Engineering and Manufacturing

Boeing Co.
PO Box #3707
S7-191 MS31-13
Seattle, WA 98124

Lockheed Advanced
 Development Co.
1011 Lockheed Way
Palo Alto, CA 93599

McDermott International
1010 Common Street
New Orleans, LA 70112

Rockwell International Corp.
MC001-D08
P.O. Box # 4250
Seal Beach, CA 90740

Space Power, Inc.
621 River Oaks Parkway
San Jose, CA 95134

Agriculture and Food Production

Agricultural Cooperative
 Development International
Suite 900
50 F Street, NW
Washington, DC 20001

Archer Daniels Midland Co.
P.O. Box #1470
Decatur, IL 62525

Cargill, Inc.
P.O. Box #9300
Minneapolis, MN 55440

Pepsico Foods International
7701 Legacy Road
Plano, TX 75024

Ralston Purina Co.
One Checkerboard Square
St. Louis, MO 63134

Automotive Manufacturing and Sales

Chrysler Corp. & Jeep/Eagle
12000 Chrysler Dr. 416-21-01
Highland Park, MI 48288

Ford Motor Co.
Room 50
P.O. Box 1899
Detroit, MI 48121

Chemical Industry

American Cyanamid Co.,
 International
One Cyanamid Plaza
Wayne, NJ 07470

Dow Chemical Co.
2020 Dow Center
Midland, MI 48674

E.I. duPont DeNemours
Nemours Bldg. 13451
1007 Market Street
Wilmington, DE 19898

FMC Corp
200 East Randolph Dr.
Chicago, IL 60601

Huntsman Chemical Corp.
2000 Eagle Gate Tower
Salt Lake City, UT 84111

Communications

AT&T
Room 3A02
100 Southgate Parkway
Morristown, NJ 07962

Bel Atlantic Corp.
1717 Arch Street
Philadelphia, PA 19103

General Electric Mobil
 Communications
421 Forbes Blvd.
Lanham, MD 20706

Hughes Communications
1990 East Grand Avenue
El Segundo, CA 90245

US West International &
 Business Development Group
Suite 210
9785 Maroon Circle
Englewood, CO 80112

**Computer and
Technology Industries**

Apple Computer
20525 Mariani Ave. MS 9ACR
Cupertino, CA 95014

BDM International, Inc.
7915 Jones Drive
McLean, VA 22102

Cadence Design Systems
555 Rover Oaks Parkway
San Jose, CA 95134

Computer Associates, Inc.
One Computer Associates Plaza
Islandia, NY 11788

Hewlett Packard Co.
P.O. Box #10301
Palo Alto, CA 94304

IBM World Trade
One Orchard Road
Armonk, NY 10504

Lotus Development Corp.
55 Cambridge parkway
Cambridge, MA 02142

Microsoft Corp.
One Microsoft Way
Redmond, WA 98052

Sun Microsystems, Inc.
2550 Garcia Ave.
MS PAC1 408
Mountain View, CA 94043

Consulting

Andersen Consulting
69 West Washington St.
Chicago, IL 60602

Bechtel Corp.
P.O. Box #193965
San Francisco, CA 94119

Booz Allen-Hamilton, Inc.
101 Park Avenue
New York, NY 10178

Boston Consulting Group
135 East 57th Street
New York, NY 10022

PlanEcon
1111 14th Street, NW
Washington, DC 20036

Planning & Development
Collaborative International, Inc.
1012 N Street NW
Washington, DC 20001

Price Waterhouse
1801 K Street NW
Washington, DC 20006

Energy and Minerals

Amoco Corporation
200 East Randolph Dr.
MC 3608
Chicago, IL 60601

Benton Oil & Gas
300 Esplanade Drive
Oxnard, CA 93030

Chevron
225 Bush Street
San Francisco, CA 94104

Conoco
1000 South Pine
Oklahoma City, OK 74603

Exxon Corp.
Suite 275
5080 North 40th Street
Phoenix, AZ 85018

Halliburton Geophysical
 Services
P.O. Box #42820
Denver, CO 80237

Marathon Oil Co.
539 South Main Street
Findlay, OH 45840

Mobil
3225 Fallows Road
Fairfax, VA 22037

Occidental Petroleum Corp.
10889 Wilshire Blvd.
Los Angeles, CA 90024

Texaco
2000 Westchester Avenue
White Plains, NY 10650

Armco International
345 Park Avenue
New York, NY 10022

INCO Aloys International
P.O. Box #1958
Huntington, WV 25720

Unocal Corp.
P.O. Box #7600
Los Angeles, CA 90051

Health Care Services

Abbott Labs International
 Division
One Abbott Park Road
Abbott Park, IL 60064

Becton Dickinson & Co.
One Becton Drive
Franklin Lakes, NJ 07417

Ciba-Geigy Corp.
444 Saw Mill River Road
Ardsley, NY 10502

Healthcare Enterprise
 International
30 West Gude Drive
Rockville, MD 20850

Russian Birth Project
1424 Washington Street
Evanston, IL 60202

Upjohn
7000 Portage Road
Kalamazoo, MI 49001

Industrial

Baker Hughes
Suite 1600
3900 Essex Lane
Houston, TX 77210

Brown & Root, Inc.
P.O. Box # 303-125
Houston, TX 77001

Ingersoll-Rand
200 Chestnut Ridge Road
Woodcliff, NJ 07675

International Harvester
 Company
401 North Michigan Avenue
Chicago, IL 60611

Parker Hannafin Corp.
17325 Euclid Ave.
Cleveland, OH 44112

York International Corp.
P.O. Box #1592-36BB
631 South Richland Avenue
York, PA 17403

Education

Academy for Educational
 Development
1255 23rd St. NW
Washington, DC 20037

Fandango Overseas Placement
1613 Escarlero Road
Santa Rosa, CA 95409

Institute for International
 Education
809 United Nations Plaza
New York, NY 10017

International Educators
 Cooperative
212 Alcott Road
East Falmouth, MA 02536

Overseas Employment
 Information for Teachers
Department of State Box #9317
Arlington, VA 22209

Overseas Placement Service for
 Educators
University of Iowa
 Student Services
Cedar Falls, IA 50614

Teaching Abroad
46 Beech View
Angmering
West Sussex 5N16 4DE
UNITED KINGDOM

AFRICA

Angola

GEOGRAPHY:
AREA: 481,351 sq. mi.
CAPITAL: Luanda
PRINCIPAL CITIES: Huambo, Lobito, Luena, Namibe
TERRAIN: Narrow coastal plain rises abruptly to vast interior plateau.
CLIMATE: Tropical to sub-tropical.

PEOPLE: Angolan
POPULATION: 9,803,576
ANNUAL GROWTH RATE: 2.67%
RELIGION: 47% indigenous beliefs; 38% Roman Catholic; 15% Protestant.
LANGUAGE: Portuguese (official); various Bantu dialects.
EDUCATION: Attendance in primary school 75%; Literacy 30%.
LIFE EXPECTANCY: Men 43; women 47 years.

GOVERNMENT: Marxist People's Republic. Popular Movement for the Liberation of Angola-Labor Party is the only legal party. Government budget: $2.7 billion.

ECONOMY:
GDP: $5.7 billion
ANNUAL GROWTH RATE: -22.6%
PER CAPITA GDP: $600.
AVERAGE RATE OF INFLATION: 1,840%
WORK FORCE: 42% of GNP is agricultural (cassava, maize, plantains); 28% of GNP is industrial (petroleum, mining, food processing, tires, textiles).
OFFICIAL EXCHANGE RATE: 90,000 kwanzas = US$
COST OF LIVING INDEX: 121

Yes, there are jobs for Westerners in Angola but think twice before applying. It is not considered a safe country in which to travel. Whereas the capital, Luanda, is relatively secure, fighting between the government and the opposition party (UNITA) has spread to most areas of the country. Guerilla attacks are not uncommon. Although there are no restrictions on Americans traveling in Angola, the United States does not maintain diplomatic relations with Angola (nor does another country represent U.S. interests) therefore the problems for Americans working and living in the country may be compounded.

Living conditions are tropical with safari suits far more typical than Western-style business suits. There is a shortage of medical personal and sophisticated medical equipment. Travelers with health problems should avoid the country. If taken ill while working seek early transportation to an area with adequate facilities. Drink only boiled or bottled water and don't travel here without a good malaria prophylaxis.

The major employer of non-Angolans are companies in the petroleum field. Mobil and Texaco are the two principle American companies in the country. Contacts:

Petroleum:

Texaco Petroleos de
 Angola S.A.R.L.
Caixa Postal 5897
Luanda

Mobil Oil Portuguesta
Caixa Postal 330
Luanda

Air Freight:

Air Express International Corp
% Jacto Cargo Ltd.
Avenida dos Combatentes 42
P.O. Box # 16326
Luanda

Financial:

INA Corporation
Glerth & Monteiro, Ltd.
Caixa Postal 562
Benguela

Data Processing:

NCR Corporation
% Angola
Rue dos Anjos 79
1011 Lisbon Codex
Portugal

Pharmaceuticals:

Pfizer, Inc.
Pfizer Central Africa Region
% Angola
P.O. Box 14764
Westland
Nairobi, Kenya

Ivory Coast
(Cote d'Ivoire)

GEOGRAPHY:
AREA: 124,000 sq. mi.
CAPITAL: Abidjan (Changed to Yamoussoukro in 1983 but not recognized by the US).
PRINCIPAL CITIES: Abidjan, Bouake, Daloa, Gagnoa.
TERRAIN: Mostly flat with undulating plains in northwest.
CLIMATE: Tropical along the coast, semi arid in the far North; three seasons: warm and dry (November to March), hot and dry (March to May), hot and wet (June to October).

PEOPLE:
POPULATION: 14,295,501
ANNUAL GROWTH RATE: 3.44%
RELIGION: 63% indigenous; 25% Muslim; 12% Christian.
LANGUAGE: French
EDUCATION: Attendance in primary school 76%; Literacy 35%.
LIFE EXPECTANCY: Men 46; women 51 years.

GOVERNMENT: One party presidential republic. President has sweeping powers. Legal system is based on French civil law. Government budget: $4.2 billion; 7% goes to military.

ECONOMY:
GDP: $21 billion
ANNUAL GROWTH RATE: NA
PER CAPITA GDP: $1,500.
AVERAGE RATE OF INFLATION: 1%
UNEMPLOYMENT RATE: 14%
WORK FORCE: One of the world's largest producers and exporters of coffee, cocoa beans and palm-kernel oil. The economy is still largely dependent on agriculture despite the government's attempts to diversify. Agriculture employs about 85% of the labor force. In the industrial sector there are some foodstuff processing plants, wood processing, oil refining, automotive assembly, and textiles.
OFFICIAL EXCHANGE RATE: 592.05 Communaute Financiere Africaine francs = US$
COST OF LIVING INDEX: 155

Despite many attempts and failures to bring the Ivory Coast's industrial capacity more in line with Western expectations this is one of the wealthiest countries in West Africa. The capital, Abidjan, is known as "Paris of West Africa." Its Ivoire Hotel is a world showplace complete with bowling alley, ice skating rink and a golf course that is as futuristic as any in the West. A new, modern Catholic cathedral dominates the skyline like the opera house in Sydney. It is the largest cathedral in the world after St. Peters.

Living and working conditions in the Ivory Coast are dependent on location. Live in the major cities and it can be a joy; life in the country requires a stronger constitution.

The major industrial employers are related to the country's struggling petroleum industry. An ESSO-led consortium brought the offshore Belier field into production in 1980. Two years later a Phillips-led consortium brought in the larger Espor field. These are the largest off shore producers today and among the major employers of Ivorians. Phillips discovered natural gas but as yet there is no commercial exploration. An oil refinery, SIR, is also a small employer of technical talent.

In addition to those with knowledge of the petroleum industry, there is always a welcome need for professionals in the health fields, social services and education.

The Ivory Coast has an embassy at 2424 Massachusetts Avenue, Washington, DC 20008 (202/483-2400). The United States Embassy is at 5 Rue Jesse Owens, Abidjan. Contacts:

Financial:

Chase International Investment
 Corp.
%BIDI, Boite Postal 4470
Abidjan

Fidelity Bank
Boite Postale V245
Abidjan

Manufacturing:

Cummins Engine Co. Inc.
01 Boite Postale 1888
Abidjan

Weatherford Products and
 Service S.A.
06 Boite Postale 705
Abidjan

Chemical:

Union Carbide Africa Ltd.
06 Boite Postal 330
Abidjan

Dow Chemical Co.
Boite Postal 1521
Abidjan

Kenya

GEOGRAPHY:
AREA: 569,250 sq. mi.
CAPITAL: Nairobi
PRINCIPAL CITIES: Mombasa, Kisumu
TERRAIN: Low plains rise to central highlands bisected by Great Rift Valley; fertile plateau in West.
CLIMATE: Tropical along coast; arid in interior.

PEOPLE:
POPULATION: 28,240,658
ANNUAL GROWTH RATE: 3.07%
RELIGION: 38% Protestant; 28% Roman Catholic; 26% indigenous beliefs.
LANGUAGE: English and Swahili (official).
EDUCATION: Attendance in primary school 83%; Literacy (in English) 25%.
LIFE EXPECTANCY: Men 51; women 55 years.

GOVERNMENT: Republic within Commonwealth. Kenya African National Union (KANU) is Kenya's sole legal political party. Legal system is based on English common law, tribal law, and Islamic law. Government budget: $2.1 billion.

ECONOMY:
GDP: $33.2 billion
ANNUAL GROWTH RATE: 0.5%.
PER CAPITA GDP $1,200.
AVERAGE RATE OF INFLATION: 55%.
WORK FORCE: Agriculture is the leading sector contributing 30% to GDP. Industries include small scale consumer goods, agricultural processing, oil refining, and cement. Unemployment unofficially is about 23.8% of the work force.
OFFICIAL EXCHANGE RATE: 68.4 Kenyan shillings = US$
COST OF LIVING INDEX: 076

Say Kenya and most people think animals, game preserves and the excitement of an African safari. Since more than 35,000 Americans visit the country each year it is only natural that tourists drawn to the Masai Mara game preserve, Tsavo National Park or Aberdare National Park return home with tales of African adventure. However, Kenya is also home base for more than 6,000 Americans including about 1,600 missionaries and more than 300 Peace Corps volunteers who concentrate on agriculture and education programs in the country's far recesses.

Americans are employed by the more than 140 U.S. firms represented in the country. U.S. business investment totals roughly $350 million, primarily in commerce, light manufacturing and tourism. The country's industrial sector is currently being restructured to make it more competitive internationally, more export oriented, and more attuned to blend with Kenya's agriculturally-based industry.

Life in Kenya can be most pleasant. Although the climate varies, for the most part light and medium weight clothing is worn most of the year. Sweaters and raincoats are needed during the rainy season. The principal cities are modern by Western standards although tribal influences are obvious throughout. Adequate hospital and outpatient treatment is available in Nairobi. The water is safe to drink in the capitol but avoid tap water elsewhere. Yellow fever, polio, typhoid, and hepatitis immunizations are recommended; take antimalarial tablets.

Employment opportunities exist in the areas of health services, education, light industry, and agricultural consultation.

Kenya has an embassy at 2249 R Street NW, Washington, DC 20008 (202/387-6101) and a consulate at 9100 Wilshire Blvd., Los Angeles, CA (213/274-6635). The United States Embassy is at Haile Selassie and Moi Avenues, Nairobi, Kenya. Contacts:

Manufacturing:

Black & Decker (Kenya) Ltd.
Dunga Road, P.O. Box # 46827
Nairobi

General Electric Technical
 Service Co. Inc.
P.O. Box # 30593
Nairobi

Food Products:

CPC Kenya Ltd.
P.O. Box # 41045
Nairobi

Pharmaceuticals:

Merck Sharp & Dohme Intl.
P.O. Box # 30676
Arwings-Kodhek Road
Nairobi

Lederle Labs
P.O. Box # 47341
Nairobi

Data Processing:

NCR Ltd.
P.O. Box # 30217
Nairobi

Liberia

GEOGRAPHY:
AREA: 43,000 sq. mi.
CAPITAL: Monrovia
PRINCIPAL CITIES: Harbel, Buchanan, Yekepa
TERRAIN: Coastal plain rising to rolling plateau. Low mountains near inland borders.
CLIMATE: Warm and humid all year. Cool to cold nights. Wet to cloudy summers with frequent heavy rain.

PEOPLE:
POPULATION: 2,972,766
ANNUAL GROWTH RATE: 3%
RELIGION: 70% traditional; 20% Muslim; 10% Christian.
LANGUAGE: English (official) used by about 20%; more than 20 local languages of the Niger-Congo language group.
EDUCATION: Attendance in primary school 35%; Literacy 25%.
LIFE EXPECTANCY: Men 55; women 60 years.

GOVERNMENT: Civilian republic. Multi-party system elects president and bicameral legislature. Government budget: $380 billion.

ECONOMY:
GDP: $2.3 billion
ANNUAL GROWTH RATE: 1.5%
PER CAPITA GDP: $800.
AVERAGE RATE OF INFLATION: 12%.
WORK FORCE: Approximately half million employed. 71% in agriculture represents only 20% of the GDP; 11% in services. Non-African foreigners hold about 95% of the top level management and engineering jobs.
OFFICIAL EXCHANGE RATE: 1 Liberian dollar = US$
COST OF LIVING INDEX: 096.

Consider Liberia an African anomaly. There is a very strong American influence throughout the country, yet it is totally African. Although the US dollar is the official paper currency you won't see any being exchanged. The greenbacks you bring with you will be in great demand and you'll be offered deep discounts if you use them. Liberia mints its own coins and its currency is "officially" directly tied to the price of the

US dollar but don't be surprised when the rates between the two may vary by as much as 50% in stores and on the black market. It is also one of only two African countries (Ethiopia is the other) that never suffered under foreign colonialism.

Its government is directly modeled on the US Constitution, yet it has more opposition parties than any other African nation. It also has one of the most corrupt governments on the continent. Civil resurrection occurred in 1990 causing the U.S. State Department to request American citizens to evacuate the country. Future such occurrences are more than likely.

The two largest cities are Monrovia and Buchanan. Do you know any other nation whose two major cities are named after American presidents? Liberia also has the largest commercial shipping fleet in the world (almost all foreign-owned). However, Liberia has a pair of negative distinctions as well. It has the wettest capital city on the continent (Monrovia averages 2.5 inches of rain per day during the six-month rainy season, May to October). And, it has the unique distinction of recording the worst economic performance in Africa during the 1980s. In the past decade, for example, per capita income has declined by more than 25%. Unemployment in Monrovia exceeds 50%.

However, despite the poor economic past and Bethlehem Steel's selling its 25% interest in LAMCO, most American companies are sticking it out. The US investment of some $500 million represents almost half of the total foreign investment in the country. In 1926, Firestone introduced rubber production. Today they manage the world's largest contiguous plantations at Harbel and remain the country's largest employer—about 10,000 workers. B.F. Goodrich also had a major investment in rubber but recently sold out to Guthrie, a Malaysian company. Mining is a growing industry with iron constituting about two thirds of Liberia's exports. The country has extensive timber resources which are just beginning to be exploited. Rain forests cover about three quarters of the country. Thus, there is a growing need for expertise in the paper/pulp industry.

Of the 15,000 foreigners living in Liberia, about 3,000 are Americans. However, with the turmoil and insurrection among governing factions, the number of Americans is declining rapidly. Medical facilities are considered marginal even in the major cities. Cholera and yellow fever immunizations are required. It is also recommended that you avoid the water. No drinking anything but bottled or boiled water and no swimming in lakes or rivers up-country. A further unsettling note: Don't walk at night in Monrovia as it is mugger's paradise. And the local police are known to hassle tourists extracting "dash" (a bribe) for any concocted offense.

Liberia has an embassy at 5201 16th Street NW, Washington, DC 20011 (202/723-9437). The United States Embassy is on United Nations Drive, Monrovia. Contacts:

Financial:

Citibank NA
Bank of Monrovia
P.O. Box # 280
Monrovia

Chemicals:

Dow Chemical Co.
2030 Dow Center
Midland, MI 48640

E.I. Du Pont de Nemours & Co.
1007 Market St.
Wilmington, DE 19898

Construction:

Leavell-Olson-Farrar
P.O. 1401
Monrovia

Rubber:

Firestone Tire & Rubber Co.
40 United States Trading Co.
P.O. Box # 140
Monrovia

Nigeria

GEOGRAPHY:
AREA: 356,700 sq. mi.
CAPITAL: Lagos
PRINCIPAL CITIES: Kano, Ibadan, Enugu
TERRAIN: Ranges from southern coastal swamps to tropical forests, open woodlands, grasslands, and semi-desert in the far north.
CLIMATE: Equatorial in the south, tropical in the center and arid in the north. Annual rainfall ranges from 150 inches along the coast to 25 inches or less in the far north.

PEOPLE:
POPULATION: 98,091,097
ANNUAL GROWTH RATE: 3.15%
RELIGION: 50% Muslim; 40% Christian
LANGUAGE: English (official) Hausa, Yoruba, Ibo also used.

EDUCATION: Attendance in primary school 42%; Literacy 25-35%.
LIFE EXPECTANCY: Men 54; women 56 years.

GOVERNMENT: Military government since 1983. Legal system is based on English common law and Islamic and tribal law. Government budget: $5.2 billion. Approximately 6% for military.

ECONOMY:
GDP: $95.1 billion
ANNUAL GROWTH RATE: 4%
PER CAPITA GDP: $1,000.
AVERAGE RATE OF INFLATION: 60%.
WORK FORCE: Approximately 37 million are employed with agriculture employing about 60% of the work force, Industry about 20% and government about 15%. Unemployment is about 28%.
OFFICIAL EXCHANGE RATE: 21.88 Naira = US$
COST OF LIVING INDEX: 124.

Nigeria is a nation in shock; from boom to bust in less than a decade. The reason is oil. What was to be the salvation of the country has turned the nation into near turmoil. The oil boom of the 1970s shifted Nigeria from an agriculturally based economy to one that now relies on oil for more than 95% of export earnings and 70% of federal budget resources. With the sharp decline in world oil prices during the early 1980s, the nation faced economic disaster.

During the oil boom there were six vehicle assembly plants in the country compared to but one in the rest of West Africa. In 1986, however, all six plants stopped production for lack of parts. Although there was a slight upswing in the price of oil in the early 1990s, by 1994 Nigeria's debt exceeded $40 billion. On the brighter side, there are more than two dozen different kinds of beer brewed in Nigeria—more than the rest of West Africa combined.

The most populous country in Africa, Nigeria accounts for one in four of sub-Saharan African people. Its population growth rate of 3% exacerbates it problems. At the present growth rate Nigeria will be the fourth most populous country on earth in but three decades. Although the government is trying to shift the economic balance by increasing the manufacturing sector, it is a long hard road. In 1987, manufacturing rose an estimated 6% and contributed 12% to the GDP.

Work conditions for foreigners are dependent on location. Work in the oil fields near Benin and you experience totally different conditions from the Northern and Eastern parts of the country. The coastal area is hot and muggy laced with lagoons and mangrove swamps. Those without proper malaria prophylaxis are asking for trouble. Oil folk coined the doggerel, "Beware, beware the Bight of Benin. Where one comes out though forty go in."

If you work in the cities you face other problems. Lagos is West Africa's largest city. And, for a national capitol it is a disgrace. Aside from being the ugliest city in Africa, it is also the dirtiest, most congested, and saddled with a very high crime rate. It is considered one of the two most dangerous cities in West and Central Africa (Kinshassa is the other). Armed robbery is the most common crime. Beware of taxi drivers as they have seem to be involved in most thefts involving foreigners. The weather is hot, muggy and generally uncomfortable. Prior to the government's devaluating the naira in the early 1980s Lagos was considered the most expensive city in the world.

Although medical facilities are adequate in the major cities most fall short by American standards. Malaria is endemic and a yellow fever vaccination is required. Tropical dress is recommended.

Despite the nation's economic problems, foreign expertise in mostly technical, oil-related, health care, manufacturing and business management areas are welcomed. Nigerian National Petroleum Corp. (NNPC) is the nation's largest petroleum complex. NNPC explores for oil and gas and holds a 53% interest in almost all oil-producing companies operating in Nigeria. They are also involved in refining and distributing oil and gas and in petrochemical production. They may be contacted at the Falomo Office Complex, P.O. Box 12701, Ikoyi, Lagos.

Nigeria has an embassy at 2201 M Street NW, Washington, DC 20037 (202/822-1500) and consulates at 575 Lexington Ave. New York, NY 10022 (212/715- 7200); 369-371 Hayes Street, San Francisco, CA 94101 (415/864-8001); and, 225 Peachtree Street, South Tower Suite 1010, Atlanta, GA (404/5774800). The United States Embassy is at 2 Eleke Crescent (P.O. Box # 554), Victoria Island, Lagos, Nigeria. Contacts:

Manufacturing:

3M Nigeria Ltd.
Isolo Road, Mushin
P.O. Box # 3062
Lagos

Ingersoll-Rand Co.
P.O. Box #109, Apapa
Lagos

Pharmaceuticals:

E.R. Squibb (Nigeria) Ltd.
P.O. Box # 12732
No. 1 Kolawoie Shonibare
Ilupeju, Lagos

Smithkline & French Nigeria,
 Ltd.
P.M.B 599, Ikeja
Lagos

Construction:

Bechtel Intl. Corp.
8-B Ademola St.
P.O. Box # 3992
Lagos

Brown & Root (Nigeria) Ltd.
38 Awolowa Rd.
P.O. Box # 2282
Lagos

Petroleum:

Exxon Standard Nigeria, Ltd.
Western House
8/10 Yakubu Gowon St.
Lagos

Geosource, Inc.
P.M.B 1315, Nigeria
Malduguri

Union of South Africa

GEOGRAPHY:
AREA: 471,445 sq. mi.
CAPITAL: Pretoria (Administrative); Cape Town (Legislative);
Bloemfontein (Judicial)
PRINCIPAL CITIES: Cape Town, Johannesburg, Durban
TERRAIN: Vast interior plateau rimmed by rugged hills
and narrow coastal plains.
CLIMATE: Mostly semi-arid; sub-tropical along the coast; sunny days,
cool nights.

PEOPLE:
POPULATION: 43,930,631
ANNUAL GROWTH RATE: 2.62%
RELIGION: Most whites and about 60% of blacks are Christian.
LANGUAGE: Afrikaans, English (official).
EDUCATION: Attendance in primary school 83%; Literacy: Almost
all whites and about half the blacks.
LIFE EXPECTANCY: Men 63; women 67 years.

GOVERNMENT: Republic with a elections at least once every five years. Tricameral legislature. Government budget: $15 billion of which 15% is for military.

ECONOMY:
GDP: $171 billion
ANNUAL GROWTH RATE: 1.1%
PER CAPITA GDP: $4,000.
AVERAGE RATE OF INFLATION: 9.7%
WORK FORCE: Most workers are engaged in manufacturing which contributes about 25% of the GDP. Mining, finance and agriculture are next in importance. The world's largest producer of gold, diamonds and chrome. Most unemployment is among the black workers, about 25 to 50%; among white workers, less than 2%.
OFFICIAL EXCHANGE RATE: 3.45 Rand = US$
COST OF LIVING INDEX: 092

The changes in South Africa, now that Nelson Mandela is President are almost impossible to predict. Despite the fact that South Africa is the strongest industrial state on the African continent, the racial turmoil that affected the nation for so many years impacted all areas of the nation's growth and development. When the white ruling minority enforced apartheid, a system of racial separation, the economy was weakened by increased black political activism, urban violence, work stoppages, economic boycotts and disinvestment by foreign companies. Although the white government attempted to modify several key pieces of discriminatory legislature in 1990, the black majority was excluded from the national parliament until the peaceful revolution that saw Mandela take control of the government in 1994.

The white government had encouraged the growth of industry to make the country self-sufficient and independent of external pressures. Factories in the southern Transvaal account for about half of the nation's manufacturing. Another 25% of manufacturing income is derived from the port cities of Cape Town, Durban, Port Elizabeth and East London. Leading industries include food processing, metalworking, and the manufacture of clothing, textiles, iron and steel and machinery.

Industry has been dependent on the white population for management, administration and higher technical skills. The average "white" earnings are about five times greater than African earnings.

Life in any of the major cities is not unlike a leading European city. Medical services, transportation and basic services are the best on the continent.

Now that many U.S. and foreign companies have begun to return there is only positive news on the job front for skilled foreigners interested in a new life in this "new country". Prior to Mandela, many South African plants had turned over their operations to local businesses. Plant management and ownership is now changing.

This is one country that is actively encouraging foreign workers to help build the nation. An excellent, detailed brochure, "Working in South Africa" is published by Medbank and is available at the South African Embassy or local consulate. A work permit and visa are required to work in or visit South Africa, but the government makes it easy to obtain either.

Many South African employment agencies are now actively recruiting. For example:

- Financial, Accounting and General Management:

  Aiken & Peat Senior Appointments
  Carlton Center
  PO Box 7400
  Johannesburg 2000
  3327111 (Tel); Fax 3327140

- Technical, Manufacturing, Engineering, Construction, Pharmaceutical:

  Brown's Personnel Consultants
  5 Coventry Road
  PO Box 757
  Cramerview 2060
  4631712 (Tel); Fax 4632349

- Agencies searching for Black workers:

  Black Executives
  89 Von
  Weilligh St.
  PO Box 7756
  Johannesburg 2000
  3334027 (Tel); Fax 3334034

South Africa has an embassy at 3051 Massachusetts Avenue NW, Washington, DC 20008 (202/232-4400) and consulates in Beverly Hills, CA., New York, NY, Houston, TX., and Chicago, IL. The United States Embassy is at Thibault House, 225 Pretorius Street, Pretoria. Contact:

Mining:

Anglo American Corporation of
South Africa, Ltd
44 Main Street
Johannesburg 2001

Industrial:

Anglovaal Limited
P.O. Box 62379
Marshalltown, Transvaal 2107

Barlow Rand Ltd
P.O. Box 782248
Sandton 2146

Premier Group Holdings
 Limited
1 Newton Avenue, Killarney
Johannesburg

Financial:

Rembrandt Group Limited
Coetzier Street, P.O. Box #456,
Stellenbosch 7600

Transportation:

South African Transport
 Services
Paul Kruger Building
Wolmarans Street
Johannesburg 2000

Utility:

Eskom
P.O. Box 1091
Johannesburg 2000

Iron & Steel:

Iscor Limited
P.O. Box 450
0001 Pretoria

Chemicals:

GAF South Africa Ltd.
P.O. Box #78838
Sandton 2146

Zaire

GEOGRAPHY:
AREA: 905,063 sq. mi.
CAPITAL: Kinshasa
PRINCIPAL CITIES: Kananga, Lubumbashi, Bukavu.
TERRAIN: Varies from tropical rain forests to mountainous terraces,

plateau, savannas, dense grasslands and mountains.
CLIMATE: Equatorial; hot and humid in much of the north and west.
Cooler and drier in the south central areas and east.

PEOPLE:
POPULATION: 42,684,091
ANNUAL GROWTH RATE: 3.1%
RELIGION: Roman Catholic: 50%; Protestant: 20%; Muslim: 10%.
LANGUAGE: French also Lingala and Swahili.
EDUCATION: Literacy 55%.
LIFE EXPECTANCY: Men 45; women 49 years.

GOVERNMENT: Republic with strong presidential authority. One party
system. Government budget: $2.0 billion.

ECONOMY:
GDP: $21 billion
ANNUAL GROWTH RATE: -6%
PER CAPITA GDP: $500.
AVERAGE RATE OF INFLATION: 35-40%
WORK FORCE: Agriculture, a key sector of the economy, employs over
75% of the population but generates only 30% of GDP. Mining and
mineral processing accounts for about a third of GDP and two-thirds of
total export earnings. High inflation compounds the labor problem.
OFFICIAL EXCHANGE RATE: 7,915,000 Zaires = US$
COST OF LIVING INDEX: 195

While Zaire has tremendous natural resources—it is the world's
largest producer of cobalt and industrial diamonds—development has
been hampered by the country's size, insufficient human resources,
inadequate transport infrastructure and continued government corruption.
Mining, particularly copper, manganese, tin and zinc, are central to the
nation's economic development. Recently, petroleum exports from small
off-shore fields, which are exploited by an American-Japanese consortium (Chevron, Unocal, and Teikoku) as well as coastal fields (Petrofina)
have become a major source of foreign exchange. Technical expertise in
the petroleum and mining businesses are always in demand.

Since the country straddles the equator living conditions generally can
be described as hot and humid. If you are fortunate enough to live and
work in the capitol of Kinshasa life can be quite pleasant. Americans
often join the elite of Zairian government circles and live in the hilly

residential area in large, well-servanted, detached homes.

With an almost runaway inflation and high cost of living it is hard to budget cost or income here. Yes, there are jobs for the skilled and there is a tremendous need here, as well as in the rest of the African heartland for experienced managers in basic business, agriculture, water resources, as well as in mining and construction.

Dress for the tropics but a light weight suit may be required for formal occasions. Hotels and restaurants in the cities are quite luxurious, but quite expensive and often over-booked. Malaria is prevalent.

Zaire has an embassy at 1800 New Hampshire Avenue NW, Washington, DC 20008 (202/234-7690). The United States Embassy is at 310 Avenue des Aviateurs, Kinshasa, Zaire. Contact:

Pharmaceuticals:

Abbott Laboratories
B.P. 9575
Kinshasa

Alcon Laboratories, Inc
B.P. 2115
306 Avenue de la Gomber
Kinshasa

**Manufacturing &
Construction:**

Armco Zaire Steel Corp.
B.P. 11899
Rue de Brasserie #12
Kinshasa

Automotive & Electronics:

General Motors Zaire S.A.R.L.
B.P. 11199
Kinshasa

ITT Bell Telephone Co.
B.P. 11210, Kin I
Kinshsasa

Zimbabwe

GEOGRAPHY:
AREA: 151,000 sq. mi.
CAPITAL: Harare
PRINCIPAL CITIES: Bulawayo, Gweru, Mutare.
TERRAIN: Central plateau with mountains along eastern border.
CLIMATE: Moderate year round. Altitude tempers the seasonal tropical

temperatures; inland position keeps humidity comfortably low. Rainy season: November—March.

PEOPLE:
POPULATION: 10,975,078
ANNUAL GROWTH RATE: 1.2%
RELIGION: 50% syncretic (part Christian, part indigenous beliefs); 25% Christian.
LANGUAGE: English (official); Shona.
EDUCATION: Attendance in primary school White, Asian, colored 100%; African 90%. Literacy 45 - 55%.
LIFE EXPECTANCY: Men 40; women 43 years.

GOVERNMENT: Parliamentary democracy. President with bicameral legislature. Government budget: $2.8 billion; 16% is devoted to military.
ECONOMY:
GDP: $15.9 billion
ANNUAL GROWTH RATE: 2%
PER CAPITA GDP: $1,400.
AVERAGE RATE OF INFLATION: 22%
WORK FORCE: Agriculture employs about 75% of the labor force but contributes only 15% to the GDP. Industry contributes about 69% to the GDP; mining accounts for about 5% of both employment and GDP.
OFFICIAL EXCHANGE RATE: 8.10 Zimbabwean dollars (Z$) = US$
COST OF LIVING INDEX: 073

Although Zimbabwe received its independence from colonial British rule in 1980, guerrilla warfare between conflicting factions has continued for the past decade. Life in the major cities is safe, but the U.S. State Department warns against sporadic violence in certain areas. "Until these conditions stabilize travelers should be cautioned when traveling in rural areas."

Zimbabwe is one of Africa's more advanced countries. It has excellent internal transportation and electrical power networks. Paved roads link the major urban and industrial centers and rail lines tie it into an extensive central African railroad network with all its neighbors.

The climate is quite pleasant. Light weight clothing is common in the summer but sweaters and woolens are often needed in the winter months. In the major cities the water is considered safe to drink but bilharzia parasites infect many lakes and rivers in rural areas. Outside the cities malaria is considered an endemic disease. Tourism remains an important factor in the nation's economy. Famed Victoria Falls draws thousands annually; many of whom travel up the Zambezi River observing native elephants, antelope and buffalo.

The country has the most broadly based economy of any country in Africa. Its industrial base is quite advanced and both its mining and construction industries are technologically advanced. Zimbabwe has an important percentage of the world's known reserves of metallurgical-grade chromite as well as significant deposits of coal, asbestos, copper, nickle, gold and iron ore. Thus, those with technologic skills in mining and metallurgy are always in demand. Contact:

Manufacturing:

Cummins Diesel Intl. Ltd.
P.O. Box # 8440, Causeway,
Harare
Mine Safety Appliances (Pvt.)
 Ltd.
P.O. Box # AY 280 AMBY
Harare

3M Zimbabwe (Pvt.) Ltd.
P.O. Box # AY 64 AMBY
Harare

Minerals:

Zimbabwe Alloys Ltd.
P.O. Box # 1108
Harare

Data Processing:

NCR Ltd.
Stanley Avenue and
Fourth Avenue
Harare

Food Products:

Olivine Industries Ltd.
P.O. Box # 797
Harare

The Coca Cola Co.
310 North Avenue, NW
P.O. Box Drawer 1734
Atlanta, GA 30313

NORTH AFRICA AND THE MIDDLE EAST

Algeria

GEOGRAPHY:
AREA: 918,497 sq. mi.
CAPITAL: Algiers
PRINCIPAL CITIES: Oran, Constantine, Annaba
TERRAIN: Mostly high plateaus and desert; some mountains with a discontinuous coastal plain.
CLIMATE: Mild winters and hot summers in coastal plain; less cold and cold winters in high plateau.

PEOPLE:
POPULATION: 27,895,068
ANNUAL GROWTH RATE: 2.29%
RELIGION: 99% Sunni Muslim.
LANGUAGE: Arabic
EDUCATION: Attendance in primary school: 94%
LITERACY: 52%
LIFE EXPECTANCY: Men 66; women 68 years.

GOVERNMENT: Republic with an elected president as chief of state. Prime Minister is head of unicameral legislature. Military budget: $23 billion, of which 4.5% is for the military.

ECONOMY:
GDP: $89 billion
ANNUAL GROWTH RATE: 1%
PER CAPITA GDP: $3,300
AVERAGE RATE OF INFLATION: 22%
WORK FORCE: Of the 4.7 million in the work force, 33% are employed in government and services; 32% industry and commerce; and, 22% agriculture. The unemployment rate is about 22%.
OFFICIAL EXCHANGE RATE: 36dinars = US$
COST OF LIVING INDEX: 101

It's been nearly three decades since Algeria gained its independence from France and in those brief years the entire economic-industrial complex of the nation has changed. In the decade following independence, Algeria nationalized all major foreign business interests as well as many major private Algerian companies and about a third of the arable farm land. Nationalization sounded good during the "revolution" but left much needed foreign investment looking elsewhere.

Recently, however, the government relaxed its regulations in an effort to bring more foreign currency and technical expertise into the country. For example, a new law allows joint ventures on hydrocarbon exploration. Now some American firms have entered into joint venture agreements with the Algerian state enterprise, all in petroleum or mining activities.

The hydrocarbon sector is of major importance to the Algerian economy representing more than 97% of the country's hard currency. The nation now accounts for about 4% of OPEC's (Organization of Petroleum Exporting Countries) total production, however, its known gas reserves are the fourth largest in the world.

Although there is not a great demand for U.S. workers in areas other than petroleum exploration and drilling, there are occasional governmental sponsored programs of economic assistance. For example, while there is no Agency for International Development or Peace Corps in Algeria, several U.S. firms are working with the Algerian government to develop an irrigation project. The U.S. Department of Agriculture is also working on a long term program to train and assist Algerian farmers.

Either working in or visiting Algeria requires a visa. To come here without a job is a waste of time as the bureaucracy involved in obtaining work can totally frustrate even a seasoned middle-Easterner. The best opportunities are with existing firms needing technical and management expertise in a country that doesn't offer many attractions to Americans.

Algeria has an embassy at 2118 Kalorama Road NW, Washington, DC 20008 (202/326-5300). The U.S. Embassy is located at 4 Chemin Cheich Bachir Brahimi, Algiers. Contacts:

Petroleum:

Metropolitan Oil Co.
7 Rue Daguerre
Algiers

Mining Supplies:

Dresser Industries Inc.
 (ALDIA, S.A.)
4/6 Blvd. Mohamed V.
Algiers

Christensen Intl.
1 Blvd. Anatole France
Algiers

Norton Co.
1 Blvd. Anatole France
Algiers

Weatherford Oil Tool GmbH.
63 Blvd. Bougara, El Biar
Algiers

Construction:

Bechtel Inc.
Villa Djenane, Mouboub 11
Chemin Acklai, B.P. 62, El Biar
Algiers

Blackwood-Hodge/France S.A.
B.P. No. 9
Ouest-Rue des Freres Lumiere
91162 Longjumeau Cedex,
Paris
France

Skidmore, Owings & Merrill
Tite Satge
Byda

Management Consultants:

Booz, Allen & Hamilton Inc.
Villa Jenny, 28 Rue Lefebure
Algiers

United Arab Emirates

GEOGRAPHY:
AREA: 30,000 sq. mi.
CAPITAL: Abu Dhabi
PRINCIPAL CITIES: Sharjah, Ras al-Khaimah, Ajman
TERRAIN: Flat, barren coastal plain merging into rolling sand dunes of vast desert wasteland; mountains in the east.
CLIMATE: Desert climate; cooler in the eastern mountains.

PEOPLE:
POPULATION: 2,791,141
ANNUAL GROWTH RATE: 4.79%
RELIGION: 96% Muslim; 4% Christian
LANGUAGE: Arabic
EDUCATION: Attendance in primary school: 82%
LITERACY: 68%
LIFE EXPECTANCY: Men 70; Women 74 years.

GOVERNMENT: Federation with specified powers delegated to the seven UAE central governments and other powers reserved to member sheikhdoms. Islamic law is supreme. There are no elections; there is no suffrage. Government budget: $4 billion of which 40% is for the military.

ECONOMY:
GDP: $63.8 billion
ANNUAL GROWTH RATE: 1%
PER CAPITA GDP: $24,000
AVERAGE RATE OF INFLATION: 3.5%.
WORK FORCE: Of the 580,000 in the work force, 80% is foreign. The majority of the work force, 85%, is engaged in industry and commerce with oil the dominant factor in the nation's economic present and future. There is no unemployment.
OFFICIAL EXCHANGE RATE: 3.65 Emirian dirmahs = US$
COST OF LIVING INDEX: 114

By most definitions this is indeed a country, however by many standards it is more a group of sheikdoms that have banded together for mutual benefit rather than a single, independent nation. In the 1820s Great Britain established protectorates over seven small sheikhdoms along the coast of the Persian Gulf between Qatar and Oman. The region was known as the Pirate Coast, later referred to as the Trucial Coast or Trucial Oman. When Great Britain announced that it would withdraw its forces from the region in 1971 the seven sheikdoms formed a federation and became independent choosing the name United Arab Emirates. (The word "emir" is Arabic meaning prince or chieftain.)

Until the discovery of oil the economy of the country was limited to the nomadic herding of sheep and camels as well as whatever cash crops could be grown and sold on the few oasis in the region. Today the United Arab Emirates has suddenly emerged from a poor, underdeveloped group of British protectorates lacking adequate housing, schools, roads, power, and medical services into a nation with one of the world's highest per capita incomes. Their social services are among the most modern with free education at all levels for every citizen. Free medical care is provided to all residents regardless of citizenship. In 1978 the Al Ain University was opened complete with an engineering and agriculture school. By 1990 the UAE had built and staffed more than 20 hospitals and 100 clinics throughout the country.

Oil brought a flood of cash as well as foreigners. Westerners provide technology and know how to the petroleum business while tens of thousands from India, Pakistan, Bangladesh, and other Asian nations provide inexpensive labor in the oil fields as well as on road crews, restaurants, etc. The major cities are now extremely modern. Roads are among the best anywhere and a building boom is just beginning to slow down. The government has set up a national bank to loan money at very low interest rates to citizens who want to build their own homes. Banking is big business here and it's not surprising to see fierce competition among the 22 Arabian banks for a piece of the action. Money breeds money and this is now a very wealthy country.

The best jobs for Americans are obviously in the fields of high tech and petroleum. In addition to such major oil producers as Mobil, Exxon, Phillips, and British Petroleum there are the usual groups of associated companies such as oil field service companies, equipment companies, and drilling groups. Although the oil companies are heavily controlled by the government, good old Yankee know how still comes at a premium. There are more than 135 U.S. multinational corporations set up in the UAE and there are occasional needs for experienced workers for these companies as well. Also, both the medical and education areas offer opportunities for Americans. In the field of education, the Jumairah American School is for children of Americans in the country. It runs from Kindergarten through the ninth grade. They are usually on the look out for qualified teachers (P.O. Box 2222, Abu Dhabi or through the International School Services, P.O. Box 5910, Princeton, NJ 08540. Roger Hove is the headmaster).

Keep in mind that this is an Arab country. American women are accepted in some areas of employment but the Arab definition of equality when it comes to women is certainly not the same as in America. As in all Arab countries women must dress according to certain standards. American women certainly do not cover their faces in public but bare arms and legs are still taboo.

To obtain a business visa you'll need a letter from a company in the UAE inviting you to discuss a job. A work permit is only issued by the government after it is satisfied that your presence is "in the best interests" of the country. Usually this just means a job in the technical field.

The United Arab Emirates has an embassy at 600 New Hampshire Avenue NW, Washington, DC 20037 (202/338-500). The U.S. Embassy is located at Al-Sudan Street, Abu Dhabi. A detailed listing of American firms operating in United Arab Emirates is available from the Foreign Commercial Service, American Embassy, P.O. Box 4009, Abu Dhabi. Contacts:

Petroleum:

Amerada Hess Oil Corporation
P.O. Box 2046
Abu Dhabi

Exxon (Al Khalij) Inc
P.O. Box 3500
Abu Dhabi

Mobil Abu Dhabi, Inc
P.O. Box 7698
Abu Dhabi

Dubai Petroleum Company
P.O. Box 2222
Dubai

**Oil Field Associated
Companies:**

Dowell Schlumberger
 (Western) S.A.
P.O. Box 4020
Abu Dhabi

Halliburton Ltd.
P.O. Box 57
Abu Dhabi

Imco Services
P.O. Box 11628
Dubai

Crescent Petroleum
P.O. Box 211
Sharjah

Construction:

Fluor Mideast Ltd.
P.O. Box 6858
Abu Dhabi

Bechtel International Corp.
P.O. Box 11101
Dubai

Computers:

Burroughs (Al Ghurair Ent.)
P.O. Box 8547
Dubai

IBM World Trade E/ME/A
P.O. Box 203
Abu Dhabi

Bahrain

GEOGRAPHY:
AREA: 260 sq. mi.
CAPITAL: Manama
PRINCIPAL CITIES: Al Muharraq, Awaii.
TERRAIN: Mostly low desert plain raising gently to low central escarpment.
CLIMATE: Arid, mild, pleasant winters. Very hot dry summers.

PEOPLE:
POPULATION: 585,683
ANNUAL GROWTH RATE: 2.96%
RELIGION: Muslim
LANGUAGE: Arabic
EDUCATION: Attendance in primary school: 98%

LITERACY: 74%
LIFE EXPECTANCY: Men 71; women 76 years.

GOVERNMENT: Traditional Monarchy. No political parties are permitted. The emir is the chief of state; the prime minister is head of government. There are no elections; no suffrage. Government budget: $1.2 billion of which 11% goes for the military.

ECONOMY:
GDP: $6.8 billion
ANNUAL GROWTH RATE: 4%
PER CAPITA GDP: $12,000
AVERAGE RATE OF INFLATION: 2%
WORK FORCE: Of the 140,000 in the work force about 42% are indigenous, 58% are expatriates. 75% work in industry and commerce; 19% services; 3% in agriculture and 3% for the government.
OFFICIAL EXCHANGE RATE: .377 Bahraini dinars = US$
COST OF LIVING INDEX: 104

Of the various Arab sheikdoms in the Middle East, Bahrain is the only archipelago, consisting of 33 islands (only 5 of which are inhabited) strung out in the Persian Gulf off the coast of Saudi Arabia. Most of the population is concentrated in the two principal cities, Manama and Al Muharraq. The indigenous people, 66% of the population, are from the Arabian Peninsula. The most numerous minorities are from Iran, India, Pakistan, Europe, and a sizable number of expatriates from America.

Bahrain was one of the first Arab states to discover oil and was the first to build a refinery. Petroleum and natural gas, the only significant natural resources in the country, dominate the economy providing 60% of the country's revenues. The first refinery was built in 1935 by Caltex Petroleum Corp, Dallas, TX. In 1980, Caltex sold 60% of the company to the state owned, Bahrain Oil Company. Saudi Arabia provides most of the crude oil for refining via pipeline. In addition to the various petroleum industries, Bahrain's other industries include Aluminum Bahrain, (which operates an aluminum smelter), Arab Iron and Steel Company, and Arab Shipbuilding and Repair Yard.

Oil-generated income has allowed the government to concentrate on improving the country's infrastructure. Roads, transportation and communication are all first rate. Schools and medical facilities are also most impressive. There is a major national university which employs many American expatriates. The new Arabian Gulf University expects to enroll 5,000 students from all parts of the gulf region. The College of Health and Sciences, operating under the Minister of Health, trains nurses, pharmacists, and paramedics. There are more than 60 private schools of which half are kindergartens. Westerners living here attend the Bahrain School in Manama which offers the American High School Diploma.

Of the 600-some international companies registered to do business in Bahrain, about 80 U.S. firms are doing business here. Some 200 off-shore banking units with assets exceeding $60 billion are well established.

Although the government has initiated the policy of replacing departing expatriates with nationals, those with specialized skills in the petroleum, petrochemical, educational, health, financial, and management areas should be able to find work here. A work visa is essential and must be secured. The initial step is to obtain a firm job offer then have your prospective employer obtain a No Objection Certificate from the Immigration Department. The cost is $30 and it is valid for 30 days. A more formal work permit will then be issued. This is not a country in which you can visit first for the purpose of job hunting. No visitors visas are being issued at present. However, by contacting U.S. or local companies and sending a detailed resume you should be able to stir up substantial interest. There is no American Chamber of Commerce in the country, however, the Commercial Officer at the U.S. Embassy should be able to supply you with a listing of American companies located here.

Bahrain has an embassy at 3502 International Drive NW, Washington, DC 20008 (202/342-0741). The U.S. Embassy is located on Sheikh Isa Road, Manama. Contacts:

Petroleum:

Amerada Hess Corporation
P.O. Box # 780
Manama

Continental Oil Company
 of Bahrain
P.O. Box 235
Manama

Esso Middle East Marketing
 Inc.
P.O. Box 5170
Manama

Gulf Middle East Trading Co.
Salahuddin Bldg.
P.O. Box 113
Manama

Chemicals:

Gray, Mackenzie & Co.
P.O. Box 210
Manama

Milicheem Intl.
P.O. Box 852
Manama

Banking:

Chemical Bank Trust Co
P.O. Box 5492
Bahrain Tower
Government Road
Manama

Irving Trust Co.
Manama Center
Manama

Manufacturers Hanover
 Trust Co.
P.O. Box 5459
Manama

Oil Field Service:

C.F. Braun & Co.
%Santa Fe International
 Services, Inc.
P.O. Box 5425
Manama

Halliburton Ltd.
P.O. Box 798
Manama

Egypt

GEOGRAPHY:
AREA: 386,650 sq. mi.
CAPITAL: Cairo
PRINCIPAL CITIES: Aswan, Alexandria, Suez, Ismailia
TERRAIN: Vast desert interrupted by Nile valley and delta.
CLIMATE: Dry and hot during the summer, moderate in the winter.

PEOPLE:
POPULATION: 60,765,028
ANNUAL GROWTH RATE: 1.96%
RELIGION: 94% Muslim, mostly Sunni
LANGUAGE: Arabic
EDUCATION: Attendance in primary school: 80%.
LITERACY: 45%
LIFE EXPECTANCY: Men 58; Women 62 years.
GOVERNMENT: Republic with an elected president every six years

who appoints cabinet, vice presidents and prime minister; bicameral legislature but People's Assembly is principal legislative body; Shura Council has consultative role. Government budget: $23 billion of which about 5% is for the military.

ECONOMY:
GNP: 13.9 million
ANNUAL GROWTH RATE: 0.3%
PER CAPITA GNP: $2,400
AVERAGE RATE OF INFLATION: 11%
WORK FORCE: Approximately 41% of the work force are engaged in agriculture; 22% in services; and, 14% industry. The unemployment rate is about 20%.
OFFICIAL EXCHANGE RATE: 3.36 Egyptian pounds = US$
COST OF LIVING INDEX: 081

Egypt has endured as a unified state for more than 5,000 years—a claim few countries of the world can make. You can't spend much time here without being constantly aware of the contrast between the ancient and the modern. It is common to see the work of the Pharaohs from the window of a newly built Holiday Inn. This is the most populous country in the Arab world and the second most populous on the African continent. Ninety-nine percent of the country's 54 million people live in Cairo and Alexandria and along the banks of the Nile. These regions are the world's most densely populated containing over 3,600 persons per square mile.

The country remains as one of the most influential members of the Arab world despite the fact that it is not a major petroleum producer. Agriculture and services each contribute about a third of the GDP with the other third split between industry, petroleum, electricity and construction. Most sizable enterprises, including virtually all heavy industries, are owned by the state. Many privately owned small and medium sized industries' prices are controlled by the state or face competition from products subsidized by the government. Only a bit more than a third of industrial production originates in the private sector, but this share is growing. Construction, non-financial services, and domestic marketing are largely private. Egypt has few natural resources other than the agricultural capacity of the Nile Valley. The major minerals are petroleum, phosphates and iron ore.

There is an ongoing need for western expertise in many areas critical to the growth and development. Computer programmers, consultants, and data processors are in demand by many industries. Those with experience in project management, marketing, accounting and fiscal planning, are also needed by many of the growing industries—particularly in the fields of textiles, food processing, metallurgy and petroleum. Also, those with a construction background or high tech experience can usually find a job here.

A visa is needed to enter the country and, of course, a work permit is required to hold a job regardless of whether you work for an Egyptian company of a foreign company with a base of operations here. The law states that only 10% of the employees of any enterprise may be non-Egyptian, but in practice this rule is often overlooked in order to hire sufficient qualified staff. Also, if you convince the authorities that you spend half of what you earn in the country you are not only permitted to take the rest out of the country but will also be exempt from any Egyptian income taxes. The State Department recommends that visitors obtain cholera, typhoid, tetanus, polio, and hepatitis immunization.

In addition to work with one of the 135 U.S. companies doing business here, there are also opportunities with the U.S. government's many AID programs. For example, U.S. assistance supports electric power, communications, housing, and transport projects. Power Plants built with American assistance generate more power than the Aswan High Dam. Some of the current AID contractors and grantees include:

Telephone Switching
AT&T
El Nasr Building, El Nil St.
Giza, Cairo
Attn: I.N. Shalaby
General Manager

Shoubra Electric Power Plant
Overseas Bechtel, Inc.
11th Floor, Heliopolis
15 A Al Ahram Street
Cairo
Attn: Mr. Said Ahmed
General Manager

Westinghouse International
 Power System
Zamalek, Box 11
Marriott Hotel
Cairo
Attn: Mr. R. Dyre
General Manager

Cairo Sewage
Ambric
P.O. Box 2265 Attaba
Cairo
Attn: Mr. Art Buffington
General Manager

English Language
 Testing/Training
American University in Cairo
113 Kasr El Aini Street
Cairo
Attn: Ms. Carol Clark
General Manager

American Culture Center
38 Farana Street
Alexandria
Mr. Robert Underland
General Manager

Fullbright Commission
1081 Corniche El Nil, Belmont
Building
Garden City
Cairo
Attn: Lynne McNamara
Chief of Party

Alexandria Sewage Project
Waste Water Consultants
 Group
End of Kafr Abdou Street
P.O. Box # 2351
Roushdi, Alexandria
Attn: Mr. Dann Maddan
General Manager

Additional information about U.S. companies doing business in Egypt is available from the U.S. Chamber of Commerce (Cairo) and a listing of the many grant and AID recipients is published in the Business Directory for Egypt 1990/91 available from United States Foreign Commercial Services at the U.S. Embassy in Cairo. Egypt has an embassy at 2310 Decatur Place NW, Washington, DC 20008 (202/232-5400) with consulates in New York, Houston, Chicago, and San Francisco. The U.S. Embassy is located at 5 Sharia Latin America, Garden City, Cairo. Contacts:

Construction:

Ebasco
49 El Mahrouky Street
Heliopolis

McCarthy Brothers
 International, Inc.
49 Abdel Khalek Sarwat Street
Cairo

Chemicals:

Dow Chemical Mideast/Africa
 SA
AEDCO
2 El Saraya El Kobra Street
Garden City, Cairo

Tam Oilfield Services
4 Guezira Street, Zamalek
Cairo

Motor Vehicles:

Ford Motor Co.
12 Mohamed Mahoud Street
Bab El Louk, Cairo

General Motors
Carlin Middle East
2A Beni Amer St.
Giza, Cairo

Electric Components:

General Electric Co.
Arab Engineering &
 Distribution Co.
2 El Saraya El Kobra Street
Garden City, Cairo

Raytheon Worldwide
14 Maahad El Sahari Street
Heliopolis, Cairo

Israel

GEOGRAPHY:
AREA: 7,850 sq. mi.
CAPITAL: Jerusalem
PRINCIPAL CITIES: Tel Aviv, Haifa, Elat, Beersheba
TERRAIN: Negev Desert in the south; low coastal plain; central mountains.
CLIMATE: Temperate. Hot and dry in desert areas.

PEOPLE:
POPULATION: 5,050,850
ANNUAL GROWTH RATE: 1.7%
RELIGION: 83% Jewish; 13% Moslem; 3% Christian
LANGUAGE: Hebrew with Arab in Moslem areas. Most people also speak English
EDUCATION: Attendance in primary school: 97%
LITERACY: Jewish: 88%; Arab: 70%
LIFE EXPECTANCY: Men 75; women 79.

GOVERNMENT: Republic. President is head of state; prime minister is head of government. Elected unicameral Knesset. Executive power vested in Cabinet. Government Budget: $23.3 billion of which 18% is for national defense.

ECONOMY:
GNP: $65.7 billion
ANNUAL GROWTH RATE: 3.5%
PER CAPITA GNP: $13,350
AVERAGE RATE OF INFLATION: 11.3%
WORK FORCE: Of the 1.5 million Israelis in the work force, 30% are involved in public and community service; 23% in industry; 12% in commerce, hotels and restaurants; 10% in finance; 7% in agriculture; 6% in construction. 90% of the labor force is organized. The unemployment rate is about 10.4%.
OFFICIAL EXCHANGE RATE: 2.97 new shekels (NIS) = US$
COST OF LIVING INDEX: 141

Since the Soviet Union altered its policy, in 1989, and allowed a mass emigration of Jews to Israel, this country's labor picture has changed drastically. Prior to the amalgamation of Soviet Jews into its culture and economy, the majority of immigrants were from Arab countries of the Near East and North Africa. As a result Israel has a labor surplus in many of the areas that its neighbors so desperately need.

Israel has a market economy with substantial governmental participation and controlled prices for basic commodities. It depends on imports of oil, food, grain, raw materials, and military equipment. It is poor in natural resources but well endowed with skilled labor. Israel's strong commitment to development and its talented work force led to economic growth rates during the nation's first two decades that frequently exceeded 10% annually. This development transformed the Israeli economy into a modern industrial and services economy with a per capita income comparable to those of Ireland, Spain and Greece.

Among the major industries that contribute to the economic growth are textiles, electronics, diamond cutting, plastics, machinery, and pharmaceuticals. The country's farms provide many of the fruits and grains that stock the shelves of Europe's super markets. Oranges and melons from Israel are common in markets in America.

What the success of the Israeli economy coupled with the influx of skilled Soviet Jews means to Americans interested in seeking work here is bad news. There simply are few good paying jobs for non-Israelis. Where neighboring Arab countries cry for skilled technical, medical, educational, and business talent, the cry here is but a distant whisper.

True, some jobs for expatriates do exist but they are very few and far between. Your best bet is not with an Israeli company but with one of the approximately 200 U.S. companies located here. A list of them is available from the Israel-American Chamber of Commerce & Industry, 35 Shaul Hamelech Blvd., P.O. Box 33174, Tel Aviv.

On the other hand if you have a desire to spend time in Israel and want to volunteer your services there are more than enough openings. From farms, kibbutzim, or archaeological digs, your time and help is often more than welcomed. For the adventurer interested in following the steps of Indiana Jones, consider joining a group of archaeologists on a Biblical dig. Volunteers from students to retirees spend anywhere from a few days to the full summer in Israel or Jordan delving into the past. Skilled archaeologists welcome help from those truly interested in probing the people, events and ancient places described in the Bible.

Some projects qualify for academic credit and can be partly tax deductible. Says noted archaeologist, Robert J. Bull, who has worked with more than 2,500 volunteers, "The kind of patience required on these digs comes best from older people. Our most productive volunteers have been retirees." For information on voluntary work contact the Israel Department of Antiquities, P.O. Box 586, Jerusalem, 91000 or the Israel Department of Antiquities, Ministry of Education and Culture, P.O. Box 586, Jerusalem 91004. A work permit is not necessary for voluntary work.

If you are fortunate enough to obtain a job in Israel your working visa is issued for a period of three months. It may be extended but not for more than 27 months. To obtain a work permit (work visa) you must first obtain either a letter of employment or signed contract from an Israeli employer. He is responsible for applying to the Ministry of Interior for your permit. You as the applicant will be informed whether this request has been granted within six weeks.

Israel has an embassy at 3514 International Drive, NW, Washington, DC 20008 (202/364-5500) with consulates in Atlanta, Boston, Chicago, Houston, Los Angeles, New York, Philadelphia, and San Francisco. The U.S. Embassy is located at 71 Hayarkon Street, Tel Aviv. (Note: Israel proclaimed Jerusalem its capitol in 1950. The United States, like nearly every other country, does not recognize this disputed area as the national capital and maintains its embassy in Tel Aviv.) Contacts:

Electronics:

Elul Technologies Ltd.
35 Shaul Hamelech Blvd.
Tel Aviv

Control Data Israel Ltd.
Brodezky 43, Ramat Aviv
Tel Aviv

Eldan Electronic Instruments
 Co., Ltd.
16 Ollav St, P.O. Box 20200
Tel Aviv

Manufacturing:

Black & Decker Mfg., Ltd.
26 Hasadna St, P.O. Box 116
Halon

Agentex Ltd.
13 Hankin St, P.O. Box 22184
Tel Aviv

Industrial Controls Ltd.
 adel Taos
17 Modlin St., P.O. Box 14095
Bnel Brak

Electra (Israel) Ltd.
19 Petach Tikva Road
P.O. Box 2180
Tel Aviv

Financial:

Horwath, Bawly, Millner & Co.
P.O. Box 777
5 Habankim Street
Haifa

American-Israel Bank Ltd.
11 Rothschild Blvd.
P.O. Box 1346
Tel Aviv

Chemicals:

ICC (Israel) Chemicals Ltd.
P.O. Box 11109
94 Ben Gurion Road
Tel Aviv

F. Gadliesh
23 Ehud Street
Zahala

Witco Chemical Ltd.
P.O. Box 975
Haifa

Jordan

GEOGRAPHY:
AREA: 35,000 sq. mi.
CAPITAL: Amman

PRINCIPAL CITIES: Irbid, Az-Zarqa, Al Aqabah
TERRAIN: Mostly high desert plateau in east; Great Rift Valley separates East and West banks of the Jordan River.
CLIMATE: Mostly arid desert; rainy season in west (November to April).

PEOPLE:
POPULATION: 3,961,194
ANNUAL GROWTH RATE: 3.6%
RELIGION: 92% Muslim; 8% Christian
LANGUAGE: Arabic
EDUCATION: Attendance in primary school: 78%
LITERACY: 71%
LIFE EXPECTANCY: Men 70; women 73 years.
GOVERNMENT: Constitutional monarchy with the king holding the balance of power. The prime minister exercises executive authority in the name of the king. Cabinet is appointed by the king. No elections.

ECONOMY:
GNP: $11.5 billion
ANNUAL GROWTH RATE: 5%
PER CAPITA GNP: $3,000
AVERAGE RATE OF INFLATION: 5%
WORK FORCE: 80% of Jordanians work in some form of agriculture; the remainder are involved in manufacturing and mining. The unemployment rate is about 20%.
OFFICIAL EXCHANGE RATE: .701 Jordanian dinars = US$
COST OF LIVING INDEX: 091

Jordan is a small country with limited natural resources. Of a total land area a bit smaller than the state of Indiana, just over a tenth of the land is arable. Even the effective use of this meager amount is restricted by water shortages. The nation's most important natural resources are phosphates, potash, and limestone. It has virtually no forests or known fossil fuels resources. In essence, Jordan is a country that is being dragged from it's century-old life as Biblical remnant into the 21st century. Without substantial aid from neighboring Arab states and western nations Jordan would remain an impoverished country. Since 1952, U.S. aid to Jordan has exceeded $2 billion!

The majority of U.S. aid has been funneled into Jordan's infrastructure (such as roads, mineral development, and electrification) and agriculture. The various aid packages have paid dividends in boosting Jordanian economic growth. Unfortunately, the political climate within the Middle East has been a constant source of frustration in the government's attempt to meet it's economic challenges. The Palestinian question, problems along the West Bank, and during late 1990 and early 1991, the flood of Iraqi refugees entering the country have been a major barrier to economic growth and development.

Jobs in Jordan are either limited exclusively to U.S. aid programs or working with one of the 26 U.S. companies located here. Although there are occasional demands for high tech skills there are very few openings. In general the job picture is bleak.

Jordan has an embassy at 3504 International Drive NW, Washington, DC 20008 (202/966-2664). The U.S. Embassy is located on Jebel Amman, Amman. Contacts:

Engineering/Construction:

Bechtel Corp.
P.O. Box 5226
Amman

CH2M Hill Inc
% Arabtech, P.O. Box 7323
Amman

Stanley Consultants Inc
P.O. Box 926571,
Central Post Office, Abdall
Amman

Wilbur Smith & Associates
P.O. Box 2572
Amman

Jacobs Engineering Group
P.O. Box 17207,
Dahiyat El-Hussein Post Office
Amman

Financial:

Chase Manhattan Bank N.A.
P.O. Box 20191, First Circle,
Jebal
Amman

First National City Bank
Jordan Insurance Bldg
Third Circle, Jebal
Amman

Arthur Young & Co
Sharia Wadi Es-Sir,
Amman

Manufacturing:

Raytheon Technical Assistance
Corp
P.O. Box 3414, Jebal
Amman

Tektronix Sales and Service   Khalil Hamarnech
 Office   P.O. Box 788, Hashimi Street
P.O. Box 35055   Amman
Amman

Kuwait

GEOGRAPHY:
AREA: 6,880 sq. mi.
CAPITAL: Kuwait City.
PRINCIPAL CITIES: Ahmadi, Jahra, Fahaheel.
TERRAIN: Primarily all desert.
CLIMATE: Extremely hot and dry in the summers; short, cool winters.

PEOPLE:
POPULATION: 1,819,322 million.
ANNUAL GROWTH RATE 4.5%.
RELIGION: Islam.
LANGUAGE: Arabic.
LITERACY: 71%.
LIFE EXPECTANCY: 74 years.

GOVERNMENT: Constitutional monarchy with the Amir serving as head of state. A National Assembly is elected by adult males who have resided in Kuwait before 1920 and their male descendants. (This represents about 8.3% of the citizenry of the country.) Government Budget: About $8 billion.

ECONOMY:
GDP $25.7 billion.
ANNUAL GROWTH RATE: 5.24%.
PER CAPITA GDP: $15,100.
WORK FORCE: Of the 675,000 in the work force (the majority being non-Kuwaitis), 45% are employed in services; 20% in construction; 12% trades; 9% manufacturing; 3% finance and real estate; 2% mining and quarrying; and 2% power and water.
OFFICIAL EXCHANGE RATE: .29 Kuwaiti Dinars = US$
COST OF LIVING INDEX: 111

Without question, one of the largest employers of Americans in the region following the Gulf War has been Kuwait. Not only did the wanton destruction wreaked by Saddam's forces destroy the majority of the country's petroleum industry but did significant damage to major highways, water pumping stations, sewage treatment plants and much of the infrastructure of the nation's largest city, Kuwait City.

In addition, many of the workers who had been employed in **every** segment of the nation's business and commerce were forced to leave Kuwait. More than a million expatriates worked in Kuwait before the war. (The largest group of non-Kuwaitis were Palestinians carrying Jordanian passports.) When most were forced to leave, consider the impact on rebuilding of the nation's economy when the war ended. Fortunately, many foreign workers are slowly drifting back looking for work. Some jobs are available; many await the continuing rebuilding process. The need for menial labor outside the construction industry is marginal; the need for skilled workers in most fields will last for many years. One expert predicts that Kuwait will have an open employment calendar well into the 21st century.

Before the war Kuwait was one of the wealthiest countries in the world. Kuwaitis, who make up but 40% of the total population, enjoy a far greater percentage of this wealth than the expatriates living in this country. The wealth of Kuwait is based both on its oil exports (accounting for about 85% of pre-war income) and a return on the country's foreign investments in overseas real estate holdings and industry. The country owns major international hotel chains, mining companies, manufacturing operations, publishing companies, and even cattle ranches in Wyoming.

The gulf war highlighted Kuwait's precarious geographic location as a small nation (slightly smaller than New Jersey) on the Persian Gulf with Saudi Arabia to the south and Iraq to the north. Kuwait's modern history began in the 18th century with the founding of the city of Kuwait by members of the Anaiza tribe from Qatar. The first contact with the Western world didn't occur until 1775 when the British operated Persian Gulf-Aleppo Mail Service was diverted through Kuwait from Persian occupied Basra (now in Iraq.)

In the 19th century, Kuwait was pressured by both the Turks and various powerful Arabian tribes to cede land. To assure some semblance of independence, Sheik Mubarak Al Sabah signed in 1899, an agreement with the United Kingdom pledging himself and his successors "neither to cede any territory nor to receive agents or representatives of any foreign power without the British government's consent." Until 1961, Kuwait enjoyed special treaty relations with the United Kingdom, which handled Kuwait's defense and foreign affairs. On June 19, 1961 Kuwait became a fully independent country.

The problems with Iraq stem from several agreements; some signed, some unsigned. In 1913 Kuwait signed an agreement with Turkey establishing the border between the area that was then part of the Ottoman Empire and the region then called Kuwait. When Iraq gained its independence from Turkey in 1932, Iraq accepted the Kuwait-Iraq border but never formerly ratified the previous 1913 Kuwait-Turkey agreement. In 1961, Iraq claimed Kuwait arguing that before British intervention the land had been part of the Ottoman Empire under Iraqi control. In other words, although the region was part of the Ottoman Empire the "fact" that Iraqis controlled it gave them the right to claim it as their own. No formal agreement was ever reached between Iraq and Kuwait as to the borders or even Kuwait's right to exist. It is this far fetched 1961 claim that Saddam resorted to when he invaded Kuwait in the summer of 1990.

The State of Kuwait has been ruled by the Sabah family since 1751. The constitution signed in 1962 contains detailed provisions on the powers and relationships of the branches of government and on the rights of citizens. For example, upon the death of the amir, the crown prince assumes his position. A new crown prince is then selected by members of the Sabah family from among descendants of Mubarak the Great.

The present ruler is Amir Jabir al-Ahmad al-Jabir Al Sabah. His successor is the crown prince and current prime minister, Sheik Saad al-Abdullah al-Salim Al Sabah. Prior to the war, the leadership of both the present amir and his predecessor gave Kuwaitis some of the most advanced social benefits in the world. The government has sponsored a wide range of social welfare benefits including: retirement income, marriage bonuses, housing loans, virtually guaranteed employment, free medical services and education at all levels. The state also provides payments to the disabled, the senile, orphans, the poor, students' families, widows, unmarried women over the age of 18, and families of prisoners. No other country has such an extensive social program.

Kuwait is also a leading practitioner of pre-birth-to-grave medical care. By the mid-1980s some of the major health problems that had plagued the country had been brought under control or eliminated. Today, the country maintains 14 hospitals, 105 dental clinics, 17 maternity centers, 28 pediatric centers and 500 school clinics. The government pays the salaries of more than 14,000 medical personnel including over 2,100 physicians and 6,000 nurses. There is one doctor for every 620 residents and one nurse for every 220 residents, a ratio no other society can match. Yet more than 4 of every five physicians is a non-Kuwaiti. About 40% of the country's doctors are Egyptians. The need for qualified medical personnel is still acute and Kuwait is on the constant look out for experienced Westerners willing to relocate here.

The literacy rate, one of the highest in the Arab world, is due to the governments support of public education. All citizens are given a free education; they may attend colleges and universities anywhere in the world with full government support. In 1990, 3,500 Kuwaitis attended school in the United States. Foreigners residing in Kuwait obtain some but not all of these welfare benefits. For example, the right to own stock in publicly traded companies, real estate, or a majority interest in a business is limited to Kuwaiti citizens.

Like other Arab countries oil transformed both the nation and its people. The discovery of the great Burgan Oil Fields in 1938 by the Kuwait Oil company (KOC)—then jointly owned by Gulf oil and British Petroleum—was one of the great mineral finds of the century. The Burgan field alone is said to be one of the world's largest and most productive petroleum pools. In 1976, the government of Kuwait nationalized the Kuwait Oil Company. The following year the government also took over on shore production in the so-called Neutral Zone between Kuwait and Saudi Arabia (boundaries in this area are still in dispute). KOC produces jointly there with Texaco which obtained a concession from Saudi Arabia to drill in the Neutral Zone.

Although petroleum is by far the largest industry in Kuwait, the country has been active in building and expanding other areas as well. Even after the devastating effects of the war, much of the country's industry is now operating and expanding. Fortunately, this also means employment possibilities for skilled Americans.

Aside from the huge drilling operation, now back to a semblance of normalcy following Iraq's setting the wells ablaze, Kuwait maintains several large export-oriented petrochemical units including refineries and a range of small petroleum-related manufacturers. The nation's industry also includes a huge water distillation facility as well as plants producing ammonia, fertilizer, bricks, and cement. Agriculture is a growing part of the country's economic development, particularly commercial fishing. The need for specialists in all types of agriculture and water resources is especially acute.

Prior to the war, Kuwait was a beacon for workers. The country had money to spare, more projects than could be easily managed, and far too few countrymen ready to tackle the growing number of jobs. The nation's economic development was achieved in part simply by importing foreign workers. Non-Kuwaitis appear prominently throughout the employment spectrum filling professional, technical, managerial, and clerical posts for which there are not enough qualified Kuwaitis.

At latest count, non-Kuwaitis held about 80% of the professional, technical, and managerial jobs in the country. At the other end of the spectrum, construction labor, is made up of about 95% expatriates. Of these foreign workers, about two-thirds are other Arabs. Almost all of the other one-third are skilled workers from Asian countries such as India, Pakistan, Bangladesh, etc. Filipinos make up much of the skilled trades and lower level supervision. Most management and supervisory positions are filled by Western professionals.

The war has obviously altered Kuwait's present and future. One thing is certain, the country will continue on its pre-war path of social, economic and most important, industrial development. The infrastructure is still a major priority with billions of dollars planned for new roads, airports, communications systems, sewage plants, water treatment facilities, schools and hospitals.

Immediately following the end of the war in January, 1991, the Kuwaiti government embarked upon a multi-stage program to rebuild the country. The initial stage was a three month damage assessment and emergency relief program. Hundreds of contracts were signed with more than $350 million going to American firms. The second stage has been rebuilding of the oil fields. Although the U.S. Corps of Engineers has been involved in this work, the primary contractor was the Bechtel Corporation, headquartered in San Francisco.

Getting information about jobs in Kuwait still isn't easy as so many companies and governments are involved in the reconstruction process. If you have skills appropriate to the type of work described in the reconstruction process, then it would be worthwhile for you to contact or send resumes to the various Ministries shown below as well as contacting the listed American companies doing business in Kuwait.

Key Ministries:

Ministry of Planning
Ministry of Public Works
Ministry of Communications
Ministry of Oil
Ministry of Interior
Ministry of Electricity and Water

Specific Addresses can be obtained from the Kuwaiti Embassy in

Washington, D.C. or any Kuwaiti Consulate. Letters can also be addressed to the particular Ministry in Kuwait City, Kuwait via Overseas Airmail. The Ministry may consider you for posts they have available for non-Kuwaiti personnel or refer your qualifications to Kuwaiti corporations.

Visiting Kuwait without a job or an invitation from the government or local sponsor is impractical if not almost impossible. A visa is necessary. However, any application to travel to Kuwait will be considered individually by either the embassy in Washington or the consulate in New York.

Most Americans working here either live in their own apartment in Kuwait City or company-operated compounds complete with modern supermarkets, schools and medical facilities. As mentioned, modern hospitals are on the rebound and many of the hospitals that had been stripped by Saddam's forces have been restocked.

Health requirements change and it is recommended that you contact the U.S. State Department before departing to determine the latest vaccination or immunization requirements. Local telephone service is back in order as well and long distance service.

As a result of the war and the Kuwaiti Government's desire to continue their social and industrial growth, the country still is in need of qualified workers in: Construction, the industrial sector, the petroleum and engineering field, medicine and education. Opportunities certainly exist and significant income can be generated.

Companies Working in Kuwait

Engineering/Construction:

The Architects Collaborative
P.O. Box 23548
Kuwait City

Bechtel Group Inc.
Eastern Bechtel Company
P.O. Box 23930 Safat
Kuwait City

Combustion Engineering Inc.
Al Julaiah General Trading &
Contracting
P.O. Box 173
Kuwait City

P.S.C. Supply Co.
P.O. Box 9465
Ahmadi

Dames & Moore
P.O. Box 26346
Safat 13124

De Leuw Cather International
P.O. Box 25582
Safat

Kirby Building Systems S.F.K.
P.O. Box 23933
Safat

McDermott Kuwait
P.O. Box 8118
Salmiya

Otis Elevator Co.
P.O. Box 9277
Dasma

VTN Corp.
VTN Resident Engineer
P.O. Box 31076
Sulaibikhat

Weatherford International
Ajal Contracting & General
 Trading Co.
P.O. Box 26256
Safat

**Technical Products &
Services:**

Carrier Air Conditioning
P.O. Box 22750
Safat

Curtiss-Wright Corp.
P.O. Box 21759
Safat

Dresser Kuwait S.A.K.
P.O. Box 4544
Safat

EG&G Inc.-Sealol Kuwait
 K.S.C.
P.O. Box 46833
Fahaheel

Grumman Aerospace & Data
 Systems
%Kuwait Computer Services
P.O. Box 5113
Safat

Onan Corp.
P.O. Box 26567
Safat

NCR Corp.
A.F. Al Fahed Trading &
 Contracting
P.O. Box 2952
Safat 13030

Raytheon Co.—Raytheon Gulf
 Systems
P.O. Box 33147
Rawda

SGS Control Services, Inc.
P.O. Box 9705
Kuwait City

UOP Inc.—Procon Middle
 East, Inc.
Safat

Petroleum & Chemicals:

Baker Oil Tools
Gulf Int'l General Trading Co.
P.O. Box 25741
Safat

Drew Chemical Corp.
P.O. Box 20423
Safat

Gamlen Chemical Co.
P.O. Box 241
Kuwait City

Getty Oil Co.
P.O. Box 187
Kuwait City

Parker Drilling Co.
P.O. Box 9277
Ahmadi

United Catalysts Inc.—VTN
P.O. Box 31076
Sulaibikhat

Vetco—Gray Inc.
Al-Julaiah General Trading &
 Contracting
P.O. Box 26142
Safat

Manufacturing:

Continental Can Co.
P.O. Box 5410
Ahmadi

John Crane Inc.
P.O. Box 26142
Safat

Foxboro Co.
Abdulaziz Abdulmohsin
 Alrashed
P.O. Box 241
Kuwait City

Financial:

Chase Manhattan Bank
The Commercial Bank of
 Kuwait
P.O. Box 2861
Safat

Merrill Lynch
P.O. Box 4906
Kuwait City

INA Corporation
Kuwait Maritime &
 Mercantile Co.
P.O. Box 78
Safat

Hotels & Contract Services:

ITT Sheraton
Kuwait Sheraton Hotel
P.O. Box 5902
Kuwait City

Marriott Corp.
P.O. Box 23933
Safat

Morocco

GEOGRAPHY:
AREA: 172,413 sq. mi.

CAPITAL: Rabat
PRINCIPAL CITIES: Casablanca, Marrakech, Fez
TERRAIN: Mostly mountains with rich coastal plains.
CLIMATE: Mediterranean, becoming more extreme in the interior.

PEOPLE:
POPULATION: 28,558,635
ANNUAL GROWTH RATE: 2.12%
RELIGION: Muslim
LANGUAGE: Arabic
EDUCATION: Attendance in primary school: 81%
LITERACY: 30%
LIFE EXPECTANCY: Men 66; women 70 years.

GOVERNMENT: Constitutional monarchy with a prime minister and ministers named by and responsible to the king. Elected unicameral legislature. Universal suffrage for those over 20. Government budget: $4 billion.

ECONOMY:
GDP: $70.3 billion
ANNUAL GROWTH RATE: 2%
PER CAPITA GDP: $2,500.
AVERAGE RATE OF INFLATION: 4.5%
WORK FORCE: Of the 6 million Moroccans in the work force, 39% are involved in agriculture; 21% commerce and services; 18% industry; 10% administration; and, 8% construction. The unemployment rate is about 16%.
OFFICIAL EXCHANGE RATE: 9.6 dirhams = US$
COST OF LIVING INDEX: 112

Although still an underdeveloped nation, Morocco is one of the more advanced of the non-petroleum Arab countries. Yet, drive from Casablanca to Marrakech and you're in a typical Biblical land. Modern agricultural equipment is rare. Mules led by Moroccans garbed in traditional caftans work the fields, often with hand-hewed wooden implements. Fences are rarely, if ever, seen. Shepherds actually do guard their flocks by night and it is not uncommon to see rows of young boys along the sides of the road holding aloft batches of mint or a fresh caught fish for your consideration. Poor roads, poorer farmers and poverty is all quite obvious. Arrive in Marrakech and cultures are in conflict. Within walking distance from a centuries-old market (complete with souks selling spices, rugs, and hand crafted copper ware) exists one of the world's most modern, luxurious hotels. It becomes quite obvious that the country is doing its best to join the 21st century.

Morocco's education system alone has been the source of national funding and special attention. Education is free and compulsory through primary school. Unlike the United States, education surpasses national defense in the government's budget—28%. Unfortunately despite government allocations, population pressure and a shortage of teachers has strained the system. Americans with an interest in teaching here have a good opportunity to be considered for a job. Write to the Moroccan Department of Education, Rabat and request information on openings for foreigners.

Although the country is fossil fuel poor it has made a significant investment building dams for both irrigation and the generation of electricity. Its richest natural resource is phosphates. It has three-quarters of the world's known phosphate reserves and is the third largest producer after the United States and the Soviet Union. The country's second biggest asset is its fisheries resource, especially off the Western Sahara. It has spent heavily developing a 180-ship high seas fishing fleet and the port infrastructure to support the fleet.

Relations with the United States have been excellent for many years. As a result, the U.S. Agency for International Development (AID) has granted millions of dollars directed primarily towards agriculture, family planning, vocational education, and renewable energy development. About 110 Peace Corps volunteers are engaged in English language training, rural sanitation, social work, vocational education, and fisheries projects. This is one of the Peace Corps' oldest and largest programs. In addition, the U.S. has just built a $175 million Voice of America transmitter here—the world's largest.

Obtaining work here is primarily limited to one of the 45 American firms doing business in the country or with one of the U.S. government AID programs. A list of American companies is available from the American Chamber of Commerce in Morocco, 30 Avenue des F.A.R., Casablanca. Although visas are not required to visit, a work permit issued through the Department of Labor is necessary to enter the country for the purpose of holding a job. Your potential employer will handle these details for you.

Morocco has an embassy at 1601 21st Street NW, Washington, DC 20009 (202/462-7979). The U.S. maintains its Embassy at 2 Avenue de Marrakech, Rabat. Contacts:

Chemicals:

Lepetit-Pharmaghreb S.A.
280 Blvd Yacoub El Manscur
Casablanca

Gamlem Chemical
Ste. Somel Peintures 62
Blvd Addellah Ben Yacine
Casablanca

Union Carbide Middle
 East Ltd.
Bureau de Liaison-Marc
6 Eme Etage-Tour Atlas
Place Zellaga
Casablanca

Manufacturing:

General Tire & Rubber Co
Boite Postale 2608
Ain-es-Sebea
Casablanca

Interlame du Maroc S.A.
Route F
Secteur Industriel 2526
Ain-Sebea, B.P. 2544
Casablanca

ITT Maroc
1 Rue Louis Guillotte
Casablanca

Otis Maroc S.A.
245 Blvd Emile Zola
Casablanca

Food Products:

CPC Maghreb S.A.
Rue St. Raphael Mariscal
Ain Bordja
Casablanca

Pharmaceuticals:

Colgate-Palmolive
11 Avenue de l'Armee Royale
Casablanca

Merck, Sharp & Dohme Intl.
Immeuble Oceania
1 Place Mirabeau
Casablanca

Pfizer Laboratories
Angle Rue Pierre Parent
 et Karatchi
Casablanca

Oman

GEOGRAPHY:
AREA: 82,030 sq. mi.
CAPITAL: Muscat
PRINCIPAL CITIES: Matrah, Ruwi, Salalah, Sohar
TERRAIN: Vast central desert plain with rugged mountains in the north
and south.
CLIMATE: Dry desert. Hot and humid along the coast; hot and dry in the

interior. Strong southeast summer monsoon (May through November) in the far south.

POPULATION: 1,701,470
ANNUAL GROWTH RATE: 3.46%
RELIGION: Muslim
LANGUAGE: Arabic
EDUCATION: Attendance in primary school: 80%
LITERACY: 30%
LIFE EXPECTANCY: Men 65; women 69 years.

GOVERNMENT: Absolute monarchy. Sultan appoints 45 member Assembly to advise him. No suffrage; no elections! Government budget: $4.2 billion of which a third goes to the military.

ECONOMY:
GDP: $16.4 billion
ANNUAL GROWTH RATE: 6.1%
PER CAPITA GDP: $10,000
AVERAGE RATE OF INFLATION: 2%
WORK FORCE: Of the 500,000 in the work force, 60% are involved in agriculture; 58% are non-Omani.
OFFICIAL EXCHANGE RATE: 0.3848 rials = US$
COST OF LIVING INDEX: 110

Were it not for oil this tiny sultanate (slightly smaller than Kansas) would still rely exclusively on agriculture, goat and camel herding, fishing and traditional handicraft to sustain its populace. With the discovery of oil in 1964 things changed radically. Although not a petroleum producer on a scale similar to its neighbors, the income generated by petroleum allowed the Sultan, Qaboos bin Sa'id, to initiate major revisions in his country. For example, the number of schools rose from 3 in 1970 to 700 in 1987, while hospital and clinic beds increased during this period from 12 to 2,800. In the Muscat capital area, both a modern international airport and a deep water port have been constructed. A national road network links the northern and southern regions.

In an effort to diversify, the government built a $200 million copper mining and refining plant at Sohar. Despite its rich oil reserves and income from petroleum, U.S. loans and grants amounting to $16 million were awarded in 1987 for water resources, fisheries, training and education. Oman has been developing many non-oil resources including manufacturing, banking, and construction.

More than half the work force is composed of non-Omanis; the vast majority from India, Pakistan, Bangladesh, Sri Lanka, Egypt and Jordan. Of these third world nationals, almost all are unskilled or semi-skilled laborers. To solve the country's serious shortage of skilled labor, the Department of Manpower initiated a program in cooperation with many private companies to select certain applicants as apprentice carpenters, motor mechanics, electricians, masons, etc. For Americans, jobs are often available in the high tech and petroleum business. The best opportunities are with existing U.S. companies. The Economic/Commercial Officer at the U.S. Embassy is the best person to contact regarding American companies in Oman.

It is almost impossible to visit Oman as a tourist. A visa or a "no objection certificate" is required of U.S. citizens for entry, and sponsorship by a resident of Oman is usually necessary. Application for a certificate can only be made by the sponsor in Oman. To obtain a work permit you must have a job before entry.

Oman has an embassy at 2342 Massachusetts Avenue NW, Washington, DC 20008 (202/387-1980). The U.S. Embassy can be reached by writing P.O. Box #966, Muscat. Contacts:

Petroleum:

Oman Refinery
 Company L.L.C.
P.O. Box 6568
Ruwi

Oil Field Supplies:

Sharikat Hani L.L.C.
Div. A-Z Intl
P.O. Box 4618, Ruwi
Muscat

Geosource Ltd
P.O. Box 9014, Mina A. Fahal
Muscat

Oman Oil Industry Supplies &
Service Co.
P.O. Box 127
Muscat

Dowell-Schlimberger (jv)
P.O. Box 9014, Mina A. Fahal
Muscat

Construction/Engineering:

Omani Constructors
P.O. Box 4851, Ruwi
Muscat

Tetra Tech Intl. Inc.
P.O. Box 4822
Muscat

Financial: Price Waterhouse & Co.
                                            Sheikh Mohammen
National Bank of Oman Ltd.   bin Ameir Bldg.
P.O. Box 3751, Ruwi   P.O. Box 5482, Ruwi
Muscat   Muscat

Coopers & Lybrand   Citibank, N.A.
P.O. Box 6075   P.O. Box 918
Al Ma'amoor Street   Muscat
Greater Muttrah, Ruwi
Muscat

Qatar

GEOGRAPHY:
AREA: 4,427 sq. mi.
CAPITAL: Doha
PRINCIPAL CITIES: Umm Said, al-Khor, Dukkan
TERRAIN: Mostly flat and barren desert.
CLIMATE: Hot and dry. Humid and sultry in the summer.

PEOPLE:
POPULATION: 512,79
ANNUAL GROWTH RATE: 2.56%
RELIGION: Muslim
LANGUAGE: Arabic
EDUCATION: Attendance in primary school: 90%
LITERACY: 50%
LIFE EXPECTANCY: Men 70; women 75 years.
GOVERNMENT: Monarchy. Amir serves as head of state and head of
government. Legislature is the State Advisory Council appointed by
Amir. Government budget: $3.4 billion.

ECONOMY:
GDP: $8.8 billion
ANNUAL GROWTH RATE: -0.5%
PER CAPITA GDP: $17,500
AVERAGE RATE OF INFLATION: 3%
WORK FORCE: Of the 105,000 in the work force, 70% work in
industry, services and commerce; 10% agriculture; and, 20% govern-

ment. The majority of the work force in the commercial sector (85%) are from India, Sri Lanka, Pakistan, and Bangladesh.
OFFICIAL EXCHANGE RATE: 3.62 Qatar riyals = US$
COST OF LIVING INDEX: 92

This tiny nation, about the size of the states of Connecticut and Rhode Island combined has one of the highest per capita incomes in the world. All thanks to that Black Gold discovered in the desert in 1939. Oil revenues provide about 90% of the country's economy. Over the past several decades the amir recognized the need to expand his country's economic base and created a major industrial center in the city of Umm Said. In full operation are a refinery with a 50,000 b/d capacity, a fertilizer plant for urea and ammonia, a steel plant, and a petrochemical plant. All these industries use gas for fuel. Most of them are joint ventures between European and Japanese firms and the state owned QGPC.

Although the United States has been a major supplier for Qatar's oil and gas industry, to date there has been little American investment here. In 1989, two U.S. oil firms, Sohio and Amoco, concluded gas/oil exploration agreements in Qatar's on-and-off shore operations. The agreements are for 25 year terms and are based upon cost sharing. Growing numbers of foreign-educated Qataris, including many educated in America, are returning to Qatar to assume key positions formerly occupied by expatriates. Over the past few years the country has tightened the administration of its foreign manpower programs. Security is an important basis for the country's strict entry and immigration rules and regulations. For example, it is almost impossible for an unmarried woman to enter the country. To work here you need a local sponsor to obtain a Non-Objection Certificate from the minister of the Interior. If you plan to stay for more than 90 days you need a residence visa that requires sheaves of paperwork to flow within and without the various bureaucratic departments. The bottom line is that your chances of working here are extremely slim unless, in the eyes of the country's moguls, there is a significant need for your particular talent and there is no Qatari available to handle the position.

There is no local U.S. Chamber of Commerce and but two dozen American companies established here. If you are fortunate to be one of the few fortunate ones granted a job permit expect a high level of pay and excellent working and living conditions.

Qatar has an embassy at Suite 1180, 600 New Hampshire Avenue NW, Washington, DC 20008 (202/338-0111). The U.S. Embassy is located in Doha at Fariq Bin Omran (opposite the television station). The address is P.O. Box 2399. Contacts:

Petroleum Related:

Baroid International
P.O. Box # 150
Doha

Drilco Inc.
P.O. Box # 150
Doha

Santa Fe International Services
 Inc.
P.O. Box 4396
Doha

Weatherford Oil Tool Middle
 East Ltd.
%Jaldah Motors & Trading
Doha

Financial:

The Commercial Bank of Qatar,
 Ltd.
P.O. Box 3232
Doha

Price Waterhouse & Co.
P.O. Box 6689
Doha

Peat, Marwick Mitchell Int'l.
P.O. Box 6689
Doha

Contractors:

Brown & Root Inc.
Doha

J. Ray McDermott & Co.
Doha

Saudi Arabia

GEOGRAPHY:
AREA: 830,000 sq. mi.
CAPITAL: Riyadh
PRINCIPAL CITIES: Jeddah, Makkah, Medina, Taif
TERRAIN: Mainly desert.
CLIMATE: Arid with great extremes of temperature.

PEOPLE:
POPULATION: 18,196,793 million (of which 4 million are foreign nationals).
ANNUAL GROWTH RATE: 3.24%
RELIGION: Islam
LANGUAGE: Arabic
EDUCATION: Attendance in primary school: 80%.
LITERACY: 52%
LIFE EXPECTANCY: Men 66; women, 69 years.

GOVERNMENT: Monarchy with council of ministers. No constitution. King is chief of state and head of the government. No legislature. Governed according to Islamic law (Sharia). No political parties; no suffrage. Government budget: $40 billion; defense is a third of total budget.

ECONOMY:
GDP: $194 billion
ANNUAL GROWTH RATE:1%
PER CAPITA GNP: $11,000.
AVERAGE RATE OF INFLATION: 1%
WORK FORCE: Of the non-oil industrial, 4%; agriculture, 3% workforce: Approximately 3 million employed, 33% are Saudi; 66% foreign. 30% of the work force are employed in agriculture; 45% in commerce and government; 15% in construction; 5% industry; 5% oil and mining. There is no unemployment
OFFICIAL EXCHANGE RATE: 3.75 riyals = US$
COST OF LIVING INDEX: 112

Like the California gold find in 1849, the discovery of oil by a U.S. company in the 1930's changed the face and future of Saudi Arabia. Today it is the world's leading oil exporter with its black gold accounting for 99% of the country's exports by value. More than 95% of all Saudi oil is produced on behalf of the Saudi government by the Arabian American Oil Company (ARAMCO) which was originally owned by four U.S. oil companies.

ARAMCO previously held a concession but now operates under new arrangements that provide for overall management of the enterprise, the rendering of various technical and administrative services, and conducting an exploration program. This arrangements means jobs for skilled Westerners. Since the sharp rise in petroleum revenues began in 1974,

Saudi Arabia has been one of the fastest growing nations in the world. This rapid growth and economic expansion coupled with the nation's need for Western technology and know-how has meant a tremendous demand for a wide range of skilled personnel. Naturally, the country is constantly searching for individuals with experience and knowledge of petroleum: technicians, geologists, engineers, construction personnel, facility managers and project directors. However, there is also a need for those in most other professions.

Saudi Arabia is the largest employer of Americans within the Arab block. In the 1970s the country initiated a series of five-year plans to bring the nation into the 20th century. The emphasis was first on the infrastructure—telecommunications, roads, ports, electricity and water. The results were impressive. The total length of paved highways tripled, power generation increased by a multiple of 28, and the capacity of the seaports grew tenfold.

The period ending in 1985 saw less spending on the infrastructure and a greater concentration on education, health and social services. The current period, through 1990, continues to emphasize growth in these areas with a strong concentration on joint projects with Western countries. Since 1985, there has been great need for individuals with experience in industry, agriculture, banking and construction.

Of course, with Iraq's invasion and usurpation of Kuwait in 1990 the entire political structure in the Middle East was shaken. Old alliances were questioned and the threat of a major war engulfing the region hovered like the sword of Damocles. Yet, the need for oil remained constant. The engines of the Western World are totally dependent upon Saudi oil and they are willing to risk total warfare to assure its continuance. As a result, the need for Western expertise in the petroleum fields is as great or greater than ever.

The need for Western talent extends throughout the country. Two new industrial cities, Jubail and Yanbu, are built around the use of indigenous oil and gas feedstock to produce steel, petrochemicals, fertilizer, and refined oil products. Naturally, the creation of a city requires a wide range of talents. Needed throughout the country are those skilled in such areas as: education (from pre-school through the highest academic levels.), construction, health care, engineers, computer personnel, project managers, operations and maintenance personnel, military, and technicians. The pay scale for Americans is among the highest paid as are the benefits.

Work permits are issued for a period of up to two years by the Ministry of Labor and Social Affairs. A residence permit is needed if you stay in the country over three years. The Ministry must also approve of any organization employing fewer than 75% Saudi employees. If there are no local workers technically competent to handle the work approval is granted.

It should be understood, however, that Saudi Arabia, like other Arab states, will not issue a work permit to any applicant who is Jewish.

Most Americans working in Saudi Arabia live in special communities designed for foreigners. For those who live on the local economy, apartments are still hard to find in Riyadh and Jeddah although housing construction has been underway for many years. Life in American complexes built close to work sites is not unlike life at home. Recreational facilities with modern swimming pools are common. Commissaries stock many American foods. The cost of food both in the housing complexes as well as in the local markets will vary. Western foods, fruits and vegetables will be high.

English is spoken in most work areas but a few words of Arabic are helpful when touring the countries, cities and back areas. All commercial transactions involving Western countries are handled in English and Arabic but any formal contract is in Arabic.

Excellent taxi and car rental services are readily available. Traffic is somewhat frenzied, however. Since women are not allowed to drive most companies provide van or bus service for them. A chaperoned taxi is another way Western women get around.

Islamic law is supreme in all areas of Saudi life. Alcoholic beverages are forbidden and anyone caught bringing them into the country faces stiff fines or imprisonment. Islamic religious code sets dress and behavior standards. Arab women still cover their faces and wear clothing that covers their entire body. Western women dress very modestly in rather longish dresses that cover the shoulders and arms. The sack-style dress is popular for both climate and culture.

One worker recently returned from Saudi Arabia and told how he and a female economist were driving in their small car. They passed a bedouin whose small pickup had broken down and stopped to offer him a ride. The driver motioned the stranded motorist into the cramped back seat whereas the bedouin shook his head, pointed to the woman seated beside the driver and motioned her to get out of the car and walk while he took her place.

In the cities, Arab men are generally courteous to Western women although they expect non-Arab women to be aware of the cultural differences and to respect those differences. It is a good policy for

American women to wear conservative clothing and not be too outspoken.

Cultural differences range from dress code to eating. Manners are an incredibly important part of Arabic cultures. Discourtesy can ruin a relationship or sour a business deal. Avoid conversations about politics and religion. In Saudi Arabia they are one in the same. Never sit with your legs crossed such that the bottom of your shoe points toward an Arab. It is considered a very rude gesture. The use of first names is appropriate only after a formal introduction. The sense of time is different from the U.S. While you are expected to arrive on time for an appointment do not expect your Saudi associate necessarily to do the same. You will be expected to wait for him without taking offense.

Obtaining a job in Saudi Arabia can be accomplished in one of two basic ways: through an American firm with an operation in Saudi Arabia; or, directly through the Saudi government or a Saudi company. There are more than 275 American multinational corporations in the country. To contact Saudi Arabian companies request a current listing from the Commercial Attache, Embassy of Saudi Arabia, 601 New Hampshire Avenue NW, Washington, DC 20037 (202/342-3800) Or, write directly to the following:

Petroleum:

Arabian American Oil
 Company (ARAMCO)
P.O. Box 1458
Dhahran

Petrochemicals:

Saudi Basic Industries Corp.
 (SABIC)
P.O. Box 5101
Riyadh

Managing Director
Saudi Petrochemical Co.
 (SADAF)
P.O. Box 10025
Jubail

Aviation:

Managing Director
Saudi Arabian Airlines, Co.
P.O. Box 620
Jeddah

Contracting:

Managing Director
Muhammad Bin Ladin
 Organization
P.O. Box 958
Jeddah

Banking & Finance:

Managing Director
National Commercial Bank
P.O. Box 3555
Jeddah

Managing Director
Saudi American Bank
P.O. Box 1
Jeddah

Manufacturing:

Abdullah Adulaziz Al-Sulaim
Managing Director
Saudi Iron & Steel Co.
 (HADEED)
P.O. Box 10053
Jubail

Diversified Companies:

Mohamed A.Y.Z. Alireza
Chairman
Xenel Industries, Ltd.
P.O. Box 2824
Jeddah

Ahmad Juffali
Managing Director
E.A. Juffali & Brothers
P.O. Box 1049
Jeddah

Ahmad Alireza
Managing Director
Haji Addulla Alireza & Co.
P.O. Box 8
Jeddah

Additional names and addresses as well as information on current hiring practices and possible companies in search of skilled employees can be obtained from:

American Businessmen's Association, Eastern Province
%SADAF
P.O. Box 10025
Madinat al-Jubail 31961
Dhahran

The American Businessmen of Jeddah
P.O. Box 5019
Jeddah

American Businessmen's Group of Riyadh
P.O. Box 259
Riyadh 11411

Saudi Arabia has an embassy at 601 New Hampshire Avenue NW, Washington, DC 20037 (202/342-3800) with consulates in Houston, Los

Angeles, New York and Los Angeles. The U.S. Embassy is located at Collector Road M, Diplomatic Quarter, P.O. Box # 9041, Riyadh 11143. Contacts:

Petroleum:

Exxon Saudi Arabia Inc.
P.O. Box # 4584
Riyadh, 11412

Mobil Saudi Arabia Inc.
P.O. Box # 40228
Riyadh, 11499

Construction:

Brown & Root Saudi Ltd.
P.O. Box # 52926
Riyadh, 11573

Marsh and McClennan Bakhsh
 Ltd.
P.O. Box # 2596
Riyadh, 11461

Manufacturing:

Johnson Controls International
P.O. Box # 753
Riyadh, 11421

Litton Saudi Arabia Ltd.
P.O. Box # 7529
Riyadh, 11472

Saudi American General
 Electric Company
P.O. Box # 10211
Riyadh, 11433

Westinghouse Saudi Arabia
 Ltd.
P.O. Box # 3779
Riyadh, 11481

Banking:

Saudi Investment Bank
(Chase Manhattan Bank)
P.O. Box # 3533
Riyadh, 11481

Aerospace:

Hughes Aircraft International
 Service Co.
P.O. Box # 7159
Riyadh, 11462

Rockwell International
P.O. Box # 2375
Riyadh, 11451

Tunisia

GEOGRAPHY:
AREA: 63,378 sq. mi.
CAPITAL: Tunis

PRINCIPAL CITIES: Sfax, Bizerte, Nabul, Al Kaf
TERRAIN: Mountainous in the north; hot dry central plain; semi arid
south merges into the Sahara.
CLIMATE: Temperate in the north with mild, rainy winters and hot dry
summers in the south.

PEOPLE:
POPULATION: 8,726,562
ANNUAL GROWTH RATE: 1.76%
RELIGION: 98% Muslim; 1% Christian; less than 1% Jewish.
LANGUAGE: Arabic (French spoken and used for business and
commerce).
EDUCATION: Attendance in primary school: 85%
LITERACY: 62%
LIFE EXPECTANCY: Men 70; women 75 years.

GOVERNMENT: Constitutional republic with an elected president as
head of both the state and the government. Unicameral National
Assembly which is largely advisory. The government budget is $3.4
billion of which about 8% is for the military.

ECONOMY:
GDP: $34.3 billion
ANNUAL GROWTH RATE: 2.6%
PER CAPITA GDP: $4,000
AVERAGE RATE OF INFLATION: 4.5%
WORK FORCE: Of the 1.8 million in the work force, 31% are involved
in agriculture, 17% in manufacturing; 15% in services; 12% in construc-
tion; and 25% other.
OFFICIAL EXCHANGE RATE: 1.05 Tunisian dinars = US$
COST OF LIVING INDEX: 089

The smallest of the North African countries, Tunisia doesn't offer
many job prospects for foreigners. For that matter it offers few job
opportunities for its own countrymen. According to CIA estimates:
"Although it is difficult to arrive at a precise figure, an estimated 50% of
the potential work force is either unemployed or underemployed."
Unemployment, aggravated by a rapidly growing work force is Tunisia's
biggest problem. Half the population is under the age of 25.

Despite its small resource base, Tunisia has succeeded in attracting
foreign investment in labor-intensive, export industries. It has also

received considerable amounts of aid from Europe, the United States, and more recently, from other Arab states such as Saudi Arabia and Kuwait. The major elements of U.S. aid are funneled through the Agency for International Development (AID), Food for Peace, and the Peace Corps which maintains about 100 American volunteers focusing on vocational education, rural development, and public health.

Basically, however, the nation's economy depends on oil, agriculture, phosphates and tourism. Americans with certain high-tech skills such as computer sciences, petroleum engineering, mining technology and certain medical specialities are more likely to be considered by local companies as they are skills sorely lacking among the present labor force. Aside from the high-tech specialities the best opportunities for work here are with American companies already established. Since there is no American Chamber of Commerce in Tunisia your best listing of U.S. companies or an insight into local job opportunities is through the U.S. Embassy in Tunis. Also, James Phippard, Director of the AID Mission, (located at the Embassy) may be able to provide information on employment or consultation possibilities for AID.

A work permit is necessary and is usually obtained by your employer. If you're just passing through on a job search you can travel for up to four months without a visa. Tunisia has no particular health hazards, but the tap water is not potable during certain times of the year, depending upon the rainfall.

Tunisia has an embassy at 1515 Massachusetts Avenue NW, Washington, DC 20005 (202/862-1850). The U.S. maintains its Embassy at 144 Avenue de la Liberte, Tunis. Contacts:

Petroleum:

Amerada Petroleum Corp.
Post Box 331
Tunis

Continental Oil Co.
100 Avenue de Lesseps
Tunis

Exxon Standard
12 Avenue de Paris
Tunis

Mobil Exploration Inc.
Post Box # 362
Tunis

Petroleum Related:

Geosource Intl.
7 Rue Ibn Messaoud, 1004 El Mesnzah
Tunis

Halliburton Ltd. (Imco
 Services Division)
4 Rue de Kenya
Tunis

Weatherford Oil Tool GmbH
Cite Pace—El Bustan
Sfax

Dresser Europe S.A.
Villa Rajeb Turki
Route de Teniour Km. 15
Sfax

Construction:

Blackwood-Hedge
Post Box # 9;
Z.I. Ouest-Rue des
 Freres Lumiere
91162 Longjumeau Cedex
Paris, FRANCE

Petty-Ray Geophysical
14 Rue Fadhel Ben Achour El
Menzah V
Tunis

Mining:

Central Resources Corp.
22 Rue Pierre de Coubertin
Tunis

N.P.K Engrais
20 Rue du Dr. Burnet
Tunis

ASIA

Myanmar (Formerly Burma)

GEOGRAPHY:
AREA: 262,000 sq. mi.
CAPITAL: Rangoon
PRINCIPAL CITIES: Mandalay, Moulmein
TERRAIN: Central lowlands ringed by steep, rugged highlands.
CLIMATE: Tropical monsoon; cloudy, rainy hot humid summers (June to September); less cloudy, scant rainfall, mild temperatures, lower humidity during winter (December to April).

PEOPLE:
POPULATION: 44,277,014
ANNUAL GROWTH RATE: 1.86%
RELIGION: Buddhist 85%; Muslim, traditional and Christian 13%.
LANGUAGE: Burmese
EDUCATION: Attendance in primary school 84%.
LITERACY: 66%
LIFE EXPECTANCY: Men 57; women 62 years.

GOVERNMENT: Military government since 1988. Although there is a constitution it isn't known which aspects are considered relevant by the governing military authorities. Government budget: $2.2 billion of which 21% goes to the military.

ECONOMY:
GDP: $41 billion
ANNUAL GROWTH RATE: 5%
PER CAPITA GDP: $950
AVERAGE. RATE OF INFLATION: 30%
WORK FORCE: Of the 14.8 million employed (there is a 10% unemployment rate in urban areas), 66% are involved in agriculture; 12% Industry; 10% trade; and 10% government.
OFFICIAL EXCHANGE RATE: 6.23 kyats = US$
COST OF LIVING INDEX: 088

Most still know this nation as Burma and recall the Kipling stories of British rule in the region. Yet today, Myanmar is a country with tremendous potential and has lived up to none of it. It has the richest natural resources in all of South East Asia, yet it is one of the poorest countries in the region. Here is a tragic example of governmental failure and mismanagement. During British rule Burma was a strong agricultural nation producing some 3.5 million tons of rice a year. Now, 15 years after independence and almost half a century after the war the country is just about producing the same quantity despite major scientific improvements in agriculture. Unfortunately, the population has doubled and its rice production no longer feeds the populace. Rice and teak still dominate Burma's exports.

In the late 1980s the socialist government recognized the need for industrialization and offered incentives to attract foreign capital. Ineptly, the military regime declined to realign the exchange rate of the kyat to more accurately reflect its true value, a move many economists see as a pre-requisite to attract foreign capital. Thus, needed foreign interests have been slow to flow into the country.

There is a need for major technological assistance in many areas of agriculture, education, light industry and mining. At present few foreigners are employed in positions other than missionary and social services. For a time visas were not easily granted but in the late 1980s the government did grant tourist visas for no more than 14 days and work visas for a longer period. Because of "internal security problems" travel to some parts of the country (along the borders, for instance) are forbidden. If you plan to do any traveling in the country count on delays. Schedules are designed to appease tourists. Few natives follow them.

Despite the state of the nations economy, this is still one of the more beautiful parts of southeast Asia. Living conditions for can be quite plush. A few words of caution however: health services are fair at best. Malaria is widespread in rural areas although not prevalent in the major cities. Unfortunately dengue fever is a problem throughout the nation. Never drink tap water.

Burma has an embassy at 2300 S Street NW, Washington, DC 20008 (202/332-9044) and a consulate in New York. The U.S. Embassy is located at 581 Merchant Street, Rangoon.

India

GEOGRAPHY:
AREA: 1,268,884 sq. mi.
CAPITAL: New Delhi
PRINCIPAL CITIES: Calcutta, Bombay, Madras, Bangladore.

TERRAIN: Upland plain in the south; flat rolling plain along the Ganges; deserts in the west, and Himalayas in the north.
CLIMATE: Varies from tropical monsoon in the south to temperate in the north.

PEOPLE:
POPULATION: 919,903,056
ANNUAL GROWTH RATE: 1.82%
RELIGION: 83% Hindu; 12% Muslim; 2.5% Christian.
LANGUAGE: Hindi, English and 14 other official languages.
EDUCATION: Literacy 36%.
LIFE EXPECTANCY: Men 58; women 59 years.

GOVERNMENT: Federal republic. National and state elections are held about once every five years. Government budget: $50.1 billion. Approximately 20% goes to military.

ECONOMY:
GNP: $1.17 trillion
ANNUAL GROWTH RATE: 3.8%
PER CAPITA GNP: $1,300
AVERAGE RATE OF INFLATION: 8%
WORK FORCE: Of the 300 million Indians in the work force (the rate of unemployment is about 10%), 70% are engaged in agriculture; 19% in industry and commerce; 8% services and government; and, 3% in transportation and communications.
OFFICIAL EXCHANGE RATE: 31.2 Indian rupees = US$
COST OF LIVING INDEX: 074

The stories of India and its struggling masses are legendary. The country occupies only 2.4% of the world's land area yet has 15% of the population. Only China has a larger population. Despite the fact that 7 out of 10 working Indians is employed in agriculture the nation has a relatively sophisticated industrial base and a large pool of skilled workers.

Cotton and jute textile production continue to be the most important industry, but public-sector output in steel, machine tools, electric and transport machinery, and chemicals have become an important economic factor over the past several decades. Although a major off shore oil source (the Bombay High Field) is showing signs of weakening, the country has had no significant petroleum discoveries in the past decade.

Also, substantial mineral resources—coal, iron ore, bauxite, and manganese—have been partially exploited.

Despite improving industrial development, Indian economic growth continues to face major internal problems: unemployment (10%), low productivity, high costs of industrial products, and bottleneck in power and transportation. Dealing with the Indians at any official level exemplifies the word "frustration." Surely if the Indian bureaucrats learned anything about the art of management and diplomacy from their British rulers it is lost today. For an American to work in India it is first necessary to obtain permission from the Reserve Bank of India. A visa is necessary to either visit or work. Obviously a work visa is far more difficult to obtain.

At least 300 American multinational companies are doing business in India. Each is requested to complete an annual report listing the number of foreigners and Indians employed at every salary level. Opportunities for high-tech workers are available throughout the country as the Indian government gradually deregulates industry and trade attempting to provide greater incentives for foreign investors. In addition there is a continued need for those interested in social services, health services, education, agriculture, and engineering.

Living conditions can be quite pleasant. Housing is reasonable and many Indians judge you by the number of servants in your employ. For many, the days of the British overlord are very much in existence. Health services are acceptable in major cities. Tap water is unsafe throughout the country.

India has an embassy at 2107 Massachusetts Avenue NW, Washington, DC 20008 (202/939-7000) and consulates in New York, Chicago, and San Francisco. The U.S. Embassy is located on Shanti Path, Chanakyapuri, New Delhi. Contact:

Pharmaceuticals:

Abbott Labs India Private Ltd.
Jehangir Bldg.
133 Mahatma Gandhi Road
Fort, Bombay 400023

Parke Davis (India), Ltd.
Saki Naka
Bombay 400072

Manufacturing:

AB Controls Ltd.
C-11 Industrial Area
Sive IV
Sahibabad, Dist. Ghaziabad
Pin 201010

Kulkarni-Black &
 Decker, Ltd.
Post Shirol Dist.
Kolhapur 416 103
Maharashtra

Kirioskar Warner
 Swasey Co.
Gokul Road, Hubil 580030
Karnataka

Chemicals:

Hercilla Chemicals, Ltd.
Bombay

Velsicol Chemical Corp.
C-32 Panch Sheel Enclave
New Delhi 110017

Agri-business:

Corn Products Co. (India)
 Private Ltd.
Shree Niwas House
Hazarimal Somani Road
P.O. Box 994
Fort, Bombay

Hi-Bred (India) Private, Ltd.
Post Bag No. 5
Karnai 132001
Haryana

Engineering:

Desein (New Delhi)
 Private Ltd.
Desein House
Greater Kailash 11
New Delhi 110048

Malaysia

GEOGRAPHY:
AREA: 127,316 sq. mi.
CAPITAL: Kuala Lumpur
PRINCIPAL CITIES: Penang, Petaling Jaya, Ipoh, Malacca.
TERRAIN: Coastal plains, and interior jungle-covered mountains.
CLIMATE: Tropical. Temperatures average around 80° year round with high humidity.

PEOPLE:
POPULATION: 19,283,157
ANNUAL GROWTH RATE: 2.28%
RELIGION: Malays (59%) nearly all Muslim; Chinese (32%) predominantly Buddhists; Indians (9%) predominantly Hindu.
LANGUAGE: Malay (official). Also English, Chinese dialects, Tamil.
EDUCATION: Attendance in primary school: 97%.
LITERACY: 80% in Peninsular; 60% in Sabah and Sarawak.

LIFE EXPECTANCY: Men 66; women 72 years.

GOVERNMENT: Federal parliamentary democracy on the Westminister model with a constitutional monarch. Government budget: $11 billion; 3.4% of which is for the military.

ECONOMY:
GDP: $141 billion
ANNUAL GROWTH RATE: 8%
PER CAPITA GDP: $7,500.
AVERAGE RATE OF INFLATION: 3.6%
WORK FORCE: Of the 7.2 million employed manufacturing employs about 28%; agriculture 18%; government 10%; mining and petroleum 9%; transportation and communication 7%; finance 10%; construction 3%, and, utilities 2%.
OFFICIAL EXCHANGE RATE: 2.7 ringgits = US$
COST OF LIVING INDEX: 107

Ask ten people to name the top three countries manufacturing semiconductor devices and the chances are no one will tell you who follows the United States and Japan. Malaysia is well known as the world's leading producer of rubber, tin and tropical timber but semiconductors? It used to be the world's tin producer but the collapse of the International Tin Council in 1985 depressed prices and forced many of the country's smaller mines to close. The country now produces about 28,000 metric tons annually.

In addition to electronic goods, air conditioners and textiles, Malaysia is taking advantage of the swing to health foods. In recent years, palm oil has overshadowed rubber as the "golden" crop. Palm oil is a vegetable oil used for a variety of purposes, such as cooking oil, soap and as an ingredient in margarine. Malaysia produces 60% of the world's palm oil with production on the increase as newly planted trees mature.

Manufacturing has supplanted agriculture in recent years as the largest sector in the economy accounting for a quarter of real GDP. However, the nation is not self-sufficient in food and a majority of the rural population subsists at a poverty level.

With the exception of a major recession in 1981-2, the growth in the nation's economy has been a rather steady climb. Economic growth is averaging about 7%-8% per year. Total foreign investment is conservatively estimated at about $10 billion. U.S. investment alone is about $4.5 billion, mostly in petroleum development and electronic component production. Oil production is about 600,000 barrels a day. The opportunity for work in Malaysia is on the upswing as well. However, recent policy states that Malaysian must own at least 70% of all businesses. This may cause a problem in time, but at present there are jobs for qualified Americans. There are 160 American multinational corporations in the country.

Living conditions in the principal cities can be very pleasant for American workers. Apartments and houses for expatriates are all air conditioned and most have swimming pools. It is expected that Americans hire their own local chauffeur (at very low wages) even if one lives within walking distance from the office. Another local custom requires you to wear a suit jacket at all times. This custom is undoubtably a holdover from the days when England ruled and in time will also go the way of the Empire. After all this is the tropics.

Life in the countryside on the other hand is rustic at best. Kuala Lumpur and other major cities are generally free from most diseases commonly associated with the Far East. Even the tap water from the municipal water system is considered safe.

Visas are not required of U.S. citizens who stay less than 15 days. If you want to stay longer contact the Malaysian Embassy. The Department of Immigration will issue a work permit when it is shown that "no Malaysian" meets the necessary qualification and experience requirements. Unfortunately, family members are not allowed to hold a job as long as you're working.

Malaysia has an embassy at 2401 Massachusetts Avenue NW, Washington, DC 20008 (202/328-2700). Consulates are located in New York, and Los Angeles. The United States Embassy is at 376 Jalan Tun Razak, Kuala Lumpur. Contact:

American Business Council
 of Malaysia
15.01, 15th floor
Amoda, Jalan Imbi,
55100 Kuala Lumpur

Electronics:

Advanced Micro Devices
 Sdn. Bhd.
Bayan Lepas Free Trade
 Zone, Phase II
Penang

General Instrument Malaysia
Sdn. Bhd.
5 Jalan S.S. 8/2, Sungei Way
Free Trade Zone
Selangor

Texas Instruments Malaysia
Sdn. Bhd.
No. 1, Lorong Enggang 33
Kuala Lumpur

Executive Search:

Korn/Ferry Intl. Dsn. Bhd.
Wisma MISC, Jalan Conjay
Kuala Lumpur 04-09

Chemicals:

Drew Ameroid Sdn. Bhd.
60/62 Jalan 52/4
New Town Centre
Petalling Jaya
Selangor

Petroline (Malaysia) Dsn.
Bhd.
Angkasa Raya Bldg.
Jalan Ampany
Kuala Lumpur 04-05

Construction:

Combustion Engineering Inc.
C-E Crest Division
Suite 12-06
Wisma Stephens
No. 88 Jalan Raja Chulan
Kuala Lumpur

Stone & Webster Malaysia
Corp.
Wisma SPK 26
Jalan Sultan Ismail
Kuala Lumpur 50250

Petroleum:

Loffland Bros. Co.
(Malaysia) Sdn. Bdh.
707 Wisma Central
Jalan Ampang
Kuala Lumpur

Offshore Drilling
Services Co.
Chase Manhattan Bank Bldg.
9 Jalan Gereja
Kuala Lumpur 01-17

Nepal

GEOGRAPHY:
AREA: 56,136 sq. mi.
CAPITAL: Kathmandu
PRINCIPAL CITIES: Patan, Bhaktapur, Pokhara.
TERRAIN: Three distinct regions: flat and fertile in the south; hill country in the center; the high Himalayas form the border with Tibet in the north.

CLIMATE: Ranges from sub-tropical in the south to cool summers and severe winters in the northern mountains.

PEOPLE:
POPULATION: 21,041,527
ANNUAL GROWTH RATE: 2.4%
RELIGION: The only Hindu state in the world. About 90% of population is Hindu; the remainder follow Buddhism and Islam.
LANGUAGE: Nepali and more than 12 others as well as 2 dozen more different dialects.
EDUCATION: Attendance in primary school 77%.
LITERACY: 33%.
LIFE EXPECTANCY: Men 52; women 52 years.

GOVERNMENT: Constitutional monarchy. King exercises autocratic control over a multi-layered government. Government budget: $733 million of which about 5% is devoted to the military.

ECONOMY:
GDP: $20.5 billion
ANNUAL GROWTH RATE: 2.9%
PER CAPITA GDP: $1,000.
AVERAGE RATE OF INFLATION: 9%
WORK FORCE: About 91% of the work force is engaged in agriculture, 2% in industry and 5% in services.
OFFICIAL EXCHANGE RATE: 49 Nepalese rupees = US$
COST OF LIVING INDEX: 082

Nepal is amongst the poorest and least developed countries in the world. It is also considered by many to be one of the most beautiful. The grandeur of the Northern Himalayas are a resplendent overseer for all Nepalese. For centuries this isolated nation depended on its own resources for its survival. Agriculture was and is the country's mainstay.

The word "undeveloped" doesn't quite describe the Nepalese economic state. Considering that half the population is under the age of 21, that there are no fewer than 36 languages and dialects, that one town may not have had contact with its neighboring town in centuries, it is hard to consider a unified approach to economic reform. The Nepalese have their own system of weights and measures. The metric system is gradually being introduced.

In 1951 the kingdom had virtually no schools, hospitals, roads, electric power, industry or civil service. With aid from India, China, and the United States, Nepal has completed a series of stages towards economic survival. Several hydroelectric projects have been completed and several small, local industries specializing in furniture, textiles and soap have been initiated. Small deposits of magnetite, limestone, zinc, copper, iron, mica and cobalt have been discovered. Mining of limestone, zinc and copper is being carried out on a limited scale. Royal Dutch Shell and the American company, Trion, are exploring for petroleum in southeastern Nepal. Work in the mining industry is one area of potential employment. Other needs involve those with knowledge in the banking industry, health services, agriculture, family planning and population control.

Visas are required but may be obtained at the airport upon entry. Medical facilities outside the few major cities are inadequate. If you plan to travel outside the capitol, malaria suppressants are recommended.

Nepal has an embassy at 2131 Leroy Place NW, Washington, DC 20008 (202/667-4550). The U.S. Embassy is at Pani Pokhari, Kathmandu.

Pakistan

GEOGRAPHY:
AREA: 310,527 sq. mi.
CAPITAL: Ishlamabad
PRINCIPAL CITIES: Rawalpindi, Karachi, Lahore, Faisalabad.
TERRAIN: Flat Indus plain in the east; mountains in the north and northwest; plateau in the west.
CLIMATE: Mostly hot dry desert; temperate in northwest; arctic in the north.

PEOPLE:
POPULATION: 128,855,965
ANNUAL GROWTH RATE: 3%
RELIGION: 97% Muslim
LANGUAGE: English and Urdu (official). Also Punjabi.
EDUCATION: Literacy 26%
LIFE EXPECTANCY: Men 56; women 58 years.

GOVERNMENT: Parliamentary with strong executive. Legal system is based on English common law but is changing to reflect Koranic injunction. Government budget: $14 billion of which about 26% goes to military.

ECONOMY:
GNP: $239 billion
ANNUAL GROWTH RATE: 3%
PER CAPITA GNP: $1,900
AVERAGE RATE OF INFLATION: 12.7%
WORK FORCE: Approximately 54% of the work force is devoted to agriculture; 33% to services; 13% to industry. Primary industrial areas are in textiles, food processing, petroleum products, construction materials, and clothing.
OFFICIAL EXCHANGE RATE: 30.2 rupees = US$
COST OF LIVING INDEX: 080

Despite the geo-political location of the country—between a hostile India to the East and turbulent Afghanistan in the north—Pakistan's economy has been expanding at a steady rate for the past decade. Although the rate of growth declined in the mid 1990s, manufacturing remains the leading sector growing at an average rate of almost 10% per year. Cotton textile output is the most important industry accounting for 20% of the manufacturing labor force and 40% of the exports. Following textile manufacturing is light engineering (electrical goods, metal working, precision equipment), food processing, cement, pharmaceuticals and rubber. Pakistan also has a substantial fertilizer industry. Iron and steel production near Karachi was recently boosted by a Soviet built plant. Fairly extensive natural gas deposits and newly discovered oil reserves have not only increased the country's energy outlook but led to greater job opportunities for Americans with technical expertise in the petroleum industry.

Visas are required. It is best to fly into the country as entry across a land border can be a problem. For example, the border with India at Wagah is only open to foreigners certain days of the week. The border between Pakistan and the Indian Punjab may require foreigners to be escorted. In all it can be a confusing situation and not worth the hassle.

There are acceptable doctors in the major cities but in the out regions medical facilities may be a problem. You'll need malarial prophylactics. Don't drink the water anywhere in the country. If the major hotels tell you the water is safe, beware! Since this is an Muslim country alcohol is not available. Don't try to bring it into the country as it may be considered a criminal offense.

Pakistani women rarely travel alone and foreign women are cautioned that traveling unaccompanied is considered an affront to Muslim males.

Pakistan has an embassy at 2315 Massachusetts Ave. NW, Washington, DC 20008 (202/939-6200). The U.S. Embassy is at Ramna 5, Islamabad. Contacts:

American Business Council
 of Pakistan
3rd Floor, Shaheen
 Commercial Complex
M.R. Kayani Road, G.P.O. Box
1322
Karachi

Pharmaceuticals:

Abbott Labs Pakistan Ltd.
Habib Bank Bldg.
Karachi 3

Parke-Davis & Co. Ltd.
P.O. Box # 3621
B/2 S.I.T.E.
Karachi 16

Chemicals:

Eastman Kodak Ltd.
60 Ghahrah-e-Quaid-e-Azam
Lahore

Dawood Hercules Chemicals
 Ltd.
48 Shahrahe Quaideazam
Lahore

Manufacturing:

Agriauto Industries Ltd.
Sidco Ave. Centre
264 R.A. Lines
Karachi

Pak-Land Corp.
Central Commercial Area
Iqbai Road.
P.E.C.H. Society
Karachi 29

Petroleum:

Esso Standard Eastern, Inc.
Dawood Center
Mouivi Tamizuddin
Kahn Road
Karachi

Tidewater Oil Co.
P.O. Box 3936
Karachi

Singapore

GEOGRAPHY:
AREA: 239 sq. mi.

CAPITAL: Singapore
PRINCIPAL CITIES: Country is a city state.
TERRAIN: Lowland.
CLIMATE: Tropical. Hot, humid, rainy. No pronounced seasons. Thunderstorms occur on 40% of all days (67% of days in April).

PEOPLE:
POPULATION: 2,859,142
ANNUAL GROWTH RATE: 1.12%
RELIGION: Majority of Chinese are Buddhists; Malays nearly all Muslim. Also Christians, Hindus, Taoists and Sikhs.
LANGUAGE: English (official) Malay (national). Also Chinese and Tamil.
EDUCATION: Attendance in primary school 94%.
LITERACY: 87%
LIFE EXPECTANCY: Men 73; women 78 years.

GOVERNMENT: Republic within the British Commonwealth. Parliamentary democracy. Government budget: $10 billion; 6% goes to military.
ECONOMY:
GDP: $42.4 billion
ANNUAL GROWTH RATE: 9.9%
PER CAPITA GDP: $15,000.
AVERAGE RATE OF INFLATION: 2.4%
WORK FORCE: 1.3 million heavily involved in industrial output: petroleum refining, electronics, oil drilling equipment, rubber processing and rubber products, food products, and financial services.
OFFICIAL EXCHANGE RATE: 1.6 Singapore Dollar = US$
COST OF LIVING INDEX: 126

In 1819 Sir Thomas Raffles, an East India Company agent, came to Singapore, realized its potential as a leading Asian trading outpost, and bought the island. Today it is one of Asia's leading trading ports and manufacturing centers. As a port it is Asia's second largest and the third largest in the world. Thanks to government intervention in the 1970s a major effort was directed towards developing successful financial incentives for export oriented industry and providing a sufficient infrastructure for manufacturing. Automation and high labor costs (by Asian standards) has led to the nation's technical modernization and efficient production standards.

This is a modern city-state with high-tech skyscrapers, efficient (yet crowded) roads, luxury hotels, and some of the world's best restaurants. With a population density of 10,357 persons per square mile, Singapore is one of the most densely populated countries in the world. Yet despite the congestion, health standards are high for the region with about 1 physician per 1,111 people (U.S. = about 1 per 700).

Extensive petroleum refining operations make that industry—in terms of total value or production—the largest in Singapore. It is closely followed by electronics, transportation equipment, and marine services (including ship repair), textiles, electrical machinery, and food industries. More than 450 U.S. multinational corporations have offices here as well as more than 50 foreign banks, insurance companies and brokerage institutions.

Many consider this city-state an anachronism in that it is "democracy" yet seems to be under the total control of Prime Minister Lee Kuan Uyew. He assures that the streets are immaculate and any form of civil disorder is not tolerated; even by Americans. Remember the caning of an 18 year old American in 1994. Yet, the system works, employment is high and the standard of living is among the world's highest.

To obtain a work permit contact the Controller of Immigration. Wives and children of Americans working in Singapore may also accept jobs after first obtaining an "employment pass" from the Controller of Immigration.

Singapore has an embassy at 1824 R Street, NW. Washington, DC 20009 (202/667-7555). The U.S. Embassy is at 30 Hill Street, Singapore 0617. Contacts:

American Business Council of
 Singapore
10-12, Shaw House
354 Orchard Road
Singapore 0923

United Chase
 Merchant Bankers, Ltd.
Straits Trading Bldg.
9 Battery Road
Singapore 1

Financial:

Bank of New York
2202-4 Ocean Bldg.
Collyer Quay
Singapore 1

Manufacturing:

York Intl. Corp.
Yen San Bldg.
268 Orchard Road
Singapore 6

Tamco Cutler-Hammer
 Pte. Ltd.
88 Second Lakyang Road.
Jurong
Singapore 22

Jamesbury Far East Pte. Ltd.
06-01 Pioneer Lane, Jurong
Singapore 2262

Construction:

De Leuw, Cather
 International Ltd.
268 Orchard Road
Singapore 0923

Turner East Asia Pte. Ltd.
1102 Wing on Life Bldg.
150 Cecil Street
Singapore 0106

Electronics:

National Semiconductors
 Pte. Ltd.
51 Goldhill Plaza
Newton Road
Singapore 1130

SCI Singapore Pte.
3 Depot Close
Singapore 0401

Sri Lanka

GEOGRAPHY:
AREA: 66,000 sq. mi.
CAPITAL: Columbo
PRINCIPAL CITIES: Kandy, Negombo, Anuradhapura.
TERRAIN: Mostly low, flat to rolling plain; mountains in south-central interior.
CLIMATE: Tropical; monsoonal.

PEOPLE: POPULATION: 18,129,850
ANNUAL GROWTH RATE: 1.18%
RELIGION: 69% Buddhist; 15% Hindu; 8% Christian; 8% Muslim.
LANGUAGE: Sinhala (official) spoken by about 74%; tamil spoken by about 18%.
EDUCATION: Attendance in primary school 62%.
LITERACY: 87%
LIFE EXPECTANCY: Men 69; women 74 years.

GOVERNMENT: Democratic Socialistic. President elected for 6 years. Unicameral Parliament. Government budget: $2.7 billion of which 11% goes to the military.

ECONOMY:
GDP: $53.5 billion
ANNUAL GROWTH RATE: 5%
PER CAPITA GDP: $3,000
AVERAGE RATE OF INFLATION: 11.6%
WORK FORCE: Of the 6.4 million employed about 45% are engaged in agriculture; 12% trade and transport; and 29% in services, etc. The unemployment rate is about 20%.
OFFICIAL EXCHANGE RATE: 49.6 rupees = US$
COST OF LIVING INDEX: 159

With a population density of about 200 people per sq. km., Sri Lanka is one of the most densely populated nations in Asia. About 70% of the population live and work in the rural areas and another 10% work on the great plantations.

A major problem facing both the Sri Lankan government as well as all perspective employees and visitors is the Tamil Question. Tamils, people of Indian descent who compromise the largest minority (about 20%), are predominantly Hindu. For years they have been demanding independence for their region of Jaffna in the north. Violence, unfortunately, has become their common form of political expression. Before accepting a job here look into the regions of "unrest" and judge accordingly.

The major cities in the south are considered safe. Medical facilities are adequate by western standards in Columbo; outside of the capital you may be in for an adventure. Tap water is not drinkable anywhere and you'll need anti-malarial tablets.

The country's economy, some 40 years after independence, still reflects the colonial structure left behind by the British when the country was known as Ceylon. Tea, rubber and coconuts are the primary source of income accounting for about 30% of GDP, about half of export earnings and almost 20% of budgetary revenues.

A major hydroelectric power plant (Mahaweli Project) is the government's hope to reverse the economy from its strong agricultural base to one geared to new industry. As a result there is a need for technical and managerial personnel to assist in these changes.

Sri Lanka has an embassy at 2148 Wyoming Avenue NW, Washington, DC 20008 (202/483-4025). The United States Embassy is at 210 Galle Road, Colombo. Contact:

Engineering:

Black & Veatch Intl.
P.O. Box #2106
Colombo

PRC Engineering
 Consultants Inc.
P.O. Box #1885
Colombo

Chemicals:

Gamlen Pty., Ltd
%Hayleys Ltd.
400 Deans Road
P.O. Box 70
Colombo 5

Monsanto
116 Stenart Place
Galle Road
Colombo 3

Manufacturing:

Rupa Transworld
23 Anderson Road
Colombo 5

Union Carbide Ceylon Ltd.
66/14 Ananda
Coomaraswamy Mawatha
Colombo 7

Thailand

GEOGRAPHY:
AREA: 198,114 sq. mi.
CAPITAL: Bangkok
PRINCIPAL CITIES: Chaing Mai, Hat Yai.
TERRAIN: Four distinct regions: populated central plain; eastern plateau; mountain range spans the country in the west; southern isthmus separates land mass with Malaysia.
CLIMATE: Tropical. Rainy southwest monsoon mid-May to September; dry and cool northeast monsoon November to mid-March; southern isthmus always hot and humid.

PEOPLE:
POPULATION: 59,510,471
ANNUAL GROWTH RATE: 1.5%
RELIGION: 95% Buddhist; 4% Muslim.
LANGUAGE: Thai

EDUCATION: Attendance in primary school 96%.
LITERACY: 89%
LIFE EXPECTANCY: Men 64; women 71 years.

GOVERNMENT: Constitutional Monarchy. King is head of state with nominal powers. Bicameral legislature. Government headed by prime minister. Government budget: $12 billion; 19% of which goes to military.

ECONOMY:
GNP: $323 billion
ANNUAL GROWTH RATE: 7.8%.
PER CAPITA GDP: $5,500
AVERAGE RATE OF INFLATION: 4.1%
WORK FORCE: Of the 31 million employed, 59% are involved with agriculture; 26% with industry and commerce and 8% with the government. Unemployment is about 3.1%.
OFFICIAL EXCHANGE RATE: 26 Baht = US$
COST OF LIVING INDEX: 130

Thailand is one of the most advanced countries in Asia. During the past decade the relative importance of agriculture to the economy has declined and presently accounts for only 16% of GDP. The industrial production growth rate of about 13% exemplifies both the Thai government's decision to improve the nation's standard of living by developing greater industrial growth as well as the continued need for technical and managerial expertise.

Large scale energy-related projects have been financed from abroad, including the development of gas resources in the Gulf of Thailand, the exploitation of lignite (brown coal) deposits in the north, and the transportation and electricity supply throughout the country. Private investment is encouraged by the government. With western cash flow also comes jobs.

Although tourism is the largest source of foreign exchange, the nation's minerals have long been sought in the west and represent a major source of foreign trade. Thailand is the world's second largest tungsten producer and the third largest tin producer. Other industries representing potential employment potential include: textiles and garments, agricultural processing, tobacco, cement and other light manufacturing such as jewelry, electric appliances, integrated circuits, etc.

Thai farmers in many isolated villages along the Golden Triangle are major suppliers of illegal opium poppy and cannabis for the international drug trade. However, the Thai government takes drug dealing very seriously. If you are caught with drugs you will be immediately imprisoned and your consulate can do nothing on your behalf. There are currently hundreds of Westerners in Thai jails for having drugs in their possession; some are serving life sentences. Venture into neighboring Burma with drugs and you may be shot. It's that serious!

You may visit for as long as 15 days without a visa however a work permit is required. Health services are advanced in Bangkok but scanty in the countryside. Malaria and hepatitis is common outside the major cities. Take precautions. Avoid tap water, raw milk, and uncooked meats and vegetables.

Remember that in a Buddhist country you remove your shoes before entering a home or temple. Don't shake hands; rather join both hands together as if in prayer. Also avoid crossing your legs because you may be pointing your foot at someone. The foot is viewed as the body's most contemptible member. The head is the body's noblest part. One high executive with a major western bank almost lost his job when he stepped on a Thai bank note to keep it from blowing away. The act was considered an appalling affront because the note carried the king's picture.

If you're planning to visit a large company in Bangkok arrange for your meeting well in advance. Some small companies will accept visits without an appointment but large ones won't. Also, keep in mind that the best months for business travel are November through March. Most business people vacation during April and May.

The American Chamber of Commerce publishes an excellent, detailed directory and member's listing which provides helpful information on working and living in Thailand.

Thailand has an embassy at 2300 Kalorama Road NW, Washington, DC 20008 (202/483-7200). Consulates are located in New York, Chicago, and Los Angeles. The U.S. Embassy is at 95 Wireless Road, Bangkok. Contact:

The American Chamber of
 Commerce in Thailand
140 Wireless Road
PO Box #11-1095
Bangkok

Manufacturing:

American Standard
 Sanitaryware
 (Thailand) Ltd.
392 Sukhumvit Road
Bangkok 10110

General Electric
International Operations
Co., Inc.
90/37 North Sathcorn Road
Bangkok 10500

Phelps Dodge Thailand, Ltd.
518/3 Ploenchit Road
Bangkok 10500

Chemicals:

Cyanamid Thailand Ltd.
1/7 Convent Road
Bangkok 10500

DuPont (Thailand) Ltd.
56 Silom Road
Bangkok 10500

Electronics:

IBM Thailand Co. Ltd.
388 Phaholyothin Road
Phyathai
Bangkok 10400

Data Equipment (Thailand)
 Ltd.
2 Silom Road
Bangkok 10500

Financial:

Bank of America NT&SA
2/2 Wireless Road
Bangkok 10500

Price Waterhouse
56 Surawongese Road
Bangkok 10500

People's Republic of China

GEOGRAPHY:
AREA: 3.7 million sq. mi.
CAPITAL: Beijing
PRINCIPAL CITIES: Shanghai, Tianjin, Guangzhou.
TERRAIN: Mostly mountainous, high plateaus, deserts in the west; plains, deltas and hills in the east.
CLIMATE: Extremely diverse. Tropical in the south; sub-arctic in the north.

PEOPLE:
POPULATION: 1.1 billion.
ANNUAL GROWTH RATE: 1.08%
RELIGION: Officially atheist. Unofficially it varies from Buddhism, Muslim, Confucianism, Daoism and a host of folk religions including ancestor worship.
LANGUAGE: Standard Chinese (Putonghua), Mandarin (based on the

Beijing dialect), Yue (Cantonese), etc.
EDUCATION: 9 years compulsory education.
LITERACY: Approximately 70%.
LIFE EXPECTANCY: Men 68; women 70 years.

GOVERNMENT: Communist state with full power vested in Party's Politburo. Government budget: Central government budget is unknown; the U.S. Central Intelligence Agency estimates the military budget to be $16 billion.

ECONOMY:
GDP: $2.61 billion
ANNUAL GROWTH RATE: 13.4%
PER CAPITA GDP: $2,200
AVERAGE RATE OF INFLATION: 17.6%
WORK FORCE: Of the approximately 500 million employed, 66% are engaged in agriculture; 21% in industry; 11% other; and approximately 3.2% are unemployed. (Note: The economic data is from the 1994 World Factbook, made available by the U.S. Central Intelligence Agency and varies considerably from U.S. State Department data or other published material, none of which is consistent.)
OFFICIAL EXCHANGE RATE: 8.7 Yuan = US$
COST OF LIVING INDEX: 108

Developing a viable economy in the world's most populated country has been a struggle for Chinese leaders for decades. However, with the liberalization of relations with western nations China has seen a steady economic growth despite the fact that it remains one of the poorest countries in the world.

Most Chinese are engaged in agriculture although only 11% of the land is cultivated. China is self-sufficient in grain and is the world's leading producer of rice, millet, barley and sorghum. China has vast and largely untapped energy and mineral supplies. As part of the government's drive to modernize the economy, China has pursued a more liberal economic policy in the '80's. Peasants are now allowed to lease land from the state and to retain earnings after meeting certain contractual obligations. Joint international ventures and foreign loans are now accepted and commercial links have been diversified.

However, from the point of view of a foreign national working in China it is a totally different story. The only employment is through a company under contract to do business with the Chinese government or a Chinese government agency, or through direct agreement with the Chinese government. Teachers, for example, may be employed through a Chinese agency to live and teach in China. Yet more than 50 American multinational corporations have offices in China and are potential sources of employment.

China needs and wants western technology and the best opportunities for work in China is in the sci-tech area. U.S. controls on technology and equipment exports to China have been gradually liberalized over the past several years (by one estimate, the value of "high-tech" exports to China increased from $144 million in 1982 to $1 billion in 1986). Even following the June '89 Tian'anmen Square debacle, which seriously affected Chinese international relations, the U.S. granted favored nation trading status to the Chinese and continues to develop closer economic and political ties.

As an independent contractor your only shot to work in China is by invitation. And, invitations are hard to come by. They often take a year or more. The Chinese can't be rushed. Exert pressure and you only upset the ingrained bureaucratic wheels of petty government. You are also at a disadvantage if you are acting as an independent or working for a small company hoping to be sent to China. The Chinese prefer dealing with large, big-name firms.

If you don't have a direct invitation from a specific Chinese organization (i.e. China National Machinery Import-Export Council, etc.) you must "qualify" for a visa as an individual. Your first step is to obtain a "Letter of Confirmation" from the China International Service (Luxingshe), Xidan Building, Beijing.

One avenue to pursue is through one of the 29 scientific and technical exchange programs being conducted under an umbrella agreement between the United States and China. A Science and Technology Commission (overseen by the White House Office of Science and Technology Policy) has the latest data on the needs and potential opportunities for work in China.

Another area to follow is through the various Chinese trade councils. Since several of China's foreign trade operations have offices in North America the trade councils will have the latest information on needs and possible job opportunities. Information may be available from:

National Council for US-China Trade
Suite 350, 1050 17th Street NW
Washington, DC 20036
202/828-8300

US Department of Commerce
International Trade Administration
Office of China and Hong Kong Affairs
Room 2317
Washington, DC 20230
202/377-3583

Also:

Committee on Scholarly Communications
 with the People's Republic of China
National Academy of Sciences
2101 Constitution Avenue NW
Washington, DC 20418
202/334-2718

National Committee on US—China Relations
777 United Nations Plaza—Room 9B
New York, NY 10017
212/922-1385

China has an embassy at 2300 Connecticut Avenue NW, Washington,
DC 20008 (202/328-2520) with consulates in New York, Houston, San
Francisco and Chicago. The U.S. Embassy is at Xiu Shui Bei Jie 3,
Beijing. Contacts:

American Chamber of
 Commerce in China
Jian Guo Hotel, Rm. 125
22 Jian Guo Men Wai Dajie
Beijing

Electronics:

Qing Hua Technical Services
Qing Hua Yuan, West Suburg
Beijing

Control Data Corp.
Beijing Hotel, Rm 3009
Beijing

Tektronix China, Ltd.
Xiyuan Hotel, Rm 102, Erligou
West Suburg
Beijing

Engineering:

CRS Sirrine Asia Ltd.
Shenshen City

Davy Corp.
2251 Minzu Hotel
Beijing

Occidental Engineering Co.
Beijing Hotel, Room 5036
Beijing

Petroleum:

Caltex Oil Corp.
Jianguo Hotel, Suite 130
Jianguo, Men Wai
Beijing

China Nanhai Reading & Bates
Drilling Corp. Ltd.
China Hotel Office Tower
Rms 506-508
Lui Hua Lu
Guangzhou

Manufacturing:

Cummings Corp.
Nationalities Cultural Palace
Rm. 701
Beijing

Navistar Intl. Export Corp.
Beijing Hotel, Suite 2089
Dong Changan Jie
Beijing

General Electric Co. Intl.
Club Jianguomeneai
Beijing

Hong Kong

GEOGRAPHY:
AREA: 411 sq. mi.
CAPITAL: Victoria.
TERRAIN: Hilly, steep sloped with large, natural harbor.
CLIMATE: Tropical monsoon. Cool and humid in the winter; hot and rainy from spring through summer. Fall is warm and sunny.

PEOPLE:
POPULATION: 5,548,754
ANNUAL GROWTH RATE: -0.09%
RELIGION: 10% Christian; 90% mixture of various Asian religions.
LANGUAGE: Chinese (Cantonese); English (Official).
EDUCATION: Literacy 75%.
LIFE EXPECTANCY: Men 76; women 83 years.

GOVERNMENT: British dependant territory until July 1, 1997 when the country returns to Chinese control. Government budget: $5.7 billion. Of which 4.3% is devoted to military (Defense is the responsibility of the U.K.).

ECONOMY:
GDP: $119 billion
ANNUAL GROWTH RATE: 5.2%
PER CAPITA GDP: $21,500.
AVERAGE RATE OF INFLATION: 9.5%
WORK FORCE: Of the 4.9 million employed, 49% are involved in industry and commerce; 27% services; 19% agriculture; and, 5% government.
OFFICIAL EXCHANGE RATE: 7.8 Hong Kong dollars = US$
COST OF LIVING INDEX: 137

This tiny Crown Colony has been the subject of international espionage encounters in both fact and fiction for decades. It is also one of Asia's leading tourist attractions and a shopper's paradise. Hong Kong's past is well documented. The colony's future however, is very much in question. The British, who have administered the colony for more than 140 years, except for the four year period during the Second World War, will turn control over to the Chinese in mid-1997. Although the Chinese have given business and industry assurances that there will be no major changes it is impossible to predict the future under a hard-line Communist regime.

Hong Kong rapidly has ascended into the front ranks of East Asia's newly industrialized countries. The United States has had a long working partnership with the colony. More than 430 American corporations are located here. The U.S. is also one of Hong Kong's primary trading partners. Among the primary commodities produced for export are: clothing, textile yarn and fabric, footwear, electrical appliances, watches and clocks, and toys. There are opportunities for employment for qualified people. One of the largest employers is the financial industry. Other opportunities exist in the high tech fields and as teachers of English. Many of the younger generation have studied abroad, speak fluent English, and are well trained in American business methods. Yet a goodly number of older Chinese merchants as well as younger men who have not traveled abroad are extremely anxious to maintain their status as "worldly businessmen."

Work in Hong Kong is not typical of the traditional Asian style of conducting business. It is active and quite personal. Despite the heat during the summer a business suit is expected. Business meetings are formal and, if conducted over the lunch or dinner table, can be very alcoholic. Be sure to have a good supply of bilingual business cards printed as they are exchanged whenever people meet.

As a tourist to this famous duty free haven, visas are not required if you stay fewer than 30 days. As an employee here, however, you will require a visa. Contact any British consulate before departing for information. Contacts:

The American Chamber of
 Commerce
Swire House, Central District
Hong Kong

The American Club
Exchange Square
Hong Kong

Executive Recruitment:

Russell Reynolds Associates
 Inc.
4107-4108 Gloucester Tower
11 Pedder Street
Hong Kong

Financial:

Bank of America NT & SA
Bank of America Tower
12 Harcourt Road
G.P.O. Box # 472
Hong Kong

Crocker Bank Intl.
1708 Alexandra House
Chater Road
Hong Kong

Chemicals:

Dow Chemical Hong Kong,
 Ltd.
Gammon House
12 Harbour Road
P.O. Box 711
Hong Kong

ICC Hong Kong, Ltd.
206 Intl. Bldg.
141 Des Voeux Road, Central
Hong Kong

Electronics:

GE Semiconductors HK Ltd.
Perfect Commercial
Bldg. # 1603
20 Austin Avenue,
Tshimshatsui, Kowloon
Hong Kong

Sprague World Trade Corp.
Block E, 8th Floor
Hop Hing Industrial Bldg.
702 Castle Peak Road
Kowloon, Hong Kong

Food Products:

Corn Products Co.
Hong Kong, Ltd.
P.O. Box # 9567,
Kwung Tong Post Office
Kowloon, Hong Kong

General Mills Hong Kong, Ltd.
(Palitoy Far East Ltd.)
Rm 1608-1610 Star House
Salisbury Road
Kowloon, Hong Kong

Wearing Apparel:

Farah Far East, Ltd.
Block E, 5th Floor
Lakshun Industrial Bldg
Chai Wan Kak St.
Kowloon, Hong Kong

Levi Strauss
9/F, Hong Kong

Spinners Industrial Bldg.
603 Tai Nan West Street
Kowloon, Hong Kong

Manhattan Industries Far East
Ltd.
136-138 Austin Road
Kowloon, Hong Kong

Indonesia

GEOGRAPHY:
AREA: 736,000 sq. mi.
CAPITAL: Jakarta
PRINCIPAL CITIES: Surabaya, Medan, Bandung.
TERRAIN: More than 13,500 islands, the larger ones consisting of
coastal plains with mountainous interiors.
CLIMATE: Tropical; hot and humid. More moderate in the highlands.

PEOPLE:
POPULATION: 200,409,741
ANNUAL GROWTH RATE: 1.59%
RELIGION: Muslim 88%; Protestant 6%; Catholic 3%.
LANGUAGE: Indonesian (Official) and local dialects the largest of
which is Javanese.
EDUCATION: Attendance in primary school 84%.
LITERACY: 85%

LIFE EXPECTANCY: Men 59; women 63 years.

GOVERNMENT: Independent republic with a president as chief of state and head of the Cabinet. Unicameral legislature. Government budget: $21.1 billion.

ECONOMY:
GDP: $75.4 billion
ANNUAL GROWTH RATE: 6.5%
PER CAPITA GDP: $2,900
AVERAGE RATE OF INFLATION: 10%.
WORK FORCE: Of the 74.5 million employed 56% are in agriculture; 23% industry and commerce; 16% services; and 2% civil service.
OFFICIAL EXCHANGE RATE: 2,116 rupiahs = US$
COST OF LIVING INDEX: 109

Indonesia is the world's fifth most populous country. The island of Java alone is one of the most densely populated areas in the world with more than 110 million people living in an area the size of New York State. Maintaining a steady economic growth of 5% (which has been maintained for the past several years) has been a successful endeavor of the Soeharto government. Fortunately, natural resources (oil and minerals) are available in generous supply. Although comprising only 21% of the country's gross national product, these sectors contribute about half its foreign exchange earnings and half its tax revenues.

The largest employer of Americans in Indonesia, aside from missionaries, is the petroleum industry. American oil companies have developed about 80% of Indonesia's oil and gas resources. The total U.S. investment in Indonesia is $3.9 billion of which $1.2 billion is in the oil and gas sectors. Oil and liquefied natural gas constitutes 55% of the country's exports: most going to Japan with about 20% to the United States.

One of the problems for U.S. companies trying to operate in Indonesia is the government's decree that the state maintain total sovereignty over all mineral resources. Therefore, foreign companies must operate as contractors to the government or one of its state enterprises.

Over the next five years the strongest mineral growth will be in coal with production expected to expand five-fold to more than 15 million tons per year, including nearly half for export. U.S. companies involved in minerals include Freeport Minerals in copper, Pennzoil in coal, and Mobil in oil.

Doing business in Indonesia can be most casual. Unlike many Asian countries it is common to visit a large company and be received without an appointment. Personal contact is very important and all business is conducted face to face. Dealing with Indonesians is a long, slow process. This is a region where "rubber time" is common; 3:00 PM can well mean 3:30 or later. Be patient. Another refreshing note: American business-women are accorded the same hospitality as men.

Visas are not required if your stay is for less than 60 days. A work permit is required if you obtain a job however. The general level of health and sanitation is below U.S. standards, Tuberculosis, malaria, dengue fever, and parasitic diseases are prevalent outside the major cities.

Indonesia has an embassy at 2020 Massachusetts Avenue NW, Washington, DC 20036 (202/775 5200). Consulates are located in New York, Los Angeles, Houston, San Francisco and Chicago. The U.S. Embassy is located at Jl. Medan Merdeka Selatan 5, Jakarta. Contacts:

American Chamber of
 Commerce in Indonesia
Citibank Bldg.
Jl. M.H. Thamrin 55
Jakarta

The Investment Coordinating
 Board
Jl. Jen 6
Gatot Subroto, Selatan
Jakarta

Petroleum:

Louisiana Land & Exploration
 Co. Indonesia
Wisma Harapan
Jl. Jenderai Sudirman Kav 34
Jakarta

Mobil Oil Indonesia, Inc.
P.O. Box # 400
Jakarta

Marathon Petroleum Indonesia
 Ltd.
P.O. Box # 3293
Five Pillars Office Park
Jl. Leklem
M.T. Haryono No. 58
Jakarta

Phillips Petroleum Co.
 Indonesia
Jl. Melawai Raya No. 16
Keb. Baru
Jakarta

Construction:

Gray Tool Intl.
%P.D. Hasil Trading Co.
P.O. Box # 2135
Pasar Baru

Kaiser Engineers Intl. Inc.
%P.T. Krakatau Steel
Jl. Taman Sunbda Kelapaneg
Jakarta

Mineral Development:

Tidex Intl., Inc.
Jl. Dayak 21, Tanung Priok
Jakarta

Conoco Irian Jaya Co.
P.O. Box # 367
Jakarta

Freeport Indonesia Inc.
Jl. Thamrin 59
P.O. Box # 3148
Jakarta

Japan

GEOGRAPHY:
AREA: 145,856
CAPITAL: Tokyo
PRINCIPAL CITIES: Osaka, Yokohama, Nagoya, Sapporo
TERRAIN: Rugged mountainous islands.
CLIMATE: Varies from sub-tropical in the south to cool temperate in the north.

PEOPLE:
POPULATION: 125,106,937
ANNUAL GROWTH RATE: 0.32%
RELIGION: Most Japanese observe both Shinto and Buddhist rites; about 16% belong to other faiths including 0.8% Christian.
LANGUAGE: Japanese
EDUCATION: Literacy 99%
LIFE EXPECTANCY: Men 76; women 82 years.

GOVERNMENT: Parliamentary democracy. Bicameral Diet with the prime minister head of government. Emperor is the symbol of the state but executive power is vested in the Cabinet selected by the prime minister. Government budget: $433 billion of which only 0.5% is devoted to the military.

ECONOMY:
GNP: $2.549 trillion
ANNUAL GROWTH RATE: 0%
PER CAPITA GNP: $20,400.
AVERAGE RATE OF INFLATION: 1.3%

WORK FORCE: Of the 60.7 million workers (40% of whom are women) 43% were involved in services; 32% in trade, manufacturing, mining and construction; 8% in agriculture and 7% in government. The unemployment rate is about 2.5%.
OFFICIAL EXCHANGE RATE: 111.5 yen = US$
COST OF LIVING INDEX: 196

For a nation slightly smaller in size than California to have achieved such remarkable economic growth and development since its defeat in World War II is truly amazing. The reservoir of industrial leadership and technicians, its intelligent and industrious work force, its high savings and investment rates, and its intensive promotion of industrial development and foreign trade have resulted in a mature industrial economy. Along with North America and Western Europe, Japan is one of the three major industrial complexes among market economies. Foreign trade is the bulwark of the economy with machinery, motor vehicles and consumer electronics being the major source of income.

American corporations have long recognized the country as a potential business partner. More than 750 U.S. multinational corporations have operations in Japan investing more than $20 billion. For Americans interested in working here, however, the number of jobs is limited. The Japanese government does not want foreigners coming here to fill jobs that can be done by nationals. Most Americans working in Japan are hired abroad and transferred by their companies. However, because of the extremely high cost of living (rent in Tokyo can run as high as $3,000 a month with utilities another $500) many U.S. companies limit the number of employees they send to Japan since they must pick up the tab for housing, cost of living differential, home leave, and educational expenses for any children.

The major exception is for teachers of foreign languages—primarily English but also German and French. Since all Japanese businessmen recognize the fact that their success depends on the English-speaking market there is a constant need for both teachers and translators. It is ironic because the Japanese school system provides a 10 year program to learn foreign languages. Graduates can read and often translate, but their conversational ability is nil. Thus the constant search for English-speaking "foreigners."

Although the need exists there is a typical Japanese bureaucratic catch 22. Unless you have been hired from abroad or transferred by your company it is against Japanese law to work in Japan without first obtaining the necessary permission while outside the country. Thus while a visitor to Tokyo can pick up the Monday edition of *The Japan Times* (published in English) and read two pages of ads submitted by the many foreign language schools in search of English teachers, the law says you can be deported by accepting such a job without prior paper work including a Letter of Guarantee assuring your job and living status, etc. Obviously there are many ways around the law including leaving the country and returning. There are also a great many Americans working in one of the many language schools "illegally." However, the best policy is to obtain a firm job before coming to Japan and obtaining all the necessary papers in advance.

Teaching jobs in Japan are also widely advertised in major U.S. papers and educational journals. These ads are the best and safest source of Japanese employment. Then, with the approval of the Ministry of Foreign Affairs, you may be employed by any enterprise.

Like most Asian countries, business cards are essential. Be sure to have your business card (called meishi) printed in English on one side and Japanese script on the other. When you hand your card to your Japanese associate be sure and face him. He will read your card, nod, then hand you his card. Read it (even if you can't understand a word) then put it in your wallet from which your own card came. Placing it in a pocket or briefcase is considered rude.

Expect to be entertained for dinner, not lunch. And, if you're married, your wife may be the only woman present—even if the evening's entertaining ends in a local geisha house.

Any Japanese National Tourist (Main office: 630 Fifth Avenue, New York, NY 10111) will provide additional information on working or doing business in Japan. They publish a wide range of brochures designed for Americans.

Japan has an embassy at 2520 Massachusetts Avenue NW, Washington, DC 20008 (202/939-6700) with consulates in a dozen U.S. cities. The U.S. Embassy is located at 10-5 Akasaka 1-chome, Minatoku, Tokyo. Contacts:

American Chamber of
 Commerce in Japan
Fukide Building, No. 2
4-1-21 Toranomon
Minato-Ku, Tokyo 105

American Club
1-2 Azabudai 2-chome
Minato-Ku, Tokyo

Electronics:

Burr-Brown Japan, Ltd.
Inoue Akasaka Bldg. 608
1-chome, Akasaka, Minato-Ku
Tokyo 107

GE Semiconductor K.K.
Meji Seimei Gotanda Bldg.
2-27-4 Nishi Gotanda
Shinagana-Ku
Tokyo 141

Manufacturing:

Nippon Brunswick K.K.
Nippon Brunswick Bldg.
27-7 Sendagaya
5-chome, Skibuya-Ku
Tokyo

Manville Japan Ltd.
2105 Mita-Kokusai Bldg.
4-28 Mita, 1-chome,
Minato-Ku
Tokyo 108

Toyo Ekco Co., Ltd.
Daiwa Bldg.
Mainamikyutaro-machi
Higashiku
Osaka 541

Financial:

First Boston Corp.
Kokusai Bldg.
11-1 Marunouchi 1-chome
Chiyoda-Ku
Tokyo 100

Mellon Bank NA
New Yurakucho Bldg.
12-1 Yuraku-chu 1-chome
Chiyoda-Ku
Tokyo 102

Management Consultants:

Boyden Associates (Japan)
Suite 1307 Aoyama Bldg.
1-2-3 Kita Aoyama, Minato-Ku
Tokyo 107

McKinsey & Co Inc.
Juji Bldg.
10th F., 2-3 Marunchi
3-chome, Chiyoda-Ku
Tokyo 100

Zehnder Egon Intl.
Sago Bldg., 11-28
Nagatc-cho, 1-chome
Chiyoda-Ku
Tokyo 100

Language School:

Berlitz
Kowa Bldg., No. 2/1-11-39
Akasaka
Minato-Ku
Tokyo 107

Employment Service:

Manpower Japan Co. Ltd.
No. 3 Kowa Bldg.
11-45 Akasaka 1-chome
Minato-Ku
Tokyo 107

South Korea

GEOGRAPHY:
AREA: 38,000 sq. mi.
CAPITAL: Seoul
PRINCIPAL CITIES: Pisan, Taegu, Inchon.
TERRAIN: Partially forested mountain ranges, separated by deep, narrow valleys; cultivated plains along the coast, particularly in the west and south.
CLIMATE: Temperate with heavier rainfall in the summer than the winter.

PEOPLE:
POPULATION: 45,082,880
ANNUAL GROWTH RATE: 1.04%
RELIGION: Strong Confucian tradition. About 28% are Christians.
LANGUAGE: Korean
EDUCATION: Attendance in primary school 99%.
LITERACY: Over 98%.
LIFE EXPECTANCY: Men 67; women 73 years.

GOVERNMENT: Republic with powers centralized in a strong executive (President). Unicameral legislature (National Assembly) Government budget: $38 billion of which about a third is devoted to the military.

ECONOMY:
GNP: $424 billion
ANNUAL GROWTH RATE: 6.3%
PER CAPITA GNP: $9,500
AVERAGE RATE OF INFLATION: 4.8%
WORK FORCE: Of the 17 million workers about 28% are employed in industry; 21% in agriculture; and, 50% in services.
OFFICIAL EXCHANGE RATE: 810 Won = US$
COST OF LIVING INDEX: 122

Over the past quarter century, Korea's economic growth has been nothing short of spectacular. This nation has advanced in a single generation from one of the poorest nations to the threshold of full industrialization, despite the need to maintain one of the world's largest military establishments. Lacking natural resources, Korea's greatest asset is its industrious, literate people. Yet despite its tremendous growth, the shadow of its mysterious and extremely dangerous brother to the north, can't be overlooked. According to one Seoul General, "North Korea is a military camp, not a country." In 1993, North Korea spent 25% of its GNP, or $2.1 billion on arms. They have a standing army in excess of 1,000,000 men compared to half that of South Korea. North Korea is, today, a heavily armed, poor third world nation, envious of the South's booming economy and high standard of living. Couple this with its nuclear arsenal and it spells potential trouble. Despite President Clinton's attempt to solve the situation the seeds of serious conflict remain.

The secret to South Korea's success has been the government's ability to institute sweeping economic reforms emphasizing exports and labor intensive light industries. Among the primary industries that have led to the nation's growth are: textiles, clothing, footwear, food processing, chemicals, steel, electronics, automobile production and ship building. More than 170 American corporations have operations in Korea.

Mining is a minor portion of the nation's growth with small deposits of tungsten, anthracite coal, iron ore, graphite, and limestone. There are no known oil reserves and energy is of concern to Korea's economic planners. The country's ambitious program to build nuclear power plants is well under way. Their eighth plant went into operation in 1993 with three more either under construction or planned.

This is not an inexpensive country in which to live or work. A decent house in the Seoul area might cost more than $4,000 a month to rent with apartments renting for about half that amount. Salaries paid to expatriates must take this high cost of living into consideration. Under Korea's Foreign Capital Inducement Act, American's working here are exempt from Korean income taxes for a specified time period. There are also no restrictions on the number of foreign employees that may be hired by a Korean firm. A U.S. passport entitles you to up to 15 days in the country without a visa. However, business travelers from the U.S. can stay as long as 48 months with a special multiple-entry visa issued by any Korean Consulate Office.

As a Westerner you'll be treated with reverence and respect. Although you probably won't be entertained in a Korean home until you know your Korean business associates quite well, you will be invited to a bar or restaurant. If more than one Korean is in the party, each one will vie for the honor of pouring you a drink. If you can't hold your alcohol ask for a soft drink as it's better than refusing their hospitality.

Health care in the major cities is better than adequate since most physicians have been trained in Western medical schools. The water is safe in the major hotels but don't eat the food from the sidewalk vendors. On the 15th of every month the air raid sirens sound. If you're on the street get to a shelter (well marked) immediately. Also, don't try and take Korean money out of the country: it's against the law! Gambling is legal in Seoul. However, if you plan to test the tables you'll need your passport for identification.

South Korea has an embassy at 2320 Massachusetts Avenue NW, Washington, DC 20008 (202/939-5600). The U.S. Embassy is located at 82 Sejong-Ro, Chongro-ku, Seoul. Contacts:

American Chamber of
 Commerce in Korea
Room 307, Chosun Hotel
Seoul

Financial:

Bank of America NT & SA
Koram Bank
1 Gong Pyung-Dong
Seoul

Mellon Bank NA
1725 Daewoo Center Bldg.
541 Namdaemun-ro, Chung-ku
Seoul

Clothing:

Bal Four Maclaine Overseas,
 Ltd.
Suite 1503; Choyang Bldg.
50-10 Ska Chungmoo-ro
Chung-ku
Seoul

Wonmi Apparel & Textile, Ltd.
%Manhattan International
1155 Avenue of the Americas
New York, NY 10036

Engineering:

Bechtel Overseas Corp.
87 Sokong-dong, Chung-ku
Seoul 100

Daniel, Mann, Johnson &
 Mandenhall
A.P.O. 96301
302-68 Ichon-dong,
Yangsan-Ku
Seoul 140

Executive Search:

Boyden/Perron Associates
1301 Lemma Bldg.
146-1 Soosong-Dong
Choong-ku
Seoul

Chemicals:

Gamlen Chemicals Co.
%Sung A. Industrials Co.
C.P.O. Box # 372
Seoul

Chemstrand, Inc.
Anglican Church Bldg. 307,
 Jeong Dong
Joong-ku
Seoul

Electronics:

Control Data Korea, Inc.,
481-11 Karibong-Dong
Yongdungpo-Ku
Seoul

General Electric Technical
 Services Co.
G.P.O. Box # 871, Seoul Bldg.
114-31 Uni-Dong, Chung-Ro
Seoul 100

Food Processing:

Knorr Korea Ltd.,
4/F Miwon Bldg.
96-48 Shinseul-Dong
Dongdaemun-Ku
Seoul

Purina Korea, Inc.
C.P.O. Box # 5112
114-5 Ohjung-dong
Buchon City
Kyonggi-do 150-71

Philippines

GEOGRAPHY:
AREA: 117,187 sq. mi.
CAPITAL: Manila
PRINCIPAL CITIES: Davao, Cebu, Quezon, Legaspi
TERRAIN: 65% mountainous with narrow coastal lowlands.
CLIMATE: Tropical marine. Aside a monsoon belt. Northeast monsoon
from November to April; southwest monsoon May to October.

PEOPLE:
POPULATION: 69,808,930
ANNUAL GROWTH RATE: 1.92%
RELIGION: 83% Roman Catholic; 9% Protestant; 5% Muslim.
LANGUAGE: Filipino (national language) and English (language of
government and higher education) Both are official.
EDUCATION: Attendance in primary school 97%.
LITERACY: 88%
LIFE EXPECTANCY: Men 62; women 68 years.

GOVERNMENT: Constitutional republic. Bicameral legislature. Next presidential election scheduled for 1992. Government budget: $1.5 billion of which 9% is devoted to the military.

ECONOMY:
GNP: $171 billion
ANNUAL GROWTH RATE: 1.4%
PER CAPITA GDP: $2,500667
AVERAGE RATE OF INFLATION: 5%
WORK FORCE: Agriculture 47%; Industry and commerce 20%; Services 13.5%; Government 10%. Unemployment rate is about 10%.
OFFICIAL EXCHANGE RATE: 27 pesos = US$
COST OF LIVING INDEX: 082

This 7,000-odd archipelago on the edge of the South China Sea has a land mass slightly smaller than Japan but a coastline twice that of the United States. Because of its dense, often inhospitable terrain, the country is only 10% occupied. Most Americans working here are located on the island of Luzon. Most corporate headquarters are located in Metro Manila, a very modern and up to date city. Mindinao, another large island offers some opportunities but is predominately Muslim and home to a very militant faction. The remaining 6,998+ islands are either uninhabited or primarily devoted to local fishing, agriculture or forestry. The primary source of foreign employment is the industrial sector with more than a handful of missionaries and Peace Corps volunteers scattered throughout the country.

The country is well endowed with minerals and non-oil resources. Test drilling for oil has been only partially successful. Philippine chromite, nickel, and copper deposits are among the largest in the world. Industrial production is centered on processing and assembling operations of items such as: food, beverages, textiles, clothing and footwear, pharmaceuticals, paper and paper products, small appliances and electronics. Heavier industries are dominated by the production of cement, glass, industrial chemicals, fertilizers, iron and steel, and refined petroleum products.

The industrial sector is concentrated in the urban areas, especially in the Manila region. Inadequate infrastructure, transportation, communication and especially electrical power inhibit a more rapid industrial growth. In recent years the production of automobiles and trucks as well as ship building have been accelerated. New plants have revitalized the sagging cement industry.

Americans working in the Philippines have little difficulty working here as foreign expertise is more than welcomed. Before you accept a job, however, obtain a work permit from the Philippine Embassy or Consulate. Work visas are usually granted for a two year period. They can be renewed for another three years once your employer submits documentation that an effort has been made to train Filipino citizens in the work you are performing.

Dealing with Filipino businessmen takes some understanding of local practices. For one thing, most Filipinos like to cultivate a personal relationship before talking business. Feel free to talk about yourself, local life, your family. Avoid politics! And, don't rush things. Business is transpired very slowly and by trying any high pressure methods will only backfire. It's better not to plan a business trip during the holiday season, June through September. Also, business lunches are just that: business. At dinner you may discuss business but it is considered far more social. Wives should be included.

Although all populated areas of the Philippines can be reached by automobile, roads are usually overcrowded and poorly maintained. Some areas of the country are plagued by civil unrest. Check with the Department of State's Office of Citizen Emergency Service in Washington (202/647-5225) or the U.S. Embassy in Manila for travel advisories. Health services in the capitol are adequate. Outside Manila dysentery is endemic so don't drink the water or eat unpeeled fruit. Contacts:

American Chamber of
 Commerce of the Philippines
P.O. Box # 1578, MCC
Manila

Electronics:

Advanced Micro Devices Inc.
MSC Compound, Km 22
S. Super Highway
Muntimiupa, Manila

NCR Corp.
P.O. Box 7020
Manila International Airport
Exchange Offices 3120
Manila

Engineering/Construction:

Amman & Whitney
V. Madrigae Bldg. 6793 Ayala Avenue
Makati, Manila

Parsons Corp., Intl. Ltd.
MCCPO Bos 2188, Makati
Manila

Food Products:

California Manufacturing Co., Inc.
P.O. Box 759
Makati Commercial Center
Makati, Manila

Kraft Foods Inc.,
Dr. A. Santos Avenue
Paranaque
Metro Manila 3128

Pioneer Hi-Bred Intl. Inc.
Mindanao

Chemicals:

Monsanto Philippines, Inc.
APMC Bldg
136 Amorsolo Street
Legaspi Village
Makati, Manila

Nalco Chemical Co.
Philippines, Inc.
P.O. 1064, MCC, Makati
Metro Manila

Pharmaceuticals:

Endo Labs Philippines
P.O. Box # 2150, MCC
Makati, Rizai D-3117

Schering Corp. Philippines Inc.
P.O. Box # 297
Manila

Warner-Lambert Labs
Philippines, Inc.
MCCPO Box # 65
Metro Manila

Taiwan

GEOGRAPHY:
AREA: 14,000 sq. mi.
CAPITAL: Taipei
PRINCIPAL CITIES: Kaohsiung, Taichung, Tainan.
TERRAIN: Largely mountainous island with flat gently rolling plains in the west.
CLIMATE: Tropical; marine, with a rainy season during the June-August monsoon. Cloudy most of the year.

PEOPLE:
POPULATION: 21,298,930
ANNUAL GROWTH RATE: 0.96%
RELIGION: Mostly Buddhist, Confucian and Taoist.
LANGUAGE: Mandarin Chinese (official).
EDUCATION: Attendance in primary school 99%.
LITERACY: 92%
LIFE EXPECTANCY: Men 72; women 78 years.

GOVERNMENT: Single party presidential regime (The Nationalist Party) dominates the political system. In 1989 the ban on political parties was lifted and by 1994 more than 40 separate parties were listed. Government budget: $30 billion of which 25% is devoted to military.

ECONOMY:
GNP: $224 billion
ANNUAL GROWTH RATE: 6%
PER CAPITA GDP: $10,600
AVERAGE RATE OF INFLATION: 3.2%
WORK FORCE: Of the 7.7 million employed, 42% work in the industrial sector; 42% in the service sector and 17% in agriculture.

OFFICIAL EXCHANGE RATE: 26 Taiwan dollars = US$
COST OF LIVING INDEX: 130

Despite the fact that Taiwan is one of the most densely populated countries in the world it has one of the world's most dynamic economies. One of the development strategies adopted by Taiwan authorities has been to assign priorities to infrastructure projects. The initial series of projects conducted between 1972 and 1982 included roadways, railroads, an airport, steel mill, shipyard, electric power and petrochemical plants. Current projects scheduled to be completed by the end of the century include solid waste disposal plants, hospital improvements, railroad electrification, a forth nuclear power plant, flood control, and a subway system in Taipei. Not only have these projects led to a greater standard of living for all Taiwanese but jobs for both natives and skilled foreigners. By 1994, more than $4 billion was invested here by Americans. Major industries include: textiles, footware, clothing, electrical and electronic equipment, chemicals, ship building and food processing.

The focus of Taiwan's move toward developing a high technology industrial base is the Hsinchu science-based industrial park, which opened in 1980 and currently employs more than 12,000 people. Almost a third of the 70 companies within the park are foreign owned, 22 are U.S. firms (there are more than 185 U.S. multinational corporations in the country). Products include computers and peripheral equipment, semiconductors, precision electronics, and telecommunications. Three biotechnological companies have also set up operations in the park.

The result of a booming economy is obvious. Living standards are high. High rise luxury hotels and apartments, fancy restaurants and expensive cars are part of modern Taipei. Taiwanese businessmen are quite aware that the success of their country's economy is based on foreign trade. Since the United States is Taiwan's largest trading partner, taking 45% of exports and supplying 22% of imports, Americans are more than welcome. Most Taiwanese businessmen either speak English or are trying to learn it. Thus, an employment opportunity for teachers of English. Interestingly, many Taiwanese want to learn English from Americans not fluent-speaking natives. There are many local language schools in Taipei that have been known to hire Americans off the street. In addition contact National Central University, Chung-Li 320 and National Taiwan University, Roosevelt Road 1, Taipei.

A few words on Taiwanese business practices. Entertaining is a major part of the working process. Deals are made in restaurants; never in a businessman's home. However, business entertaining may last until the early morning hours so be prepared. When you are the host for a business dinner it is considered good practice to also invite the wife of your guest. If you plan many such meetings have business cards printed: English on one side and Mandarin on the other. Card companies in Taipei will print them for you in 48 hours. Many businessmen take their vacations between January and March so plan accordingly.

To work in Taiwan you must obtain approval and an entry visa issued by the Ministry of Foreign Affairs. First however, your application must be submitted by the local employer to the Ministry of Economic Affairs for initial approval. You'll be asked to specify the position, monthly remuneration and length of employment. This data will be confirmed by your local employer who must also submit a document guaranteeing your position. One excellent source of employment data is the American Chamber of Commerce, Room 1012, Chia Hsin Building Annex, 96 Chung Shan North Road, Sector 2, Taipei.

The more common Asian health problems are extremely rare in Taiwan. It is far more common to suffer the effects of high pollen counts and air pollution than more serious maladies. It is safe to drink the water in Taipei's major hotels. Elsewhere be cautious.

Since Taiwan is still considered an official part of China there is no separate embassy in the United States. Unofficial commercial and cultural relations are maintained through a private organization, the Coordination Council for North American Affairs with headquarters in Taipei and field offices in Washington and 10 other U.S. cities. In Taipei contact the American Institute in Taiwan (AIT) 7 Lane 134, Hsin Yi Road, Sector 3. Contacts:

American Chamber of
Commerce in Taiwan
P.O. Box # 17-277
Taipei

Electronics:

Ampex Taiwan Ltd.
P.O. Box 188
Taoyuan, Taipei

Lumax Intl. Corp.
P.O. Box 81-228
Taipei

Texas Instruments Taiwan Ltd.
142, Sector 1, Hsin Nan Road
Chung Ho City, Taipei Hsien
Taipei

Financial:

Bank of California NA
8 Hsiang Yang Road
Commercial Bank Building
Taipei

Citibank NA
105 Chung Cheng 4th Road
Kaohsiung
Taipei

Construction:

Wayne Hoh Corp.
Je Ai Road, Sector 4 #33, P.O.
Box 24-77
Taipei

Ebasco Overseas Corp.
P.O. Box 3, Sanchin
Taipei Hsien
Taipei

Engineering:

Gibsin Engineers Ltd.
P.O. Box 68-3161
Taipei

Chemicals:

Asia Silicones Ltd.
Formosa Plastics Bldg.
96 Chung Shan North Road
Sector 2
Taipei

Atlas Taiwan Corp.
11A Morrison Plaza
25 Jen Ai Road, Sector 4
Taipei

Monsanto Far East Ltd.
36 Chang An East Road
Sector 1
Taipei

Employment:

Manpower Temporary Services
201/30 Tun Hua North Road
Taipei

SOUTH PACIFIC

Antarctica

GEOGRAPHY:
AREA: 5,405,000 sq. mi.
CAPITAL: None
PRINCIPAL CITIES: None
TERRAIN: 98% thick continental ice sheet with mountain ranges transecting part of continent. Coastal areas free of ice most of the year. Ice sheet slopes from a thickness of more than a mile in the interior to several hundred meters along the coast.
CLIMATE: Severe low temperatures vary with latitude and season. Winter along the coast may range from -80° F. to 0° F. Inland the world's coldest temperature was recorded at -163°F. The summer may see temperatures as high as 40° F along the coast. Coastal conditions during the dry summer months can be quite pleasant. The continent is basically a desert with precipitation rarely exceeding 14 inches a year—all in the form of ice and snow.

PEOPLE:
POPULATION: None

GOVERNMENT: No government. Treaty signed in 1959 limits the area to scientific purposes only. No military weapons are allowed.

Yes, there are jobs in Antarctica. Strange as it may seem, although there are no formal cities, there are major developed areas established by the scientific communities of many nations. The U.S., for example, has a major outpost along the Ross Sea called McMurdo. The inhabitants are all seasonal with few ever spending more than 12 months here at a time. A major nuclear power station supplies energy for the several thousand inhabitants that may be here during the warmer summer months—November through March. Ten miles from the McMurdo Base the New Zealand scientific community has also established a sizable scientific community.

Although the various U.S. science and research personnel are representing either a university or privately funded research group the many support personnel are either hired by the U.S. Navy or are under the supervision of the National Science Foundation. Thus, support civilian jobs in the areas of construction, engineering, and other related fields come under the aegis of NSF. To obtain data about their needs and seasonal requirements contact them directly: National Science Foundation, Operation Deepfreeze, 1800 G Street NW., Washington, DC 20550. NSF may lead you to specific research groups in need of your non-scientific talents or will update you on the current NSF-Antarctica program requirements. Most jobs on the continent last no longer than six months as to "winter over" essentially means a complete cut off from outside support and supply. These choice opportunities are almost always given to the military support teams (often SeaBees) and the individual scientists who volunteer for the privilege.

Australia

GEOGRAPHY:
AREA: 2,966 million sq. mi.
CAPITAL: Canberra
PRINCIPAL CITIES: Sydney, Melbourne, Brisbane.
TERRAIN: Mostly low plateau with deserts; fertile plain in southeast.
CLIMATE: Relatively dry ranging from temperate in the south to semitropical in the north.

PEOPLE:
POPULATION: 18,077,419
ANNUAL GROWTH RATE: 1.38%
RELIGION: Anglican 26%; Roman Catholic 24%; other Christian 24%.
LANGUAGE: English
EDUCATION: Attendance in primary school 100%.
LITERACY: 99%
LIFE EXPECTANCY: Men 74, women 80 years.

GOVERNMENT: Democratic, federal-state system recognizing British monarch as sovereign. Bicameral parliament with prime minister head of government. Government budget: $93 billion, 10% of which is for the military.

ECONOMY:
GNP: $339.7 billion
ANNUAL GROWTH RATE: 4%
PER CAPITA GNP: $19,100
AVERAGE RATE OF INFLATION: 1.1%

WORK FORCE: Of the 8 million employed 63% are involved in services; 26% in mining, manufacturing and utilities; 6% in agriculture; and, 5% in public administration and defense.
OFFICIAL EXCHANGE RATE: 1.4 Australian Dollar = US$
COST OF LIVING INDEX: 120

This beautiful island continent, slightly smaller in size than the United States, has a diversified economy with a relatively high level of prosperity comparable to levels in West European countries. Australia has immense mineral and energy resources. It is one of the world's leading producers of and exporters of aluminum, alumina, bauxite, cobalt, copper, industrial diamonds, gold, iron ore, lead, nickel, and silver. In addition, abundant supplies of coal, natural gas, liquid petroleum gas, and uranium add to the country's energy resources.

The manufacturing sector is limited by Australia's small domestic market and relatively high labor costs arising from a strong union movement. However, Australia has developed a broad based manufacturing sector largely due to an extensive and effective range of tariffs and other protective measures. Building and construction is a major industry with manufacturing the largest employer of labor. The economy's mainstay however is beef and lamb, wool, coal and iron ore.

Living standards and wages are high. Costs are comparable to those in America. The life style is, by and large, far more relaxed. Australians are not class conscious and almost always will make time for visitors even without an appointment. Business dealings are relaxed and very informal. If, for example, you're invited to a party, don't talk business. There is play time and business time; the two don't mix. Be honest and up front. Say what you mean and mean what you say. Aussies can detect a phony faster than a kangaroo at full gait.

Although Australia used to have an open immigration policy welcoming foreigners to live and work, the heavy influx of immigrants from Asia and England forced the government to alter their procedures. Today Americans working in Australia must first be granted a temporary resident status issued by the Commonwealth Department of Immigration and Ethnic Affairs. Your prospective employer vouches for you and claims that you possess certain job skills that cannot be found locally.

With more than $40 billion (1991) invested in Australia, there are a number of American firms that employ both locals as well as Yanks that meet the technical requirements.

One of the best sources of job information is the American Chamber of Commerce in Australia. They publish *Who's Who in U.S. Business in Australia*, a 400 page guide listing names and addresses of more than 1,000 U.S. companies in Australia, their affiliates, directors and product or service specialities. Address: 8th floor, 50 Pitt St., Sydney, NSW 2000 (Tel 02 241-1907). Another good reference guide is the *Australia Employment Directory* (1989—Centralia, WA. Pierce Publications, Inc.).

Australia has an embassy at 1601 Massachusetts Avenue NW, Washington, DC 20008 (202/797-3000) with consulates in New York, Chicago, San Francisco, Los Angeles, Houston, and Honolulu. The U.S. Embassy is at Moonah Place, Yarralumia, Canberra. Contacts:

American Chamber of
 Commerce in Australia
Level 41, 80 Collins Street
Melbourne, Victoria 3000

Executive Search:

Korn/Ferry International Pty.
 Ltd.
11th Floor, Kyle House
31 Macquarie Place
Sydney
New South Wales 2000

Boyden International
Level 35, MLC Center
Martin Place
Sydney
New South Wales 2000

Western Personnel Services
 Pty. Ltd.
GPO Box # 1071
Brisbane, Queensland 4001

Construction:

Brown & Root Ltd.
31 Rothesay Street
Kenmore, Queensland 4069

Raymond Engineers Australia
 Pty. Ltd.
Locked Bag No. 9
Cloisters Square
Perth, Western Australia 6000

Mining:

Philbro Energy (Australia) Pty.
 Ltd.
P.O. Box # N273
Grosvenor Street
Sydney
New South Wales 2000

Western Mining Corporation
 Holdings Ltd.
GPO Box 860K
Melbourne, Victoria 3001

Manufacturing:

J.I. Case (Australia) Pty. Ltd.
Windsor Road
Northmead
New South Wales 2152

GE Australia	Frontline Ford Pty. Ltd.
100 Cope Street	477 Northeast Road
Waterloo	Hillcrest, South Australia 5086
New South Wales 2017	

Guam

GEOGRAPHY:
AREA: 509 sq. mi.
CAPITAL: Agana
PRINCIPAL CITY: Timoneng
TERRAIN: Island of volcanic origin surrounded by coral reefs, relatively flat coraline limestone plateau (source of most fresh water) with steep coastal cliffs. Mountains in the south.
CLIMATE: Tropical marine; generally warm and humid. Dry season from January to June; rainy season from July to December. Little seasonal temperature variation.

PEOPLE:
POPULATION: 149,620
ANNUAL GROWTH RATE: 2.48%
RELIGION: 98% Roman Catholic
LANGUAGE: English (official) and Chamorro. Most residents are bilingual. Japanese also widely spoken.
EDUCATION: Attendance in primary school 94%.
LITERACY: 90%
LIFE EXPECTANCY: Men 72; women 76 years.

GOVERNMENT: Unincorporated territory of the United States. Governor elected to 4 year term. Elections for unicameral legislature every 2 years. Guamanians are U.S. citizens but do not vote in U.S. presidential elections. Government budget: $175 million.

ECONOMY:
GNP: $2.0 billion
ANNUAL GROWTH RATE: NA
PER CAPITA GNP: $14,000
AVERAGE RATE OF INFLATION: 4.9%
WORK FORCE: Of the 42,000 in the labor market 45% work for the government; the remainder are involved in petroleum refining, construc-

tion, concrete products, textiles and clothing, and tourism. The unemployment rate is about 2%.
OFFICIAL EXCHANGE RATE: Currency is the $US.

This isolated island, about three times the size of Washington, D.C., is primarily an American military outpost in the middle of the Pacific Ocean. Tokyo is 1,350 miles to the North; and Honolulu 3,300 miles to the east. The entire economy is based on U.S. military spending and on revenues from tourism. Over the past 20 years tourism has grown rapidly, creating a construction boom for new hotels and the expansion of older ones. Visitors numbered about 600,000 in 1990. About 55% of the labor force works for the private sector the rest for the government. Most food and industrial goods are imported, with about 75% from the U.S. In 1988, the unemployment rate was but 3% down from 10% in 1983.

The primary sources of employment on Guam are the military, construction and teaching. One of the larger construction contractors is Dillingham Construction Corp, 5944 Inglewood Dr., Pleasanton, CA (or Hawaiian Rock Products, P.O. Box # DS, Agana, Guam 96910). For teaching positions on the island contact the Personnel Director, Department of Education, Agana, Guam 96910. Also: Office of the High Commissioner, Trust Territory of the Pacific Islands, Saipan, Mariana Islands; and for teaching military dependents: Office of Dependent Schools, Department of Defense, Washington, DC 20301. Contacts:

Banking:

California First Bank
Hernan Cortes Avenue
Agana 96910

Chase Manhattan Bank. N.A.
PDN Bldg., O'Hara Street
P.O. Box # AE
Agana 96910

Accounting:

Touche Ross & Co.
Pacific News Bldg.
238 O'Hara Street
Agana 96910

Peat, Marwick Mitchell & Co.
Guam International Trade
 Center
P.O. Box # 3
Agana 96910

Petroleum:

Mobil Petroleum Co., Inc.
P.O. Box # EU
Agana 96910

Chemicals:

Connell Bros. Co. Ltd.
P.O. Box # DS
Agana 96910

Marketing:

Milbrands Inc.
P.O. 9016
Timoneng 96911

Micronesia

GEOGRAPHY:
AREA: 702 sq. mi. Forms, with Palau, the archipelago of Caroline Islands, consisting of the states of Yap, Truk, Pohnpei, and Kosrae in western Pacific Ocean.
CAPITAL: Kolonia
TERRAIN: Islands vary geographically from high mountainous to low, coral atolls. Some volcanic outcropping.
CLIMATE: Tropical. Heavy year-round rainfall, especially in the eastern islands.

PEOPLE:
POPULATION: 120,347
ANNUAL GROWTH RATE: 3.36%
RELIGION: Mostly Christian; divided between Roman Catholic and Protestant.
LANGUAGE: English (official) with local languages as well. EDUCA-TION: Attendance in primary school 95%.
LITERACY: 92%.
LIFE EXPECTANCY: Men 65; women 69 years.

GOVERNMENT: Constitutional government in free association with the U.S. Unicameral legislature. President is elected every four years from ranks of popularly elected senators. Government budget: Revenues of $110 million mostly from the U.S.

ECONOMY:
GNP: $150 million
ANNUAL GROWTH RATE: Not applicable.
PER CAPITA GNP: $1,500
AVERAGE RATE OF INFLATION: Not applicable. Unemployment rate of 27%.
OFFICIAL EXCHANGE RATE: Official currency is the dollar.

COST OF LIVING INDEX: 109

On these remote islands better known as former World War II battle-grounds than much else, financial assistance from the U.S. is the primary source of revenue. Micronesia also earns about $4 million a year from the exploitation of commercial fishing concerns. With the exception of some high grade phosphate deposits there are few minerals worth mining. The potential for tourism exists but the remoteness of the islands, a lack of adequate facilities and hot, humid weather hinders development.

So where are the jobs? In essence, with four out of five locals out of work there are only a few areas where Americans can find work. The largest supplier of non-locals is the education system. There are a few construction jobs but unless you have high-tech construction know-how there is no way to compete with the natives for unskilled work. For possible teaching positions contact the Director of Personnel, Department of Education, Kolonia, Micronesia as well as: Office of the High Commissioner, Trust Territory of the Pacific Islands, Saipan, Mariana Islands; and for teaching military dependents, Office of Dependent Schools, Department of Defense, Washington, DC 20301.

New Zealand

GEOGRAPHY:
AREA: 103,886 sq. mi.
CAPITAL: Wellington
PRINCIPAL CITIES: Auckland, Christchurch.
TERRAIN: Highly varied from snow capped mountains to lowland plains.
CLIMATE: Temperate with sharp regional contrasts.

PEOPLE:
POPULATION: 3,388,737
ANNUAL GROWTH RATE: 0.57%
RELIGION: 81% Christian; 18% none or unspecified.
LANGUAGE: English
EDUCATION: Attendance in primary school 100%.
LITERACY: 99%
LIFE EXPECTANCY: Men 72; women 80 years.

GOVERNMENT: Independent state within the British Commonwealth.

No formal constitution. Unicameral parliament. Government budget: $15.6 billion of which 4% is devoted to the military.

ECONOMY:
GNP: $53 billion
ANNUAL GROWTH RATE: 3%
PER CAPITA GNP: $15,700
AVERAGE RATE OF INFLATION: 2%
WORK FORCE: Of the 1.7 million employed, 47% are involved in services and government; 41% in industry and commerce; and 12% in agriculture and mining. Unemployment is about 9%.
OFFICIAL EXCHANGE RATE: 1.7 New Zealand Dollars = US$
COST OF LIVING INDEX: 106

New Zealand is experiencing an economic maelstrom. For years the country was one of the world's most efficient producers of agricultural products; primarily wool, lamb and beef (actually there are more sheep in New Zealand than people). However the economy suffered severely with a drop in world commodity prices and shrinking quotas in the key European Community markets. In 1988 unemployment reached a near record low (11.3%) while inflation climbed to about 5%. Interest rates have been at a high of 20%.

In the early 1990s, however, the country witnessed an outstanding reversal with a change in government. In 1993-94, the budget was not in deficit, as it had been habitually. Rather, the nation experienced a surplus of about 0.6% of GDP! And the economy grew at 5.3% compared with 2.3% the previous fiscal year. Finance Minister, Bill Birch, stated that he expects the economy to continue this growth for the remainder of the century. As a result of this economic spurt, there is a growing need for skilled labor to buttress the existing local labor pool. Unskilled labor is not needed as a majority of the unemployed are amongst this group as are Asians who have come to this beautiful country in search of greater opportunity. The country is rich in wool production (actually the supply exceeds demand) and is searching for greater industrial opportunities with increased foreign investment.

Although all foreign investment requires prior government approval, the New Zealand government is trying to lure foreign investment when it can be tied to local enterprises. As a result there are opportunities for skilled workers in the area of oil refining, aluminum smelting, automobile parts assembly, chemicals, food preparation, finance, and forest products. Best sales prospects are in the areas of computers, software, sporting goods, and telecommunications equipment.

There are strict regulations regarding business dealings. The nation's manufacturing industry, for example, is protected by very stringent regulations. An item can't be imported if it can be manufactured locally. Yet, the country is eager to obtain experts in those fields that will improve the overall economy. If you possess a special skill you may be classified as a "visiting expert." As a result your overall income tax liability is limited to 35% of gross income for a period of up to two years. A work permit issued by the Department of Labor is issued for a six month period, renewable for an additional six months. If your special skill is not generally available in New Zealand you can usually extend your stay as long as you like.

Living conditions are similar to any major U.S. or European city. Standards are high. Most New Zealanders are outdoors people. A family camping vacation is commonplace.

New Zealand has an embassy at 37 Observatory Circle NW, Washington, DC 20008 (202/328-4800) with a consulate in Los Angeles. The U.S. Embassy is located at 29 Fitzherbert Terrace, Thornton, Wellington. Contacts:

American Chamber of
 Commerce of New Zealand
P.O. Box # 3408
Wellington

Chemicals:

A.C. Hatrick (NZ) Ltd.
22 York Street
P.O. Box # 2359
Parnell
Auckland 1

Stauffer Chemical Co. (NZ)
 Ltd.
P.O. Box 37-022
272 Parnell Road
Parnell
Auckland 1

Petroleum:

Occidental Petroleum Co. (NZ)
 Ltd.
P.O. Box # 2786
Auckland 1

Mobil Oil (NZ) Ltd.
Atlantic Union Oil (NZ) Ltd.
Aurora House
48-64 The Terrace
P.O. Box # 2497
Wellington 1

Food Products:

Corn Products (NZ) Ltd.
49-55 Anzac Avenue
Auckland 1

General Mills Creative Products
Ltd.
11A Tawari Street
Mount Eden Auckland

Automotive Parts:

General Motors Ltd.
Trentham Plant # 1, Private Bag
Upper Hutt

Pharmaceuticals:

Merck, Sharp & Dohme (NZ)
Ltd.
Plunket Avenue
P.O. Box # 23-244
Papatoe, Wirl
Auckland

Parke, Davis & Co.
405 Hutt Road
P.O. Box # 2407
Wellington
Lower Hutt

Engineering:

PLT Engineering Inc.
17 Albert Street, 7th Floor
Auckland

Bechtel Pacific Corp.
32 The Terrace
Wellington

Papua New Guinea

GEOGRAPHY:
AREA: 178,260 sq. mi.
CAPITAL: Port Moresby
PRINCIPAL CITIES: Lae, Rabaul, Goroka, Madang
TERRAIN: Mostly mountainous with coastal lowlands and rolling foothills.
CLIMATE: Tropical; northwest monsoon December to March, southeast monsoon May to October. Slight seasonal temperature variation.

PEOPLE:
POPULATION: 4,196,806 million
ANNUAL GROWTH RATE: 2.3%
RELIGION: More than 50% Christian (of which half are Roman Catholic); remainder various indigenous beliefs.
LANGUAGE: 715 indigenous languages. English spoken by about 2%. Pidgin English is widespread.
EDUCATION: Attendance in primary school 65%.
LITERACY: 32%

LIFE EXPECTANCY: Men 55; women 57 years.

GOVERNMENT: Independent parliamentary state recognizing the British monarch. Unicameral parliament. Government budget: $1 billion of which about 4% goes to the military.

ECONOMY:
GDP: $8.2 billion
ANNUAL GROWTH RATE: 1.2%
PER CAPITA GDP: $2,000
AVERAGE RATE OF INFLATION: 4.5%
WORK FORCE: Of the 1.8 million workers agriculture (subsistence or small land holders) employs about 82%; services 8%; government 4%; and, commerce and industry about 3%.
OFFICIAL EXCHANGE RATE: 1 kina = US$
COST OF LIVING INDEX: 122

For those interested in one of the more exotic work experiences coupled with a glimpse of a true remnant of a stone age culture consider Papua New Guinea (PNG). This remote and wild archipelago brings back memories of World War II with General MacArthur overseeing military activities from his headquarters in Port Moresby.

Since the war, the country has maintained its economic pace as a result of three major factors: an annual grant from Australia, the huge copper mines at Bougainville, and economically viable coffee and cocoa plantations. Oil and gas exploration have been active since the 1930s. More than 120 wells have been drilled, and the discoveries—two oil fields, five gas and condensate fields, and four dry gas fields—have led to tentative estimates of hydrocarbon reserves of about 10 trillion cubic feet of gas, 135 million barrels of condensate, and 345 million barrels of oil. Commercial exploitation, however, will be expensive given the high cost of infrastructure and operating in remote regions.

Agriculture provides a subsistence livelihood for more than half the population. Mining (copper and gold) accounts for about two-thirds of the nation's export earnings. However without outside financial aid PNG would have serious economic difficulties. In addition to Australia, other major sources of aid to PNG are New Zealand, Germany, Japan and various international organizations (i.e. World Bank, Asian Development Bank, UN, etc.). U.S. aid emphasizes assistance to agriculture, marine resources, health, and private enterprise development. Although employment opportunities exist in these areas, most foreigners are volunteers. In addition to Peace Corps volunteers, some 2,000 missionaries work in churches, hospitals and schools. Several churches have their own economic development projects.

U.S. investment in PNG is about $500 million. AMOCO is the largest American investor with one-third ownership of the OK Tedi mine. Chevron has a significant interest in oil exploration. Several ancillary companies operate in PNG and employ Americans who meet specific criteria. Columbia Helicopters, for example, has about 40 Americans on their payroll.

The PNG government seeks foreign help in developing their mineral resources, energy production, agriculture, and manufacturing. Foreign managers and technicians are allowed to work and live in Papua New Guinea but investors are expected to train local people and nationalize key positions within a reasonable length of time.

Tourist visas are valid for 60 days and are readily available at any PNG mission. A 30 day visa is available at the local airport in Port Moresby. A work permit, however, can only be obtained before arrival. A word of caution: Don't bring any "adult" magazines into the country. They are defined as pornography and are subject to confiscation with the importer subject to heavy fines. Health conditions in PNG are generally adequate. Most serious endemic diseases are not a problem. Malaria, including chloroquine resistant strains, is endemic.

Papua New Guinea has an embassy at 1330 Connecticut Avenue NW, Washington, DC 20036 Suite 350 (202/659-0858). The U.S. Embassy is located at Armit Street, Port Moresby. Contacts:

Mining:

AMOCO
OK Tedi, Inc.
P.O. Box 1
Tabubil

Annapurna Pty. Ltd.
(AMPAC Mining, Inc.)
P.O. Box 133
Konedobu

Chevron Niugini Pty. Inc.
P.O. Box 842
Port Moresby

Kennecott Niugini Mining Joint Venture
P.O. Box 1931
Rabaul

Parker Drilling
Rt 1, Box 210
Odessa, TX 79765

New Guinea Mining
P.O. Box 31
Kainantu

Electronics:

Bull (PNG) Pty, Ltd.
P.O. Box 1349
Port Moresby

Consultants:

Business Advisory PNG
P.O. Box 107
Port Moresby

Christensen Research Institute
P.O. Box 105
Madang

Aircraft:

Columbia Helicopters, Inc.
P.O. Box 1021
Port Moresby

7

HELPFUL
PLANNING HINTS

PASSPORTS AND VISAS

Your U.S. passport is a legal document issued by the government guaranteeing that you are an American citizen. It conveys no special privileges but it is required to travel abroad. As a matter of fact, if you fly overseas, the airlines won't board you without seeing your passport.

A visa is a document, usually a fancy stamp impressed on a page in your passport, issued by a foreign government stating that you have that government's permission to visit their country for a specified period of time. Visa requirements vary from country to country and are fully outlined in the pamphlet "Visa Requirements of Foreign Governments" available at any passport agency.

In the old days every country required you to apply well in advance for a visa. Every time you crossed a national border your passport and visa were scrupulously inspected by an officious bureaucrat and stamped with great ceremony. Today, unless you are planning to stay for several months, most countries require only a valid passport for entry, not a visa.

If you are planning to work in a country it then becomes essential to acquire a specific work visa prior to entering the country. Only one or two countries will issue a work visa once you are within the country.

Passport stamping is also a thing of the past in many parts of the world. Now a border immigration inspector checks your nationality, assures himself that your passport has not expired, and waves you through. However if you plan to visit the Middle East, Asia or Eastern Europe to check out job potentials you may obtain a tourist visa which allows you to visit—but not work—for 30 to 90 days and your passport gets stamped with that time period. When I took my family to China one vacation, we requested the immigration officer to stamp our passports so we would have a "red star" as a souvenir of our visit, which he very graciously did. Upon returning to our home in the Middle East, this created somewhat of a stir at immigration in that we had visited a "communist country"! The officer then refused to stamp our re-entry on the same page (a minor protest) and waved us through. So, sometimes it's best to leave well enough alone and get a stamp only if its required. If you visit Israel and then plan to travel on to another Mideast country afterwards, you might not be admitted if there is an Israeli stamp in your passport.

A U.S. passport is valid for ten years and costs $35.00 plus a $7.00 processing fee if you are applying in person (No processing fee when renewing your passport by mail). The standard passport has twenty-four pages, most of which are blank and are for entry/exit stamps and visas. If you are planning to travel widely in countries that require visas you may want a forty-eight or ninety-six page passport, available at no extra charge.

To obtain your passport, apply at:

- A U.S. Passport Agency in Boston, Chicago, Detroit, Honolulu, Houston, Los Angeles, Miami, New Orleans, New York, Philadelphia, San Francisco, Seattle, Stamford, CT, or Washington, DC.

- Most local county courthouses.

- Selected Post Offices.

You will need:

- Two identical photographs 2 inches square, color or black and white, on non glossy paper, and taken within the last six months.

- Your birth certificate, naturalization certificate, or an expired passport that was issued you after age sixteen.

- Proof of identity, e.g. drivers license (if you apply in person).

Remember that when you enter a foreign country, you come under the jurisdiction of their laws, administered by their police. Your U.S. passport doesn't carry much weight.

If your passport is lost or stolen while abroad, call the nearest American Embassy or consulate. Be sure you record your passport's number and its place and date of issue. Keep this data with your traveler's check numbers in a separate, secure place.

MONEY AND BANKING

One of the most asked questions of soon-to-become expatriates is, "How much money should I take with me?" This is a most subjective question and can only be answered on an individual basis. For one thing you will find that your major credit card —American Express, Master Card (incorporating Access and EuroCard), Diner's Club, and Visa—are accepted almost everywhere. We have found Visa to be the most widely accepted despite the ads ballyhooing American Express. If you maintain an active bank account in the States you can have your credit card invoices sent to your foreign address and pay with your personal check drawn on your American account.

Travelers checks are accepted nearly everywhere as well. If you bring enough from home to get you started it is easy to buy more abroad. Every American Express office, and they are everywhere, will sell you AmEx travelers checks and, if you're an AmEx card holder, cash your personal check as well. Another advantage: you'll find that you get a better exchange rate when using traveler's checks and credit cards.

It's not a bad idea to establish a local bank account abroad but don't expect banking to be like at home. Naturally each country has its own banks and banking regulations. Despite the aggravation we've all had at our local bank, there really is no comparison between dealing with an American bank and a foreign bank. In modern London, for example, you may find that your local bank will not cash a check drawn on a branch of the same bank. Deposit a check in a French bank and wait more than a week before it clears. Cash a traveler's check in an Italian bank and discover you must first present your passport, fill out several forms, then often wait while your check passes through several levels of banking bureaucracy. Most foreign banks won't open an account for you unless you can show that you're a bona fide resident.

The best rule is to keep your account open in the states, carry travelers checks to your new location then ask your employer's personnel advisor about local banks and banking. It may even be that your company has an in with a local bank which may work to your advantage.

CUSTOMS

There is no country in which you can avoid the process of passing through immigrations or customs. In Europe you now can cross borders with little more than a wave of a passport but don't assume the customs and immigrations folk aren't at the border. In some countries the entry and exit process is more of an ordeal than others. Whenever there is a wave of international terrorism the simple border crossing becomes more complicated. In all cases you should be aware of what to expect in entering and leaving a foreign country **and** in returning home.

Since each country has its own unique customs and immigrations rules and regulations it is important to check with that Embassy or consulate before leaving the States. A standard guide book such as Fodors or Fieldings will contain a section outlining the basic regulations. In most cases you will have no problems. However, if you're a hunter and wish to bring your own firearms into a country you better find out if they are allowed. Generally you can assume that there are limits on the amount of tobacco or alcohol you're allowed to import. You can usually exceed this amount by paying a duty or tax.

In some Moslem countries, the importation of any alcoholic beverage is strictly forbidden. They are very serious about this! Try to sneak a bottle of Scotch or beer into the country for a future celebration and you're asking for trouble. If you're caught you may be expelled—if you're lucky. You can be imprisoned. And, don't expect the American Embassy to help; it's out of their jurisdiction, you must remember you are a guest of that country and must abide by local laws.

Some countries allow an unlimited amount of currency to be brought in but limit the amount you can take out. Items such as fresh meat, plants, vegetables, and pets are also controlled. If you are planning on traveling with any of these items plan ahead and determine whether you can bring them with you.

Needless to say, drugs are outlawed everywhere. Don't even consider trying to sneak any controlled substance into a foreign country. The drug laws in America are nothing compared to some parts of the world. In a few southeast Asian countries the possession of drugs is a capital crime. Prescription drugs, on the other hand, can usually be brought with you without any problem; but, be sure you have your doctor write you out a prescription so that you may get it refilled locally. Many countries will not require a prescription for non-narcotic drugs, but its best to be safe. When you return to the States you also will pass through customs. Each member of your family is allowed to bring back up to $400 worth of gifts or items for your personal use duty-free. If you are traveling with such foreign made items as cameras, binoculars or watches that you bought before heading abroad either take a Xerox copy of the receipts with you or register them with U.S. Customs before leaving America. This may save you considerable time and a great deal of aggravation upon your return.

If you buy a car or motorcycle abroad and plan to bring it home you will be liable to duty. The amount of duty depends upon the items, etc. If you have any questions regarding American custom rules and regulations write to the U.S. Customs Service, Box #7407, Washington, DC 20044.

CULTURAL DO'S AND DON'TS

It won't take you long to discover that no matter where you are overseas, people will do things different from the way you're most familiar. Even if it's a simple matter of eating, we just don't do things the same way. Of course visitors to America say the same thing; and they are right. For example, why do we switch our knife and fork between hands every time we cut our food? Most Europeans hold their knife in the right hand and their fork in their left. Our basic mannerisms are unique to us. However, it is a good idea to understand that in every country there are also certain customs, ways of dress, and business methods that are particular to those people as well.

The customs and traditions in the Middle East are now pretty well appreciated but it never hurts to review some of the basics before heading for a Moslem country. Manners are an incredibly important of Arabic cultures. For example, be careful never to sit with your legs crossed so the bottom of your shoe faces an Arab. This a considered a very rude gesture. Also, the use of first names is appropriate only after formal introductions. It is not good manners to eat with your left hand and don't be surprised if you are invited to an Arabic home to find no utensils on the table. Remember, eat with your right hand. You will find, however, that most local restaurants will be as Westernized at home.

Even in "cultured" Great Britain you'll find unique customs and manners. Touching your nose indicates secrecy or confidentiality. Take out a package of cigarettes and it is expected that you'll offer smokes all around. In Germany it is inconsiderate if you smoke at a meal before coffee is served.

It will take a bit of time to become accustomed to the local lifestyles. Expect to make mistakes! But also don't be afraid to ask your hosts to explain the local mores. You'll become an expert in the local lifestyle more quickly than you realize. And, as the French say, Viva la Difference!

FURTHER READING

Aulick, June. *Looking for Employment in Foreign Countries*. 7th Edition. New York: World Trade Academy Press, 1985.

Cantrell, Will & Marshall, Terry. *101 Ways to Find an Overseas Job*. Oakton, VA, 1988.

Directory of American Firms Operating in Foreign Countries, 12th Edition. New York: World Trade Academy Press, 1991.

Foreign Policy Association, *Guide to Careers in World Affairs* (Manassas Park, VA: Impact Publications, 1993.

International Directory of Employment Agencies. Quebec: Overseas Employment Service, 1986.

Knoppman, Edward, ed., *American Jobs Abroad*. Detroit, MI: Visible Ink Press, 1994.

Kocher, Eric. *International Jobs*. Reading, MA: Addison-Wesley, 1984.

Krannich, Ronald L. & Caryl Rae, *Almanac of International Jobs and Careers*, 2nd Edition. Manassas Park, VA: Impact Publications, 1994.

Krannich, Ronald L. & Caryl Rae, *The Complete Guide to International Jobs and Careers*, 2nd Edition. Manassas Park, VA: Impact Publications, 1993.

Lay, David C. *Getting Your Job In The Middle East*. Tampa, FL: DCL Publishing; PO Box 16347, Tampa, FL 33687-6347.

Liebers, Arthur. *How to Get the Job You Want Overseas*. New York: Pilot Books, 1983.

Lipinski, Alex. (ed.) *The Directory of Jobs and Careers Abroad*. Oxford: Vacation Work, 1989.

Parsons, Kenneth O. *Strategies for Getting an Overseas Job*. New York: Pilot Books, 1989.

Phillips, David Atlee. *Careers in Secret Operations, How to be a Federal Intelligence Officer*. Bethesda: Stone Trail Press, 1984.

Powers, Linda (ed.). *Careers in International Affairs*. Washington, DC: Georgetown University, School of Foreign Service, 1986.

Sanborn, Robert, *How to Get a Job in Europe*. Chicago, IL: Surrey Books, 1994.

Sanborn, Robert, *How to Get a Job in the Pacific Rim*. Chicago, IL: Surrey Books, 1992.

Williams, John. *Evaluating an Overseas Job Opportunity*. New York: Pilot Books, 1979.

Win, Davis. *International Careers*. Charlotte, VT: Williamson Publishing, 1987.

INDEX